Pediatric Forensic Neuropsychology

Pediatric Forensic Neuropsychology

Edited by

Elisabeth M.S. Sherman, PhD

Brian L. Brooks, PhD

OXFORD
UNIVERSITY PRESS

UNIVERSITY PRESS

Oxford University Press, Inc., publishes works that further
Oxford University's objective of excellence
in research, scholarship, and education.

Oxford New York
Auckland   Cape Town   Dar es Salaam   Hong Kong   Karachi
Kuala Lumpur   Madrid   Melbourne   Mexico City   Nairobi
New Delhi   Shanghai   Taipei   Toronto

With offices in
Argentina   Austria   Brazil   Chile   Czech   Republic France   Greece
Guatemala   Hungary   Italy   Japan   Poland   Portugal   Singapore
South Korea   Switzerland   Thailand   Turkey   Ukraine   Vietnam

Copyright © 2012 by Oxford University Press, Inc.

Published by Oxford University Press, Inc.
198 Madison Avenue, New York, New York 10016
www.oup.com

Oxford is a registered trademark of Oxford University Press

Library of Congress Cataloging-in-Publication Data

Pediatric forensic neuropsychology / edited by Elisabeth M.S. Sherman
and Brian L. Brooks.
p. ; cm.
Includes bibliographical references and index.
ISBN 978-0-19-973456-6
1. Forensic Neuropsychology—methods. 2. Brain Injuries—diagnosis. 3. Child.
4. Mental Disorders—diagnosis. 5. Neuropsychological Tests.
I. Sherman, Elisabeth M. S. II. Brooks, Brian L.
RJ486.5.P426 2011
618.92'8—dc22
2011009178

This material is not intended to be, and should not be considered, a substitute for clinical, legal or other professional advice. Clinical and legal approaches described in this material are highly dependent on the individual circumstances, and although this material is intended to be current as of the time it was written, readers should ensure that content is consistent with current codes of conduct and legal statutes appropriate to their practice area. The publisher, authors, and editors make no representations or warranties to readers, express or implied, as to the accuracy or completeness of this material. The publisher, authors and editor do not accept, and expressly disclaim, any responsibility for any liability, loss or risk that may be claimed or incurred as a consequence of the use and/or application of any of the contents of this material.

Also, case material for this book has been purposefully de-identified by the authors, and any resemblance to actual persons living or dead is purely coincidental.

9 8 7 6 5 4 3 2 1
Printed in USA
on acid-free paper

ACKNOWLEDGMENT

The editors would like to thank all of the authors who contributed their work to this collection. Without their expertise, interest, and commitment to the project, this book would have remained only as an idea. We are extremely fortunate to have been able to benefit from their knowledge, and thank them for their dedication to advancing the field. We are also very appreciative to the reviewers of our original proposal for their feedback on this project.

We are immensely grateful to Joan Bossert, Vice President/Editorial Director, Medical Division, at Oxford University Press. Without her enthusiasm for the book, which was evident upon our first informal meeting, none of this would have been possible. We would also like to thank Susan Lee, Tracy O'Hara, and Jennifer Milton at Oxford University Press. Thanks as well to Aravind Kannankara and the production staff at Cenveo Publisher Services who met tight editing deadlines with grace and professionalism.

Finally, we would like to thank, in alphabetical order, Helen Carlson, Lonna Ivey, Basil Kadoura, and Emily Tam, who helped with aspects of the preparation, proof-reading, and completion of this project.

CONTRIBUTORS

Ida Sue Baron, PhD, ABPP (CN)
Independent Practice,
 Potomac, MD
Department of Neurosciences,
 Inova Fairfax Hospital, Falls
 Church, VA
Visiting Professor, Department of
 Pediatrics
University of Virginia School of
 Medicine
Charlottesville, VA

Brian L. Brooks, PhD
Neurosciences Program, Alberta
 Children's Hospital
Departments of Pediatrics and Clinical
 Neurosciences
University of Calgary
Calgary, Alberta, Canada

Shane S. Bush, PhD, ABPP, ABN
Long Island Neuropsychology, P.C.
Lake Ronkonkoma, New York

Jacobus Donders, PhD, ABPP
Mary Free Bed Rehabilitation
 Hospital
Grand Rapids, Michigan

Gerard A. Gioia, PhD
Chief, Division of Pediatric
 Neuropsychology
Director, Safe Concussion Outcome,
 Recovery & Education (SCORE)
 Program
Children's National Medical Center
Associate Professor, Depts. of Pediatrics
 and Psychiatry
George Washington University School
 of Medicine
Washington, DC

Alan L. Goldberg, Psy.D., ABPP; J.D.
Private Practice (and Disability
 Determination Services
 Administration of Arizona)
Tucson, Arizona

Lisa G. Hahn, PhD
Neuropsychology Associates of
 New Jersey
Madison, New Jersey

Peter K. Isquith, PhD
Private Practice
Dartmouth Medical School
Norwich, Vermont

Grant L. Iverson, PhD
Professor, Department of Psychiatry
University of British Columbia
Vancouver, B.C., Canada

Michael W. Kirkwood, PhD,
ABPP (CN)
Department of Physical Medicine and
    Rehabilitation
University of Colorado-Denver and
    Children's Hospital Colorado
Aurora, Colorado

Danielle N. Landwher
Division of Neuropsychology
Mount Washington Pediatric Hospital
Baltimore, Maryland

Antolin M. Llorente, PhD
Division of Neuropsychology
Mount Washington Pediatric Hospital
Baltimore, Maryland

William S. MacAllister, PhD,
ABPP-CN
NYU Comprehensive Epilepsy Center
New York, New York

Arthur MacNeill Horton, Jr. Ed.D.,
ABPP (CL), ABN, ABPP (BP)
Chief, Neuropsychology Section,
Psych Associates of Maryland LLC,
Towson, Columbia and Bethesda,
    Maryland

Jeffrey E. Max, MBBCh
Department of Psychiatry
University of California, San Diego
Director, Neuropsychiatric Research
Rady Children's Hospital, San Diego

Joel E. Morgan, PhD, ABPP (CN)
Department of Neurology and
    Neurosciences
UMDJ-New Jersey Medical School
Newark, New Jersey

Tisha J. Ornstein, PhD, C.Psych
Department of Psychology
Ryerson University
Toronto, Ontario, Canada

Cecil R. Reynolds, Ph.D., ABN,
ABPdN
Emeritus Professor of Educational
    Psychology,
Professor of Neuroscience,
Distinguished Research Scholar,
Texas A & M. University,
College Station, Texas

Russell J. Schachar, PhD
Departments of Psychiatry
Neurosciences and Mental Health
Research Institute
The Hospital for Sick Children
University of Toronto
Toronto, Ontario, Canada

Elisabeth M.S. Sherman, PhD
Neurosciences Program, Alberta
    Children's Hospital
Departments of Pediatrics and Clinical
    Neurosciences
University of Calgary
Copeman Healthcare Centre
Calgary, Alberta, Canada

Daniel J. Slick, PhD
Neurosciences Program, Alberta
    Children's Hospital
Departments of Pediatrics and Clinical
    Neurosciences
University of Calgary
Calgary, Alberta, Canada

Jerry J. Sweet, PhD
NorthShore University
    HealthSystem and
University of Chicago Pritzker
    School of Medicine
Chicago, Illinois

Christopher G. Vaughan, PhD
Division of Pediatric Neuropsychology
Children's National Medical Center
Assistant Professor, Depts. of Pediatrics
  and Psychiatry
George Washington University School
  of Medicine
Washington DC

**Keith Owen Yeates, PhD,
ABPP (CN)**
Departments of Pediatrics, Psychology,
  and Psychiatry
The Ohio State University and
Nationwide Children's Hospital
Columbus, Ohio

CONTENTS

PREFACE

This book is the very first text dedicated specifically to pediatric forensic neuropsychology. The authors who contributed to this volume represent an elite, knowledgeable, and expert group of clinician-researchers who are among the best in the field, and whose work sets the standard for the practice, science, and discipline of neuropsychology. The book was created with the hope that it may become the definitive reference text on the practice and process of forensic neuropsychological assessment of children.

This book was created for several reasons. First and foremost was the simplest: We could not find a book to refer to in our forensic work that covered the practical, clinical, and theoretical topics that are essential to pediatric forensic neuropsychology. Pediatric forensic neuropsychological assessment involves a more complex collection of knowledge than any of its constituent parts. It requires knowledge of forensic, ethical, psychometric, and developmental issues, and blending this knowledge with child clinical neuropsychological assessment skills requires a fair degree of expertise and training. This book seemed like a good place to begin to put these different topics together. Second, there appeared to be larger need for this book beyond our own. Pediatric neuropsychology is one of the fastest-growing branches of neuropsychology, and neuropsychology is one of the fastest growing branches in the entire discipline of clinical psychology (Heben & Milberg, 2002). Likewise, forensic neuropsychology is growing at an exponential rate (see Chapter 1). Yet references that meld together pediatrics, neuropsychology, and forensics are few and far between. For instance, the entire collection of existing forensic neuropsychology books published during the last decade include only a small fraction of content specific to pediatric forensic neuropsychology. There are case reports (Heilbronner, 2005; Heilbronner, 2008; Morgan & Sweet, 2009) and single chapters on assessing children as part of larger works on forensic assessment (Denney & Sullivan, 2008; Horton & Hartlage, 2003; Larrabee, 2005; Sweet, 1999), but the majority of forensic neuropsychology books do not cover pediatric issues at all. Conversely, general books on forensic assessment of children rarely include coverage of neuropsychological assessment or do not contain sufficient coverage of all of the practical and theoretical issues that are encountered. For instance, one of the best-known reference texts on forensic mental health assessment of children and adolescents contains only a single chapter devoted to pediatric neuropsychological assessment (Sparta & Koocher, 2006).

Pediatric Forensic Neuropsychology is intended primarily to be used by neuropsychologists who engage in forensic work. However, this book does not discriminate: It is intended for all neuropsychologists, regardless of whether they are retained by plaintiff or defense, or in the case of school-mandated evaluations, by parents or school districts. Importantly, the authors in this book represent a large range of practices, experiences, and approaches to forensic neuropsychological assessment. At times, their perspectives and opinions differ from one another, and they may differ from our own. We hope that this diversity of opinion enriches the book considerably and mirrors to some extent forensic practice, where there are necessary ambiguities and complexities on the way to establishing a legal truth.

Clinical work can become forensic either unexpectedly or by design. Although we hope that the book will be helpful for the pediatric forensic neuropsychologist who is an expert at his or her craft, the topics in this book should prove useful for those who do not usually engage in forensic work, such as clinicians who find themselves at the end of a subpoena or summons to appear in court relating to a clinical case. This book is intended to set down some guideposts for helping navigate such a situation. Therefore, the information provided in this book may be of utility for any neuropsychological assessment, regardless of whether there is a forensic reason for the referral.

The book is divided into three main sections. First, theoretical and conceptual topics in the assessment of children for forensic purposes are covered. This includes legal and process issues pertaining to forensic neuropsychological assessment of children, such as the role of pediatric neuropsychology in the courtroom and practical issues encountered in private forensic practice (Chapter 1), as well as the ethical issues that need to be considered (Chapter 2). Foundational topics in the psychometrics of forensic neuropsychological assessment are also covered, and these include core topics such as neuropsychological test selection (Chapter 3), understanding the prevalence of low scores when interpreting performance on pediatric neuropsychological test batteries (Chapter 4), and interpreting change across repeated assessments (Chapter 5). These chapters are particularly important because they form the basis of the interpretation of test findings—a foundation that is necessary for any clinician and critical for forensic work. Of necessity, given the forensic context where cases occur, the book also covers topics germane to exaggeration, malingering, and suboptimal performance, including conceptual distinctions between poor effort and nonadherence to test instructions (Chapter 6), and a diagnostic framework for the detection and identification of malingering and related conditions in children. The practical implications of these issues for interpreting test scores and a detailed review of techniques for detecting suboptimal performance are also provided in Chapter 7. Cross-cultural issues are also well addressed in a comprehensive chapter (Chapter 8), and confounding factors that complicate interpretation of findings such as premorbid functioning and comorbid conditions are covered in another chapter (Chapter 9).

In the second part of the book, the forensic evaluation of specific pediatric populations is introduced. Here, we focus purposefully on clinical groups seen by neuropsychologists in forensic practice. Many of the clinical chapters include case studies, to help bring the topics to life. Topics include concussions and mild traumatic brain injuries (Chapter 10), as well as moderate to severe traumatic brain injuries (Chapter 11). In addition, because it is a question that frequently arises in the forensic evaluation of children, secondary attention-deficit/hyperactivity disorder (ADHD) in the context of traumatic brain injury is covered in its own chapter (Chapter 12). Medical malpractice cases (Chapter 13) and independent educational evaluations (Chapter 14) are also discussed in detail.

The third part of this book contains the pediatric forensic toolbox. This includes a sample consultant-attorney contract (Exhibit A), examples of brief (Exhibit B) and lengthier (Exhibit C) consent forms, samples letters for parents (Exhibit D) and teachers (Exhibit E), a consent form for release of school information (Exhibit F), a clinical interview checklist (Exhibit G), a sample interview form specifically for traumatic brain injury cases (Exhibit H), and a background questionnaire that can be used in forensic assessments (Exhibit I). These sample forms are intended primarily for use by the clinical practitioner but can also be informative for any professional involved in a forensic case that includes neuropsychological assessment. Clinicians are free to use these as a template for creating their own forms, or these documents can also be downloaded directly from the Oxford University Press Web site and modified according to circumstance or jurisdiction.

Importantly, this book is designed to cover topics germane to civil litigation, the legal domain where the majority of pediatric neuropsychologists practice. The book purposefully omits topics relevant to criminal litigation, such as competence to stand trial, competence to waive *Miranda* rights, determination of legally defined insanity, topics pertaining to the juvenile justice system, as well as topics related to child custody or child abuse evaluations. Unlike the practice areas included in this book (e.g., the cognitive assessment of children with traumatic brain injuries), these areas of practice in criminal law are usually not the sole domain of the neuropsychologist. Instead, they are relevant to a broader clinical psychology audience. Several excellent books address these topics, and the interested reader is encouraged to refer to general sources for further information (e.g., Grisso, 2005; Sparta & Koocher, 2006; Wynkoop, 2008).

In addition, this book only has limited coverage of assessments with children who are exposed to environmental and industrial contaminants (see Chapter 1). Childhood toxin exposure is a complex, sometimes controversial topic that is well covered elsewhere. In particular, lead exposure in children is covered both within (McCaffrey, Horwitz, & Lynch, 2009; Stanford, 2005) and outside (e.g., Bisbing, 2006) the field of neuropsychology. There is also a rapidly expanding literature concerning the effects of childhood exposure to polychlorinated biphenyls (PCBs), lead, mercury, radioactive substances, carbon monoxide, mold, and industrial waste and substances used in manufacturing. At this time, the reader is encouraged to also refer to key sources for information on exposure to toxic substances, including references on forensic neuropsychology and the neurotoxic tort (Bolla, 2005, Berent & Albers, 2005–2008; Hartman, 1995, Hartman, 1999), and on the many issues that need to be considered, including noncredible claims (Artiola i Fortuny, 2009).

The book should also be a useful resource for attorneys, both to better understand the process of neuropsychological assessment and its considerable assets in the forensic arena, as well as its limitations. Additionally, some topics will also be of interest to neuropsychologists who conduct forensic evaluations of adults; adult forensic work often involves the consideration of preexisting or premorbid childhood conditions, and several chapters include this important topic. Other professionals involved in forensic evaluations, such as clinical psychologists, psychiatrists, neurologists, and physiatrists may also find this book useful. Because most neuropsychologists, at one time or another, will engage in forensic work, coverage of forensic neuropsychology as part of clinical neuropsychology training should be a requirement of any good training program, and we hope the book will be used by graduate training programs and postdoctoral programs as part of training future neuropsychologists. Furthermore, this book presents psychometric, diagnostic, and assessment issues that can be generalized to forensic practice in a wide range of countries, with the main focus of legal and process issues specific to the United States and Canada. Importantly, this book is intended as an introduction to basic legal, clinical, and forensic aspects of pediatric neuropsychology. Individual readers should consult appropriate legal, clinical, and forensic materials in their jurisdiction.

It is our hope that, thanks to the invaluable contribution of the expert chapter authors, this book represents a first step in establishing a solid foundation of theoretical, practical, and clinical knowledge that reflects the current state of the art in forensic neuropsychological evaluation of children.

REFERENCES

Artiola i Fortuny, L. (2009). Alleged mold toxicity. In J. E. Morgan & J. J. Sweet (Eds.), *Neuropsychology of malingering casebook* (pp. 294–306). New York: Psychology Press.

Berent, S., & Albers, J. W. (2005–2008). *Neurobehavioral toxicology: Neurological and neuropsychological perspectives.* New York: Taylor Francis.

Bisbing, S. B. (2006). A pediatric lead litigation primer: Foundations for mental health assessment. In S. V. Sparta & G. P. Koocher (Eds.), *Forensic mental health assessment of children and adolescent* (pp. 285–300). New York: Oxford University Press.

Bolla, K. I. (2005). Neurotoxic injury. In G. J. Larrabee (Ed.), *Forensic neuropsychology: A scientific approach* (pp. 271–297). New York: Oxford University Press.

Denney, R. L., & Sullivan, J. P. (2008). *Clinical neuropsychology in the criminal forensic setting.* New York: Guilford Press.

Grisso, T. (2005). *Evaluating juveniles' adjudicative competence: A guide for clinical practice.* Sarasota, FL: Professional Resource Press.

Hartman, D. E. (1995). *Neuropsychological toxicology: Identification and assessment of human neurotoxic syndromes* (2nd ed.). New York: Plenum Press.

Hartman, D. E. (1999). Neuropsychology and the neuro(toxic) tort. In J. J. Sweet (Ed.), *Forensic neuropsychology: Fundamentals and practice* (pp. 339–368). New York: Taylor & Francis.

Heilbronner, R. L. (2005). *Forensic neuropsychology casebook.* New York: Guilford Press.

Heilbronner, R. L. (2008). *Neuropsychology in the courtroom: Expert analysis of reports and testimony.* New York: Guilford Press.

Heben, N., & Milberg, W. (2002). *Essentials of neuropsychological assessment.* New York: John Wiley & Sons.

Horton, A. M., & Hartlage, L. C. (2003). *Handbook of forensic neuropsychology.* New York: Springer Publishing.

Larrabee, G. J. (2005). *Forensic neuropsychology: A scientific approach.* New York: Oxford University Press.

Lees-Haley, P. R. (2003). Toxic mold and mycotoxins in neurotoxicity cases: Stachybotrys, Fusarium, Trichoderma, Aspergillus, Penicillium, Cladosporium, Alternaria, Trichothecenes. *Psychological Reports, 93,* 561–584.

McCaffrey, R. J., Horwitz, J. E., & Lynch, J. K. (2009). Child forensic neuropsychology: A scientific approach. In C. R. Reynolds & E. Fletcher-Janzen (Eds.), *Handbook of clinical child neuropsychology* (3rd ed.), pp. 729–743. New York: Plenum Press.

Morgan, J. E., & Sweet, J. J. (2009). *Malingering casebook.* New York: Psychology Press.

Sparta, S. V., & Koocher, G. P. (2006). *Forensic mental health assessment of children and adolescents.* New York: Oxford University Press.

Stanford, L. (2005). Lead astray: The controversies of childhood lead poisoning. In R. L. Heilbronner (Ed.), *Forensic neuropsychology casebook* (pp. 218–235). New York: Guilford Press.

Sweet, J. J. (1999). *Forensic neuropsychology: Fundamentals and practice.* New York: Taylor & Francis.

Wynkoop, T. F. (2008). Neuropsychology in the juvenile justice system. In R. L. Denney & J. P. Sullivan (Eds.), *Clinical neuropsychology in the criminal forensic setting* (pp. 295–325). New York: Guilford Press.

PART ONE

Theoretical, Conceptual, and Psychometric Issues in Pediatric Forensic Neuropsychology

Chapter 1

Pediatric Neuropsychology in Forensic Proceedings: Roles and Procedures in the Courtroom and Beyond

JERRY J. SWEET
MICHAEL WESTERVELD

INTRODUCTION

Forensic neuropsychology involves the provision of evaluation or consultative services related to an individual involved in a proceeding that is potentially adversarial in nature in that two or more parties must reach a resolution of a common concern or disagreement, but have differing interests, related to which they have potentially conflicting or antagonistic positions. This chapter will address specific aspects of forensic practice related to the developing subspecialty of pediatric forensic neuropsychology.

To truly understand the nature and scope of pediatric forensic neuropsychology, as well as the specific activities of a pediatric neuropsychologist whose practice involves forensic cases, one first needs to appreciate a number of general factors. Therefore, the chapter begins with discussion of basic background information, including *(1)* the scope of involvement of clinical neuropsychologists in forensic cases, *(2)* reasons that forensic opinions are sought from neuropsychologists, *(3)* the nature of the settings in which forensic consultations occur, and *(4)* differences between routine clinical and forensic activities, as they pertain to particular forensic venues. Subsequently, important relevant literature and professional issues that are germane to forensic practice and not encountered in routine clinical settings will be discussed. At various points, the chapter will narrow to include roles and procedures that are associated with pediatric forensic activities. Throughout this chapter the writing style and content will undoubtedly reflect that of neuropsychologists writing for a readership of other neuropsychologists in straightforward language. For more detailed and precise reference material written by mental health forensic experts, some of whom are also lawyers, the reader should consult Barsky and Gould (2002), Goldstein (2003), and Melton, Petrila, Poythress, and Slobogin (2007).

EXTENT OF INVOLVEMENT

Data from a variety of sources and practice experience have converged to form the inescapable conclusion that *clinical neuropsychologists can run, but cannot expect to successfully hide from attorneys*. Thus, it is for most clinicians merely a question of whether to choose to learn about forensic activities, in order to be prepared for the inevitable, or instead to wing it when the eventuality of being involved in a forensic scenario occurs. For those who are early in their careers or who have not yet entered the field, we can begin with a summary of available data.

Taylor (1999) was perhaps the first to offer empirical data suggesting that the involvement of clinical neuropsychologists in litigated cases had become substantial, and to identify the point in time after which the majority of growth had occurred. In 1997, Taylor performed a computerized search of the term "neuropsychologist" in a database of court decisions. At the point that his search was conducted, 400 state and federal decisions contained the word "neuropsychologist." Of interest, 98% of these citations occurred after 1980, 83% occurred within the prior decade, and 56% were within the preceding 5 years.

Recently, Sweet and Giuffre Meyer (2011) gathered citation data in a similar manner from the legal search engine LexisNexis Academic to demonstrate that the number of litigated cases involving neuropsychological issues and experts has continued to increase very dramatically since Taylor's original research. By decade, the number of publications for attorneys (e.g., law reviews, legal journal articles) containing the terms "neuropsychologist," "neuropsychology," or "neuropsychological" were as follows: 1960 to 1969 = 0; 1970 to 1979 = 2; 1980 to 1989 = 18; 1990 to 1999 = 193; and 2000 to August 2009 = 502. Clearly, attorneys over time have increasingly mentioned the specialty of clinical neuropsychology. Particularly since 1990, these inclusions in case summaries have been substantial.

For the present chapter, we have updated a portion of the citation data pertaining to state and federal cases that have been cited in LexisNexis Academic presented in Sweet and Giuffre Meyer (2011). These updated data are presented in Figure 1.1, which depicts a very impressive increase across time in the number of state and federal cases that refer to neuropsychologists and descriptions of neuropsychological content. Such data support the earlier mentioned catchphrase implying a very high likelihood that practicing neuropsychologists will encounter attorneys in their work. It is noteworthy that this type of case frequency data only includes formally litigated cases, and therefore it does not consider informal forensic proceedings, such as disability determination and due process educational hearings. But the question can be asked as to whether these data represent more or less activity across time in other specialties. That is, perhaps litigation in general is growing and related to this growth increasingly involves a number of other specialists, not just those in clinical neuropsychology. Interestingly, Kaufmann (2009) has offered data that are fairly convincing in suggesting that neuropsychologists over time are in fact in greater contact with litigated cases than are other specialty practitioners. Figure 1.2 shows Kaufmann's data comparing searches relevant to neuropsychology, forensic psychology, forensic psychiatry, and neuropsychiatry. Based on search results, polynomial regression projections were plotted, showing a distinct

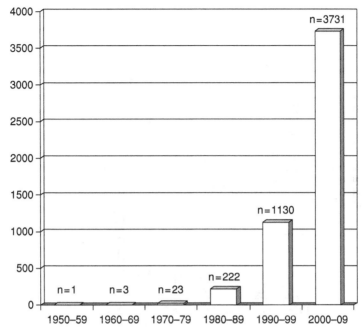

FIGURE 1.1 Cases identified in legal search engine LexisNexis Academic by decade that mention "neuropsychologist" or "neuropsychology" or "neuropsychological". Note that the information in this figure represents data previously published in Sweet and Giuffre Meyer (2011) and updated for the present chapter through May 2010. The "Power" search function was used, which specifically targets "Federal and State Cases, Combined."

difference with psychiatry specialists. Even compared to psychologists whose specialty is forensics, neuropsychologists as a whole appear to have a greater degree of involvement, and the predicted trajectory suggests they will remain the most frequently involved specialists in psychology.

We should note that the proportion of the litigated cases identified by the legal search engine in these various searches that involve *pediatric* neuropsychology has not been identified. However, relevant survey data from clinical neuropsychologists (e.g., Sweet, Nelson, & Moberg, 2006) indicate that there are fewer pediatric practitioners than adult practitioners and that the former group has reported substantially less involvement in forensic practice than the latter group, though individuals who are involved in pediatric *and* adult practice report the highest proportion of forensic practice.

REASONS FOR INVOLVEMENT

So why is it that neuropsychologists are so commonly involved in forensic activities? A number of factors have been suggested as related, and perhaps determinative, in creating an attractiveness of neuropsychologists for attorneys and decision makers involved in forensic proceedings. The fact that the bedrock foundation of

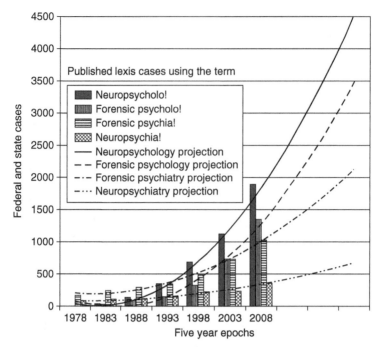

FIGURE 1.2. Number of United States federal and state cases using the root terms Neuropsycholo!, Forensic Psycholo!, Forensic Psychia!, and Neuropsychia! in 5-year epochs for the past 30 years used as a basis for polynomial regression projections for the next 15 years. (From Kaufman, 2009. Used with permission.)

clinical neuropsychology is its scientist-practitioner approach has been mentioned as a primary reason for the frequency of involvement in forensic activities (Larrabee, 2005; Sweet, 1999; Sweet, Ecklund-Johnson, & Malina, 2008). Lees-Haley and Cohen (1999) described a similar sentiment in stating that the most substantial contribution of a neuropsychologist expert is a scientifically based opinion.

Of course, attorneys and decision makers in forensic venues must find relevance to the experts whose opinions are sought, and without question the subject matter of consultations routinely provided by clinical neuropsychologists regarding (1) the question of whether brain dysfunction has been acquired and, if so, the effects of the acquired brain dysfunction on fundamental abilities that have the potential to impact day-to-day activities and responsibilities, (2) the psychological effects of injury, disease, and exposure to emotional trauma, and (3) knowledge of clinical conditions that are commonly the subject of formal and informal forensic proceedings (e.g., traumatic brain injury, depression, learning disability, chronic pain, posttraumatic stress disorder, neurotoxic exposure). We previously described this notion (Sweet, 2009a) as follows:

Ideally, a clinical neuropsychologist minimizes the use of intuition, "gut feelings," and a vague sense of knowing, in favor of drawing conclusions based upon empirical data, which is itself able to be compared to published peer-reviewed data from individuals whose clinical conditions are well documented.

In short, impressions give way to facts, which in both clinical and forensic contexts are viewed as acceptable, even desirable bases of opinions. (p. 4)

In fact, the clinical literature created and relied upon by clinical neuropsychologists to guide their practice is broad and deep with regard to subject matter that is often at issue in forensic settings, such as traumatic brain injury (Dikmen, Machamer, Winn, & Temkin, 1995; Donders, 2011; Goldstrohm & Arffa, 2005; Kirkwood, et al., 2008; Price, Joschko, & Kerns, 2003). Considering that this may also be true for other disciplines, such as neurology, what is salient to the frequent use of neuropsychologists as forensic experts is the near unique status of the specialty as having established a very large and ever-growing literature related to dealing with a quintessential question within all forensic settings. That question is whether the examinee provided valid information on which a trier of fact can reliably make a decision. An inventory of topics published within the three most popular clinical neuropsychology peer-reviewed journals found that during the period from 1990 through 2000 the annual article content related to forensic topics was as high as 16%, with 86% of these articles related to the general topic of response validity (Sweet, King, Malina, Bergman, & Simmons, 2002). With regard to this important issue, the specialty of clinical neuropsychology has an enormous empirical research literature pertinent to determining whether symptoms have been reported accurately and whether performances on ability measures reflect sufficient effort and are credible with regard to the claimed disorder (see Sweet, 2009b, for extensive bibliographic listing by topic; see also textbooks by Boone, 2007, and Larrabee, 2005, and extensive case descriptions in Morgan & Sweet, 2009). No other health care discipline or specialty has a comparable literature. Whether the development of this neuropsychology literature occurred in response to, or is a cause of, the substantial involvement of clinical neuropsychologists in forensic proceedings is arguable. However, there is no argument with the observation that the knowledge and the specific assessment tools related to this research literature allows clinical neuropsychologists to address questions that are central to forensic consultations.

SPECIFICS OF PEDIATRIC FORENSIC NEUROPSYCHOLOGY

Much has been written about the type of patient interactions that lead to forensic encounters, but most of what has been written is focused on adults. Although many of the process issues (e.g., defining the relationship with the attorney and/or patient; dealing with confidentiality limits) are similar in adult and pediatric forensic consultations, working with children presents several unique challenges. First, there may be psychosocial factors that complicate the conduct of the examination. For example, divorced parents may be at odds and in some cases one parent may be party to the litigation through allegations of neglect or responsibility for the injury. Second, the type of clinical consultation that may end up in the hands of attorneys may differ in that cases may not involve a clear, identifiable proximal cause (e.g., neurodevelopmental disorders alleged to result from exposure to teratogens; postnatal exposure to toxins). Finally, the nature and certainty of the conclusions regarding the extent of impairment resulting from the alleged injury can be more obscure, particularly when the determination is attempted within the context of ongoing neurobehavioral development that occurs in childhood.

Nature of Cases

The types of consultation in which the pediatric neuropsychologist engages vary with the setting and nature of the injury. The most common type of forensic consultation concerns the evaluation of a child who has an acquired brain injury or alleged cognitive and developmental impairment as a result of trauma from an accident in which an unrelated party is responsible. However, pediatric neuropsychologists may be asked to provide expert opinions in multiple settings or circumstances, some of which blur the line between the role of objective provider of information to the court and advocate for the child. For example, a child who suffers a neurological injury with cognitive effects may also be involved in process issues related to placement and access to services in the school setting. In nonforensic clinical work as a treating neuropsychologist, a key element of the consultation process involves determining recommendations for school that will allow the child to function most effectively. However, in a forensic context the questions may be limited to the presence or absence of cognitive impairment resulting from injury to the brain, and the severity and impact of any identified problems. It is important that the neuropsychologist be aware that advocacy in one setting may undermine credibility as an expert through eroding perceptions of objectivity in another setting.

Pediatric neuropsychologists may also be asked to become involved in cases where an injury is caused by physical abuse or neglect, and one or both parents are alleged to be responsible. In such cases, the issues may go beyond the nature and extent of the injury to include determination of causality, with parental rights at stake (Wills & Sweet, 2006). In some instances, newly discovered abuse or neglect may be uncovered during the course of the examination. Neuropsychologists, (mandated reporters in many jurisdictions), may be required by law to report abuse, which can introduce complications into the assessment process. When a pediatric neuropsychologist determines that abuse or harmful neglect is present, standard reporting procedures should be followed. Even though there is an attorney–client relationship (see Chapter 2 for further elaboration), failure to report could result in liability on the part of the neuropsychologist, particularly if there is further injury after the abuse is discovered that could have reasonably been prevented.

In adult forensic consultations, there is typically an alleged proximal cause that is the subject of litigation, such as an automobile or work-related accident. While this may also be true in many child cases, in some children there may be a long-standing disorder in search of a cause. For example, autism is a neurodevelopmental disorder that is alleged in some instances to have been caused, or contributed to, by administration of the MMR (measles, mumps, rubella) vaccine in children (Wakefield, 1998). Following revelations of conflict of interest related to forensic interests that led 10 of the 13 coauthors to disavow the original interpretation (Mayor, 2004), the original article was retracted by the journal in which it was initially published (Dyer, 2010). More important, subsequent research has failed to support a link (Baird et al., 2008; Hornig et al., 2008), yet the notion persists. This is likely due to the inherent appeal that a causal explanation or liable party for developmental disorders, such as autism, holds for frustrated parents seeking answers for their child's disability. It is important that pediatric neuropsychologists familiarize themselves with and critically evaluate relevant literature when becoming involved in forensic consultation and testimony.

There are numerous substances for which there is an established link between exposure and increased risk for neurodevelopmental syndromes. Such cases may involve a pediatric neuropsychologist whose expertise is solicited to establish a link between exposure and a child's developmental status. In some cases, the evidence is circumstantial and a direct link is difficult to establish because there may be other confounding factors that contribute to cognitive and behavioral problems in a given child. Establishing causation and injury with a "reasonable degree of neuropsychological certainty" in a specific individual case may prove difficult. For example, although there is a clear neurobiological basis for neurological injury in lead poisoning, there are individual differences in the specific effects depending on age and level of exposure, and there remains controversy about the effects of low-level exposure (<10 mc/dl). Early controversies regarding lead also considered the environmental and psychosocial influences on outcome, such as socioeconomic status (Bellinger, 1995). Thus, although lead is a known neurotoxin with clearly established neurobehavioral effects at the population level, quantifying damage at the individual level may be more challenging.

Pediatric neuropsychologists may be asked to determine a link between prenatal exposure to prescription medications taken during pregnancy and adverse neurodevelopmental outcomes. While teratogenic effects may include obvious physical defects immediately apparent at birth, more attention is also being given to long-term neurodevelopmental effects such as learning disability and attention-deficit disorder. For example, recent evidence has been accumulating that children born to mothers with epilepsy who take antiepileptic medications during pregnancy have a higher rate of learning disabilities (Meador, Baker, Cohen, Gaily, & Westerveld, 2007). However, methodological issues with this type of research limit the confidence of attribution to a specific cause in any given child.

As one may imagine, the scope of incidents that can result in brain injury or cognitive and behavior change suspected to be due to neurological injury is virtually limitless and an exhaustive list is beyond the scope of this chapter. However, the important point is that in clinical practice, pediatric neuropsychologists should not consider themselves to be isolated from potential legal involvement when a child presents for evaluation. The chance of being drawn into a forensic matter is present even in what may appear to be relatively benign medical consultations. Beyond routine clinical referrals, so-called stealth referrals or attorney-involved referrals that are channeled through a pediatrician or other medical specialist are relatively common. Careful history taking to uncover potential forensic issues is important in any clinical case.

Aside from injury-related forensic consultations, pediatric neuropsychologists may be asked to consult in a variety of other circumstances. A common venue for involvement is school-related process issues where a child's neurological injury or neurodevelopmental disorder status creates special needs that require detailed assessment and explanation (see Chapter 14 for more details). Pediatric neuropsy-chologists may also be asked to consult in criminal proceedings. Understanding normal developmental trends regarding cognitive development, particularly with respect to decision making and ability to anticipate consequences of an act can be important factors in determining criminal culpability. Neurological injury or disease resulting in "intellectual disability" or "mental retardation" may, in the most severe cases, also be a mitigating factor in determining punishment. The U.S. Supreme Court ruled in 2002 (*Atkins v. Virginia*) that it was unconstitutional to execute per-sons with intellectual disability, although they did not define the term.

Assessing Severity of Injury

The questions of *extent* and *permanence* of adverse neurocognitive and behavioral symptoms can be particularly challenging. When working with an adult, there is often an extensive premorbid educational and occupational history that allows for estimation of premorbid function against which the effects of injury can be compared and recovery gauged. However, in the developing child there are several issues that come into play that complicate estimation of extent and permanence. For example, in a child who is alleged to have prenatal exposure to teratogens, or in whom a birth injury is alleged, what is the basis for estimating how the child would have developed had the injury not occurred? Also, even in children who suffer an injury at a later age the concept of return to baseline as a measure of recovery is inadequate because the baseline is a moving target. While, on the one hand, the premorbid estimation may be easier because the data are contemporary rather than historical, these data are less useful in assessing the degree of impairment or gauging recovery because of the nature of brain development and ongoing acquisition of skills.

Wills and Sweet (2006) identified multiple factors that have an effect on extent and permanence of damage, including the nature of the injury and the age and developmental stage at which the injury occurs. There is strong evidence that abili-ties are more vulnerable to effects of neurological injury during phases of rapid development (Donders, 2011) and that the specific pattern of outcome will be related to the age of onset and stage of development that the child is in at the time of injury. However, the age at which the child is assessed is also an important factor. Assessing a young child may not reveal the long-term effects on abilities that have yet to emerge. This may be particularly true for impairment in "executive functions" that are dependent on frontal lobe maturation.

NATURE OF FORENSIC VERSUS CLINICAL SETTINGS

Clinicians are familiar with the routine clinical setting of providing services, in which the practicing neuropsychologist and the patient work together toward a mutually identified goal, usually to identify or ameliorate a health problem, in the best inter-est of the patient. In other words, the clinician and the patient share the same goal. One of the characteristics of this *treating* relationship, a term used even when the clinical service is evaluative or diagnostic, is confidentiality of the patient's health care information, which is only shared with the informed consent of the patient. Because of the types of patients that are referred to neuropsychologists in routine clinical settings, it is very likely that there will be patients who have been involved in accidents or who have undergone extensive medical treatments because of central nervous system or other medical disorders, subsequent to which psychological or neuropsychological injuries may be claimed. These patients may file civil lawsuits or disability claims, related to which a clinician who provided services as a *treater*, which is simply the term used in civil legal proceedings when referring to a health care professional whose role is restricted to that of a clinician, may be requested to provide records or deposition or trial testimony. If this occurs, the patient will have essentially agreed, by virtue of placing his or her health status in question, to allow other individuals, agencies, and perhaps the court to have access to his or her health information. In other words, the former confidentiality that applies to the original neuropsychologist–patient relationship will no longer apply.

Context-Specific Procedures Pertaining to Information Sharing

Application for educational accommodations, disability claim, product liability lawsuit, medical malpractice lawsuit, or personal injury lawsuit filed by a current or former patient will result in written permission of the patient to have her or his health records gathered by a third party for review. Thus, a neuropsychologist is very likely to learn that a former or current patient is pursuing a claim or litigation when a request from the third party, accompanied by a signed release from the patient, arrives in the mail. When individuals are involved in civil lawsuits, the notification to a treater that records and/or testimony are requested most often comes in the form of a *subpoena*. There are several forms that a subpoena can take, but all are considered a legal directive that commands a person to "appear before a court or other tribunal, subject to a penalty for failing to comply" (from *Black's Law Dictionary*, Garner, 1999). A common type of subpoena served on health care professionals is a *subpoena duces tecum*, which specifies records or materials that the witness is to bring to the location at which testimony is to be given. Neuropsychologists should take seriously the requests represented by a subpoena. The American Psychological Association (APA) has compiled advice from psychologist lawyers who comprise the Committee on Legal Issues (American Psychological Association Committee on Legal Issues, 2006) regarding strategies that can assist psychologists in determining how to respond to subpoenas and compelled testimony, as these requests pertain to patient records, test materials, and particularly the ethical obligation incumbent to the psychologist to avoid misuse of assessment techniques and data. As noted by the APA committee, a subpoena may be modified or even completely voided if the demand is, for some reason, not legally enforceable. A psychologist who is in possession of treatment records can contact and inform a patient whose records have been requested. That patient may or may not in turn decide to seek to protect her or his own records. The psychologist can also choose to negotiate with the requesting body or in some instances seek guidance from the court regarding the subpoena. In addition to the APA's advice on more formal legal responses to subpoenas, Kaufmann (2009) also offers detailed advice regarding such legal responses as a *motion to quash* or a *protective order*, which can be filed either by the patient or the psychologist with the assistance of an attorney. Kaufmann notes, in particular, "A discovery demand may also be modified if it involves items that are irrelevant or if the request is unduly burdensome" (p. 1145). The last phrase "unduly burdensome" refers broadly to demands in some subpoenas that are excessive and beyond reasonableness, such as being requested to compile a list of every single litigant or claimant ever evaluated by the neuropsychologist to whom the same exact tests were administered. Such lists are not kept as a matter of routine, and they could not be compiled retrospectively. This would be quite different than the legitimate request that parallels the requirement related to U.S. federal cases that expert witnesses are required to provide a list of cases in which they have testified in the preceding 4 years.

Some requests for release of records received by neuropsychologists may be inappropriate. In most states it is important to confirm that the written release you have received covers more than simply "medical records". Specifically, legitimate release of information requests identify that the examinee has given permission for release of "mental health" or "psychological" or "neuropsychological" records, not simply "medical records." In some states, such as Illinois, a request to release "raw data" and test materials to a patient, a lawyer, or an agency would violate state law. As noted by Kaufmann (2009),

> With the rapid growth in forensic consulting, unrestrained discovery of raw data and psychological test materials during litigation erodes the reliability and validity of the test procedures. Dissemination of test materials reduces the interpretive value of the tests and promotes cheating, turning our best methods into junk science in the courtroom. (p. 1130)

Readers should note that "raw data" does not refer to summary test scores, but to the testing forms on which are depicted the test instructions, test stimuli, questions, and examinee answers. In fact, it is now commonplace for clinical neuropsychologists to attach a summary sheet of salient test scores to formal reports, as a means of documenting information in the medical record that can be referred to in the future care, including possible reevaluation, of the patient.

To be clear, it is not the case that neuropsychologists seek to obstruct or withhold information from lawyers and agencies that genuinely need information to resolve litigation, claims, or disputes. Rather, neuropsychologists and test publishers seek to keep test materials and raw data secure to avoid invalidation of testing and assessment procedures in the future. Moreover, there are reasonable and legitimate means by which such information can be shared, while maintaining test security. For example, providing educational information on the subject of test security to the interested parties may lead to release of copies of raw data and test materials from one psychologist to another, or, if necessary, release of information under the protection of a judge's order. Kaufmann (2009) has provided an extensive review of relevant rulings and the full range of actions that can be taken when dealing with an inappropriate request. This topic is best understood and dealt with by clinicians within the context of their own state laws and regulations, as well as within the specific forensic venue in which the information request is generated.

A final word on the topic of sharing information in response to legal requests that may be received by neuropsychologists pertains to a *court order* or *judicial order*, which is "a written direction or command delivered by a court or judge" (Garner, 1999, p. 1123). This type of request generally represents the outcome of a prior discussion in court before the judge, which has resulted in a directive to be carried out by the recipient of the order. As such, when receiving a court order, a neuropsychologist is expected to comply. If compliance appears to violate the law or requires professional behavior that is deemed unacceptable, it is best to seek advice from an attorney.

Context-Specific Roles: Fact Versus Opinion Witness

As noted earlier, when engaged in routine clinical activities, a health care specialist gathers information that is subsequently of interest to a forensic proceeding, that clinician is termed a *treater*. There are different expectations and different procedural boundaries associated with the circumstance of being involved as a clinician versus being formally retained as an expert witness. Treaters are experts related to their scope of practice, which explains why they were involved in the care of the individual who went on to become a litigant or claimant. A neuropsychologist who becomes a *retained* expert witness was not originally involved in the care of the individual who is now a litigant or claimant, but instead has been retained to provide opinions regarding that individual. Both treaters and retained witnesses are *expert* witnesses because of their relevant professional expertise, but the former is considered a *fact witness*, whereas the latter is considered an *opinion witness*.

The primary difference between these types of expert witnesses is in the limits of testimony, with the fact witness limited to the factual information from the era of the involvement with the litigant or claimant when that individual was in the role of patient. Consideration of facts relating to events that occurred after the clinical interactions and the expression of new opinions that were not formed at the time of the clinical interaction are deemed inappropriate for comment by a fact witness, who, as noted earlier, is also termed a *treater*. In contrast, the opinion witness often has much more information on which to base opinions than does a treater and is free to explore all information that becomes relevant to issues in the forensic matter at hand that are within the expert's scope of practice. Additionally, there is no confidentiality between a litigant or claimant who interacts with a retained expert witness, a fact that the examinee should be apprised of at the time of an examination, if one occurs.

Note that we describe these two categories as though they are mutually exclusive, which is a widely held position among forensic authorities (e.g., Greenberg & Shuman, 1997), who believe that it is an ethical conflict for one individual to attempt both roles. Though there are a number of reasons that these two roles are considered to be in conflict, a primary underlying concern is that in the role of being a treater the fundamental goal is to help the patient in some manner. This role is viewed as carrying with it the potential of reducing the necessary objectivity that should accompany the primary goal of the retained forensic expert, which is simply to "get it right" (i.e., to provide objective information and opinion that will assist the "trier of fact," whether that is helpful to the litigant or not). It is very important to note that in both instances, whether in the role of treater or in the role of retained expert, what the legal system expects and desires is honesty and objectivity. In fact, as noted by Malina, Nelson, and Sweet (2005), whether initially performed in clinical context or expressly performed within and for a forensic context, the work of professionals in providing information in forensic proceedings does not involve any advocacy, other than advocating one's own opinions, not in advocating anything else. As previously described (Sweet, Grote, & Van Gorp, 2002), ". . . whether in the role of treater or retained expert, neuropsychologists must strive to remain fully objective in their work and opinions" (p. 108).

Types of Opinion Witness Roles

In civil lawsuit proceedings, not all retained expert witnesses actually offer opinions publicly, which basically means officially on the record to the opposing parties. Expert witnesses can be retained as *undisclosed consultants*, whose opinions are only known to the retaining party, who is usually an attorney. An undisclosed consulting expert is primarily retained to educate the retaining party about clinical or technical matters that will be of assistance in litigating the case at hand. This consultation may include formulating relevant questions that will be asked in gathering information from witnesses who are providing testimony.

Experts are sometimes used as *disclosed consultants*, with the only difference being that both sides involved in the lawsuit may know the name of, and share information with, the consultant, but the consultant's opinions are not revealed to both sides. However, in some jurisdictions and some venues, disclosure of the identity of the consultant would leave open the possibility that the expert's opinions could be sought and placed officially on the record, which is the reason that consultant names are often not disclosed. In either instance, the primary role of both undisclosed and disclosed nontestifying experts is educational.

Neuropsychologists who are retained as testifying opinion witnesses need to be mindful of a number of expectations of this role. Many retained experts are testifying witnesses, and as such their opinions will be placed officially on the record, in the form of a deposition, which is a formal proceeding used to introduce relevant information from witnesses, or trial testimony. In some jurisdictions there is a distinction between a *discovery* deposition and an *evidence* deposition. A discovery deposition is a formal proceeding in which a court reporter documents the questions asked by attorneys, as well as the verbal responses of a witness. Because the intent of this type of deposition is to uncover all relevant information, the time required to complete this proceeding can at times be lengthy. Some of the details and the bases of an expert's opinions, such as the expert's report and peer-reviewed articles, may be attached to the transcribed testimony and referred to as *exhibits*. It is advisable for expert witnesses to be aware that any records created in the process of working on a case, any form of written communication, including letters, notes, and e-mails, as well as all ancillary materials, such as billing records, are discoverable. In other words, such materials, if deemed relevant, may be obtained by attorneys working on the case and placed officially on the record.

Subsequent to the discovery deposition, if the case continues to move forward to trial, an expert's opinion may be presented live at trial, or, when circumstances do not allow live testimony, an evidence deposition is often the chosen alternative. The evidence deposition may be videotaped and shown in court, which, as is common in live courtroom testimony, typically is shorter in duration and more focused on only salient issues. In jurisdictions that rely on discovery depositions prior to trial, an expert's opinions are not expected to change from the former to the latter, except in the instance that new relevant information is provided to or found by the expert. In fact, changing one's opinions between the initial discovery stage and the subsequent evidence deposition or live courtroom testimony without new facts being introduced may lead to a court ruling that the new opinions are not admissible.

Expectations of Legal System for Opinion Witnesses

What is useful to the legal system is not *personal* opinion, despite the characterization of the expert as an opinion witness. Instead, the legal system expects honesty and fairness in the presentation of opinions relevant to the expert's area of knowledge and experience. There is no question that when it comes to formal courtroom proceedings, the general trend across time is to raise the thresholds of evidentiary standards in a manner that minimizes or even excludes capricious, idiosyncratic, personal, and nonscientific opinions. The *Frye standard* (*Frye v. United States*, 1923), which stated that evidence provided by experts must be "generally accepted" within the particular field from which it was derived, was an initial attempt to set a lower limit on quality of expert testimony. This criminal case involved a low-level biometric "lie detector" in the form of a blood pressure measurement procedure, which was not commonly accepted in the relevant professional community, and therefore was ruled inadmissible as evidence at trial. Over the decades that the *Frye* ruling predominated in the U.S. legal system, additional more specific and stringent evidentiary standards were developed. In a 1934 Rules Enabling Act of Congress, the U.S. Supreme Court was given authority to develop rules and procedures for federal judges. This authority was eventually transferred in 1958 to a Judicial Conference, which eventually created the Federal Rules of Evidence, which Congress enacted in 1975 (see Rice & Delker, 2000 for detailed history and ongoing developments). Eventually, a 1993 federal court decision known as the *Daubert* decision (*Daubert v. Merrell Dow Pharmaceuticals*, 1993) offered an alternative to the minimalistic *Frye* standard focus on general consensus, by adding that judges should also evaluate a witness's methods for empirical testing that could determine its falsifiability, whether the methods had been subject to peer review, and consideration of the known error rate of the methods. There has been much ensuing debate and a lack of consensus regarding whether experts have been held to a higher standard by judges in allowing or excluding witness evidence in the post-*Daubert* era (cf. Cheng & Yoon, 2005; Dahir et al., 2005; Groscup, Penrod, Studebaker, Huss, & O'Neil, 2002).

Kaufmann (2008) has reviewed the admissibility of neuropsychological evidence in criminal cases, noting that pertaining to criminal proceedings, psychologists are recognized as "experts in matters of competence, insanity, criminal culpability, and mitigation, with few exceptions" (p. 61). Kaufmann advises that there is a specialized body of knowledge, including numerous specialized rules (e.g., rules governing declarations of competency to enter a plea or to stand trial), that applies to specific tasks of expert witnesses in criminal proceedings. Thus, psychologists who provide expert witness testimony in criminal proceedings need first to learn about the types of information deemed relevant and the special processes involved in providing neuropsychological evidence and testimony in criminal proceedings. In general, Kaufmann's review conveys that if neuropsychologists adhere to procedural rules related to criminal proceedings and evidentiary rules that apply to the court system in general, their work product and testimony are capable of being accepted as relevant and worthy of consideration by the criminal court system.

Consistent with Kaufmann (2008), Sweet, Ecklund-Johnson, and Malina (2008) provided a detailed overview of evidentiary rulings that involved psychologists and neuropsychologists and found no cause for concern regarding the specialty of neuropsychology in general as to whether the evidentiary requirements for expert witnesses can be met by neuropsychologists. Though some individuals have been excluded when their opinions were not relevant or did not have appropriate bases or their particular methods used in a case were not appropriate, there has been no evidence of a trend toward exclusion of neuropsychologists as witnesses, and, as stated previously and depicted in Figures 1.1 and 1.2, the trend is clearly toward greater involvement of the specialty with each passing year. In other words, the results of applications of evidentiary standards that may exclude experts from testifying are case specific. Because neuropsychologists are particularly well grounded in the scientist-practitioner model of training and practice, they are particularly well suited to withstand the scrutiny of the criminal and civil courts' gatekeepers.

Objectivity and Bias

Unfortunately, a stereotype of retained experts has arisen, based on apparent examples of such witnesses providing biased information that does not fairly characterize the salient facts in the case. In fact, when federal judges and lead attorneys were polled in 1991 and in 1998 regarding perceived problems with expert witness testimony, the results of both surveys indicated the number-one problem: "Experts abandon objectivity and become advocates for the side that hired them" (Krafka, Dunn, Johnson, Cecil, & Miletich, 2002, p. 314). In this survey, ranked third and fourth, respectively, as problematic were the following: "Expert testimony appears to be of questionable validity or reliability" and "Conflict among experts that defies reasoned assessment." It seems obvious that courts commonly encounter expert witnesses whose testimony is problematic. *This is no more or less true for neuropsychologist expert witnesses than for any other psychology specialty or any other discipline.*

Relevant literature contains a number of recommendations that can be used by expert witnesses to minimize bias. From the general decision-making literature, multiple experts have emphasized using actuarially based clinical decision making (i.e., algorithms, formulae, and empirically derived rules), rather than clinician-based judgments (cf. Dawes, Faust, & Meehl, 1989; Garb, 1998; Mellers, Schwartz,

& Cooke, 1998). Particularly relevant to the present topic, the strength of actuarial decision making is that such an approach can be applied without prejudice, which is to say not selectively or in a manner that would favor the position of the side that retained the expert.

As useful as an actuarial approach is for evaluating individual test results, there remain very few actuarial formulae for integrating aggregated information to answer the frequent broad questions that are evident in forensic proceedings, such as those pertaining to civil causation, criminal culpability, a criminal defendant's mental state at the time of a crime, specific implications of acquired brain dysfunction, prognoses, and whether an examinee is consciously feigning a condition. Such "big picture" opinions can definitely benefit from actuarial methods as bases, in part, but they ultimately also require clinical judgment. In nearly all applications relevant to clinical neuropsychology, one would expect that these clinical judgments benefit greatly from empirical support in peer-reviewed literature, or an expert witness could risk exclusion on the basis of not meeting evidentiary standards. (See Chapter 3 for additional discussion of clinical vs. actuarial, i.e., statistical, prediction.)

Expert witnesses encounter powerful influences that are not part of routine clinical experience as they participate in forensic activities. Within an adversarial forensic context, which can at times cause emotions to run high, it is possible for an expert's objectivity to be altered and possibly diminished. Related, some forensic writers have offered guidance regarding strategies that can be employed in the form of self-corrective techniques that may serve to maintain expert objectivity, even under trying circumstances. Sweet and Moulthrop (1999) offered nine general self-examination questions and eight report-related self-examination questions that forensic consultants could ask themselves. These questions included the following general items, among others:

Do I almost always reach conclusions favorable to the side that retains me? Have I taken a position, in very similar cases, when retained by an attorney from one side that I did not take when retained by an attorney from the opposite side? Do I routinely apply the same decision-rules for establishing brain dysfunction no matter which side retains me?

Report-related questions included the following items, among others:

How will I defend each statement in the report, if required to do so? Have I placed only the amount of confidence in my interpretive statements that is warranted by each test's psychometric characteristics? Have I included statements that are at odds with the mainstream literature on this subject?

Though we cannot assume that self-examination will cure the most serious bias in experts, a well-intentioned expert who desires only to "get it right" will take on the extra burden of carefully scrutinizing her or his own work products and testimony in an effort to maintain objectivity.

Brodsky (1991, 1999) has offered detailed and invaluable advice to psychologists who aspire to being expert witnesses. Among his recommendations is the suggestion (Brodsky, 1999) that an expert fight the "pull to affiliate with the side that calls us to testify" (p. 75) by performing integrity checks. Brodsky describes the calculation of a proportion of cases in which an expert agrees with the retaining party. This can be calculated as a *contrary quotient*, if framed as proportion of cases in which the expert disagrees with the retaining party's preferred position.

Though there is no magic number that represents the dividing line between objectivity and bias, it is logical that a substantial proportion of cases brought to a health care expert would not have been accurately characterized in advance by the retaining party, who is in fact a legal expert and not a health care expert. This obvious fact is the very reason that expert witnesses are needed by the legal system.

Certainty: Probable Versus Possible

There are numerous points in providing expert witness testimony that the question being asked of the expert will be framed by the phrase "Is it your opinion *to a reasonable degree of neuropsychological certainty* that . . ." At these moments, the testifying neuropsychologist is being asked to assert the strength of the opinion being expressed, in terms of a relevant legal standard. Though scientific probability is often expressed in statistical values, such as a probability of less than .05 or .01 that the mean performances of two groups are significantly different, the legal standard is quite different. Lewin (1998) provided an excellent review of the history and evolution of the legal concept of "medical certainty," noting that numerous authorities have indicated what may appear to scientist-practitioners to be a lax threshold by comparison to statistical conventions. Using the related concept of "more probably true than not," the minimum threshold for "certainty" is a mere 51% probability of being true. This 51% threshold separates two key concepts in forensic venues, that of *probable* and that of simply *possible*. Court systems generally are concerned with what is probable and not what is merely possible, which again comports with the scientific underpinnings of an expert witness in clinical neuropsychology.

Effort Is Essential

The evaluation of effort on ability tests is absolutely essential when evaluating individuals within a forensic context (American Academy of Clinical Neuropsychology, 2007; Bush et al., 2005; Heilbronner, Sweet, Morgan, Larrabee, & Millis, 2009). This is no less true for pediatric cases than for adult cases. The literature related to assessing effort in pediatric forensics has lagged behind the effort literature pertaining to adults, but it is gaining traction, as evidenced by the increasing number of articles addressing this topic in neuropsychology practice journals (see Chapters 6 and 7). There may be key differences regarding how effort contributes to performance in children versus adults. Understanding that there are various and potentially different reasons for insufficient or compromised effort in pediatric cases begins with an appreciation of developmental trends in the ability to deceive. In adults, developmental issues are rarely evident in examining compromised effort on neuropsychological tests, which in a forensic context is often linked to secondary gain. Claimants with financial incentive may underperform on neuropsychological tests with the expectation that they will be financially rewarded for their "disability." Often, the claimant has a poor understanding of how credible neurobehavioral effects of neurological injury will present, resulting in performance that does not make sense based on extensive knowledge regarding how the brain works. As a result, assessment of effort has rapidly become a standard component of forensic consultations, and it is also now increasingly seen as important in nonforensic clinical examinations.

Clinical lore posits that children are less capable of deception than adults (Rohling, 2004; Kirkwood, Kirk, Blaha, & Wilson, 2010). However, there is a developmental trend in capabilities related to deception that is age related. The ability to manage one's behavior and alter presentation for secondary gain requires an emerging ability to connect long-term outcomes with immediate behavior as well as an ability to take the perspective of another and maintain a consistent message (Kirkwood et al., 2010), abilities that are not fully developed until late childhood and early adolescence. Nevertheless, measures that are designed to assess effort in adults have been applied to pediatric populations, with relatively good success. Although some of this research is aimed at demonstrating that the tasks are so easy that children can pass them (providing additional evidence of noncredible performance in adults), application of these tests to detecting poor effort in children naturally followed. Much of this research has focused on the ability of children to pass measures of effort (e.g., Kirkwood & Kirk, 2010), with less emphasis on identification of embedded measures of effort on other neuropsychological tests. Children as young as 5 years old have been able to pass effort measures such as the Test of Memory Malingering (TOMM; Tombaugh, 1996), whereas other effort measures requiring facility with numbers and letters (e.g., Green's Word Memory Test; WMT) may not be appropriate for children of this age (Kirkwood et al., 2010). Instead, it is very likely that age-specific or developmental-skill-specific limits vary across effort tests. For example, failures on Green's WMT are much less likely to occur in children who possess at least a third-grade reading level (Green & Flaro, 2003).

There are several important gaps in the understanding of suboptimal effort and noncredible test performance in children. First, much of the research has focused on tests of memory, yet children may present with poor effort in other functional domains. For example, McKinzey, Prieler, and Raven (2003) demonstrated in a sample of 44 children aged 7–17 years that all but 2 children were able to produce lower scores on the Raven Progressive Matrices test when instructed, but that a formula for identifying these children had a very high false-negative rate (64%). Second, a complete understanding of factors related to suboptimal performance in children is lacking. Although Kirkwood and colleagues identified a variety of psychosocial factors, an important point of that small case series is that motives may not be obvious and that single measures of effort may not be sufficient to detect anomalous patterns of performance that can alert the clinician to poor effort or attempts to manipulate presentation on neurocognitive tests. Additional research is needed to address the possibility that genuine factors may masquerade as compromised effort in children, as well as to develop more effective and age-appropriate methods for detecting simulated performance in pediatric samples (Heilbronner et al., 2009). This is especially true related to the sophisticated methods of evaluating effort that have been developed related to so-called embedded measures derived from atypical performance patterns on neuropsychological tests with adults (see Morgan & Sweet, 2009, for extensive list of procedures). Despite the sophistication of these methods for adults, efforts to apply embedded measures with children have been particularly lacking.

OVERVIEW

Pediatric neuropsychologists are likely, at some point in their career, to find themselves involved in a forensic matter. In cases where the consultation is explicitly forensic (i.e., solicited by an attorney seeking expert opinion regarding functional implications of alleged injury to the brain) basic legal and procedural issues are similar to those in adults. Explanation of limits of confidentiality and the nature of the consulting relationship with both the patient/family and the attorney should be made at the outset. Informed consent may be supplemented by assent of the child, with clear explanations of procedures in a manner understandable by the child based on the child's age and level of functioning. However, in pediatric consultations complicating factors may arise, such as custody and consent issues when parents are divorced, and they should be identified prior to commencing the evaluation. When the consultation is initially clinical, the neuropsychologist may be asked to render an expert opinion based on clinical examination of the child. When this occurs, it is important for the pediatric neuropsychologist to consider carefully whether he or she is able to objectively provide an opinion based on the available information and to consider the roles of treating neuropsychologist versus expert witness. There may be cases in which it is acceptable to function as an advocate for the child (e.g., school proceedings regarding placement or access to support services), rather than an objective source of information for the court.

In both explicitly forensic, as well as clinical-turned-forensic, settings it is important that the pediatric neuropsychologist is aware of the limitations of his or her procedures, accounting for factors that may affect the validity of test results and conclusions regarding causal relationships between an alleged event and a child's neurodevelopmental status. Issues regarding effort may not be related to malingering or secondary gain (see Chapters 6 and 7 for additional information), but they may still play an important role in determining the validity of the test with respect to inferences about neurological injury. It is important to keep the concepts of effort and deception/malingering separate in children and to maintain awareness of the possible nonneurological clinical influences that can affect performance. In addition, judgments regarding permanence should take into account the developmental literature and consider factors, such as the potential effect of future interventions on long-term cognitive and behavioral outcome. These points are developed in more detail in the chapters that follow.

REFERENCES

American Academy of Clinical Neuropsychology. (2007). American Academy of Clinical Neuropsychology (AACN) Practice Guidelines for Neuropsychological Assessment and Consultations. *The Clinical Neuropsychologist, 21,* 209–231.

American Psychological Association Committee on Legal Issues (2006). Strategies for private practitioners coping with subpoenas or compelled testimony for client records or test data. *Professional Psychology: Research and Practice, 37,* 215–222.

Baird, G., Pickles, A., Simonoff, E., Charman, T., Sullivan, P., Chandler, S., et al. (2008). Measles vaccination and antibody response in autism spectrum disorders, *Archives of Disease in Childhood, 93*(10), 832–837.

Barsky, A. E., & Gould, J. W. (2002). *Clinicians in court: A guide to subpoenas, depositions, testifying and everything else you need to know*. New York: Guilford Press.

Bellinger, D. C. (1995). Interpreting the literature on lead and child development: The neglected role of the "experimental system." *Neurotoxicology and Teratology, 17*(3), 201–212.

Boone, K. (Ed.). (2007). *Assessment of feigned cognitive impairment: A neuropsychological perspective*. New York: Guilford Press.

Brodsky, S. L. (1991). *Testifying in court: Guidelines and maxims for the expert witness*. Washingon, DC: American Psychological Association.

Brodsky, S. L. (1999). *The expert expert witness: More maxims and guidelines for testifying in court*. Washington, DC: American Psychological Association.

Bush, S. S., Ruff, R. M., Tröster, A. I., Barth, J. T., Koffler, S. P., Pliskin, N. H., et al. (2005). Symptom validity assessment: practice issues and medical necessity NAN policy & planning committee. *Archives of Clinical Neuropsychology, 20*(4), 419–426.

Cheng, E. K., & Yoon, A. H. (2005). Does *Frye* or *Daubert* matter? A study of scientific admissibility standards. *Virginia Law Review, 91*, 471–513.

Dahir, V., Richardson, J. T., Ginsburg, G. P., Gatowski, S. I., Dobbin, S. A., & Merlino, M. L. (2005). Judicial application of Daubert to psychological syndrome and profile evidence: A research note. *Psychology, Public Policy, and Law, 11*, 62–82.

Dawes, R. M., Faust, D., & Meehl, P. E. (1989). Clinical versus actuarial judgment. *Science, 243*(4899), 1668–1674.

Dikmen, S. S., Machamer, J. E., Winn, H. R., & Temkin, N. R. (1995). Neuropsychological outcome at 1-year post head injury. *Neuropsychology, 9*, 80–90.

Donders, J. (2012). Forensic aspects of pediatric traumatic brain injury. In G. J. Larrabee (Ed.), *Forensic neuropsychology: A scientific approach* (2nd ed.). New York: Oxford University Press.

Dyer, C. (2010). Lancet retracts Wakefield's MMR paper. *British Medical Journal, 340*, c696.

Garb, H. (1998). *Studying the clinician: Judgment research and psychological assessment*. Washington, DC: American Psychological Association.

Garner, B. A. (Ed.). (1999). *Black's law dictionary*. St. Paul, MN: West Group.

Goldstein, A. (2003). Forensic psychology. In I. Weiner (Ed.), *Handbook of psychology* (Vol. 11). New York: Wiley.

Goldstrohm, S. L., & Arffa, S. (2005). Preschool children with mild to moderate traumatic brain injury: An exploration of immediate and post-acute morbidity. *Archives of Clinical Neuropsychology, 20*(6), 675–695.

Green, P., & Flaro, L. (2003). Word Memory Test performance in children. *Child Neuropsychology, 9*(3), 189–207.

Greenberg, S. A., & Shuman, D. W. (1997). Irreconcilable conflict between therapeutic and forensic roles. *Professional Psychology: Research and Practice, 28*, 50–57.

Groscup, J. L., Penrod, S. D., Studebaker, C. A., Huss, M. T., & O'Neil, K. M. (2002). The effects of Daubert on the admissibility of expert testimony in state and federal criminal cases. *Psychology, Public Policy, and Law, 8*, 339–372.

Heilbronner, R. L., Sweet, J. J., Morgan, J. E., Larrabee, G. J., & Millis, S. R. (2009). American Academy of Clinical Neuropsychology Consensus Conference Statement on the neuropsychological assessment of effort, response bias, and malingering. *Clinical Neuropsychologist, 23*(7), 1093–1129.

Hornig, M., Briese, T., Buie, T., Bauman, M. L., Lauwers, G., ... Lipkin, W. I. (2008). Lack of association between measles virus vaccine and autism with enteropathy: A case-control study. *PLoS ONE 3*(9): e3140. doi:10.1371/journal.pone.0003140.

Kaufmann, P. M. (2008). Admissibility of neuropsychological evidence in criminal cases: Competency, insanity, culpability, and mitigation. In R. Denney & J. Sullivan (Eds.), *Clinical neuropsychology in the criminal forensic setting* (pp. 55–90). New York: Guilford.

Kaufmann, P. M. (2009). Protecting raw data and psychological tests from wrongful disclosure: A primer on the law and other persuasive strategies. *Clinical Neuropsychologist, 23*(7), 1130–1159.

Kirkwood, M. W., & Kirk, J. W. (2010). The base rate of suboptimal effort in a pediatric mild TBI sample: Performance on the Medical Symptom Validity Test. *Clinical Neuropsychologist, 24*(5), 860–872.

Kirkwood, M. W., Kirk, J. W., Blaha, R. Z., & Wilson, P. (2010). Noncredible effort during pediatric neuropsychological exam: A case series and literature review. *Child Neuropsychology, 16*(6), 604–618.

Kirkwood, M. W., Yeates, K. O., Taylor, H. G., Randolph, C., McCrea, M., & Anderson, V. A. (2008). Management of pediatric mild traumatic brain injury: a neuropsychological review from injury through recovery. *Clinical Neuropsychologist, 22*(5), 769–800.

Krafka, C., Dunn, M. A., Johnson, M. T., Cecil, J. S., & Miletich, D. (2002). Judge and attorney experiences, practices, and concerns regarding expert testimony in federal civil trials. *Psychology, Public Policy, and Law, 8*, 309–332.

Larrabee, G. J. (Ed.) (2005). *Forensic neuropsychology: A scientific approach.* New York: Oxford University Press.

Lees-Haley, P., & Cohen, L. (1999). The neuropsychologist as expert witness: Toward credible science in the courtroom. In Sweet J. J. (Ed.), *Forensic neuropsychology: Fundamentals and practice* (pp. 443–468). Lisse, Netherlands: Swets & Zeitlinger.

Lewin, J. (1998). The genesis and evolution of legal uncertainty about "reasonable medical certainty." *Maryland Law Review, 57*, 380–504.

Malina, A., Nelson, N., & Sweet, J. J. (2005). Framing the relationships in forensic neuropsychology: Ethical issues. In S. Bush (Ed.) Ethics in forensic neuropsychology [Special issue]. *Journal of Forensic Neuropsychology, 4*, 21–44.

Mayor, S. (2004). Authors reject interpretation linking autism and MMR vaccine. *British Medical Journal, 328*(7440), 602.

Meador, K. J., Baker, G., Cohen, M. J., Gaily, E., & Westerveld, M. (2007). Cognitive/behavioral teratogenetic effects of antiepileptic drugs. *Epilepsy and Behavior, 11*(3), 292–302.

McKinzey, R. K., Prieler, J., & Raven, J. (2003). Detection of children's malingering on the Raven's Progressive Matrices. *British Journal of Clinical Psychology, 42*(Pt 1), 95–99.

Mellers, B. A., Schwartz, A., & Cooke, A. D. (1998). Judgment and decision making. *Annual Review of Psychology, 49*, 447–477.

Melton, G. B., Petrila, J., Poythress, N. G., & Slobogin, C. (2007). *Psychological evaluations for the courts: A handbook for mental health professionals and lawyers* (3rd ed.). New York: Guilford Press.

Morgan, J., & Sweet, J. J. (2009). *Neuropsychology of malingering casebook.* New York: Psychology Press.

Price, K. J., Joschko, M., & Kerns, K. (2003). The ecological validity of pediatric neuropsychological tests of attention. *Clinical Neuropsychologist, 17*(2), 170–181.

Rice, P., & Delker, N-E. (2000). *The Federal Rules of Evidence Advisory Committee: A short history of too little consequence 191 F.R.D. 678.* Retrieved April 2011, from the American University Washington College of Law web site: http://www.wcl.american.edu/pub/journals/evidence/short_history.pdf?rd=2011.

Rohling, M. (2004). *Who do they think they're kidding: A review of the use of symptom validity tests with children. APA Division 40 Newsletter, Volume 22 number 2.*

Sweet, J. J. (Ed.) (1999). *Forensic neuropsychology: Fundamentals and practice.* New York: Taylor & Francis.

Sweet, J. J. (2009a). Forensic bibliography: Effort/malingering and other common forensic topics encountered by clinical neuropsychologists. In Morgan J. & Sweet J. (Eds.), *Neuropsychology of malingering casebook* (pp. 566–630). New York: Psychology Press.

Sweet, J. J. (2009b). Neuropsychology and the law: Effort/malingering and other common forensic topics encountered by clinical neuropsychologists. In Morgan J. & Sweet J. (Eds.), *Neuropsychology of malingering casebook* (pp. 3–8). New York: Psychology Press.

Sweet, J. J., Ecklund-Johnson, E., & Malina, A. (2008). Overview of forensic neuropsychology. In J. Morgan & J. Ricker (Eds.), *Textbook of clinical neuropsychology* (pp. 869–890). New York: Taylor & Francis.

Sweet, J. J., Grote, C., & Van Gorp, W. (2002). Ethical issues in forensic neuropsychology. In S. Bush & M. Drexler (Eds.), *Ethical issues in clinical neuropsychology* (pp. 103–133). Lisse, Netherlands: Swets & Zeitlinger.

Sweet, J. J., & Giuffre Meyer, D. (2012). Trends in forensic practice and research. In G. J. Larrabee (Ed.), *Forensic neuropsychology: A scientific approach* (2nd ed., pp. 501–506). New York: Oxford University Press.

Sweet, J. J., King, J. H., Malina, A. C., Bergman, M. A., & Simmons, A. (2002). Documenting the prominence of forensic neuropsychology at national meetings and in relevant professional journals from 1990 to 2000. *Clinical Neuropsychologist, 16*(4), 481–494.

Sweet, J. J., & Moulthrop, M. (1999). Self-examination questions as a means of identifying bias in adversarial cases. *Journal of Forensic Neuropsychology, 1,* 73–88.

Sweet, J. J., Nelson, N. W., & Moberg, P. J. (2006). The TCN/AACN 2005 "salary survey": professional practices, beliefs, and incomes of U.S. neuropsychologists. *Clinical Neuropsychologist, 20*(3), 325–364.

Taylor, J. S. (1999). The legal environment pertaining to clinical neuropsychology. In J. J. Sweet (Ed.), *Forensic neuropsychology: Fundamentals and practice* (pp. 421–442). New York: Taylor & Francis.

Tombaugh, T. N. (1996). *Test of Memory Malingering (TOMM).* North Tonawanda, NY: Multi-Health Systems.

Wakefield, A. J. (1998). Autism, inflammatory bowel disease, and MMR vaccine. *Lancet, 351,* 1356.

Wills, K., & Sweet, J. J. (2006). Neuropsychological considerations in forensic child assessment. In S. Sparta & G. Koocher (Eds.). *Forensic mental health assessment of children and adolescents* (pp. 260–284). New York: Guilford Press.

COURT DECISIONS

Atkins v. Virginia, 536 U.S. 304 (2002).

Daubert v. Merrell Dow Pharmaceuticals, 113 (S. Ct. 2786 1993).

Frye v. United States (293 F. 1013 D.C. Cir. 1923).

Chapter 2

Ethical Issues in Pediatric Forensic Neuropsychology

SHANE S. BUSH
WILLIAM S. MAcALLISTER
ALAN L. GOLDBERG

INTRODUCTION

The intersection of pediatric neuropsychology and forensic neuropsychology affords clinicians the opportunity to inform attorneys, courts, triers of fact, and administrative decision makers about the brain-behavior relationships of children and adolescents involved in adjudicative proceedings. Although the term *forensic* is typically applied when neuropsychologists are retained by parties other than the child's parents or guardian, some pediatric patients are brought for *clinical* neuropsychological evaluation or treatment services by their parents or guardian prior to the initiation of litigation or during litigation, thus bringing the neuropsychologist into a forensic context despite not having been (knowingly) retained for that purpose at the outset. Regardless of how neuropsychologists who work with pediatric populations come to be involved in forensic matters, they are likely to encounter ethical issues and challenges that differ from those frequently encountered in strictly clinical contexts. Clinicians who anticipate and prepare in advance to address complex ethical issues will typically be well positioned to make sound ethical decisions and achieve adequate solutions. The purposes of this chapter are to present ethical issues and potential ethical pitfalls that are commonly confronted by neuropsychologists working in pediatric forensic contexts, and to provide structured guidance for avoiding and addressing ethical challenges while pursuing high standards of ethical conduct.

COMMON ETHICAL CHALLENGES AND SOURCES OF CONFLICT

Neuropsychologists who work in forensic contexts with pediatric populations are likely to confront a unique blend of ethical issues. Many of these issues are encountered in various manifestations by psychologists and neuropsychologists in other areas of practice. Neuropsychologists working in pediatric forensic contexts will face many of the same ethical issues that are faced by psychologists (Pope & Vetter, 1992), neuropsychologists (Bush, 2007; Bush, Grote, Johnson-Greene, & Macartney-Filgate, 2008), pediatric neuropsychologists (Bush & MacAllister, 2010), and forensic psychologists (Bush, Connell, & Denney, 2006). However, the blending of these professional roles, combined with diversity in practice settings, results in some variation of ethical priorities and likely challenges for practitioners. The following ethical issues are likely to be of considerable importance in most pediatric forensic neuropsychology practice contexts.

Professional Competence and Scope of Practice

Professional competence is the foundation of ethical practice. Such competence is established through appropriate education, training, and/or professional experience (American Psychological Association [APA], 2002, Ethical Standard 2.01, Boundaries of Competence, subsections a & b; Association of State and Provincial Psychology Boards [ASPPB], 2005, Section III A1, Limits on Practice). Professional competence is the foundation needed for practitioners to provide beneficial services without harming the individuals or institutions with whom the practitioner works (APA General Principle A, Beneficence and Nonmaleficence; APA Ethical Standard 3.04, Avoiding Harm; Beauchamp & Childress, 2001). Without being competent to undertake the requested professional services, practitioners may very well do a disservice to the examinee, referral source, legal system, and reputation of neuropsychology. Despite what may be well-intentioned efforts, practitioners who lack the necessary education, training, or professional experience to perform their work competently will likely be of limited value in the litigation process and may be a harmful presence in the legal case.

Neuropsychologists who provide services to pediatric populations in forensic contexts need to have education, training, or experience in (a) neuropsychology, (b) development of normal or healthy children and adolescents, (c) neuropathology and psychopathology of childhood and adolescence, (d) the forensic context in which services are provided, and (e) the integration of those four aspects of professional knowledge. Evidence of competence in neuropsychology can be determined through review of board certification credentials, among other means. Board certification, however, does not imply competence in all aspects of neuropsychological practice, and there is currently no board certification option in pediatric forensic neuropsychology "by way of an accepted, rigorous peer review process sponsored by a nonprofit professional organization" (Sweet, Grote, & van Gorp, 2002; p. 14). As a result, neuropsychologists who provide services to pediatric populations in forensic contexts are guided by their professional ethics, personal values, and scope of practice laws.

According to the *Specialty Guidelines for Forensic Psychology*, 6th revision draft (SGFP6; Committee on the Revision of the Specialty Guidelines for Forensic Psychology, 2011), even practitioners who have achieved expertise in a particular area of practice may be well served by consulting with colleagues (4.01, Scope of Competence). Additionally, "forensic practitioners adequately and accurately inform all recipients of their services (e.g., attorneys, tribunals) about relevant aspects of the nature and extent of their experience, training, credentials, and qualifications, and how they were obtained" (Committee on the Revision of the Specialty Guidelines for Forensic Psychology, 2011, section 2.03, Representing Competencies, p. 5). Often the adversarial litigation process allows practitioners who provide substandard services to be identified and challenged.

Informed Consent and Assent

In forensic work, practitioners identify *the client* at the outset of their involvement in the case because ethical and practical considerations are directly related to the relationship with the client. The client often is not the person being evaluated. Rather than only determining who the client is, neuropsychologists are better served by determining what ethical obligations are owed to each of the parties involved in cases (Fisher, 2009). For example, the practitioner's agreement with the retaining party covers logistics, such as fees and billing, framing the referral question, and the manner in which the results will be conveyed, to name just a few. Each of these aspects of the neuropsychologist's involvement in the case has associated ethical and legal obligations.

In addition to the ethical obligations owed to the retaining party, the neuropsychologist has ethical obligations to the examinee, the examinee's parents or other guardian, the judicial system, and society at large. Although the usual relationship between a treating doctor and patient does not exist in forensic contexts (Bush, Barth, Pliskin, Arffa, Axelrod, Blackburn, et al., 2005), the neuropsychologist nevertheless has ethical obligations to the examinee. For example, the examinee has the right to be treated with courtesy (APA General Principle E, Respect for People's Rights and Dignity; Ethical Standard 3, Human Relations) and to receive services of adequate quality (Ethical Standard 2.01, Boundaries of Competence).

The essential consideration for clinicians is to determine and clarify (with all parties at the outset of involvement in the case) the nature of the relationships among involved parties and the implications for the neuropsychological services and the information and data obtained (Ethical Standard 3.07, Third Party Requests for Services). Such information is considered by potential examinees when deciding whether to participate in neuropsychological evaluations (Ethical Standards 3.10, Informed Consent and 9.03, Informed Consent in Assessments; Johnson-Greene & NAN Policy & Planning Committee, 2005). In forensic contexts in which examinees are ordered by the court or otherwise mandated to undergo neuropsychological evaluation, practitioners must nevertheless provide *notification of purpose*, which details the purpose, nature, and parameters of the evaluation (Bush, Connell, & Denney, 2006; Ethical Standards 3.10, Informed Consent, subsection c, and 9.03, Informed Consent in Assessments; SGFP6, 6. Notification, Assent, Consent, and Informed Consent).

Similarly, when evaluating persons who have significant cognitive compromise and are legally incapable of providing consent, practitioners have the following ethical obligations (APA, 2002):

(1) provide an appropriate explanation, (2) seek the individual's assent,
(3) consider such persons' preferences and best interests, and (4) obtain

appropriate permission from a legally authorized person, if such substitute consent is permitted or required by law. When consent by a legally authorized person is not permitted or required by law, psychologists take reasonable steps to protect the individual's rights and welfare. (Ethical Standard 3.10, Informed Consent, subsection b).

When providing forensic neuropsychological services to children or adolescents, the minor examinee, with some exceptions, does not have the legal right to provide consent for services. As a result, the consent must be obtained from the parent(s) or other legal guardian. If the parents are divorced or separated, it is preferable to obtain consent from both parents rather than only from the custodial parent whenever possible (Rae, Brunnquell, & Sullivan, 2003). In most jurisdictions, parental consent is not required once the examinee has reached 18 years of age; however, laws regarding the age at which juveniles can legally provide consent for neuropsychological services vary by state. *Emancipated minors*, defined as persons under age 18 who are married, serving in the military, or living independently of their parents and supporting themselves, have the same rights as persons who are 18 years of age or older. Similarly, in some jurisdictions minors have the legal right to consent to specific types of psychological or neuropsychological services, such as suicide assessment or substance abuse treatment (Rae, Brunnquell, & Sullivan, 2003).

Even in cases in which the examinee has not reached the age of consent, it is recommended that assent be obtained from the child or adolescent whenever possible. *Assent* refers to the examinee's agreement to participate in the evaluation. The process of obtaining assent from pediatric examinees involves, at a minimum, providing a description of the nature and purpose of the evaluation, the roles of the people involved, the expectations placed on the examinee, and the advantages and disadvantages of undergoing the evaluation, allowing for discussion as needed (Bush & MacAllister, 2010). Such descriptions and discussion are provided using developmentally appropriate language. Eliciting the minor's assent to undergo the evaluation can help foster rapport and improve cooperation, thereby increasing the likelihood that the results are a valid representation of the examinee's optimal functioning. Whenever possible, informed consent should be obtained in writing, with informed assent from minors obtained in writing or orally. Appropriate documentation is vital.

Limits to Confidentiality

The informed consent and assent process includes discussion of privacy and confidentiality as described in jurisdictional laws and professional ethics codes. APA (2002) Ethical Standard 4.02 (Discussing the Limits of Confidentiality) requires the following:

(a) Psychologists discuss with persons (including, to the extent feasible, persons who are legally incapable of giving informed consent and their legal representatives) and organizations with whom they establish a scientific or professional relationship (1) the relevant limits of confidentiality and (2) the foreseeable uses of the information generated through their psychological activities.

(b) Unless it is not feasible or is contraindicated, the discussion of confidentiality occurs at the outset of the relationship and thereafter as new circumstances may warrant.

In forensic contexts, the expectations for privacy and confidentiality are much different than in most clinical contexts. When persons place their mental state (or those of their children/wards) at issue in a litigated matter, they do not have the same rights to privacy as they would in typical clinical contexts (Federal Rules of Evidence, 1987). In fact, information obtained may be considered to be protected by lawyer–client privilege rather than psychologist–patient privilege. Persons undergoing psychological evaluations in forensic contexts do not have the same right to review and amend their records as is afforded by the Health Insurance Portability and Accountability Act (HIPAA; Department of Health and Human Services, 2003) for clinical contexts (Connell & Koocher, 2003; Fisher, 2003). According to HIPAA, information compiled in anticipation of use in civil, criminal, and administrative proceedings is not subject to the same right of review and amendment as is health care information obtained in clinical contexts [§164.524(a)(1)(ii)] (U.S. Department of Health and Human Services, 2003). Perhaps more succinctly, Grote (2005) stated that HIPAA does not apply to forensic neuropsychological practice. Additionally, according to HIPAA's Privacy Rule, covered practitioners can and must disclose protected health information in response to a court order, with such disclosures limited to the information explicitly covered by the court order (§164.524).

Even in forensic contexts, examinees and/or their legal representatives are informed of the anticipated recipients of neuropsychological reports and other documentation, as well as the possible exposure of such materials if they become part of the public record. Clinicians have a responsibility to protect test materials, whether under copyright/fair trade use law or, as test purchasers, under contractual duty to the test publishers. In addition to the expected dissemination of information obtained during the neuropsychological evaluation, examinees are informed that clinicians are mandated to break confidentiality in specific circumstances, such as when the examinee threatens suicide or when there is reason to suspect child abuse. Jurisdictional laws provide direction regarding the instances in which practitioners must violate patient confidentiality, typically to protect the welfare of others. Therefore, all parties must understand that reports or evidence of child abuse or neglect will be reported to the appropriate agencies.

The APA Insurance Trust and the National Academy of Neuropsychology offer on their Web sites (http://www.apait.org/apait/resources/riskmanagement/FINF.htm; http://nanonline.org/NAN/Files/PAIC/PDFs/NANIMEpaper.pdf) consent form templates for forensic contexts that help to clarify (a) the nature of the relationships between the involved parties, (b) confidentiality exceptions, (c) which party maintains control of the results, and (d) the fact that although the examinee (and more often parents or guardians acting as decision makers) can decline to participate in the evaluation, there may be legal consequences for doing so

(Malina, Nelson, & Sweet, 2005). Sample informed consent forms for pediatric forensic neuropsychology are provided in the Appendix to this book.

Assessment

Neuropsychologists select and use assessment measures and procedures based on the value of such methods for answering referral questions. In forensic contexts with children, neuropsychological evaluations tend to be comprehensive, utilizing multiple methods. Such methods include review of medical and educational records, interviews of parents and/or other collateral sources of information (often including educators), observations of the child, and the administration of neuropsychological tests. The emphasis of the evaluation is on providing the trier of fact with information that is most relevant to the psycholegal issue (SGFP6, 10.01, Focus on Legally Relevant Factors).

Normative Data

The choice of normative data can be a particularly important decision when preparing for a pediatric forensic neuropsychological evaluation. The normative data sets for some commonly used tests are limited by having few subjects for certain age ranges, some tests have no norms at all for certain pediatric age ranges, and some norms are so dated that the Flynn effect has compromised their usefulness (Bridges & Holler, 2007; Bush & MacAllister, 2010). Samples sizes between 50 and 75 subjects per cell have been recommended for tests of constructs for which population means are assumed to be normal (e.g., intelligence tests, memory tests), with smaller sample sizes posing serious problems for diagnostic use (Bridges & Holler, 2007).

Symptom Validity

The conclusions derived from neuropsychological evaluation depend on the validity of the data obtained, and validity is largely dependent on the examinee's effort and honesty. Pediatric examinees may not put forth their best effort for a variety of reasons, including severe anxiety about being evaluated, presence or absence of a parent in the room, presence of other third parties, possible oppositional behavior, a lack of understanding or appreciation of the testing and the importance of trying one's best, or instruction by others to do poorly. Consistent with current standards of practice (American Academy of Clinical Neuropsychology, 2007; Bush et al., 2005; Heilbronner, R. L., Sweet, J. J., Morgan, J. E., Larrabee, G. J., Millis, S., and Conference Participants, 2009), neuropsychologists who evaluate pediatric populations in clinical contexts have clinical and ethical responsibilities to assess effort through both qualitative and quantitative methods. Ethical Standard 9.01 (Bases for Assessments) requires psychologists to base their conclusions on information and methods that are sufficient to support the conclusions. In the context of pediatric forensic neuropsychology, quantitative measures or indicators of symptom validity are needed to substantiate conclusions about all but the most significantly impaired examinees, and recent research has validated several symptom validity tests, originally designed for adult populations, for use with children (Blaskewitz, Mertens, & Kathmann, 2008; Constantinou & McCaffrey, 2003;

Courtney, Dinkins, Allen, & Kuroski, 2003; Donders, 2005; Green & Flaro, 2003; MacAllister, Nakhutina, Bender, Karantzoulis, & Carlson, 2009). A more complete review of this issue, and detailed review of tests for use with children, can be found in Chapters 6 and 7.

THIRD-PARTY PRESENCE

Some young children become quite anxious when their parents leave the office in which test administration will take place. Sensitive, and sometimes creative, examiners are often successful at putting such children at ease, allowing the evaluation to proceed according to standardized procedures. Although the easier solution of allowing the parent to remain in the room can be tempting, standardized testing procedures and the ability to confidently apply norms based on those procedures require that only the examiner and the child are present during testing. Research has demonstrated that the presence of third parties, including parents, affects performance on neuropsychological tests, often in unknown ways (McCaffrey, Fisher, Gold, & Lynch, 1996; McCaffrey, Lynch, & Yantz, 2005; Yantz & McCaffrey, 2009), which can compromise the validity of the results and the value of the evaluation. Professional organizations have provided position papers that advise clinicians in most practice contexts to prohibit third parties from being present during neuropsychological evaluations because of the impact that such presence has on the reliability and validity of the test data (American Academy of Clinical Neuropsychology, 2001; National Academy of Neuropsychology, 2000a).

In extreme situations in which it would be impossible to engage the child in testing without the parent's presence, the examiner must decide whether to proceed with the testing, cognizant that such an accommodation will likely affect the results. When practitioners determine that a parent must be in the room to promote the child's cooperation and effort during test administration, the parent must understand the importance of remaining as unobtrusive as possible. At no time should attorneys or their representatives be present, either in person or through observation, including recording devices, during neuropsychological evaluations. Furthermore, secretive recording of neuropsychological evaluations is not appropriate (Bush, Pimental, Ruff, Iverson, Barth, & Broshek, 2009). Anytime that nonstandard procedures are utilized, it is vital to document such deviations in reports. Third-party presence during test administration is but one example of a nonstandard procedure needing to be documented.

Recommendations, Feedback, and Interventions

Most pediatric neuropsychological evaluations performed for clinical (vs. forensic) purposes conclude with recommendations for treatment, academic accommodations, or other ways of improving the well-being of the child. Consistent with good clinical and ethical practice, such recommendations are commonly discussed with the child's parents or guardian, and, as appropriate, with the child (Standard 9.10, Explaining Assessment Results). In addition, verbal and/or written feedback is often provided to educators, therapists, and physicians, in accordance with professional ethics (e.g., Standard 9.04, Release of Test Data) and jurisdictional laws.

In contrast to the ethical obligations regarding feedback for clinical evaluations, neuropsychologists do not have the same ethical mandate to provide feedback to examinees in forensic evaluation contexts, and such feedback is frequently contraindicated. The APA Ethics Code (Standard 9.10, Explaining Assessment Results) states, "psychologists take reasonable steps to ensure that explanations of results are given to the individual or designated representative unless the nature of the relationship precludes provision of an explanation of results (such as in some organizational consulting, pre-employment or security screenings, and forensic evaluations), and this fact has been clearly explained to the person being assessed in advance." The SGFP also states that, when feedback is precluded, the practitioner explains to the examinee (and/or parents/guardian) prior to the evaluation that feedback will not be provided by the practitioner (Committee on Ethical Guidelines for Forensic Psychologists, 1991; Committee on the Revision of the Specialty Guidelines for Forensic Psychology, 2011). In some situations the neuropsychologist may inform the examinee, parent, or guardian about how he or she can obtain a copy of the report.

Managing Records and Test Security

Neuropsychologists create, maintain, and disseminate records according to professional necessity and ethical and legal requirements. When indicated, neuropsychologists inform retaining parties of their record-keeping practices, including time frames in which records will be destroyed (SGFP6 10.07, Recordkeeping). At minimum, compliance with jurisdictional laws and rules for professional conduct must be maintained. Some states have codified the APA Ethics Code into practice rules or statutes, making the Code the standard for professional conduct. In forensic practice and in many clinical contexts, exchange of raw test data between neuropsychologists facilitates performance comparisons and peer review. In contrast, release of raw test data to attorneys and other nonpsychologists threatens the validity of future evaluation results by increasing the likelihood that examinees will be exposed to test materials prior to their evaluations (Bush & Martin, 2006; Bush, Rapp, & Ferber, 2010). As a result, most sources of ethical authority have emphasized the need to minimize the potential for misuse and misinterpretation of test results by maximizing test security (Attix et al., 2007; Bush, Connell, & Denney, 2006; National Academy of Neuropsychology, 2000b, 2003). However, jurisdictional laws often do not distinguish raw test data from other types of records, resulting in neuropsychologists being compelled by courts to release raw test data to meet evidentiary requirements.

The SGFP6 advise forensic practitioners to make available all documentation, including test data, pursuant to subpoenas, court orders, or other consent from authorized persons (SGFP6 10.06, Provision of Documentation). However, there are steps that can be taken to clarify whether raw test data actually needs to be provided and, if so, to help safeguard the materials. When requested or compelled to release raw test data, neuropsychologists can provide ethical and legal information to educate the court and other interested parties about the importance of test security for society, and they can take steps to minimize the dissemination of their test data (Attix et al., 2007; Kaufmann, 2009; National Academy of Neuropsychology, 2000b, 2003). Again, copyright and fair trade law issues may also be involved.

Maximizing Objectivity

There are many threats to the objectivity of forensic practitioners and their opinions (Crown, Fingerhut, & Lowenthal, 2003; Kaufmann, 2005; Martelli, Bush, & Zasler, 2003; Slick & Iverson, 2003; van Gorp & McMullen, 1997). For example, working with children can bring out feelings ranging from compassion to frustration, and working with the parents can similarly elicit feelings ranging from sympathy to disappointment. There may be a natural tendency to consider letting such feelings influence one's methods or opinions. Alternatively, the process of having feelings impact one's practices may occur outside of the neuropsychologist's awareness. Either way, there is an ethical obligation to identify the impact that various sources of bias have on one's practices and opinions. "Forensic practitioners strive for accuracy, objectivity, fairness, and independence" (SGFP6, 1.02, Impartiality and Fairness, Committee on the Revision of the Specialty Guidelines for Forensic Psychology, 2011, p. 4). Although the APA Ethics Code does not address the issue of bias directly, Ethical Standard 3.01 (Unfair Discrimination) applies.

When the practices or opinions of neuropsychologists are swayed by financial incentive, personal feelings toward an examinee or others involved in the forensic matter, or other factors that are not directly related to answering the psycholegal question as objectively as possible, the neuropsychologists are engaging in discrimination, which will be unfairly advantageous or disadvantageous to the involved parties. Such bias is counter to the ethical responsibility to act with integrity (APA General Principle C, Integrity), promote fairness (APA General Principle D, Justice), and avoid or minimize harm (APA General Principle A, Beneficence and Nonmaleficence). Sweet and Moulthrop (1999a; also see Lees-Haley, 1999 and Sweet & Moulthrop, 1999b) provided recommendations for reducing bias in one's neuropsychological activities.

USE OF ETHICAL AND LEGAL RESOURCES IN THE DECISION-MAKING PROCESS

As with clinical decision making, sound ethical decision making involves the application of a body of relevant information to a structured decision-making process.

General Bioethical Principles

Bioethical principles are based on the shared values of a society applied to health care. Such general principles underlie the specific ethical standards mandated by professional organizations. Beauchamp and Childress (2001) proposed four general bioethical principles that have been widely adopted in health care and are reflected in the 2002 APA Ethics Code. The four principles are (a) respect for autonomy, (b) beneficence, (c) nonmaleficence, and (d) justice. Additionally, fidelity (Bersoff & Koeppl, 1993; Kitchener, 1984) and general beneficence (Knapp & VandeCreek, 2006) are principles that supplement the four described by Beauchamp and Childress (2001) and are directly applicable to forensic neuropsychology. Fidelity refers to the practitioner's obligation to be truthful and faithful, keep promises, and maintain loyalty, while general beneficence refers to a responsibility to the public at large (i.e., society). When ethical challenges are considered or confronted, practitioners are often well served by reviewing these underlying bioethical principles. However, "theory and principle are only starting points and general guides for the development of norms of appropriate conduct. They are supplemented by paradigm cases of right action, empirical data, organizational experience, and the like" (Beauchamp & Childress, 2001, p. 2).

Resources

Ethical decision making involves the review and consideration of a variety of resources. Because professional ethics are by design general in nature, more specific direction is often needed from resources within a practice specialty. In addition to the general bioethical principles and professional ethics codes previously described, neuropsychologists who provide pediatric forensic services may benefit from reviewing the *Code of Conduct* of the Association of State and Provincial Psychology Boards (2005); position papers of professional organizations, such as the National Academy of Neuropsychology (e.g., Silver et al., 2006; Silver et al., 2008); scholarly ethics publications (e.g., Fennell, 2002, 2005; Goldberg, 2005; Woody, 1997); and empirical investigations of ethical questions (e.g., McCaffrey, 2005). Additionally, the jurisdictional laws and rules that relate to and govern neuropsychological practice (e.g., Behnke et al., 2003; Latham & Latham, 1998; Woody, 1997; Wulach, 1993) and those that apply in specific ways to pediatric populations (e.g., Individuals with Disabilities Education Act, 2004; section 504 of the Rehabilitation Act of 1973; No Child Left Behind Act, 2001; Child Abuse Prevention and Treatment Act, 1974) should be considered. Furthermore, the counsel of experienced and knowledgeable colleagues may be particularly helpful when confronted with an ethical dilemma. As part of an ongoing commitment to maintaining ethical competence, continuing education courses are often of considerable value.

Decision-Making Models

Ethical decision making benefits from structure. Such structure assists practitioners with identifying and clarifying the problem, developing possible solutions, considering probable outcomes and alternative solutions, implementing the preferred solution, and evaluating the outcome (Knapp & VandeCreek, 2003). Specific decision-making models have been proposed for forensic psychology (Bush, Connell, & Denney, 2006), neuropsychology (Bush, 2007), and pediatric neuropsychology (Bush & MacAllister, 2010). The primary value of such models is that they provide a step-by-step approach to problem resolution, which increases the probability that most of the important aspects of the problem and possible solutions will be considered in a thorough and logical manner. Table 2.1 provides an ethical decision-making model for pediatric forensic neuropsychology contexts.

TABLE 2.1. Ethical Decision-Making Model for Pediatric Forensic
Neuropsychology Contexts: A 12-Question Approach

1. What is the ethical problem?
2. What is the significance of the context and purpose of the service?
3. What are the needs and roles of the patient and family?
4. What obligations are owed to involved parties (e.g., child/adolescent, parents, retaining party, trier of fact)?
5. Which ethical and legal resources have been used, and which are still needed?
6. How are the practitioner's personal beliefs and values affecting the decision-making process?
7. What are the possible solutions to the ethical problem?
8. What are the likely consequences of each possible solution?
9. Which course of action is best?
10. What was the outcome?
11. Is a different solution or a modification of the previous solution needed?
12. Has the ethical decision-making process been documented?

SOURCE: Adapted from Bush and MacAllister (2010).

Resolving Conflicts Between Ethical and Legal Obligations

Ultimately, practitioners must comply with laws. However, laws often do not reflect ethical ideals, leaving practitioners to determine what course of action should be taken to resolve the conflict in a manner that satisfies ethical ideals but does not violate the law. For example, in some jurisdictions examinees are legally allowed to be accompanied by a third party of their choice during some independent medical (in this case "neuropsychological") examinations. However, as previously described in this chapter, the presence of third parties affects the validity of the test results, rendering the findings of questionable value. By employing an ethical decision-making model, practitioners can discover approaches to resolve problems, such as by educating the involved parties, which may result in withdrawal of the request to have a third party present. Of course, such attempts at education are not always successful, leaving practitioners to determine whether to proceed with the evaluation. We recommend that, in nearly all instances, neuropsychologists elect not to perform evaluations rather than allow a third party to be present, despite the possibility that the evaluations will be performed anyway, and often by colleagues who appear to be less qualified.

According to sections of the APA (2010) Ethics Code (Introduction and Applicability section; Ethical Standard 1.02 Conflicts Between Ethics and Law, Regulations, or Other Governing Legal Authority), psychologists address conflicts between ethics and laws by striving to meet the higher ethical standard. However, the Code also states, "If this Ethics Code establishes a higher standard of conduct than is required by law, psychologists make known their commitment to this Ethics Code and take steps to resolve the conflict in a responsible manner in keeping with basic principles of human rights." (Introduction and Applicability section). With the 2010 amendments, the Code no longer explicitly states that, when confronted with conflicts between ethics and law, psychologists may follow the law. Forensic practitioners strive to comply with applicable ethics codes, laws, and regulations, utilizing appropriate sources of professional authority to inform their decision making and behavior.

ETHICS AS A PRIMARY PROFESSIONAL COMMITMENT

Positive Ethics

Ethical and legal requirements outline a minimum level of professional responsibility. Thus, laws and enforceable ethical standards provide the bottom line for acceptable professional conduct; practitioners must meet their requirements or face disciplinary action. Alternatively, aspirational ethical principles and professional guidelines, such as position papers, describe a higher level of ethical conduct, adherence to which is not enforceable. Positive ethics involves the active promotion of the highest ethical ideals, which includes risk management and the avoidance of misconduct (Handelsman, Knapp, & Gottlieb, 2002; Knapp & VandeCreek, 2006). Although pursuing a high standard of ethical conduct requires time, effort, and expense beyond that required by minimum enforceable standards, such a commitment ultimately benefits practitioners, recipients of neuropsychological services, and the profession.

The Four A's of Ethical Practice and Decision Making

The four A's of ethical practice provide a framework for maintaining high levels of ethical practice (see Fig. 2.1).

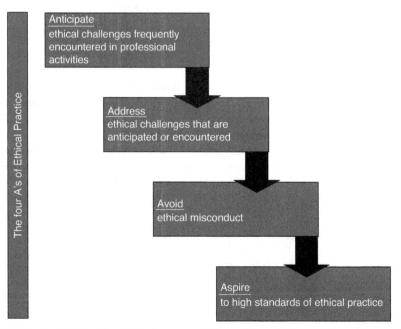

FIGURE 2.1. The four A's of ethical practice. (Adapted from Bush, 2009.)

Practitioners who adhere to the four A's *(a) anticipate* and prepare in advance for ethical challenges that are frequently encountered in professional activities, *(b)* strive to *avoid* ethical misconduct, *(c) address* ethical challenges that are anticipated or encountered, and *(d) aspire* to high standards of ethical practice (Bush, 2009). Practitioners who periodically review and reaffirm their commitment to the four A's of ethical practice facilitate ethical practice.

CONCLUSIONS

Neuropsychologists providing services to pediatric populations in forensic contexts face numerous professional and ethical issues, some of which may become problematic ethical challenges for insufficiently prepared practitioners. By keeping in mind that pediatric populations are vulnerable populations in general and that neurologically compromised children and adolescents are particularly vulnerable, neuropsychologists are likely to maintain sensitivity to their welfare (Rae, Brunnquell, & Sullivan, 2003), even in forensic contexts. Such sensitivity to both pediatric examinees and associated ethical issues will position practitioners well to assist triers of fact and to practice at a high level of ethical competence.

REFERENCES

American Academy of Clinical Neuropsychology (2001). Policy statement on the presence of third party observers in neuropsychological assessment. *The Clinical Neuropsychologist, 15,* 433–439.

American Academy of Clinical Neuropsychology. (2007). Practice guidelines for neuropsychological assessment and consultation. *The Clinical Neuropsychologist, 21,* 209–231.

American Psychological Association. (2002). Ethical principles of psychologists and code of conduct. *American Psychologist, 57,* 1060–1073.

American Psychological Association. (2010). *Ethical principles of psychologists and code of conduct: 2010 amendments.* Retrieved May 2011 from http://www.apa.org/ethics/code/index.aspx.

Association of State and Provincial Psychology Boards. (2005). *ASPPB Code of Conduct.* Retrieved May, 2011 from / http://www.asppb.net/i4a/pages/index.cfm?pageid=3353.

Attix, D. K., Donders, J., Johnson-Greene, D., Grote, C. L., Harris, J. G., & Bauer, R. M. (2007). Disclosure of neuropsychological test data: Official position of Division 40 (Clinical Neuropsychology) of the American Psychological Association, Association of Postdoctoral Programs in Clinical Neuropsychology, and American Academy of Clinical Neuropsychology. *The Clinical Neuropsychologist, 21,* 232–238.

Beauchamp, T. L., & Childress, J. F. (2001). *Principles of biomedical ethics* (5th ed.). New York: Oxford University Press.

Behnke, S. H., Perlin, M. L., & Bernstein, M. (2003). *The essentials of New York mental health law.* New York: W.W. Norton.

Bersoff, D., & Koeppl, P. (1993). The relations between ethical codes and moral principles. *Ethics and Behavior, 3,* 345–357.

Blaskewitz, N., Mertens, T., & Kathmann, N. (2008). Performance of children on symptom validity tests: TOMM, MSVT, and FIT. *Archives of Clinical Neuropsychology, 23,* 379–391.

Bridges, A. J., & Holler, K. A. (2007). How many is enough? Determining optimal sample sizes in pediatric neuropsychology. *Child Neuropsychology, 13*(6), 528–538.

Bush, S. S. (2007). *Ethical decision making in clinical neuropsychology.* New York: Oxford University Press.

Bush, S. S. (2009). *Geriatric mental health ethics: A casebook.* New York: Springer Publishing Company.

Bush, S. S., Barth, J. T., Pliskin, N. H., Arffa, S., Axelrod, B. N., Blackburn, L. A., et al. (2005). Independent and court-ordered forensic neuropsychological examinations: Official statement of the National Academy of Neuropsychology. *Archives of Clinical Neuropsychology, 20,* 997–1007.

Bush, S. S., Connell, M. A., & Denney, R. L. (2006). *Ethical issues in forensic psychology: A systematic model for decision making.* Washington, DC: American Psychological Association.

Bush, S. S., Grote, C., Johnson-Greene, D., & Macartney-Filgate, M. (2008). A panel interview on the ethical practice of neuropsychology. *The Clinical Neuropsychologist, 22,* 321–344.

Bush, S. S., & MacAllister, W. S. (2010). Ethical and legal guidelines for pediatric neuropsychologists. In A. S. Davis (Ed.), *Handbook of pediatric neuropsychology* (pp. 1005–1016). New York: Springer.

Bush, S. S., & Martin, T. A. (2006). The ethical and clinical practice of disclosing raw test data: Addressing the ongoing debate. *Applied Neuropsychology, 13*(2), 115–124.

Bush, S. S., Pimental, P. A., Ruff, R. M., Iverson, G. L., Barth, J. T., & Broshek, D. K. (2009). Secretive recording of neuropsychological testing and interviewing: Official position of the National Academy of Neuropsychology. *Archives of Clinical Neuropsychology, 24,* 1–2.

Bush, S. S., Rapp, D. L., & Ferber, P. S. (2010). Maximizing test security in forensic neuropsychology. In A. M. Horton, Jr. & L. C. Hartlage (Eds.), *Handbook of forensic neuropsychology* (2nd ed., pp. 177–195). New York: Springer.

Bush, S. S., Ruff, R. M., Tröster, A. I., Barth, J. T., Koffler, S. P., Pliskin, N. H., et al. (2005b). Symptom validity assessment: Practice issues and medical necessity. Official position of the National Academy of Neuropsychology. *Archives of Clinical Neuropsychology, 20,* 419–426.

Child Abuse Prevention and Treatment Act, 42 USC § 5101; 42 USC § 5116 (1974).

Committee on Ethical Guidelines for Forensic Psychologists. (1991). Specialty guidelines for forensic psychologists. *Law and Human Behavior, 15,* 655–665.

Committee on the Revision of the Specialty Guidelines for Forensic Psychology. (2011). *Specialty guidelines for forensic psychology,* 6th draft. Retrieved May 2011, from http://www.ap-ls.org/aboutpsychlaw/3182011sgfpdraft.pdf.

Connell, M., & Koocher, G. (2003). HIPAA & forensic practice. *American Psychology Law Society News, 23,* 16–19.

Constantinou, M., & McCaffrey, R. J. (2003). Using the TOMM for evaluating children's effort to perform optimally on neuropsychological measures. *Child Neuropsychology, 9,* 81–90.

Courtney, J. C., Dinkins, J. P., Allen, L. M., & Kuroski, K. (2003). Age-related effects in children taking the Computerized Assessment of Response Bias and Word Memory Test. *Child Neuropsychology, 9,* 109–116.

Crown, B. M., Fingerhut, H. S., & Lowenthal, S. J. (2003). Conflicts of interest and other pitfalls for the expert witness. In In A. M. Horton, Jr. & L. C. Hartlage (Eds.), *Handbook of forensic neuropsychology* (pp. 383–421). New York: Springer.

Donders, J. (2005). Performance on the Test of Memory Malingering in a mixed pediatric sample. *Child Neuropsychology, 11,* 221–227.

Federal rules of evidence for United States courts and magistrates. (1987). St. Paul, MN: West Publishing Company.

Fennell, E. B. (2002). Ethical issues in pediatric neuropsychology. In S. S. Bush & M. L. Drexler (Eds.), *Ethical issues in clinical neuropsychology* (pp. 75–86). Lisse, Netherlands: Swets & Zeitlinger.

Fennell, E. B. (2005). Ethical challenges in pediatric neuropsychology, part I. In S. S. Bush (Ed.), *A casebook of ethical challenges in neuropsychology* (pp. 133–136). New York: Psychology Press.

Fisher, C. B. (2003). Release of test data and the new APA ethics code: What psychologists need to know. *National Psychologist, 12,* 12–13.

Fisher, M. A. (2009). Replacing "Who is the client?" with a different ethical question. *Professional Psychology: Research and Practice, 40,* 1–7.

Goldberg, A. L. (2005). Ethical challenges in pediatric neuropsychology, part II. In S. S. Bush (Ed.), *A casebook of ethical challenges in neuropsychology* (pp. 137–144). New York: Psychology Press.

Green, P., & Flaro L. (2003). Word Memory Test performance in children. *Child Neuropsychology, 9,* 189–207.

Grote, C. L. (2005). Ethical challenges in forensic neuropsychology, Part II. In S. Bush (Ed.), *A casebook of ethical challenges in neuropsychology* (pp. 23–29). New York: Psychology Press.

Handelsman, M. M., Knapp, S. J., & Gottlieb, M. C. (2002). Positive ethics. In C. R. Snyder & S. J. Lopez (Eds.), *Handbook of positive psychology* (pp. 731–744). New York: Oxford University Press.

Heilbronner, R. L., Sweet, J. J., Morgan, J. E., Larrabee, G. J., Millis, S., and Conference Participants (2009). American Academy of Clinical Neuropsychology Consensus Conference statement on the neuropsychological assessment of effort, response bias, and malingering. *The Clinical Neuropsychologist, 23,* 1093–1129.

Individuals with Disabilities Education Act, 20 USC § 1400 (2004).

Johnson-Greene, D., & National Academy of Neuropsychology Policy, Planning Committee. (2005). Informed consent in clinical neuropsychology practice: Official statement of the National Academy of Neuropsychology. *Archives of Clinical Neuropsychology, 20,* 335–340.

Kaufmann, P. M. (2005). Protecting the objectivity, fairness, and integrity of neuropsychological evaluations in litigation: A privilege second to none? *Journal of Legal Medicine, 26,* 95–131.

Kaufmann, P. M. (2009). Protecting raw data and psychological tests from wrongful disclosure: A primer on the law and other persuasive strategies. *The Clinical Neuropsychologist, 23,* 1130–1159.

Kitchener, K. S. (1984). Intuition, critical evaluation and ethical principles: The foundations for ethical decisions in counseling psychology. *The Counseling Psychologist, 12,* 43–55.

Knapp, S., & Vandecreek, L. (2003). *A guide to the 2002 revision of the American Psychological Association's Ethics Code.* Sarasota, FL: Professional Resource Press.

Knapp, S., & VandeCreek, L. (2006). *Practical ethics for psychologists: A positive approach.* Washington, DC: American Psychological Association.

Latham, P. S., & Latham, P. H. (1998). Selected legal issues. In C. E. Coffey & R. A. Brumback (Eds.), *Textbook of child neuropsychiatry* (pp. 1491–1506). Washington, DC: American Psychiatric Press.

Lees-Haley, P. (1999). Commentary on Sweet and Moulthrop's debiasing procedures. *Journal of Forensic Neuropsychology, 1*, 43–57.

MacAllister, W. S., Nakhutina, L., Bender, H. A., Karantzoulis, S., & Carlson, C., (2009). Assessing effort during neuropsychological evaluation with the TOMM in children and adolescents with epilepsy. *Child Neuropsychology, 15*, 521–531.

Malina, A. C., Nelson, N. W., & Sweet, J. J. (2005). Framing the relationships in forensic neuropsychology: Ethical issues. *Journal of Forensic Neuropsychology, 4*, 21–44.

Martelli, M. F., Bush, S. S., & Zasler, N. D. (2003). Identifying, avoiding, and addressing ethical misconduct in neuropsychological medicolegal practice. *International Journal of Forensic Psychology, 1*(1), 26–44.

McCaffrey, R. J. (2005). Special Issue: Third party observers. *Journal of Forensic Neuropsychology, 4*(2).

McCaffrey, R. J., Fisher, J. M., Gold, B. A., & Lynch, J. K. (1996). Presence of third parties during neuropsychological evaluations: Who is evaluating whom? *The Clinical Neuropsychologist, 10*, 435–449.

McCaffrey, R. J., Lynch, J. K., & Yantz, C. L. (2005). Third party observers: Why all the fuss? *Journal of Forensic Neuropsychology, 4*, 1–16.

National Academy of Neuropsychology Policy and Planning Committee. (2000a). Presence of third party observers during neuropsychological testing: Official statement of the National Academy of Neuropsychology. *Archives of Clinical Neuropsychology, 15*, 379–380.

National Academy of Neuropsychology Policy and Planning Committee. (2000b). *Test security. Official position statement of the National Academy of Neuropsychology.* Retrieved May 2011, from http://nanonline.org/NAN/Files/PAIC/PDFs/NANPositionSecurity.pdf.

National Academy of Neuropsychology Policy and Planning Committee. (2003). *Test security: An update. Official statement of the National Academy of Neuropsychology.* Retrieved May 2011, from http://nanonline.org/NAN/Files/PAIC/PDFs/NANTestSecurityUpdate.pdf.

No Child Left Behind Act, 20 USC § 6319. (2001).

Pope, K. S., & Vetter, V. A. (1992). Ethical dilemmas encountered by members of the American Psychological Association: A national survey. *American Psychologist, 47*, 397–411.

Rae, W. A., Brunnquell, D., & Sullivan, J. R. (2003). Ethical and legal issues in pediatric psychology. In M. C. Roberts (Ed.), *Handbook of pediatric psychology* (3rd ed., pp. 32–49). New York: Guilford Press.

Rehabilitation Act of 1973, 29 USC § 794 (1973).

Silver, C. H., Blackburn, L. B., Arffa, S., Barth, J. T., Bush, S. S., Koffler, S. P.,... Elliot, R. W. (2006). The importance of neuropsychological assessment for the evaluation of childhood learning disorders. Official statement of the National Academy of Neuropsychology. *Archives of Clinical Neuropsychology, 21*, 741–744.

Silver, C. H., Ruff, R. M., Iverson, G. L., Barth, J. T., Broshek, D. K, Bush, S. S.,... NAN Policy & Planning Committee. (2008). Learning disabilities: The need for neuropsychological evaluation. *Archives of Clinical Neuropsychology, 23*, 217–219.

Slick, D. J., & Iverson, G. L. (2003). Ethical issues in forensic neuropsychological assessment. In I. Z. Schultz & D. O. Brady (Eds.), *Psychological injuries at trial* (pp. 2014–34). Chicago, IL: American Bar Association.

Sweet, J. J., & Moulthrop, M. A. (1999a). Self-examination questions as a means of identifying bias in adversarial assessments. *Journal of Forensic Neuropsychology, 1*(1), 73–88.

Sweet, J. J., & Moulthrop, M. (1999b). Response to Lees-Haley's commentary: Debiasing techniques cannot be completely curative. *Journal of Forensic Neuropsychology, 1,* 49–57.

Sweet, J. J., Grote, C., & van Gorp, W. G. (2002). Ethical issues in forensic neuropsychology. In S. S. Bush & M. L. Drexler (Eds.), *Ethical issues in clinical neuropsychology* (pp. 103–33). Lisse, Netherlands: Swets & Zeitlinger.

U.S. Department of Health and Human Services. (2003). *Public Law 104–191: Health Insurance Portability and Accountability Act of 1996.* Retrieved April 2011, from http://www.hhs.gov/ocr/privacy/.

van Gorp, W. & McMullen, W. (1997). Potential sources of bias in forensic neuropsychological evaluations. *The Clinical Neuropsychologist, 11,* 180–187.

Woody, R. H. (1997). Psycholegal issues for clinical child neuropsychology. In C. R. Reynolds & E. Fletcher-Janzen (Eds.), *Handbook of clinical child neuropsychology* (2nd ed., pp. 712–725). New York: Plenum Press.

Wulach, J. S. (1993). *Law and mental health professionals: New York.* Washington, DC: American Psychological Association.

Yantz, C. L., & McCaffrey, R. J. (2009). Effects of parental presence and child characteristics on children's neuropsychological test performance: Third party observer effect confirmed. *The Clinical Neuropsychologist, 23,* 118–132.

Chapter 3

Basic Psychometrics and Test Selection for an Independent Pediatric Forensic Neuropsychology Evaluation

CECIL R. REYNOLDS
ARTHUR MacNEILL HORTON, JR.

INTRODUCTION

Clinical neuropsychology is the assessment of brain–behavior relationships (Meier, 1974) and focuses on the clinical problems of assessment and treatment of disorders of higher cortical functions in humans, including children, adults, and the elderly. Clinical neuropsychologists use objective psychological tests that meet recognized psychometric standards of validity and reliability (Horton & Wedding, 1984). This clinical specialty area differs from and is similar to other related areas of psychological practice, such as clinical psychology (Sechrest, Stickle, & Stewart, 1998) and behavioral neurology, to name but two related areas, in terms of the populations served, the neuropsychological problems addressed, and the procedures and techniques employed (American Academy of Neurology, 1996). Pediatric neuropsychology is the subspecialty that focuses upon children, and pediatric forensic neuropsychology is when pediatric neuropsychology in practiced within the legal arena (Hartlage, 2010).

Differences between pediatric neuropsychology and pediatric forensic neuropsychology include the following: relating pediatric neuropsychological findings to legal issues in the forensic setting, the greater need for symptom validity or effort testing, and effectively communicating pediatric neuropsychological implications for legal issues in ways that attorneys, judges, and juries, who may not have scientific backgrounds, can comprehend and understand (Heilbrun et al., 2003). Also, forensic pediatric neuropsychologists must deal with the adversarial nature of legal proceedings and the critical implications of the adversarial nature for the practice of forensic pediatric neuropsychology (Weithorn, 2006). Courtroom procedures evolved from armed combat trials to settle disputes in the Middle Ages. In the legal setting, forensic issues are vigorously contested and the pediatric forensic neuropsychology findings will be regarded by many lawyers depending on whether the pediatric forensic neuropsychology findings support the lawyer's specific case (Zillmer & Green, 2006). The legal combat is different from the traditional clinical setting, where a pediatric neuropsychologist is treated with great respect by colleagues. In forensic proceedings, the degree of respect offered is often proportional to the degree that the forensic pediatric neuropsychology findings support the lawyer's specific case. Nonetheless, the pediatric forensic neuropsychologist must fairly report and objectively interpret the implications of the forensic pediatric neuropsychological findings for the legal questions posed (Horton & Hartlage, 2010). The pediatric forensic neuropsychologist, it should be recalled, has a supportive role in the legal proceedings. Answering the ultimate legal question, of course, is the sole responsibility of the triers of fact, the judge, and jury (Blau, 1998).

Communicating pediatric neuropsychological findings to attorneys, judges, and jury members, who may not have scientific backgrounds, requires great care. As noted by Greiffenstein and Cohen (2005), the neuropsychological report language should be clear and understandable to the general public; technical terms should be avoided, and neuropsychological concepts should be explained simply. The pediatric forensic neuropsychology report is intended to inform the lawyers, judges, and jury members about the implications of the pediatric neuropsychological assessment findings for the legal questions at hand (Heilbrun et al., 2003).

RELIABILITY: CORE CONCEPTS AND TEST USAGE

The concept of reliability refers to the consistency and accuracy with which scores taken from a measuring instrument estimate various knowledge, skills, and abilities (Reynolds, 1998). Reliability is the key concept in measurement theory because it relates to the practical usefulness of all types and systems of measurement. Reliability is also a characteristic of a specific test score and not a test. All human measurements contain error, whether the measurements are of objects or constructs. When measuring a construct that is stable, scores with high reliability will yield consistent results across time. If the underlying construct is subject to fluctuating values, then test scores will not be consistent over time; however, this is not an issue with the reliability of the obtained test scores, but rather with the relative stability of the underlying trait. Reliability is particularly important when tests are used to assess neurological, medical, mental health, and educational difficulties, and in other areas where decisions about individuals are based in whole or even in some part on test scores (Reliability is also discussed in Chapter 5.)

The study of test score reliability centers on estimating the amount of error associated with score derivation (Cronbach, 1990). When error variance is investigated, results are usually reported in terms of a reliability coefficient, a special use of the correlation coefficient. For scores yielded by a test to be considered appropriately reliable for individual diagnostic applications, reliability coefficients that approximate .80 in magnitude are needed and coefficients of .90 or above are considered preferred (Aiken, 2000; Cronbach, 1990; Nunnally & Bernstein, 1994). However, any such pronouncements are relative in nature. Some constructs are simply far more difficult to measure accurately than others and, in such instances, lower values might well be acceptable so long as they provide the most accurate measurements possible and exceed chance or subjective estimations (e. g., see Reynolds & Livingston, 2012). Test scores in this context are useful to the extent they reduce error in the estimation of some value. Error in test scores is commonly attributable to three key sources: content sampling (i.e., test content), time sampling (i.e., when the person was tested), and scorer and administration differences.

Content Sampling

Error associated with content sampling is associated with the degree of homogeneity among items within a test or subtest and how well the items sample the domain of all items associated with the construct being measured. The purpose of a test is to measure a specific knowledge, skill, trait, state, or ability and thus the more items are related to each other (homogeneity), the smaller the error in the test will be (Cronbach, 1990). If the test items are unrelated to each other, they are most likely measuring different constructs, and the amount of error due to content sampling would be greater (and the reliability of the test would be lower as a result) due to the multidimensionality of the score, meaning it is being influenced by extraneous variables. Tests can include both speed and power tests: With speeded tests the individuals' scores depend on how fast they complete the task correctly. With power tests, the number of correct answers obtained in an untimed situation determines the scores obtained. Speeded tests can confound motor speed with decision speed, and it is important to be able to distinguish the components related to each component. The standard error of measurement (SEM) is simply the standard deviation of the error variance around a particular test score. The SEM can be used to develop a confidence interval that surrounds a particular test score. For example, consider an obtained test score of 100. If the associated SEM is 6, it can be said with 68% confidence that the true score lies in a range from one SEM below (94) and one SEM above (106).

Reliability of a test score for a general population (U.S. population) may be different for subgroups within that population (e.g., brain-injured persons, cognitively disabled, gifted, etc). Test score reliability information for subgroups who are likely to be tested or who, because of racial, ethnic, disability, or linguistic differences, might experience test bias (Reynolds, 1998) is needed. The reliability estimates for the selected subgroups within the normative sample can demonstrate the consistency of measurement in different subgroups. Selected subgroups should represent a broad spectrum of identifiable groups, embracing gender and identified ethnic groups. Cronbach's coefficient alpha is the most accurate and most widely used measure of the internal consistency reliability of a test score. It represents the average interitem correlation of all items contributing to the test score which is then corrected for the total number of items. Another way to conceptualize alpha is that it is the mean of all possible split-halves of the items making up the score corrected for the length of the total number of items.

Time Sampling

Error due to time sampling refers to the extent to which an individual's test performance is constant over time. Reliability over time is usually estimated by the test-
retest method. The test-retest method requires that the test is given to a group of
individuals, a period of time is allowed to pass, and the same individuals are tested
again and the results of the two testings are compared. Test-retest studies also afford
an opportunity to examine practice effects. Novel tasks and nonverbal tasks tend to
show the greatest impact from having taken the test on a previous occasion. In general, as the complexity and novelty of the task increases, so does the practice effect
(Franklin, 2010). If one assumes a perfectly stable trait, any differences in scores
over time not attributable to practice effects are due to errors of measurement.

Scorer and Administrator Differences

Examiner variability is another type of reliability. Examiner variability refers to the
amount of test score error due to examiner variability in test administration and
scoring. The most common sources of unreliable scoring are clerical errors or
improper applications of standard scoring criteria on the part of an examiner. Test
reliability for scorer error should be demonstrated statistically for the amount of
error in their tests due to different scorers (Anastasi & Urbina, 1997). Alterations in
standardized procedure also results in lessened reliability of the obtained scores on
a test. To the extent examiners in clinical practice make the same number of scoring
and administrative errors as existed in the standardization sample, alpha will include
such contributions in the error terms in the SEM because such errors lower the
average interitem correlation—if a specific examiner makes more or fewer scoring
or administrative errors, the test score reliability will move up or down.

VALIDITY: CORE CONCEPTS

Test validity referrers to the appropriateness of the interpretation given to the measurement taken and is different from reliability (Messick, 1989). Reliability is
important for validity, but a measurement can be consistent (foot size as a measure
of intelligence) but not true.

    According to the American Educational Research Association, American
Psychological Association, and National Council on Measurement in Education
(AERA, APA, NCME, 1999) *Standards for Educational and Psychological Testing*,
validity refers to "... the degree to which *evidence* and *theory* support the interpretations of test scores entailed by proposed users of tests" (emphasis added, p. 9).
Reynolds (1998) defines validity similarly, averring that validity refers to the appropriateness and accuracy of the interpretation of performance on a test (usually represented as a test score). Validation of the meaning of test scores is also a process
that involves an ongoing effort to accumulate evidence for a scientific basis for proposed test score interpretations (AERA et al., 1999; Reynolds, 1998; Reynolds &
Livingston, 2012). Validation is a constantly moving goal. Validity will always be an
evolving concept since the validity (i.e., evidence to support an interpretation of

performance on a test) of an interpretation may vary according to the purpose for which test scores are being used, the types of individuals or populations being examined, and the specific test interpretations being made.

Validation continues as new research studies are completed and published, and test users should not be constrained by the necessary limitations imposed on time-linked information in a dated test manual and should follow the accumulated contemporary research literature of the ongoing process of test validation. This premise is also supported in the *Standards* (AERA et al., 1999), which note that "validation is the joint responsibility of the test developer and test user" (p. 11). The 1999 *Standards* provides a suggested scheme for organizing sources of evidence to evaluate proposed interpretations of test scores. The *Standards* propose five categories of evidence that will vary in their respective importance according to how test scores are used, the consequences of test results' interpretive errors, the consequences of not using an objective psychological test, and the population to which the test is applied. Users of tests consequently must carefully weight the specific test validation evidence presented, be knowledgeable of current research literature, and make their own empirical and clinical evaluation of the research evidence for the clinical use they intend to make of the test in question. The empirically based evidence is organized into the five areas suggested in the 1999 *Standards*, shown in Figure 3.1.

Theory as well as empirical evidence in support of test score interpretations is considered to be important in the standards. The *Standards* also note that evidence

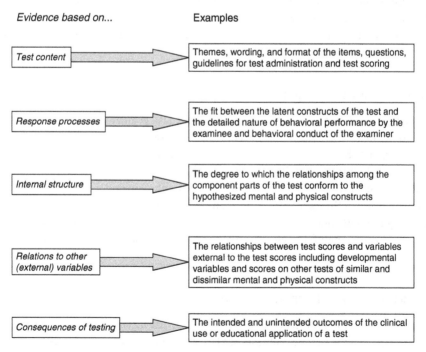

FIGURE 3.1. Kinds of validity evidence to consider when evaluating psychological tests. (Adapted from AERA et al., 1999.)

may be logical and not just empirical, especially with regard to evidence based on content and response processes.

Theory-Based Evidence

Models of brain function and other contemporary conceptualizations of neuropsychological function can be cited as validity evidence for neuropsychological tests (Carroll, 1993; Horton & Wedding, 1984; Joseph, 1996: Zillmer & Spiers, 2001). A considerable amount of evidence has accumulated linking various neuropsychological tests and brain systems. When choosing a neuropsychological test, it is especially important to determine whether the research literature evidence supports the linkage between the specific neuropsychological tasks or specific tests to actual brain systems (Horton & Wedding, 1997; Reynolds & Horton, 2006).

Evidence Based on Test Content

The *Standards* (AERA et al., 1999) state that test content refers to the "... themes, wording, and format of the items, tasks, or questions ..." as well as guidelines "... for administration and scoring" (p. 11). In discussing the types of evidence that may be appropriate in this context, the *Standards* conclude that evidence related to test content may be logical or empirical and that expert judgments of the relationships between the test scores and the constructs intended to be assessed by the test are appropriate as evidence of validity. Direct examination and a comparison of the stimuli and the format of the subtests to other very well-researched tasks in clinical neuropsychology can be a measure of positive evidence of validity based on the test content. Expert judges may also be employed to evaluate the content evidence for test interpretation.

Evidence Based on Response Processes

Evidence based on the response processes of the task evaluates the fit between the nature of the performance or actions in which the examinee is actually engaged and the constructs being assessed. Eliciting stimuli and the response processes may be very strongly intertwined. To rule out peripheral perceptual or motor confounds that may impair the validity of tasks as a measure of neuropsychological functioning, a number of things may be done. Comparison of subtests with common cognitive requirements but different response formats (e. g., motor enhanced and motor reduced) can be helpful in elucidating the presence of possible peripheral perceptual and motor confounds.

Evidence Based on Internal Structure

Analyses of the internal structure of a test can provide information about the interrelationships of the items or subtests of a larger test and evaluate the degree to which this internal structure conforms to the hypothesized construct(s) being assessed (AERA et al., 1999). Analysis of internal structure evidence requires both empirical and logical analyses. Evidence from studies of internal consistency and studies of the intercorrelation matrix (Cattell, 1978) among subtests is evaluated relative to the context of proposed interpretations of the test scores provided (e.g., see Jensen, 1998).

Internal Structure Among Selected Gender, Ethnic, and Clinical Groups

As noted in the *Standards* (AERA et al., 1999) and Reynolds (1998), an analysis of the internal structure segregated by various nominal groupings can shed light on the stability and robustness of the results with smaller sample sizes and reveal whether the latent structure of the component subtests is constant across groups.

Common results across gender, ethnic, and other subgroups will argue in favor of a common set of interpretations across groups.

Evidence Based on Relations to Other (External) Variables

Evaluation of the relationship of scores on the instrument of interest to variables that are external to the test itself is a crucial aspect of the test validation process. This includes relationships with other tests that may measure some similar or dissimilar constructs, diagnostic categorizations, educational success, and relationships with developmental constructs such as age (Reynolds & Horton, 2006). The *Standards* (AERA et al., 1999) note that different relationships will have different degrees of importance to examiners in different settings or when using the test for different purposes. Test users have the responsibility to evaluate the evidence and determine its adequacy for the intended use of the instrument. As mentioned earlier, validation of the meaning of test scores is always an ongoing process and continuing investigation of tests and especially their relationships to various questions of interest and their relative levels of specificity and sensitivity across various clinical conditions, different races and ethnic groups, demographic characteristics, and geographical locations is clearly warranted and indeed is actually required for reasonable use of a test (Reynolds & Horton, 2006).

ISSUES RELATING TO NORMS SAMPLES

Normative Groups

To interpret a neuropsychological test, it is necessary to understand how the patient compares to an appropriate reference group or normative sample. What reference group is most appropriate depends upon the type of question one is attempting to answer as well as characteristics of the patient. If you want to know how the patient's neuropsychological test performance ranks relative to the general population of age mates in the United States, then a population proportionate stratified random sample of the same-age peers in the United States is the right reference group. However, one may be interested instead in knowing how the extant patient compares to a specific patient population, for example, how is this pediatric leukemia patient's neuropsychological test performance relative to that of same-age peers who are also receiving chemotherapy for leukemia? The latter question requires a different reference sample. Confusion of reference groups (aka normative samples) for tests is a common issue not just in practice, but in research as well (e.g., see Reynolds, 2010).

Considerations regarding neuropsychological tests norms include the normative sample selected, the demographic characteristics of the sample, and the types of normative scores provided. However, the overriding question is the question to be answered about the patient and this will most often dictate the appropriate reference group for comparison(Lyman, 1988).

Sample Selection

The normative sample selected should be based on the intended purpose and use of the pediatric neuropsychological test. If the test is intended to be used primarily in the United States, then the normative sample should be selected in the United States and should be representative of the U.S. population. For a test intended to be used primarily in Canada or Australia, then those tests might need normative samples selected in and representative of the populations of those countries. Specific interpretations for specific patient populations also need to be considered as noted earlier, and multiple reference groups may be desired. In choosing tests, one should consider carefully the questions to be answered via testing and the availability of reference groups for test performance in answering the posed questions.

Demographic Characteristics

The characteristics of the sample with regard to geographic region, gender, race, ethnicity, age, and education should be reported and the percentages for these characteristics should be compared with those reported in the *Statistical Abstracts of the United States* (U.S. Bureau of the Census, 2010), for any normal samples. The percentages reported by the Bureau of the Census (2010) are the most accurate reflection of the demographic characteristics available to describe the population residing in the United States.

Normative Scores

Normative scores facilitate interpretation of data. This section relates the statistical properties of these normative scores and the procedures used to compute them (Cronbach, 1990).

T SCORES
Norms are often presented in the form of T scores which have a mean of 50 and a standard deviation of 10. T scores are commonly used in measures of child and adolescent personality and behavior such as the Behavior Assessment System for Children-Second Edition (BASC-2, Reynolds & Kamphaus, 2004) and less so in cognitive measures, purely by habit and convention in most cases.

The T scores for a test like the BASC-2 are age-corrected, deviation-scaled scores based on the cumulative frequency distributions of the raw scores made by examinees of varying ages. That is, they are computed directly from the percentiles associated with the raw scores made by individuals in the standardization sample. The resulting data were smoothed somewhat to allow for a consistent progression across age levels, but the scores are not normalized; rather, they are linear transformations. Linear transformations are more appropriate when the latent distributions are not normal in shape as is the case with most behavioral variables. For aptitude scores, normalized curvilinear transformations are most often chosen by test developers because aptitudes such as intelligence, spatial ability, and the like are approximately normally distributed in the population.

PERCENTILES

Percentiles are derived scores that indicate the percentage of persons (or scores) that occur at or below a particular raw score. Although percentiles are convenient and popular, examiners should be familiar with their advantages and disadvantages as explained by Aiken (2000), McLoughlin and Lewis (2000), Reynolds (1998), Salvia and Ysseldyke (2001), and Wallace, Larsen, and Elksnin (1992).

AGE (OR GRADE) EQUIVALENTS

Age (or grade) equivalents are simply the mean raw score of individuals at a particular age (or grade), but they are not recommended for clinical use. It is not correct to compute the mean or average of a group of age equivalents (or grade equivalents for that matter) or any other type of test score that exists on a nominal or ordinal scale of measurement. Age- and grade-equivalent scores are ordinal forms of measurement (see Reynolds & Livingston, 2012, for a more detailed explanation). After the age of about 13 to 14 on nearly all developmental phenomena, age equivalents do not make psychometric sense (Reynolds, 1998), and at every age they contribute to interpretive problems because age (grade) equivalents may exaggerate small differences in actual performance and such scores are not comparable across variables or across age.

The Flynn Effect and Test Revisions

There are numerous population-related factors that influence the accuracy of tests that measure neuropsychological abilities. The most prominent are as follows:

1) The normative sample from which scores are derived should be representative of a recent population of interest and one that addresses the questions to ask of performance on the test. In the United States, it is an age-appropriate sample of the U.S. population. The U.S. population demographics have been shown to change rapidly and to the extent the reference or normative sample is out of date, the scores will be inaccurate in describing a patient to some unknown degree.

2) Test items exist in a cultural context that is temporal. As broad changes occur in the cultural patterns, test items that include cultural references

can easily become archaic, again causing score estimations to be inaccurate in describing a patient to some unknown degree.

3) The Flynn effect requires more frequent calibration of IQ test scores and may have similar implications for pediatric neuropsychological tests in general. Research by James Flynn (1987, 1998), a political scientist at the University of Otago in Dunedin, New Zealand, made detailed comparisons of children's scores on measures of intelligence across time and countries and demonstrated a steady increase in intelligence test performance throughout the 20th and into the 21st century. This increase in intelligence performance is consistent and measurable. This phenomenon of rising IQ, called the Flynn effect, has indicated that across countries and across conditions there is a real growth in intelligence of up to 25 points per generation. This increase may be the result of better nutrition, smaller families, and wider access to education and video games, but empirical evidence regarding etiology is unclear. The implication for intelligence tests, however, is that intelligence tests should be recalibrated every 10 years or so to account for the Flynn effect. In the interim period or in the case of use of an older test, a Flynn correction should be applied to the scores (see Reynolds, Niland, Wright, & Rosenn, 2010, for specifics).

Once a new version or revision of an intelligence test is available, the Flynn effect suggests the most recent version or revision should be used. Two documents of the American Psychological Association (APA) also aver use of the most recent version or revision. First, the APA *Ethical Principles of Psychologists* indicates that "Psychologists do not base such decisions or recommendations on tests and measures that are obsolete and not useful for the current purpose" (APA, 2002, p. 14). Second, another set of standards makes a similar statement. The APA, along with the American Educational Research Association (AERA) and the National Council on Measurement in Education (NCME), makes the same point regarding using the most recent version or revision in the *Standards for Educational and Psychological Tests* (AERA et al., 1999). Whenever a psychologist uses an older version of a test, the *Standards* place the burden of proving it was an appropriate choice over the newer version squarely on the shoulders of the user: "If an older version of a test is used when a newer version has been published or made available, test users are responsible for providing evidence that the older version is as appropriate as the new version for that particular test use" (AERA et al., 1999, p. 48).

STANDARDS FOR TEST INTERPRETATION IN THE FORENSIC SETTING

In recent years, there has been a revolution in the scientific approach to the interpretation of intelligence test scores. In the past, clinicians had been trained to interpret subtests of intelligence tests by performing ipsative comparisons among these subtests (calculating the mean of a person's scores on subtests of a battery of tests and then comparing individuals against themselves by comparing each subtest score to the mean of the individual's subtests) (Rapaport, Gill, & Schafer, 1945–1946).

Clinicians would find the examinee's mean subtest score across the subtests administered and calculate a series of difference scores by then subtracting each subtest score from this mean. If the difference score was statistically significantly different from the mean, the clinician would interpret these individual subtests to reflect a pattern of cognitive strengths and weaknesses that support various diagnoses.

Research over the last 20 years, however, has not validated this traditional practice. Rather, the global scores that assessed verbal and nonverbal intelligence and their composite had the greatest evidence for their interpretability (Livingston, Jennings, Reynolds & Gray, 2003; Stanton & Reynolds, 2000; Reynolds & Kamphaus, 2003). Beliefs about subtest-level data, based upon training and experience, were found to be myths (Watkins, 2000). Current research indicates that the better a test measures intellectual functioning, the less likely subtest-level profile analysis will aid in differential diagnosis (e.g., Livingston, Jennings, Reynolds, & Gray, 2003; McDermott, Fantuzzo, Glutting, Watkins & Baggaley, 1992; Reynolds & Kamphaus, 2003). A primary problem with subtest profiling is that subtest score differences are all too common in normal individuals to be used to identify learning disabilities, emotional disorders, or brain damage (Watkins & Kush, 1994). Base rates (the frequency of occurrence in the normal, standardization sample) of various profiles indicate too much overlap among groups to predict group membership based upon subtest scores (Glutting, McDermott, Watkins, Kush, & Konold, 1997). Due in large part to the base rate issue, subtest-level profiles of intelligence tests cannot distinguish normal from abnormal intellectual patterns on an individual case basis. Another problem with subtest-level interpretations of intelligence tests is that subtest profiles (difference scores) lack reliability (Pritchard, Livingston, Reynolds, & Moses, 2000). Reliability is used in measurement theory as shorthand for looking at the relative precision as well as degree of error in a measurement. Subtest-level profile ipsative scores for interpretation rarely have reliability coefficients that reach .50 or higher (e.g., see Livingston, Jennings, Reynolds, & Gray 2003; McDermott et al., 1992; and Reynolds & Kamphaus, 2003). Therefore, the predominant source of variation in ipsative profile scores at the subtest level is error variance (the percentage of error variance in a score is simply 1 minus the reliability coefficient). However, when subtests are combined in a composite index, the composite index scores become highly reliable and can then be interpreted.

Individual subtest scores, or even small groupings of subtest scores of larger intelligence batteries, do not predict well and the profiles they produce are substantially unreliable over time (Livingston et al., 2003; McDermott, et al., 1992; also see review in Chapter 1 of Reynolds & Kamphaus, 2003). The implication of this body of research is that great care needs to be taken not to overinterpret individual subtests and profiles of subtests.

On neuropsychological test batteries, a high level of test specificity and test score reliability can overcome these problems, but little research has been done with most batteries to ascertain the validity of profile interpretation. Most clinicians simply assume it is proper practice. It is best to avoid interpretation of subtests or components from batteries where the average subtest intercorrelations are moderate to high (e. g., .60 or higher); in such cases it is best to focus on the interpretation of composite scores.

CLINICAL VERSUS FORENSIC PEDIATRIC NEUROPSYCHOLOGY ASSESSMENT INSTRUMENTS

Test selection in forensic pediatric neuropsychology is frequently similar to a clinical pediatric neuropsychological evaluation with the following exceptions. There is a much greater reliance on the assessment of effort (Iverson, 2003; see also Chapters 6 and 7), the identification and careful review of health, school and employment records, and interviews with collateral informants. Also, specialized questionnaire/tests/structured interview measures developed to answer specific legal questions may be added. Most forensic pediatric neuropsychologists use a core group of neuropsychological tests that they administer to most patients but augment the core battery depending on the specific legal questions that required the forensic neuropsychological evaluation; the patient's physical abilities, mental capabilities, or fatigue level and time available for evaluation; and the setting and circumstances under which the forensic neuropsychological evaluation is to be conducted (i.e., hospital bedside or detention facility) as well as on the patient's particular educational, medical, neurological, and social characteristics.

Batteries of forensic pediatric neuropsychological tests typically include measures to assess the neuropsychological domains of sensory-perceptual functioning, motor skills, language abilities, visual/spatial skills, executive functioning, attention and memory, emotional status, and personality functioning and effort (Horton & Wedding, 1984, Iverson, 2003). A conundrum is that there is a relative dearth of specifically developed forensic pediatric neuropsychology instruments that focus solely on legal questions.

In many cases, the forensic pediatric neuropsychologist may use instruments developed to assess brain injury to answer legal questions other than brain injury (Cullum, Heaton, & Grant, 1991). In such cases, great caution is needed. A crucial question with forensic pediatric neuropsychological test selection, however, is the degree to which reliance can be placed on a neuropsychological test or various groupings of neuropsychological tests to answer specific legal questions (Horton, 1997). If a forensic pediatric neuropsychologist wishes to rely on a group of neuropsychological tests in a forensic neuropsychology setting, rather than on a single neuropsychological test, then it is best if the group of neuropsychological tests has previously been empirically considered, as a group of tests, for the legal question being asked (Reitan & Wolfson, 1992, 1993) and that base rates of profiles in the normal population are understood, and that data regarding false-positive and false-negative error rates in particular are available or can be estimated accurately. If a group of neuropsychological tests has not been considered as a group for the specific legal question being asked, then the established accuracy level would have to be considered to be equal to the best accuracy for any single neuropsychological test (Reitan, 1958) that has been empirically validated for the legal question being asked (Project on Scientific Knowledge and Public Policy, 2003). In short, forensic pediatric neuropsychological findings should have an empirical/actuarial basis (Project on Scientific Knowledge and Public Policy, 2003) and not be based on speculation about how batteries might combine to reflect brain function.

ADMISSIBILITY CRITERIA

There are various legal standards for the admissibility of expert witness testimony in the courts (see Cohen, 2010, for a review).

Frye Standard

In a 1923 Court of Appeals for the District of Columbia ruling in *Frye v. the United States,* the decision stated that the expert witness' opinion must be based on theories or principles that are generally accepted in that expert's scientific/professional community. Many states still use this "general acceptance" standard.

Daubert Standard

In *Daubert v. Merrell Dow Pharmaceuticals* (1993), the U.S. Supreme Court determined the *Daubert* standard for deciding the characteristics of expert testimony that would be allowed into courtrooms as evidence. The Supreme Court's intent was to eliminate expert testimony that was not based on scientific findings. The issue of expert testimony that was not based on science has been a significant concern of the legal system for many years. The *Daubert* opinion criteria clarify for judges what expert testimony should be permitted. The *Daubert* decision indicated four key criteria among others by which judges could determine whether the science in proposed expert testimony should be admissible (see Table 3.1).

Many states have moved to adopt the *Daubert* standard and the trend is toward wide acceptance of the *Daubert* standard. The Supreme Court has warned against using the list as "a definitive checklist or test," and judges themselves, according to some legal scholars, have not been consistent in applying *Daubert* criteria in all cases. Extended discussion of this important legal issue goes beyond the scope of this chapter, but there is an excellent extended discussion put forth by the Project on Scientific Knowledge and Public Policy (2003) and readers are encouraged to review that reference and other forensic neuropsychology resources (Cohen, 2010; Horton & Hartlage, 2003). Also, if the forensic pediatric neuropsychological tests that form the basis of an opinion have clear evidence to support the interpretations given by the neuropsychologist, then a *Daubert* challenge is unlikely (Greiffenstein & Cohen, 2005).

TABLE 3.1. The Four Key Criteria from the *Daubert* Decision

1. Is the evidence based on a testable theory or technique?
2. Has the theory or technique been peer reviewed?
3. In the case of a particular technique, does it have a known error rate and standards controlling the technique's operation?
4. Is the underlying science generally accepted?

NOTE: These criteria, among others, are to be used by judges to determine whether the science in proposed expert testimony should be admissible.

Kumho Tire Case

The *Kumho Tire v. Carmichael case* (1999) extended the *Daubert* standard beyond scientific testimony to also include testimony based on technical and specialized knowledge.

SCOPE OF THE TYPICAL FORENSIC PEDIATRIC NEUROPSYCHOLOGICAL ASSESSMENT

The pediatric forensic neuropsychological evaluation methods and procedures will vary depending on several factors. These factors include the referral question, the nature of the legal issues, specific circumstances of the child or adolescent (e.g., age, education, ethnicity, and gender), special impairments of the child or adolescent, and available resources of finances, time, and setting, among others.

CONTROVERSIES OVER FIXED VERSUS FLEXIBLE BATTERIES AND COURTS

Some forensic pediatric neuropsychologists have a rigid conceptualization of "fixed test batteries." They suggest that fixed battery proponents never deviate from a fixed battery of tests whereas flexible battery proponents select a battery of tests based on the patient's individual needs (see Strauss, Sherman, & Spreen, 2006 for further discussion of these issues and concepts). In addition, an intermediate approach position is postulated where similar patients are given a common grouping of tests. The intermediate position is characterized as a flexible battery approach where a common core of neuropsychological tests is administered and then additional tests may be given based on the patient's performance on the core battery. The presentation of a fixed neuropsychology battery approach as never deviating from a set group of neuropsychological tests is a myth. Forensic pediatric neuropsychologists who use fixed batteries often supplement the pediatric neuropsychology battery to assess specific areas and often modify the pediatric neuropsychology battery when patient needs dictate modifications are necessary. Rather, proponents of standardized (rather than fixed) neuropsychological test batteries aver that when a combination of neuropsychological tests is used to reach a clinical neuropsychological decision there should have been validation of the specific combination of tests for the specific purpose at the level of the individual patient (Reitan & Wolfson, 1993). In other words, to make a decision with a group of neuropsychological tests, it is best to have empirically based research on the ability of the specific group of tests.

That is not to say that in the absence of empirical research with a group of pediatric neuropsychological tests that individual neuropsychological tests cannot be used for clinical decision making with patients but rather the ability to make decisions is limited to the power of the individual tests rather than the specific combination of tests. Nothing is wrong with developing forensic opinions on the basis of a limited specific group of pediatric neuropsychological tests because frequently it is not possible to employ more extensive neuropsychological testing; however, the scientific creditability of the decision making is limited to the scientific research evidence for the individual measures. It can also be problematic since the more individual tests that are given, where the base rates of false positive and false negatives are unknown, the more likely one is to accrue "abnormal" findings that are common in the normal population.

Very low scores on some neuropsychological tests are common in the normal population and as tests are added, the probability of such occurrences in the absence of any brain dysfunction increases (Iverson, Brooks, White, & Stern, 2008; Koushik, Brooks, Iverson, Horton, & Reynolds, 2009; see also Chapter 4). A more sophisticated model of test selection would appreciate that specific batteries of pediatric neuropsychological tests have been or should be validated for specific legal questions and that neuropsychological test selection should rest on research results as to which groups of neuropsychological tests, or neuropsychological batteries, are most effective for answering the specific legal questions being asked. Rather than expect clinical neuropsychologists to make up a new battery of neuropsychological tests for every new patient it is better to rely on research findings that document which sets of neuropsychological tests have been empirically validated for answering specific legal questions. While this represents a challenge to all in practice, the inclusion of a common core battery (a fixed component) assists in solving many of the practical issues encountered.

ISSUES WITH TEST ADMINISTRATION

Important matters regarding administering tests include information about (a) eligibility for testing, (b) examiner competence, (c) environment for testing, and (d) accounting for situational and subject error/specific instructions for administering and scoring.

Eligibility for Testing

Individuals with significant vision problems may perform poorly due to limited sight visual tests. Visual-perceptual difficulties, if severe, may also impede performance and if such problems are suspected, the examiner may wish to include in the evaluation the Developmental Test of Visual Perception-Adolescent and Adult (DTVP-A; Reynolds, Voress, & Pearson, 2002) for individuals aged 11 years and up and the Developmental Test of Visual Perception-2 (Hammill, Pearson, & Voress, 1992) for younger ages, both instruments designed for this purpose. Persons with significant expressive aphasic symptoms would be expected to have difficulty with the language loaded tests such as the Clinical Evaluation of Language Fundamentals, Fourth Edition (Semel, Wiig, & Secord, 2003) and any poor results could be due to oral motor performance problems rather than other problems. Examinees with significant fine or gross motor impairments in the dominant hand or with a significant peripheral neuropathy may have difficulty with tests that require a perceptual-motor response. Subsequent administration with the Comprehensive Trail Making Test (Reynolds, 2002) may be helpful in clarifying the contributions of various psychomotor abilities.

Examiner Competence

Examiners who give and interpret tests should have formal training in assessment. This training should result in a thorough understanding of test statistics; general procedures governing test administration, scoring, and interpretation; and specific information about the evaluation of children. Examiners are expected to be knowledgeable about the current edition (at the time of testing) of the *Standards for Educational and Psychological Testing* and to follow the standards whenever possible. Supervised practice in administering, scoring, and interpreting individually administered tests is essential.

Environment for Testing

The testing environment should be a room arranged to minimize distractions. The testing room should be free from noise and other people and well lit. The table used during testing should be large enough to allow the examiner and the examinee to sit at the same table and young children may need seat cushions to elevate them to a more appropriate height. In addition, the table should be large enough to allow the examinee to lay the record booklet completely on the table in order to make the necessary markings and to accommodate the stimulus cards. There is a great deal of research demonstrating that third-party observers (Binder & Johnson-Greene, 1995; McCaffrey, Fisher, Gold, & Lynch, 1996; Kehrer, 1999) may influence neuropsychological test results, so the best policy is not to allow third-party observers during forensic pediatric neuropsychological test administration (National Academy of Neuropsychology, 2000). This is also discussed in more detail in Chapters 1 and 2.

Situational/Subject Error

Reynolds (1998) noted that the reliability of any test can be impaired by inherent sources of error that include (*a*) examinee and (*b*) situation. The two sources of error variance arise from physical location factors and within the examiners themselves. An examiner has the very important responsibility to control and/or account for the obvious external/situational variables that can affect the examinee's performance adversely (e.g., noisy room, no rest breaks, poor lighting, a chair that is too low, and uncomfortable furniture). Test examiners must be alert to certain individual conditions (e.g., fatigue, state of physical health, lack of sleep, nervousness, attitude toward the test, attention level). Test examiners also have an important responsibility to adhere exactly to the guidelines for standardized administration of the tests they administer because even seemingly minor variations in administration can greatly influence the test results (Lee, Reynolds, & Willson, 2003). And especially unfortunate is the finding of these same researchers that not only the degree but also the direction of score changes is often unpredictable and counterintuitive in many instances.

SENSITIVITY AND SPECIFICITY

Forensic opinions given by pediatric neuropsychologists are made after evaluations of multiple data sources such as neuropsychological test results, behavioral observations, interviews, self-reported histories, collateral reports of significant others, and careful review of various types of health, educational, and criminal justice records. In the case of a forensic opinion that can be reduced to a yes or no diagnostic decision, the most common situation in forensic matters, there are four potential outcomes (Larrabee, 2005). The outcomes are as follows:

(1) Correct about the presence of a disorder, a true-positive condition
(2) Incorrect about the presence of a disorder, a false-positive condition
(3) Correct about the absence of a disorder, a true-negative condition
(4) Incorrect about the absence of a condition, a false-negative condition.

This decision scheme is illustrated with respect to evidence for poor effort during neuropsychological test administration in Figure 3.2.

For example, if a forensic pediatric neuropsychologist makes the conclusion that a patient has given poor effort during neuropsychological testing, the forensic pediatric neuropsychologist may be correct—a true-positive condition—or the forensic pediatric neuropsychologist may be incorrect—a false-positive condition. On the other hand, if a forensic pediatric neuropsychologist makes the conclusion that a patient has given good effort during the neuropsychological test administration, the forensic pediatric neuropsychologist may be correct—a true-negative condition, or the forensic pediatric neuropsychologist may be incorrect—a false-negative condition. Briefly, there are four possible outcomes of any yes/no decision.

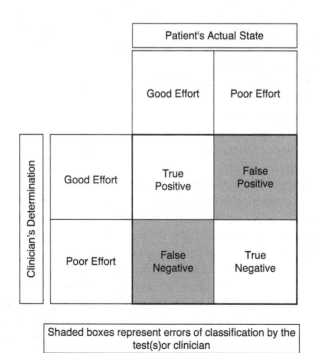

FIGURE 3.2. Diagnostic outcomes in the evaluation of sensitivity and specificity.

In the best of all cases, the forensic pediatric neuropsychologist will make either a true-positive or true-negative condition decision regarding the patient's effort, but in the worst of cases, the forensic pediatric neuropsychologist would be incorrect and make either a false-positive or false-negative condition decision. Cutoff scores can be set to maximize true-positive and true-negative conclusions (correct answers) and minimize both false-positive and false-negative conclusions (errors). Base rates and the relative benefits/costs of each condition in terms of therapeutic outcome, monetary impact, medical, psychological, and social costs are primary factors considered in deciding how to maximize correct answers and minimize errors. Increasing and decreasing rates of different conditions require a tradeoff among the various conditions mentioned previously. Using more conservative or more liberal cutoffs in decision making will affect the accuracy of true-positive and true-negative diagnostic decision rates. There are reasons to maximize/minimize one type of error over another (Reynolds, 1984).

CLINICAL VERSUS STATISTICAL PREDICTION

The forensic pediatric neuropsychologist uses neuropsychological test scores and interview results, behavioral observations, collateral reports and reviews of health, educational, and criminal justice as well as mental health and neurological records to form forensic opinions. There are two fundamental approaches a clinician can apply to prediction (Kleinmuntz, 1990). The first approach relies on the human judgment of the forensic pediatric neuropsychologist evaluating all of the available data in conjunction with prior experiences and knowledge of the psychological literature. This is the *clinical method* and relies primarily on the clinical acumen of the individual forensic pediatric neuropsychologist to make a prediction. Alternately, the forensic pediatric neuropsychologist may apply a previously developed and empirically validated formal algorithm or set of mathematical equations to make a predication. The use of an algorithm or mathematical equation approach is *the statistical method* (Meehl, 1954).

There has been extensive research over many decades on the ability of clinicians to use test data and other clinical information to make predictions. Meehl (1954) concluded that the statistical method (formula-based technique) was superior to the clinical method (individual clinicians) in predicting clinical conditions and human behavior. In 70+ years of research the statistical method has consistently been shown to be superior to the clinical method (Faust & Ackley, 1998). In 136 studies since 1928, over a wide range of prediction tasks, the actuarial method was invariably equal to or superior overall to clinical methods (Grove & Meehl, 1996). Put another way, John Henry lost to the steam engine.

Statistical methods are superior because clinicians cannot assign optimal weights to variables used to make decisions, do not apply decision-making rules consistently, and are influenced by relatively unreliable data (e.g., see Dawes, 1995; Dawes, Faust, & Meehl, 1989; Faust, 1984; Grove & Meehl, 1996; Meehl, 1954). See Chapter 1 for additional discussion of statistical (actuarial) prediction in neuropsychological assessment.

SHORT FORMS AND BRIEF SCREENING MEASURES

Short forms and brief screening tests are designed to be screening instruments such that if a person scores below or above a preset cutting score, more extensive testing would be required to document an ability level. Short forms and brief screening tests are not intended or designed to be substitutes for or part of a comprehensive forensic pediatric neuropsychological evaluation. Short forms and brief screening tests are useful to identify individuals who are in need of a comprehensive neuropsychological assessment (e.g., Pagano, Cassidy, Little, Murphy, & Jellinek, 2000). For example, in discussing the Reynolds Intellectual Screening Test (RIST), a short form of the RIAS, Reynolds and Kamphaus (2003) state emphatically "... the screener [the RIST] is not used to make classification decisions" (p. 117). Using such a test in the face of such assertions by test authors is clearly inappropriate. Shortened versions of tests are less reliable than the full version of the test (the shortened-version test scores contain larger error components) and have less scientific evidence available to support the interpretation of the shortened version of the test.

Smith, McCarthy, and Anderson (2000) have noted the common weak application of psychometric principles in the development and validation of short forms. These authors identify and develop two general and nine specific methodological "sins" that are frequent in their occurrence in short-form development.

THE IMPACT OF LANGUAGE AS A CONFLICTING VARIABLE

The forensic pediatric neuropsychological assessment of bilingual individuals is particularly complex when English is their second language. Entire volumes have been produced on the topics of cross-cultural and bilingual assessment of neuropsychological abilities (e.g., Fletcher-Janzen, Strickland, & Reynolds, 2002). These issues are discussed in more detail in Chapter 8.

Puente and McCaffrey (1992) have noted that individuals with a bilingual status fall into three different types of functional bilingualism.

Coordinate Bilingualism

This bilingual person learned two languages simultaneously as a child and the two languages are arranged along a continuum with easy access to both languages. This individual is fluent in both languages. This individual can potentially be assessed in either language with similar results.

Compound Bilingualism

This bilingual person has merged two languages and is not fluent in either language and tends to switch back and forth based on the situation at hand. This is often called language mixing or code switching. Verbal ability scores will be depressed in either language due to the merging of the two languages.

Subordinate Bilingualism

This bilingual person learned one language during childhood and learned another language after childhood and speaks and thinks in one language and translates thoughts to the second language. The bilingual test taker should be assessed by a bilingual examiner as to the type of bilingual status exhibited along with a measurement of the level of ability within a specific bilingual type. Sattler (1992) noted that "few, if any instruments for bilingual assessment meet acceptable psychometric standards" (p. 576). Some instruments have been translated into various languages, but this often does not solve the problem, even if norms are developed in the additional language because there are often many dialects of the language.

PITFALLS IN ESTIMATING PREMORBID COGNITIVE FUNCTION

The vast majority of research on estimation of premorbid cognitive functioning has been on estimation of intellectual functioning (Barona, Reynolds, & Chastain, 1984). The estimation of premorbid functioning in neuropsychological domains such as attention, visual spatial abilities, learning, memory, and executive functioning has received much less attention (Lynch & McCaffrey, 1997). At present, there is very little empirical data regarding the estimation of premorbid neuropsychological functioning domains (McCaffrey & Vanderslice, 2010). Estimations of premorbid intellectual functioning are most often made by regression analyses based on historical and contemporary clinical test data and often fail to account for individual differences (McCaffrey & Vanderslice, 2010). Estimations of premorbid intellectual functioning are also often associated with such large confidence intervals (c.f., Strauss, Sherman, & Spreen, 2006) as to render the accuracy of estimated premorbid intelligence scores of limited value when applied to an individual patient.

SUMMARY

Pediatric forensic neuropsychology provides the legal system with scientific evidence with which to assist judges and juries in making crucial legal decisions. Forensic neuropsychology results are seen as based on empirical research findings and assist in the dispensing of justice. The psychometric foundations of neuropsychological tests are the empirical basis upon which neuropsychological testing rests. To the extent that the pediatric forensic neuropsychologist is seen as unbiased will determine the degree to which the forensic pediatric neuropsychologist will be welcome in the forensic arena in the future (Zillmer, 2004). The hope and expectation is that pediatric forensic neuropsychology will positively contribute to fair judicial decision making.

REFERENCES

Aiken, L. (2000). *Psychological testing and assessment* (10th ed.). Boston, MA: Allyn & Bacon.

American Academy of Neurology. (1996). Assessment: Neuropsychological testing of adults: Considerations for neurologists. *Neurology, 47*, 592–599.

American Educational Research Association, American Psychological Association, & National Council on Measurement in Education. (1999). *Standards for educational and psychological testing.* Washington, DC: American Educational Research Association.

American Psychological Association. (2002). *Ethical principles of psychologists.* Washington, DC: Author.

Anastasi, A., & Urbina, S. (1997). *Psychological testing* (7th ed.). Upper Saddle River, NJ: Prentice Hall.

Barona, A., Reynolds, C. R., & Chastain, R. (1984). A demographically based index of premorbid intelligence for the WAIS-R. *Journal of Consulting and Clinical Psychology, 52,* 885–887.

Binder, L. M., & Johnson-Greene, D. (1995). Observer effects on neuropsychological performance: A case report. *The Clinical Neuropsychologist, 9,* 74–78.

Blau, T. H. (1998). *The psychologist as an expert witness* (2nd. ed.). New York: Wiley.

Carroll, J. B. (1993). *Human cognitive abilities: A survey of factor analytic studies.* New York: Cambridge University Press.

Cattell, R. B. (1978). Matched determiners vs. factor invariance: A reply to Korth. *Multivariate Behavioral Research, 13*(4), 431–448.

Cohen, L. (2010). The admissibility of neuropsychological evidence: a primer. In A. M. Horton, Jr. & L. C. Hartlage (Eds), *Handbook of forensic neuropsychology* (2nd ed., pp. 411–430). New York: Springer.

Cronbach, L. J. (1990). *Essentials of psychological testing* (5th ed.). Boston, MA: Addison-Wesley.

Cullum, C. M., Heaton, R. K., & Grant, I. (1991). Psychogenic factors influencing pediatric neuropsychological performance: Somatoform disorders, factitious disorders, and malingering. In H. O. Doerr & A. S. Carlin, A. S. (Eds.), *Forensic neuropsychology: Legal and scientific bases* (pp. 141–171). New York: Guilford.

Dawes, R. M. (1995). Standards of practice. In S. C. Hayes, V. M. Follette, R. M. Dawes, & K. E. Grady (Eds.), *Scientific standards of psychological practice: Issues and recommendations* (pp. 31–43). Reno, NV: Context Press.

Dawes, R. M., Faust, D., & Meehl, P. E. (1989). Clinical versus actuarial judgment. *Science, 243*(4899), 1668–1674.

Faust, D. (1984). *The limits of scientific reasoning.* Minneapolis, MN: University of Minnesota Press.

Faust, D., & Ackley, M. A. (1998). Did you think it was going to be easy? Some methodological suggestions for the investigation and development of malingering detection techniques. In C. R. Reynolds (Ed.), *Detection of malingering during head injury litigation* (pp. 1–54). New York: Plenum Press.

Fletcher-Janzen, E., Strickland, T., & Reynolds, C. R. (Eds.). (2002). *Handbook of cross-cultural neuropsychology.* New York: Plenum Press.

Flynn, J. R. (1987). Massive IQ gains in 14 nations: What IQ tests really measure. *Psychological Bulletin, 101,* 171–191.

Flynn, J. R. (1998). IQ gains over time: Toward finding the causes. In U. Neisser (Ed.), *The rising curve: Long term gains in IQ and related measures* (pp. 25–66). Washington, DC: American Psychological Association.

Franklin, R. D. (2010). When change matters: Objective methods for measuring change in neuropsychological test scores. In A. M. Horton, Jr. & L. C. Hartlage (Eds.), *Handbook of forensic neuropsychology* (2nd ed., pp. 333–365). New York: Springer.

Glutting, J. J., McDermott, P. A., Watkins, M. M., Kush, J. C., & Konold, T. R. (1997). The base rate problem and its consequences for interpreting children's ability profiles. *School Psychology Review, 26*(2), 176–188.

Grove, W. M., & Meehl, P. E. (1996). Comparative efficiency of informal (subjective, impressionistic) and formal (mechanical, algorithmic) prediction procedures: The clinical-statistical controversy. *Psychology, Public Policy, and Law, 2*(2), 293–323.

Greiffenstein M. F., & Cohen, L. (2005). Neuropsychology and the law: Principles of productive attorney—neuropsychologist relations. In G. Larrabee (Ed.), *Forensic neuropsychology: A scientific approach* (pp. 29–91). New York: Oxford University Press.

Hammill, D. D., Pearson, N. A., & Voress, J. K. (1992). *Developmental Test of Visual Perception* (2nd ed.). Austin, TX: PRO-ED.

Hartlage, L. C. (2010). Neuropsychology in the courtroom. In A. M. Horton, Jr. & L. C. Hartlage (Eds.), *Handbook of forensic neuropsychology* (pp. 315–333). New York: Springer.

Heilbrun, K., Marczyk, G., DeMatteo, D., Zillmer, E., Harris, J., & Jennings, T. (2003). Principles of forensic mental health assessment: Implications for pediatric neuropsychological assessment in the forensic context. *Assessment, 10*, 329–343.

Horton, A. M., Jr. (1997). Halstead Reitan Neuropsychology Test Battery. In A. M. Horton, Jr. & D. Wedding (Eds.), *The neuropsychology handbook* (2nd ed.). New York: Springer.

Horton, A. M., Jr., & Hartlage, L. C. (2003). *Handbook of forensic neuropsychology.* New York: Springer.

Horton, A. M., Jr., & Hartlage, L. C. (2010). *Handbook of forensic neuropsychology* (2nd ed.). New York: Springer.

Horton, A. M., Jr., & Wedding, D. (1984). *Clinical and behavioral neuropsychology.* New York: Praeger.

Horton, A. M., Jr., & Wedding, D. (1997). *The neuropsychology handbook* (2nd ed.). New York: Springer.

Iverson, G. L. (2003). Detecting malingering in civil forensic evaluations. In A. M. Horton, Jr. & L. C. Hartlage (Eds.), *Handbook of forensic neuropsychology* (pp. 137–177). New York: Springer.

Iverson, G. L., Brooks, B. L., White, T., & Stern, R. A. (2008). Neuropsychological Assessment Battery: Introduction and advanced interpretation. In A. M. Horton, Jr. & D. Wedding, (Eds.), *The neuropsychology handbook* (3rd ed., pp. 279–343). New York: Springer.

Jensen, A. R. (1998). *The g factor: The science of mental ability.* Westport, CT: Praeger.

Joseph, R. (1996). *Neuropsychiatry, neuropsychology, and clinical neuroscience: Emotion, evolution, cognition, language, memory, brain damage, and abnormal behavior* (2nd ed.). Baltimore, MD: Williams & Wilkins.

Kehrer, C. A. (1999). The effects of a significant-other observer on neuropsychological test performance. *Dissertation Abstracts International: Section B: The Sciences & Engineering, 59*(9-B), 5167.

Kleinmuntz, B. (1990). Why we still use our heads instead of the formulas: Toward an integrative approach. *Psychological Bulletin, 107*, 296–310.

Koushik, N. S., Brooks, B. L., Iverson, G. L., Horton, A. M., Jr., & Reynolds, C. R. (2009, October). *Base rates of low scores on the Test of Verbal Conceptualization and Fluency (TVCF) in healthy children and adolescents.* Poster Presented at the Annual Meeting of the National Academy of Neuropsychology (NAN), New Orleans, LA.

Larrabee, G. L. (2005). Assessment of malingering. In G. Larrabee (Ed.), *Forensic neuropsychology: A scientific approach* (pp. 115–158). New York: Oxford University Press.

Lee, D., Reynolds, C. R., & Willson, V. L. (2003). Standardized test administration: Why bother? *Journal of Forensic Neuropsychology, 3*, 55–81.

Livingston, R. B., Jennings, R. B., Reynolds, C. R., & Gray, R. M. (2003). Multivariate analyses of the profile stability of intelligence tests: High for IQ's, Low to very low for subtest analysis. *Archives of Clinical Neuropsychology, 18*, 487–507.

Lyman, H. B. (1998). *Test scores and what they mean* (6th ed.). Needham Heights, MA: Allyn & Bacon.

Lynch, J. K., & McCaffrey, R. J. (1997). Premorbid intellectual functioning and the determination of cognitive loss. In R. J. McCaffrey, A. D. Williams, J. M. Fisher, & L. C. Lang (Eds.), *The practice of forensic neuropsychology: Meeting challenges in the courtroom* (pp. 91–115). New York: Plenum.

McCaffrey, R. J., Fisher, J. M., Gold, B. A., & Lynch, J. K. (1996). Presence of third parties during neuropsychological evaluations: Who is evaluating whom? *The Clinical Neuropsychologist, 10*, 435–449.

McCaffrey, R. J., & Vanderslice, J. L. (2010). Estimation of premorbid IQ. In A. M. Horton, Jr. & L. C. Hartlage (Eds.), *Handbook of forensic neuropsychology* (2nd ed., pp. 333–365). New York: Springer.

McDermott, P. A., Fantuzzo, J. W., Glutting, J. J., Watkins, M. W., & Baggaley, A. R. (1992). Illusions of meaning in the ipsative assessment of children's ability. *Journal of Special Education. 25*, 504–526.

McLoughlin, J. A., & Lewis, R. B. (2000). *Assessing special students.* (4th ed.). New York: Merrill.

Meehl, P. (1954). *Clinical versus statistical prediction.* Minneapolis, MN: University of Minnesota Press.

Meier, M. J. (1974). Some challenges for clinical neuropsychology. In R. M. Reitan & L. A. Davison (Eds.), *Clinical neuropsychology: Current status and application.* (pp. 289–324) New York: John Wiley.

Messick, S. (1989). Validity. In R. L. Linn (Ed.), *Educational measurement* (3rd ed., pp. 13–103). Upper Saddle River, NJ: Merrill/Prentice Hall.

National Academy of Neuropsychology. (2000). Presence of third party observers during neuropsychological testing. *Archives of Clinical Neuropsychology, 15*, 379–380.

Nunnally, J. C., & Bernstein, I. H. (1994). *Psychometric theory* (3rd ed.). New York: McGraw-Hill.

Pagano, M. E., Cassidy, L. J., Little, M., Murphy, J. M., & Jellinek, M. S. (2000). Identifying psychosocial dysfunction in school aged children: The Pediatric Symptom Checklist as a self-report measure. *Psychology in the Schools, 37*, 91–106.

Pritchard, D. A., Livingston, R. B., Reynolds, C. R., & Moses, J. A., Jr. (2000). Modal profiles for the WISC-III. *School Psychology Quarterly, 15*(4), 400–418.

Puente, A. E., & McCaffrey, R. J. (1992). *Handbook of neuropsychological assessment: A biopsychosocial perspective.* New York: Plenum Press.

Project on Scientific Knowledge and Public Policy. (2003). *Daubert: The most influential Supreme Court ruling you've never heard of.* Retrieved January 2007, from the DefendingScience.org web site, http://www.defendingscience.org/courts/Daubert-report-excerpt.cfm.

Rapaport, D., Gill, M., & Schafer, R. (1945-1946). *Diagnostic psychological testing* (Vols. 1–2). Chicago, IL: Year Book Publishers.

Reitan, R. M. (1958). Validity of the Trail Making Test as an indicator of brain damage. *Perceptual and Motor Skills, 8*, 271–276.

Reitan, R. M., & Wolfson, D. (1992). *The Halstead-Reitan Neuropsychological Test Battery for Adults.* Tucson, AZ: Neuropsychology Press.

Reitan, R. M., & Wolfson, D. (1993). *The Halstead-Reitan Neuropsychological Test Battery for Older Children*. Tucson, AZ: Neuropsychology Press.

Reynolds, C. R. (1998). Fundamentals of measurement and assessment in psychology. In A. Bellack & M. Hersen (Series Eds.) & C. R. Reynolds (Volume Ed.), *Comprehensive clinical psychology: Vol. 4. Assessment* (pp. 33–56). Oxford, England: Elsevier Science.

Reynolds, C. R. (2002). *Comprehensive Trail-Making Test*. Austin, TX: PRO-ED.

Reynolds, C. R. (2010). Measurement and assessment: An editorial view. *Psychological Assessment*, 22(1), 1–4.

Reynolds, C. R., & Horton, A. M., Jr. (2006). *Test of Verbal Conceptualization and Fluency: Examiner's manual*. Austin, TX: ProEd.

Reynolds, C. R., & Kamphaus, R. W. (2003). *Reynolds Intellectual Assessment Scales*. Odessa, FL: PAR.

Reynolds, C. R., & Kamphaus, R. W. (2004). *Behavioral Assessment System for Children* (2nd ed.). Bloomington, MN: Pearson Assessments.

Reynolds, C. R., & Livingston, R. A. (2012). *Mastering psychological testing*. Boston, MA: Allyn & Bacon.

Reynolds, C. R., Livingston, R. A., & Willson, V. L. (2006). *Measurement and assessment in education*. Boston, MA: Allyn & Bacon.

Reynolds, C. R., Niland, J., Wright, J., & Rosenn, M. (2010). Failure to apply the Flynn Correction in death penalty litigation: Standard practice of today maybe, but certainly malpractice of tomorrow. *Journal of Psychoeducational Assessment*, 28, 477–481.

Reynolds, C. R., Pearson, N., & Voress, J. (2002). *Developmental Test of Visual Perception Adolescent and Adult*. Austin, TX: PRO-ED.

Salvia, J., & Ysseldyke, Z. J. E. (2001). *Assessment* (8th ed.). Boston, MA: Houghton Mifflin.

Sattler, J. M. (1992). *Assessment of children*. (3rd ed., text rev.). San-Diego, CA: Jerome M. Sattler.

Sattler, J. M. (2001). *Assessment of children: Cognitive applications* (4th ed.). La Mesa, CA: Jerome M. Sattler.

Sechrest, L., Stickle, T. R., & Stewart, M. (1998). The role of assessment in clinical psychology. In A. Bellak & M. Hersen (Series Eds.) & C. R. Reynolds (Vol. Ed.), *Comprehensive clinical psychology: Vol. 4. Assessment* (pp. 1–32). Oxford, England: Elsevier Science.

Semel, E., Wiig, E. H. & Secord, W. A. (2003). *Clinical Evaluation of Language Fundamentals* (4th ed.). San Antonio, TX: Harcourt Assessments, Inc.

Strauss, E., Sherman, E. M. S., & Spreen, O. (2006). *A compendium of neuropsychological tests: Administration, norms, and commentary* (3rd ed.). New York: Oxford University Press.

Smith, G. T., McCarthy, D., & Anderson, K. G. (2000). On the sins of short-form development. *Psychological Assessment*, 12, 102–111.

Stanton, H. C., & Reynolds, C. R. (2000). Configural frequency analysis as a method of determining Wechsler profile types. *School Psychology Quarterly*, 15(4), 434–448.

U.S. Bureau of the Census. (2001). *Current population survey, March 2001*. [Data file]. Washington, DC: Author.

Wallace, G., Larsen, S. C., & Elksnin, L. (1992). *Educational assessment of learning problems* (2nd ed.). Needham Heights, MA: Allyn & Bacon.

Watkins, M. W. (2000). Cognitive profile analysis: A shared professional myth. *School Psychology Quarterly*, 15(4), 465–479.

Watkins, M. W., & Baggaley, A. R. (1992). Illusions of meaning in the ipsative assessment of children's ability. *Journal of Special Education*, 25, 504–526.

Watkins, M. W., & Kush, J. C. (1994). Wechsler subtest analysis: The right way, the wrong way, or no way? *School Psychology Review, 23*(4), 640–651.

Weithorn, L. A. (2006). The legal contexts of forensic assessments of children and families. In S. N. Sparta & G. P. Koocher (Eds.), *Forensic mental health assessment of children and adolescents* (pp. 11–29). New York: Oxford University Press.

Zillmer, E. A., & Green, H. K. (2006). Neuropsychological assessment in the forensic setting. In R. P. Archer (Ed.), *Forensic uses of clinical assessment instruments* (pp. 209–227). Mahwah, NJ: Erlbaum.

Zillmer, E. A., & Spiers, M. V. (2001). *Principles of neuropsychology.* Belmont, CA: Wadsworth.

Zillmer, E. A. (2004). The future of neuropsychology. *Archives of Clinical Neuropsychology, 19,* 713–724.

COURT DECISIONS

Frye v. United States, (1979). 408 A2d 364.

Daubert v. Merrell Dow Pharmaceuticals, Inc. (1993). 509 US S.Ct.

Kumho Tire Co. v. Carmichael (1999). 526 US S. Ct.

Chapter 4

Improving Accuracy When Identifying Cognitive Impairment in Pediatric Neuropsychological Assessments

BRIAN L. BROOKS
GRANT L. IVERSON

INTRODUCTION

Pediatric neuropsychological assessments focus on the measurement and quantification of brain–behavior relationships. No other specialty has developed, normed, and validated measures of cognitive abilities in the same manner as neuropsychology. As a result, neuropsychology is well positioned to provide valuable information to the forensic process about whether a child's cognitive abilities have been negatively affected by a disease or injury, the extent of the change in cognitive functioning, and the impact of cognitive problems on day-to-day functioning.

This chapter is focused on the assessment of cognitive functioning in children and adolescents, with a goal of *improving* the accuracy of identifying and quantifying cognitive impairment in children and adolescents. The concepts discussed in this chapter have direct application to any neuropsychological assessment. The issues discussed in this chapter are not specific to any neurological, medical, or psychiatric disorder, but they apply to any cause of possible changes in cognitive functioning. This chapter will include discussions on how cognitive impairment is defined, the complexity and comprehensiveness of a pediatric neuropsychological assessment, and the psychometric concepts to consider when interpreting cognitive test scores.

DEFINING COGNITIVE IMPAIRMENT

There is no single, universal, accepted definition of cognitive impairment. *The Diagnostic and Statistical Manual for Mental Disorders, Fourth Edition, Text Revision* (*DSM-IV-TR*; American Psychiatric Association, 2000) and the *International Classification of Diseases, Tenth Edition* (*ICD-10*; World Health Organization, 1992) indicate that cognitive impairment is observed in various diagnoses, but they do not provide well-delineated information on what actually constitutes cognitive impairment or how it is measured. Without clear direction on what "cognitive impairment" is, clinicians are left to decide whether 1.0, 1.5, or 2.0 standard deviations (or somewhere in between) should be interpreted as "impaired."

To add to the complexity of trying to define what constitutes cognitive impairment, consider the lack of consensus on describing levels of cognitive abilities by various test developers. Table 4.1 summarizes some of the classifications presented in the technical manuals of common pediatric tests. Several conclusions can be drawn from this table. First, agreement for classifications across tests, even across tests from the same test publisher, is limited. It can be agreed upon that a score close to the 50th percentile is "average," a score more than two standard deviations below the mean is very low, and a score more than two standard deviations above the mean is very high. Classification of scores in between these markers is variable. Second, even when different tests agree on the cutoff scores for different levels of classifications, the terms used can have semantic differences. For example, a scaled score of 5 is called "borderline" on the Wechsler Preschool and Primary Scale of Intelligence, Third Edition (WPPSI-III; Wechsler, 2002), "below expected level" on the NEPSY, Developmental Assessment, Second Edition (NEPSY-II; Korkman, Kirk, & Kemp, 2007b), "deficient" on the Test of Memory and Learning, Second Edition (TOMAL-2; Reynolds & Voress, 2007), or "mildly-to-moderately impaired" on the Wisconsin Card Sorting Test (WCST; Heaton, Chelune, Talley, Kay, & Curtiss, 1993). Each of these descriptors can potentially have very different meanings to the recipient of a report (e.g., a lawyer, judge, or family). Third, tests provide various gradations of low performance that attempt to parse out different cognitive weaknesses. However, many tests do not provide similar attention to the classifications above the 50th percentile. As such, using the classification system for those tests (e.g., NEPSY-II, WCST) might not fully describe a child's relative or absolute strengths.

As noted, the inability to agree on the classifications for performance on cognitive tests can have an impact on the communication of a person's results. *We recommend that, regardless of which classification system is chosen for interpretation, the classification system be clearly identified in the forensic report and the same terminology be used throughout the report for interpreting all test scores.* Using different classification descriptions for different tests in the same report is conceptually confusing for the reader.

COMPLEXITY AND COMPREHENSIVENESS OF A PEDIATRIC NEUROPSYCHOLOGICAL ASSESSMENT

Forensic neuropsychological assessments of children and adolescents are often thorough, lengthy, and designed to cover a wide range of cognitive abilities. For example, Figure 4.1 illustrates some of the domains that might be assessed. It is important to note that this is not necessarily an exhaustive list of domains that might be evaluated (e.g., does not include adaptive functioning, psychological functioning, or behavioral functioning). In addition, there is not an expectation that a neuropsychological assessment will cover all of these domains, although forensic

TABLE 4.1. Descriptions for Standard Score Performances Across Selected Pediatric Neuropsychology Tests

Standard Scores					Descriptive Classifications for Scores on Various Pediatric Neuropsychological Tests							
Z Score	Percentile	Index/ IQ Score	Scaled Score	T Score	Wechsler Indexes	Wechsler Subtests	NEPSY-II	TOMAL-2	RIAS	K-ABC	WCST	WJ-III
3.0	99.9	145	19	80								
2.7	99.6	140	18	76/77		Very superior		Very superior	Significantly above average	Upper Extreme		
2.3	98.6	133	17	72/73	Very superior		Above expected level					Very Superior
2.0	97.7	130	16	70				Superior				Superior
1.7	95	124/125	15	66	Superior	Superior			Moderately above ave.	Above Average	Above Average	
1.3	91	120	14	63/64				Above average	Above average			High Average
1.0	84	115	13	60	High average	High average						
0.7	75	110	12	56/57								
0.3	63	105	11	53/54								
0	50	100	10	50	Average	Average	At expected level	Average	Average	Average	Average	Average
−0.3	37	95	9	46/47								
−0.7	25	90	8	43/44								
−1.0	16	85	7	40	Low average	Low average		Below average	Below average		Below Average	Low Average
−1.3	9	80	6	36/37		Borderline	Borderline			Below Average	Mild Impaired	
−1.7	5	75/76	5	34	Borderline			Deficient	Moderately below ave.		Mild-Moderate Impaired	Low
−2.0	2.3	70	4	30			Below expected level					
−2.3	1.4	67	3	27/28	Extremely low	Extremely low	Well below expected level	Very deficient	Significantly below average	Lower Extreme	Mod. Impaired	Very Low
−2.7	0.4	60	2	23/24							Mod-Severe Impaired	
−3.0	0.1	55	1	20								

NOTES: Descriptive classifications for various test scores are obtained from the respective test manuals. Wechsler classifications are used for tests published by Pearson/The Psychological Corporation (Children's Memory Scale, Cohen, 1997; Wechsler Primary and Preschool Intelligence Scale, Third Edition, Wechsler, 2002; Wechsler Intelligence Scale for Children, Fourth Edition, Wechsler, 2003); NEPSY-II, Developmental Neuropsychological Assessment–Second Edition (Korkman et al., 2007a); TOMAL-2, Test of Memory and Learning–Second Edition (Reynolds & Voress, 2007); RIAS, Reynolds Intellectual Assessment Scale (Reynolds & Kamphaus, 2003); K-ABC, Kaufman Assessment Battery for Children (Kaufman & Kaufman, 2004); WCST, Wisconsin Card Sorting Test (Heaton et al., 1993); WJ-III, Woodcock-Johnson–Third Edition, Test of Cognitive Abilities (Woodcock et al., 2001).

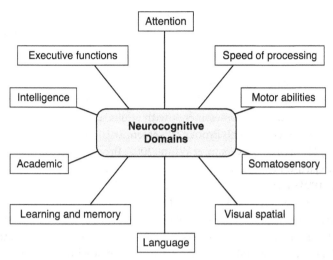

FIGURE 4.1. Sample of neurocognitive and behavioral domains that might be evaluated in a forensic pediatric neuropsychological assessment. Some domains might not be included in some evaluations, and other domains not listed in this figure could also be included.

evaluations are usually quite thorough (e.g., Sweet, Peck, Abramowitz, & Etzweiler, 2002).

The comprehensive nature of neuropsychological evaluations for forensic cases is important for ensuring that a wide range of domains is assessed. This comprehensiveness, however, ultimately means that a substantial number of tests are administered and interpreted. In the next section, several key concepts or principles that need to be considered when interpreting multiple test scores are presented and discussed. Understanding these concepts is important for improving accuracy of interpretation of multiple scores, thus minimizing the chances of misdiagnosis and even missed diagnosis.

INTERPRETATION OF MULTIPLE NEUROPSYCHOLOGICAL TEST SCORES

The administration and simultaneous interpretation of several test scores in order to identify cognitive impairment secondary to an injury or illness is the foundation of pediatric neuropsychology. When a single score is administered, then the rules of a Gaussian or univariate distribution (i.e., bell curve) apply for interpretation of that single score. For example, if a person obtains a score at the 16th percentile, then it is known that the score is comparable to or better than 16% of people. However, when multiple tests are administered and simultaneously interpreted, then the interpretation becomes multivariate and the results can (and most often do) differ from single-score interpretation. These multivariate analyses, which provide information on the "prevalence of low scores" or the "base rate of low scores," are psychometrically driven and are intended to ultimately minimize the chances of misinterpreting test scores.

Obtaining some low scores on a neuropsychological assessment is common and expected in a substantial minority of healthy people (Binder, Iverson, & Brooks, 2009). There has been considerable research over the past decade that supports what clinicians have long known—if several tests are administered and interpreted, there will be test-score scatter (i.e., differences between the lowest and highest scores) and a portion of healthy people will obtain low scores. This has been demonstrated repeatedly in neuropsychological assessments with adults and older adults (Axelrod & Wall, 2007; Binder et al., 2009; Brooks & Iverson, 2010; Brooks, Iverson, Holdnack, & Feldman, 2008; Brooks, Iverson, & White, 2007; Brooks, Iverson, & White, 2009c; Crawford, Garthwaite, & Gault, 2007; de Rotrou et al., 2005; Heaton, Grant, & Matthews, 1991; Heaton, Miller, Taylor, & Grant, 2004; Ingraham & Aiken, 1996; Iverson, Brooks, & Holdnack, 2008a; Iverson, Brooks, White, & Stern, 2008b; Palmer, Boone, Lesser, & Wohl, 1998; Schretlen, Testa, Winicki, Pearlson, & Gordon, 2008), with results holding true across various test batteries. In addition to demonstrating the concept, several papers have also *(a)* provided ready-to-use tables that can be used as part of clinical interpretation in a neuropsychological evaluation (Brooks et al., 2007; Brooks et al., 2008; Brooks et al., 2009c; Iverson et al., 2008a; Iverson et al., 2008b), *(b)* developed new psychometrically based criteria for identifying cognitive impairment based upon the prevalence of low scores (Brooks, Iverson, Feldman, & Holdnack, 2009a), and *(c)* demonstrated the ability for these base-rate analyses to identify cognitive problems in adult or older adult clinical groups (Brooks, Holdnack, & Iverson, 2011; Brooks et al., 2009a; Iverson, Brooks, & Haley, 2009a; Iverson, Brooks, & Young, 2009b; Iverson, Brooks, & Young, 2009c).

Only recently has the prevalence of low scores been examined for different neuropsychological measures in children and adolescents. For example, published manuscripts with readily available data that can be used by clinicians in forensic and day-to-day clinical neuropsychological assessments are available for the Children's Memory Scale (CMS; Cohen, 1997) in Brooks, Iverson, Sherman, and Holdnack (2009b), for the NEPSY-II (Korkman, Kirk, & Kemp, 2007a) in Brooks, Sherman, and Iverson (2010b), and for the Wechsler Intelligence Scale for Children, Fourth Edition (WISC-IV; Wechsler, 2003) in Brooks (2010; 2011) and in Crawford et al. (2007). Analyses involving the prevalence of low scores on the CNS Vital Signs, a brief computerized neuropsychological battery, have also been used to identify cognitive problems in children and adolescents with depression (Brooks, Iverson, Sherman, & Roberge, 2010a). There are clear advantages to having published data on the prevalence of low scores because it allows clinicians to interpret overall performance across a large battery of tests using empirical data, it potentially reduces the chances of clinician biases (see discussion of potential biases in Iverson et al., 2008a), and it is designed to improve the accuracy of clinical interpretation.

When interpreting multiple test scores in a pediatric forensic neuropsychological assessment, it is important for clinicians to understand several key concepts that differ from interpreting a single score in isolation. These concepts have been previously reviewed using adult and older adult test batteries (Brooks, Strauss, Sherman, Iverson, & Slick, 2009d; Iverson & Brooks, 2011), but it is important to extend the discussion to children and adolescents. For example, clinicians interpreting multiple neuropsychological scores need to understand the following: *(a)* test-score scatter or variability is common; *(b)* having some low scores is common; *(c)* the number of low scores is related to the cutoff score used for interpretation; *(d)* the number of low scores depends on the number of tests administered; and *(e)* the number of low scores varies by characteristics of the examinees (e.g., level of child's intelligence and number of years of parental education). Failing to appreciate these five multivariate concepts can lead to increased chances of misdiagnosis of cognitive impairment. A discussion of each concept is presented in the sections that follow, along with examples using common pediatric neuropsychological measures that were computed from either actual standardization samples (adapted from Brooks, 2010; Brooks et al., 2009b; Brooks et al., 2010b) or using the Crawford et al. (2007) computer program to estimate prevalence rates. Although the accuracy of the computer program for estimating the prevalence of low scores has been supported in adult populations (Brooks & Iverson, 2010; Schretlen et al., 2008), it should be noted that the numbers presented are to illustrate the principles; prevalence rates could potentially differ if computed using the actual standardization sample of children and adolescents.

Test-Score Variability Is Common in Healthy Children

Test score scatter refers to the difference between high and low scores across a specific battery of tests (e.g., WISC-IV subtests). In a forensic assessment, a clinician is able to readily determine how common it is for a child to have at least one, two, three, or even four standard deviations (SDs) between lowest and highest scores based on information presented within some technical manuals. Figure 4.2 presents the cumulative percent of healthy children with different amounts of test-score variability on the WPPSI-III (Wechsler, 2002) and the WISC-IV (Wechsler, 2003). When examining the variability for the 10 primary subtests from the WISC-IV, nearly the entire standardization sample has at least a three-scaled-score spread (i.e., ≥ one SD) between their highest and lowest subtest scores. Having at least a six-scaled-score (i.e., ≥ two SDs) or nine-scaled-score (i.e., ≥ three SDs) spread between highest and lowest subtest scores is found in approximately three-quarters and one-quarter of healthy children, respectively. Examples of six-point spreads (i.e., two-SD spread) include 4–10 (2nd percentile to 50th percentile), 6–12 (9th percentile to 75th percentile), and 9–15 (37th percentile to 95th percentile). Examples of nine-point spreads (i.e., three-SD spreads) include 1–10 (<1st percentile to 50th percentile), 5–14 (5th percentile to 91st percentile), and 10–19 (50th percentile–>99th percentile). Clearly, having some test score scatter and variability is common. In fact, it is uncommon to *not* have scatter (i.e., only 0.4% of children on the WISC-IV and 3.3% of 4–7-year-olds on the WPPSI-III had all subtest scores within zero, one, or two scaled-score points).

Low Scores Are Common Across All Neurocognitive Tests in Healthy Children

A substantial percentage of healthy children and adolescents obtain some low scores on pediatric neuropsychological test batteries (Brooks, 2010; Brooks, 2011;

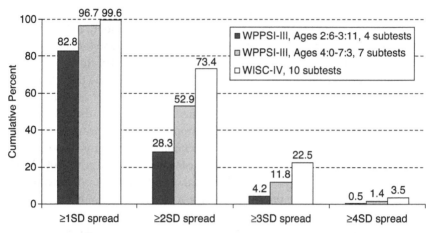

FIGURE 4.2. Cumulative percentages of healthy children and adolescents who have large spreads between their highest and lowest primary subtest scores on intelligence measures. These analyses include the primary subtests that comprise the index scores. The average scaled score for subtests is 10 with a standard deviation (SD) of 3 points and a range of 1–19. 2SD spread = 6 scaled score points; 3SD spread = 9 scaled score points; and 4SD spread = 12 scaled score points. This figure was adapted from data presented in Table B.6 of the WPPSI-III Administration and Scoring Manual (Wechsler, 2002) and Table B.6 of the WISC-IV Administration and Scoring Manual (Wechsler, 2003).

Brooks et al., 2009b; Brooks et al., 2010b; Crawford et al., 2007). Having some low scores is universal and is not an artifact of a specific standardization sample or a specific type of neurocognitive test. Figure 4.3 illustrates the prevalence of one or more low scores (≤5th percentile) on the 10 primary subtests from the WISC-IV (Wechsler, 2003), the eight immediate and delayed memory scores from the CMS (Cohen, 1997), 14 selected NEPSY-II subtests for 7–16-year-olds (Korkman et al., 2007a), eight memory scores for 5–8-year-olds on the Wide Range Assessment of Memory and Learning, Second Edition (WRAML-2; Sheslow & Adams, 2003), and the five memory scores from the WJ-III Tests of Cognitive Abilities (Woodcock, McGrew, & Mather, 2001). These percentages are derived by considering the performance of all scores *simultaneously* and determining how many children have at least one score below the cutoff (i.e., ≤5th percentile).

Consider that if interpreting each score from each test in isolation, a clinician would expect 5% of the sample to fall below the cutoff of ≤5th percentile (i.e., traditional univariate analysis, based on the bell curve). As seen in Figure 4.3, a substantial minority of healthy children and adolescents has one or more scores ≤5th percentile on various batteries when multiple scores are considered simultaneously (i.e., multivariate analyses). These cumulative percentages differ considerably from 5%. In fact, having one or more subtest scores ≤5th percentile is found in approximately 1 in 5 healthy 6–8-year-olds on the WJ-III (considering only 5 scores), in approximately 1 in 3 healthy children on the WISC-IV (considering 10 scores), CMS (considering 8 scores), and WRAML-2 (considering 8 scores), and in nearly 1 out of 2 healthy 7–16-year-olds on the 14-subtest version of the NEPSY-II. Thus, having some low

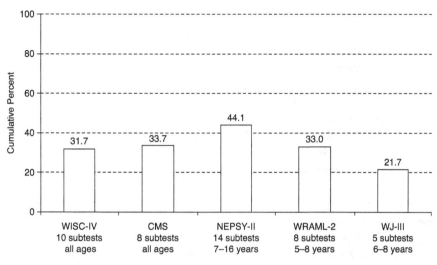

FIGURE 4.3. Low scores are common: Prevalence of one or more scores ≤5th percentile on common pediatric tests. WISC-IV base rates include 10 primary subtests that are used to derive the four index scores. NEPSY-II base rates include a two-hour battery for 7–16-year-olds (i.e., 14 selected subtests), as described in Brooks et al. (2010b). Prevalence rates of low subtest scores on the CMS, WRAML-2, and WJ-III were computed using the Crawford et al. (2007) computer program and subtest intercorrelations in each of the respective technical manuals. CMS intercorrelations for all ages included the following eight scores: Dot Locations Learning and Long Delay; Stories Immediate and Delayed; Faces Immediate and Delayed; and Word Pairs Learning and Long Delay. WRAML-2 intercorrelations for ages 5–8 years included the following eight scores: Story Memory and Story Memory Recall; Design Memory and Design Recognition; Verbal Learning and Verbal Learning Recall; and Picture Memory and Picture Memory Recognition. WJ-III intercorrelations for ages 6–8 years included the following five scores: Visual-Auditory Learning and Visual-Auditory Learning Delayed; Picture Recognition; and Story Recall and Story Recall Delayed. Prevalence rates of low scores were adapted from Brooks (2010) for the WISC-IV and Brooks et al. (2010b) for the NEPSY-II.

scores is common in healthy children and adolescents and is found across pediatric neuropsychological batteries.

The Number of Low Scores Depends on Where a Clinician Sets the Cutoff

Table 4.1 demonstrates that there is minimal agreement by test publishers on what should constitute a low score. Moreover, there has yet to be universal agreement on the definition of a low score and it is up to individual clinicians to set their own standard for where to set a cutoff for interpretation of cognitive impairment. Exactly where a clinician sets the cutoff for a low score is arbitrary, can vary from one clinician to another, and will invariably dictate test interpretation. Furthermore, where a clinician sets a cutoff score will have an impact on the sensitivity and specificity of the tests for detecting cognitive impairment. Higher cutoff scores are more likely to correctly identify those who have cognitive problems (improved sensitivity), but they are also more likely to include those who do not have cognitive problems (reduced specificity).

When interpreting a battery of test scores through the multivariate process, the prevalence of low scores varies considerably based on the cutoff score used. In various publications, we have presented the prevalence of low scores for several cutoff scores, including the 25th, 16th, 10th, 5th, and 2nd percentiles (e.g., Brooks, 2010; Brooks, 2011; Brooks et al., 2007, 2010; Brooks et al., 2008; Brooks et al., 2009b; Brooks et al., 2010b; Iverson et al., 2008a; Iverson et al., 2008b; Iverson et al., 2009a). Providing information for various cutoff scores allows clinicians to select their own preferred cutoff score. As shown in Figure 4.4, the cutoff selected can substantially change the interpretation of the prevalence of low subtest scores on pediatric memory batteries. These memory batteries are presented as examples, but the concept is applicable to all pediatric batteries. When using the 25th percentile as a cutoff (i.e., a scaled score of 8), having one or more low subtest scores ranges from 59% on the WJ-III to 77.1% on the CMS. A consistent trend demonstrating a reduction in the prevalence of one or more low scores as the cutoff score becomes further away from the population mean is obvious. When the 2nd percentile (i.e., standard score of 4)

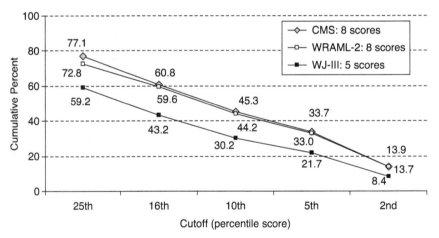

FIGURE 4.4. The number of low scores depends on where a cutoff is set: Prevalence of one or more low scores across various cutoff scores on selected pediatric memory batteries. Prevalence rates of low scores were computed using the Crawford et al. (2007) software and subtest intercorrelations from the respective technical manuals for each test in the figure. CMS intercorrelations for all ages included the following eight scores: Dot Locations Learning and Long Delay; Stories Immediate and Delayed; Faces Immediate and Delayed; and Word Pairs Learning and Long Delay. WRAML-2 intercorrelations for ages 5–8 years included the following eight scores: Story Memory and Story Memory Recall; Design Memory and Design Recognition; Verbal Learning and Verbal Learning Recall; and Picture Memory and Picture Memory Recognition. WJ-III intercorrelations for ages 6–8 years included the following five scores: Visual-Auditory Learning and Visual-Auditory Learning Delayed; Picture Recognition; and Story Recall and Story Recall Delayed.

is used as the cutoff, having one or more low scores is relatively rare and is found in 8.4%–13.9% of healthy children on these three pediatric memory batteries.

Until there is universal agreement on what constitutes a low score, and the definition can vary for lower versus higher functioning persons, clinicians will continue to select a cutoff based on training, preference, and various personal factors. It is important to understand that the prevalence of low scores when considering all scores simultaneously, much like univariate analyses with a single score, will vary based on the cutoff selected.

The Number of Low Scores Depends on the Number of Tests Administered

As more tests are administered and more scores are interpreted, it becomes more common to have low scores. In a pediatric forensic neuropsychological assessment, a clinician is likely to administer several hours of testing and interpret a large number of scores. Consider that the length of a clinical assessment ranges from 4.49 to 6.48 hours, with the average length of a forensic assessment being 9.47 hours (Sweet et al., 2002). Although these numbers are not exclusively derived from pediatric neuropsychological assessments, they do give an indication as to the thorough nature and potential number of tests being administered (see Fig. 4.1). For example, consider the number of subtest scores (primary and secondary) that might be obtained in the following pediatric neuropsychological assessment with a 10-year-old[1]: measurement of intelligence using the WISC-IV yields 10 primary scores; measurement of attention, learning, and memory using the CMS yields up to 14 subtest scores, using the WRAML-2 yields up to 15 subtest scores, and using the TOMAL-2 yields up to 16 subtest scores; measurement of language comprehension, production, and fluency using the NEPSY-II yields 6 primary subtest scores; measurement of visuospatial skills using the NEPSY-II yields up to 8 primary subtest scores; and measurement of executive functioning using just four selected tests from the Delis-Kaplan Executive Function System (D-KEFS; Delis, Kaplan, & Kramer, 2001) (i.e., verbal fluency, design fluency, color-word interference, and trail making test) yields 16 primary scores (plus numerous contrast scores). This would be a comprehensive assessment, and yet it still leaves other domains to potentially be assessed. Regardless, it is important to consider that the sample tests mentioned earlier, covering the domains of intelligence, attention, learning and memory, language, visuospatial, and executive functions yields between 54 and 56 subtest scores. The more scores administered and interpreted, the more likely it is that low scores will appear in the child's neuropsychological profile.

Figure 4.5 illustrates the prevalence of low scores across batteries of varying length, when considering all scores simultaneously. For example, having one or more scores ≤5th percentile is found in 44.1% of healthy children when considering 17 subtest scores (i.e., NEPSY-II, 2-hour battery for 7–16-year-olds), in 34.8% when

---

1. These tests are used only to provide an example of the number of scores that could be obtained in an evaluation. Inclusion of these tests does not provide support or evidence for use of these specific measures in a forensic assessment.

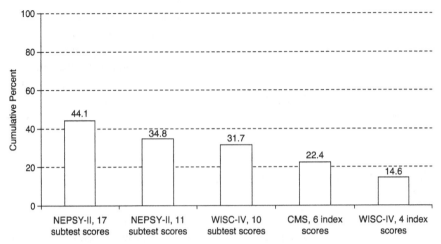

FIGURE 4.5. The number of low scores depends on the number of tests administered: Prevalence of one or more scores ≤5th percentile. The NEPSY-II includes a two-hour battery (17 scores) for 7–16-year-olds and a 1-hour (11 scores) battery that was originally proposed in Brooks et al. (2010b). WISC-IV base rates include the 10 primary subtests that are used to derive the four index scores. CMS base rates include the following scores: Dot Locations Learning and Long Delay; Stories Immediate and Delayed; Faces Immediate and Delayed; and Word Pairs Learning and Long Delay. Prevalence rates of low scores were adapted from Brooks et al. (2010b) for the NEPSY-II, Brooks (2010) for the WISC-IV, and Brooks et al. (2009b) for the CMS.

considering 11 subtest scores (i.e., NEPSY-II, 1-hour battery for 7–16-year-olds), in 31.7% when considering 10 subtest scores (i.e., WISC-IV), in 22.4% when considering 6 CMS index scores, and in 14.6% when considering 4 WISC-IV index scores.

The Number of Low Scores Varies by Examinee Characteristics

Neuropsychological test performance is related to various factors, including culture, language, and socioeconomic status (see Chapter 8 for further discussion of some of these variables). How a child performs on testing must be considered within the context of these different types of variables. One area of consideration when interpreting neuropsychological measures in children is the level of intellectual abilities. Children with lesser intelligence are, inherently, expected to get more low scores (Horton, 1999; Steinberg, Bieliauskas, Smith, & Ivnik, 2005; Steinberg, Bieliauskas, Smith, Ivnik, & Malec, 2005; Tremont, Hoffman, Scott, & Adams, 1998; Warner, Ernst, Townes, Peel, & Preston, 1987). This does not necessarily mean that all scores are low, but when compared to a child with higher intelligence, more scores should fall below a priori cutoff scores. If the goal of testing is to identify the presence of acquired cognitive impairment, especially a decline attributable to a neurological injury or disease, then diagnostic accuracy may be improved if relevant demographic characteristics are considered in the interpretation of test performance.

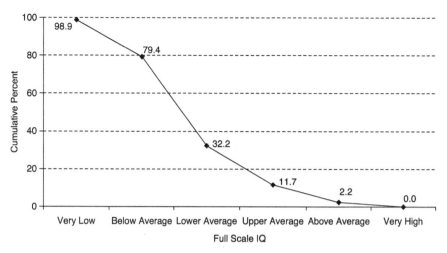

FIGURE 4.6. The number of low scores varies by a child's level of intelligence:
One or more WISC-IV scores ≤5th percentile. Intellectual abilities are based on
the child's WISC-IV full scale IQ (FSIQ). Very Low, FSIQ < 80; Below Average,
FSIQ = 80–89; Lower Average, FSIQ = 90–99; Upper Average, FSIQ = 100–109;
Above Average, FSIQ = 110–119; Very High, FSIQ ≥ 120. WISC-IV base rates include
10 primary subtests that are used to derive the four index scores. Prevalence rates of low
WISC-IV subtest scores were adapted from Brooks (2010).

When interpreting the prevalence of low scores, it is important to consider prevalence rates for groups of children who have similar levels of intelligence as the examinee. This level of analysis can provide additional insight into whether a child's cognitive performance is common or uncommon compared to others with a similar level of intelligence. For example, it might be common for a child with low intelligence to have several low memory scores. Figure 4.6 illustrates the differences in the prevalence of one or more WISC-IV subtest scores ≤5th percentile across levels of overall intelligence (Full Scale IQ). Nearly all of the children with very low (FSIQ < 80) intelligence had at least one low subtest score, in comparison to 11.7% with "upper" average intelligence (FSIQ = 100–109), 2.2% with above average intelligence (FSIQ = 110–119), and none of the children with very high intelligence (FSIQ ≥ 120). Of course, a somewhat circular argument occurs here, where the very scores that comprise the overall level of intelligence are the scores being examined. Ergo, if you consider a child with a low Full Scale IQ, then more low scores (which contribute to the overall low Full Scale IQ score) will be found. However, the concept holds true with test batteries other than IQ, but the effect might not be as substantial.

Other examples of the relationship between intellectual abilities and the prevalence of low scores might help to convince the reader that this is an important consideration. For example, Figure 4.7 illustrates the prevalence of low CMS index scores (≤5th percentile) across levels of intelligence (i.e., WISC-III FSIQ). Notice that as the level of intelligence increases, the prevalence of at least one low CMS index score decreases. In children with below average intelligence (i.e., WISC-III FSIQ < 90), one-third of the sample has at least one low CMS index score.

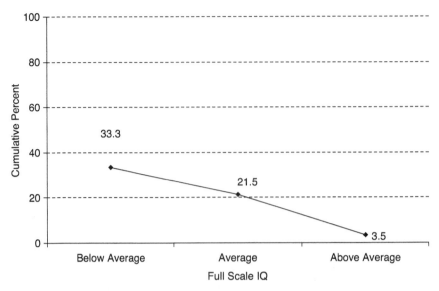

FIGURE 4.7. The number of low memory scores varies by a child's level of intelligence: One or more CMS index scores ≤5th percentile. Intellectual abilities are based on the child's WISC-III Full Scale IQ (FSIQ). Below Average, FSIQ <90; Average, FSIQ = 90–109; and Above Average, FSIQ >109. Analyses of the prevalence of low CMS index scores included six index scores (Learning, Verbal Immediate, Visual Immediate, Verbal Delayed, Verbal Delayed Recognition, and Visual Delayed). The Attention/Concentration and General Memory indexes were not included in the analyses. Prevalence rates of low CMS index scores were adapted from Brooks et al. (2009b).

When children with average intelligence (i.e., WISC-III FSIQ = 90–109) are considered, only 1 in 5 children has at least one low CMS index score. Finally, in children with above average intelligence (i.e., WISC-III FSIQ > 109), having one or more CMS index scores ≤5th percentile is relatively uncommon. Clearly, a child's level of intelligence is related to the prevalence of low scores, with below average intelligence associated with more low scores and above average intelligence associated with far fewer lower scores.

What about an examination of the prevalence of low scores according to other demographic variables? Previous research has reported a positive relationship between parental education and child neurocognitive functioning (e.g., Devlin, Daniels, & Roeder, 1997; Schoenberg, Lange, Brickell, & Saklofske, 2007a; Schoenberg, Lange, & Saklofske, 2007b; Thomas, Sukumaran, Lukose, George, & Sarma, 2007; van der Sluis, Willemsen, de Geus, Boomsma, & Posthuma, 2008). Because of this positive (albeit relatively weak) correlation (i.e., Schoenberg et al., 2007a found that parental education and ethnicity only accounts for 21% of the variance in a child's FSIQ score), parental education has been used as a predictive variable for estimating cognitive and intellectual abilities in those between 6–16 years (Schoenberg et al., 2007a) and in those between 16–19 years (Pearson Assessment, 2009).

Using the premise that parental education is related to a child's cognitive abilities, it is possible to examine whether differences occur in a child's prevalence of low

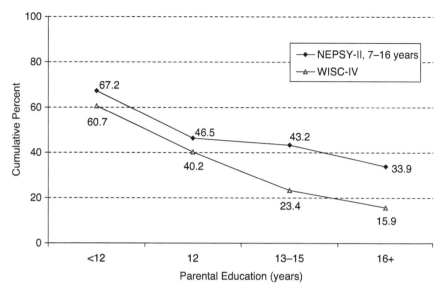

FIGURE 4.8. The number of low scores varies by parents' education level: One or more subtest scores ≤5th percentile. NEPSY-II includes a two-hour battery (17 scores) for 7–16-year-olds that was originally described in Brooks et al. (2010b). Prevalence of low NEPSY-II subtest scores adapted from Brooks et al. (2010). WISC-IV includes 10 primary subtests for the analyses. Prevalence of low WISC-IV scores adapted from Brooks (2010).

scores when stratified by level of his or her parents' education. As described later, this has important applications when a pediatric measure, such as a learning and memory battery, is not co-normed with a measure of intelligence. Brooks, Sherman, and Iverson (2010b) reported that the prevalence of low NEPSY-II scores decreased as the level of parental education increased (see Fig. 4.8). In those families where the average parental education is less than high school, 67.2% of 7–16-year-olds had one or more scores ≤5th percentile compared to 33.9% of those children who come from a family with average parental education of at least an undergraduate degree. Similar findings were also reported for the WISC-IV (Brooks, 2010). In this study, children of parents with less than high school education were eight times more likely to have one or more subtest scores ≤5th percentile compared to children of parents with at least an undergraduate degree. The positive relation between a parent's level of education and a child's level of intelligence, although clearly far from a perfect correlation, allows for stratification of the prevalence of low scores using a variable that requires no extra testing time and is readily available in nearly every assessment.

USING MULTIVARIATE ANALYSES IN A PEDIATRIC FORENSIC NEUROPSYCHOLOGICAL ASSESSMENT

Publications on the prevalence of low scores on pediatric batteries provide important information that can be used clinically. However, these publications (Brooks, 2010; Brooks, 2011; Brooks et al., 2009b; Brooks et al., 2010b) include a large amount of information. As such, some key rules for the use of the prevalence tables in clinical and forensic neuropsychological assessments are presented next.

- The information on the prevalence of low scores is specific to the tests included in the analyses. Tests or index scores cannot be substituted for those identified in the analyses (i.e., if one test is not given, but another one is substituted in its place, the information in the tables cannot be considered accurate).
- The exact same number of tests included in the tables must be administered and interpreted (i.e., if eight scores are included in the analyses, but only six of those scores are obtained in the assessment, the tables cannot be used).
- The information provided for a specific test is only applicable to that specific test (e.g., the prevalence rates on the WISC-IV cannot be used to interpret performance on the WPPSI-III).
- The prevalence rates in published tables tell a clinician how many healthy children and adolescents obtain one or more, two or more, three or more, etc. low scores on the same battery of tests. In other words, the values represent the cumulative percent of children who obtain *at least the same number or more* low scores.
- Different cutoffs are often provided, ranging from the 2nd percentile to the 25th percentile. Because a universal cutoff score has not been identified, clinicians may choose the cutoff of their preference.
- When stratification by level of intelligence, parental education, or other demographic variable is not available, clinicians may consider the prevalence of low scores in the entire sample. However, clinicians need to be aware that the prevalence rates are likely higher for lower functioning children, and lower for higher functioning children.
- Because interpreting more scores results in a higher chance of obtaining some low scores, some caution is warranted when interpreting the prevalence of low scores for a single battery or a single domain in isolation from the rest of the measures in a lengthy neuropsychological assessment. In other words, the base rates of low scores in each domain (e.g., memory) or for each battery (e.g., WISC-IV) are known—but the base rates of low scores for combinations of domains and batteries are not known.
- Knowing the prevalence of low scores is designed to supplement, *not replace*, clinical judgment. Like any other psychometric information that is provided for test-score interpretation, it is up to the clinician to make a determination based on all pieces of information and in the context of the specific details of the case.

CASE EXAMPLES

The clinical application of the prevalence of low scores is demonstrated using two case examples. Table 4.2 presents CMS index scores for a 14-year-old boy who sustained a remote concussion two years prior to the assessment when he fell on an icy sidewalk. At the time of the neuropsychological assessment, he had returned to

TABLE 4.2. Performance on the Children's Memory Scale (CMS) Indexes in a 14-Year-Old Boy Who Sustained a Concussion

CMS Index Scores	Standardized Performance and Descriptions		
	Index Score	Percentile Rank	Classification
Learning	103	58	Average
Visual Immediate	103	58	Average
Visual Delayed	84	14	Low Average
Verbal Immediate	115	84	High Average
Verbal Delayed	106	66	Average
Delayed Recognition	103	58	Average

NOTES: Index scores have a mean = 100 and a standard deviation = 15. Classifications are based on the Wechsler system. The General Memory and Attention/Concentration Indexes are not included in the base rates of low scores analyses.

school, was achieving similar grades compared to before his concussion, and his family had reported that they did not perceive residual cognitive effects from an injury. As can be seen in this table, the patient obtained one index score at the 14th percentile (Visual Delayed Index = 84), but other index scores ranged from the 58th to the 84th percentiles. Figure 4.1 from Brooks et al. (2009b) indicates that having one or more index scores <16th percentile is found in 37.6% of the CMS standardization sample. This adolescent's level of intelligence was within the average range. Again, considering the information in Figure 4.1 of Brooks et al. (2009b), having one or more scores <16th percentile is found in approximately the same percent of healthy children and adolescents with average intelligence (i.e., 36.6%). This information assists clinical judgment by allowing the clinician to determine how common one or more, two or more, or even three or more low scores are in healthy children and adolescents. In other words, it is a mistake to rigidly apply deficit measurement theory and the principles of the bell curve to the interpretation of this Visual Delayed Index score in isolation. Rather, the clinician is encouraged to consider that the index score corresponded to the 14th percentile (below average), but having one or more below average index scores on the CMS is fairly common (i.e., it occurs in more than one-third of children). Based on all of the available information, the clinician concluded that this boy's neuropsychological profile on the CMS was not unusual compared to healthy adolescents and was unlikely to represent cognitive impairment secondary to his injury (i.e., consistent with the family's report).

Table 4.3 presents a second case example of a previously healthy, 11-year-old girl who sustained a severe traumatic brain injury when she was an unrestrained passenger in a high-speed motor vehicle collision (i.e., Glasgow Coma Scale score at the scene was 4/15, posttraumatic amnesia and fluctuating orientation for 10 days, and numerous findings on a brain magnetic resonance imaging (MRI) scan, including petechial hemorrhages throughout the white matter consistent with diffuse axonal injury, a nonhemorrhagic lesion in the brainstem, and subarachnoid hemorrhages in frontal, parietal, ventricular, and tentorial regions of the left hemisphere).

TABLE 4.3. Performance on Selected NEPSY-II Subtests in an 11-Year-Old Girl Who Sustained a Severe Traumatic Brain Injury

NEPSY-II Domains and Subtests	Standardized Performance and Descriptions		
	Scaled Score	Percentile	Classification
Attention and Executive Functioning			
Animal Sorting Total Correct Sorts	6	9	Borderline
Auditory Attention Total Correct	6	9	Borderline
Response Set Total Correct	5	5	Borderline
Inhibition: Naming Total Completion Time	6	9	Borderline
Inhibition: Inhibition Total Completion Time	4	2	Extremely Low
Inhibition: Switching Total Completion Time	2	<1	Extremely Low
Language			
Comprehension of Instructions Total	11	63	Average
Phonological Processing Total	9	37	Average
Speeded Naming Total Completion Time	7	16	Low Average
Memory and Learning			
Memory for Designs Total	9	37	Average
Memory for Designs Delayed Total	8	25	Average
Narrative Memory Free & Cued Recall Total	6	9	Borderline
Narrative Memory Free Recall Total	5	5	Borderline
Word List Interference Repetition Total	8	25	Average
Word List Interference Recall Total	7	16	Low Average
Visuospatial Processing			
Block Construction Total Score	10	50	Average
Geometric Puzzles Total Score	12	75	Average

NOTE: Scaled scores have a mean = 10 and a standard deviation = 3. Classifications are based on the Wechsler system.

Neuropsychological assessment at 1.5 years post injury included, among other measures, selected subtests from the NEPSY-II (i.e., these are the selected subtests presented in Table 1 from Brooks et al., 2010b). Examining her performance on the NEPSY-II subtests (see Table 4.3), it can be seen that she had several low scores. Specifically, she had 12 scores ≤25th percentile, 8 scores ≤10th percentile, 4 scores ≤5th percentile, and 2 scores ≤2nd percentile. Using the information provided on the prevalence of low NEPSY-II scores (the reader is referred to Table 4 from Brooks et al., 2010b), the clinician determined that having at least this many low NEPSY-II scores, regardless of the cutoff score used, is uncommon in healthy children (i.e., prevalence rates range from 0.9% to 5.2% depending on the cutoff score). When considering that both of her parents had at least some university education (i.e., 13–15 years), her performance was still considered uncommon across all cutoff scores. Based on all of the available information, the clinician concluded that this young girl's neuropsychological profile on the NEPSY-II was consistent with cognitive deficits secondary to her injuries sustained in the motor vehicle collision. In this second example, the clinician is able to use the prevalence of low scores to determine that the overall "profile" is uncommon and to supplement clinical judgment.

CONCLUSIONS

Pediatric forensic neuropsychological assessments are geared toward the detection and quantification of cognitive impairment secondary to an acquired injury or illness. In these assessments, numerous tests across different neurocognitive domains are administered, which results in the interpretation of multiple test scores. Clinicians must simultaneously interpret performance across all measures, but without psychometric data to inform clinicians, it is possible to overinterpret one or more low scores. This is because when multiple tests are administered and numerous test scores are interpreted, it is common to have some low scores. Although the bell curve is applicable for a single-score distribution, the classic and mainstream interpretation principles derived from the bell curve are misleading when applied to a group of test scores. In other words, if a single memory test yielding a single score is interpreted, the likelihood of obtaining a score ≤ 5th percentile is 5%. However, if multiple memory scores are interpreted simultaneously, as is always the case in comprehensive evaluations, the likelihood of obtaining one very low score goes up dramatically. Without psychometrically derived information on the prevalence of low scores (i.e., multivariate analyses), clinicians must rely solely on their judgment as to whether the number of low scores obtained is common or uncommon. Therefore, the multivariate analysis of test scores can be used to aid clinical judgment in a pediatric forensic neuropsychological assessment.

As discussed in this chapter, multivariate analyses have provided some key concepts that a pediatric neuropsychologist must consider when interpreting test performance. Clinicians must appreciate that (a) test-score scatter or variability is common; (b) having some low scores is common in a substantial minority of children; (c) the number of low scores is related to the cutoff score used for interpretation; (d) the number of low scores depends on the number of tests administered; and (e) the number of low scores varies by characteristics of the examinees (e.g., level of child's intelligence and number of years of parental education). By understanding these concepts and having ready-to-use interpretive tables, clinicians can bolster the scientific underpinnings of their clinical judgment in the forensic process. It is also important to note that multivariate analyses can be applied to the numerous discrepancy score comparisons that are often generated for test batteries (i.e., Verbal Comprehension Index v. Perceptual Organization Index; for examples of the prevalence of low index score comparisons, see Brooks et al., 2009d; Crawford et al., 2007) and to the numerous test-retest score comparisons (i.e., change from

time 1 to time 2 across a battery of tests; see Chapter 5) that occur in neuropsychological assessments, both of which are likely subject to increased prevalence rates
when multiple analyses are conducted.

To date, published data on the prevalence of low scores across a test battery have
been available for many adult and older adult tests, but less information has been
published using pediatric tests. There are three methods for obtaining the prevalence
of low scores on a pediatric test battery: (a) from the test publisher as part of the
interpretive manual; (b) through independent research using the standardization
sample after the publication of the test; and/or (c) by using information already provided in the test manual (i.e., subtest intercorrelations) and an available computer
program that can estimate the base rates (i.e., Crawford et al., 2007). At the time
of this writing, there has yet to be a published battery of pediatric tests that provides clinically usable information on the base rates of low scores in the test manual.
The information that is available to clinicians has come from independent research.

Information on the prevalence of low scores clinically and forensically is designed
to assist clinical judgment and promote evidence-based practice. The prevalence
rates of low scores are utilized in the context of determining whether an examinee's
overall profile (i.e., the number of low scores) is common or uncommon in healthy
children and adolescents. It is important for the clinician to remember that the presence of more low scores than would be expected in healthy children is not diagnostic of a specific clinical condition and is not necessarily diagnostic of pathology.
Rather, the tables provided can be used to determine whether the number of low
scores obtained is atypical in healthy children and adolescents, thus leaving clinical
acumen to determine whether the low scores reflect the consequences of injury or
disease, or if some other factor(s) account for the number of obtained low scores.
An individual suffering a neurological injury may have more low scores than
expected as a consequence of his or her injury or as a consequence of other factors
that may need to be considered (e.g., premorbid functioning, medication effects,
effort, other medical conditions, and/or normal variability).

It is essential to appreciate that there is always a balance between sensitivity and
specificity that is directly related to false-positive and false-negative diagnostic conclusions. A child who sustains a severe traumatic brain injury, has good recovery,
and obtains a "normal" number of low scores on a battery of tests might still, of
course, have acquired cognitive deficits. That child might have been functioning in
the upper average to superior range cognitively prior to injury and recovered to the
lower average range. Rigidly applying the principles of multivariate analyses to that
case might result in the failure to identify residual acquired cognitive deficits in that
child (i.e., a false negative).

There can be some clinical evaluations (e.g., educational, vocational, psychological) that are not directed at determining whether a decline or change in neurocognitive functioning has occurred as a result of an injury or illness, but are more focused
on identifying a profile of cognitive strengths and weaknesses. For example, having
a low index score might not necessarily be an uncommon finding in healthy children but could still reflect relative weakness for a particular child, have a negative
impact on daily functioning, require academic accommodations or compensatory
strategies, and impact future vocational choices. In these situations, the base-rate

information may be of interest to the clinician but potentially might not be used in the same manner as when determining the effects of an injury in a pediatric forensic neuropsychological assessment.

REFERENCES

American Psychiatric Association (2000). *Diagnostic and statistical manual of mental disorders* (4th ed., text rev.). Washington, DC: Author.

Axelrod, B. N., & Wall, J. R. (2007). Expectancy of impaired neuropsychological test scores in a non-clinical sample. *International Journal of Neuroscience, 117*(11), 1591–1602.

Binder, L. M., Iverson, G. L., & Brooks, B. L. (2009). To err is human: "Abnormal" neuropsychological scores and variability are common in healthy adults. *Archives of Clinical Neuropsychology, 24*, 31–46.

Brooks, B. L. (2010). Seeing the forest for the trees: Prevalence of low scores on the Wechsler Intelligence Scale for Children, Fourth Edition (WISC-IV). *Psychological Assessment, 22*(3), 650–656.

Brooks, B.L. (2011). A study of low scores in Canadian children and adolescents on the Wechsler Intelligence Scale for Children, Fourth Edition (WISC-IV). *Child Neuropsychology, 17*(3), 281–289.

Brooks, B. L., Holdnack, J. A., & Iverson, G. L. (2011). Advanced clinical interpretation of the WAIS-IV and WMS-IV: Prevalence of low scores varies by level of intelligence and years of education *18*(2), 156–167. *Assessment,* doi: 10.1177/1073191110385316.

Brooks, B. L., & Iverson, G. L. (2010). Comparing actual to estimated base rates of "abnormal" scores on neuropsychological test batteries: Implications for interpretation. *Archives of Clinical Neuropsychology, 25*, 14–21.

Brooks, B. L., Iverson, G. L., Feldman, H. H., & Holdnack, J. A. (2009a). Minimizing misdiagnosis: psychometric criteria for possible or probable memory impairment. *Dementia and Geriatric Cognitive Disorders, 27*(5), 439–450.

Brooks, B. L., Iverson, G. L., Holdnack, J. A., & Feldman, H. H. (2008). Potential for misclassification of mild cognitive impairment: A study of memory scores on the Wechsler Memory Scale-III in healthy older adults. *Journal of the International Neuropsychological Society, 14*(3), 463–478.

Brooks, B. L., Iverson, G. L., Sherman, E. M. S., & Holdnack, J. A. (2009b). Healthy children and adolescents obtain some low scores across a battery of memory tests. *Journal of the International Neuropsychological Society, 15*(4), 613–617.

Brooks, B. L., Iverson, G. L., Sherman, E. M., & Roberge, M. C. (2010a). Identifying cognitive problems in children and adolescents with depression using computerized neuropsychological testing. *Applied Neuropsychology, 17*(1), 37–43.

Brooks, B. L., Iverson, G. L., & White, T. (2007). Substantial risk of "Accidental MCI" in healthy older adults: Base rates of low memory scores in neuropsychological assessment. *Journal of the International Neuropsychological Society, 13*(3), 490–500.

Brooks, B. L., Iverson, G. L., & White, T. (2009c). Advanced interpretation of the Neuropsychological Assessment Battery (NAB) with older adults: Base rate analyses, discrepancy scores, and interpreting change. *Archives of Clinical Neuropsychology, 24*(7), 647–657.

Brooks, B.L., Sherman, E. M. S., & Iverson, G. L. (2010b). Healthy children get some low scores too: Prevalence of low scores on the NEPSY-II in preschoolers, children, and adolescents. *Archives of Clinical Neuropsychology, 25*, 182–190.

Brooks, B. L., Strauss, E., Sherman, E. M. S., Iverson, G. L., & Slick, D. J. (2009d). Developments in neuropsychological assessment: Refining psychometric and clinical interpretive methods. *Canadian Psychology, 50*(3), 196–209.

Cohen, M. J. (1997). *Children's Memory Scale*. San Antonio, TX: The Psychological Corporation.

Crawford, J. R., Garthwaite, P. H., & Gault, C. B. (2007). Estimating the percentage of the population with abnormally low scores (or abnormally large score differences) on standardized neuropsychological test batteries: a generic method with applications. *Neuropsychology, 21*(4), 419–430.

de Rotrou, J., Wenisch, E., Chausson, C., Dray, F., Faucounau, V., & Rigaud, A. S. (2005). Accidental MCI in healthy subjects: a prospective longitudinal study. *European Journal of Neurology, 12*(11), 879–885.

Delis, D. C., Kaplan, E., & Kramer, J. H. (2001). *Delis-Kaplan Executive Function System*. San Antonio, TX: The Psychological Corporation.

Devlin, B., Daniels, M., & Roeder, K. (1997). The heritability of IQ. *Nature, 388*, 468–471.

Heaton, R. K., Chelune, G. J., Talley, J. L., Kay, G. G., & Curtiss, G. (1993). *Wisconsin Card Sorting Test*. Lutz, FL: Psychological Assessment Resources, Inc.

Heaton, R. K., Grant, I., & Matthews, C. G. (1991). *Comprehensive norms for an extended Halstead-Reitan Battery: Demographic corrections, research findings, and clinical applications*. Odessa, FL: Psychological Assessment Resources, Inc.

Heaton, R. K., Miller, S. W., Taylor, M. J., & Grant, I. (2004). *Revised comprehensive norms for an expanded Halstead-Reitan Battery: Demographically adjusted neuropsychological norms for African American and Caucasian adults, professional manual*. Lutz, FL: Psychological Assessment Resources.

Horton, A. M., Jr. (1999). Above-average intelligence and neuropsychological test score performance. *International Journal of Neuroscience, 99*(1–4), 221–231.

Ingraham, L. J., & Aiken, C. B. (1996). An empirical approach to determining criteria for abnormality in test batteries with multiple measures. *Neuropsychology, 10*, 120–124.

Iverson, G. L., & Brooks, B. L. (2011). Improving accuracy for identifying cognitive impairment. In M. R. Schoenberg & J. G. Scott (Eds.), *The black book of neuropsychology: A syndrome-based approach* (pp. 923–950). New York: Springer.

Iverson, G. L., Brooks, B. L., & Haley, G. M. (2009a). Interpretation of the RBANS in inpatient psychiatry: Clinical normative data and prevalence of low scores for patients with schizophrenia. *Applied Neuropsychology, 16*(1), 31–41.

Iverson, G. L., Brooks, B. L., & Holdnack, J. A. (2008a). Misdiagnosis of cognitive impairment in forensic neuropsychology. In R. L. Heilbronner (Ed.), *Neuropsychology in the courtroom: Expert analysis of reports and testimony* (pp. 243–266). New York: Guilford Press.

Iverson, G. L., Brooks, B. L., White, T., & Stern, R. A. (2008b). Neuropsychological Assessment Battery (NAB): Introduction and advanced interpretation. In A. M. Horton, Jr. & D. Wedding (Eds.), *The neuropsychology handbook* (3rd ed., pp. 279–343). New York: Springer.

Iverson, G. L., Brooks, B. L., & Young, A. H. (2009b). Identifying neurocognitive impairment in depression using computerized testing. *Applied Neuropsychology, 16*(4), 254–261.

Iverson, G. L., Brooks, B. L., & Young, A. H. (2009c). Rapid computerized assessment of neurocognitive deficits in bipolar disorder. *Applied Neuropsychology, 16*(3), 207–213.

Kaufman, A. S., & Kaufman, N. L. (2004). *Kaufman Assessment Battery for Children, Second Edition*. Circle Pines, MN: AGS Publishing.

Korkman, M., Kirk, U., & Kemp, S. (2007a). *NEPSY-II: A Developmental Neuropsychological Assessment*. San Antonio, TX: The Psychological Corporation.

Korkman, M., Kirk, U., & Kemp, S. (2007b). *NEPSY-II: Clinical and Interpretive Manual*. San Antonio, TX: The Psychological Corporation.

Palmer, B. W., Boone, K. B., Lesser, I. M., & Wohl, M. A. (1998). Base rates of "impaired" neuropsychological test performance among healthy older adults. *Archives of Clinical Neuropsychology, 13*(6), 503–511.

Pearson Assessment. (2009). *Advanced clinical solutions for the WAIS-IV/WMS-IV*. San Antonio, TX: NCS: Pearson.

Reynolds, C. R., & Kamphaus, R. W. (2003). *Reynolds Intellectual Assessment Scales*. Lutz, FL: Psychological Assessment Resources.

Reynolds, C. R., & Voress, J. K. (2007). *Test of Memory and Learning, Second Edition*. Austin, TX: Pro-Ed, Inc.

Schoenberg, M. R., Lange, R. T., Brickell, T. A., & Saklofske, D. H. (2007a). Estimating premorbid general cognitive functioning for children and adolescents using the American Wechsler Intelligence Scale for Children-Fourth Edition: Demographic and current performance approaches. *Journal of Child Neurology, 22*(4), 379–388.

Schoenberg, M. R., Lange, R. T., & Saklofske, D. H. (2007b). A proposed method to estimate premorbid full scale intelligence quotient (FSIQ) for the Canadian Wechsler Intelligence Scale for Children-Fourth Edition (WISC-IV) using demographic and combined estimation procedures. *Journal of Clinical and Experimental Neuropsychology, 29*(8), 867–878.

Schretlen, D. J., Testa, S. M., Winicki, J. M., Pearlson, G. D., & Gordon, B. (2008). Frequency and bases of abnormal performance by healthy adults on neuropsychological testing. *Journal of the International Neuropsychological Society, 14*(3), 436–445.

Sheslow, D., & Adams, W. (2003). *Wide Range Assessment of Memory and Learning, Second Edition*. Wilmington, DE: Wide Range Inc.

Steinberg, B. A., Bieliauskas, L. A., Smith, G. E., & Ivnik, R. J. (2005). Mayo's Older Americans Normative Studies: Age- and IQ-adjusted norms for the Trail-Making Test, the Stroop Test, and MAE Controlled Oral Word Association Test. *The Clinical Neuropsychologist, 19*(3–4), 329–377.

Steinberg, B. A., Bieliauskas, L. A., Smith, G. E., Ivnik, R. J., & Malec, J. F. (2005). Mayo's Older Americans Normative Studies: Age- and IQ-adjusted norms for the Auditory Verbal Learning Test and the Visual Spatial Learning Test. *The Clinical Neuropsychologist, 19*(3–4), 464–523.

Sweet, J. J., Peck, E. A., III, Abramowitz, C., & Etzweiler, S. (2002). National Academy of Neuropsychology/Division 40 of the American Psychological Association practice survey of clinical neuropsychology in the United States, Part I: practitioner and practice characteristics, professional activities, and time requirements. *The Clinical Neuropsychologist, 16*(2), 109–127.

Thomas, S. V., Sukumaran, S., Lukose, N., George, A., & Sarma, P. S. (2007). Intellectual and language functions in children of mothers with epilepsy. *Epilepsia, 48*(12), 2234–2240.

Tremont, G., Hoffman, R. G., Scott, J. G., & Adams, R. L. (1998). Effect of intellectual level on neuropsychological test performance: A response to Dodrill (1997). *The Clinical Neuropsychologist, 12*, 560–567.

van der Sluis, S., Willemsen, G., de Geus, E. J., Boomsma, D. I., & Posthuma, D. (2008). Gene-environment interaction in adults' IQ scores: measures of past and present environment. *Behavioral Genetics, 38*(4), 348–360.

Warner, M. H., Ernst, J., Townes, B. D., Peel, J., & Preston, M. (1987). Relationships between IQ and neuropsychological measures in neuropsychiatric populations: within-laboratory and cross-cultural replications using WAIS and WAIS-R. *Journal of Clinical and Experimental Neuropsychology, 9*(5), 545–562.

Wechsler, D. (2002). *Wechsler Preschool and Primary Scale of Intelligence, Third Edition.* San Antonio, TX: The Psychological Corporation.

Wechsler, D. (2003). *Wechsler Intelligence Scale for Children-Fourth Edition.* San Antonio, TX: The Psychological Corporation.

Woodcock, R. W., McGrew, K. S., & Mather, N. (2001). *Woodcock-Johnson III Tests of Cognitive Abilities.* Itasca, IL: Riverside Publishing.

World Health Organization. (1992). *International classification of diseases* (10th ed.). Geneva, Switzerland: Author.

Chapter 5

Interpreting Change on Repeated Neuropsychological Assessments of Children

GRANT L. IVERSON

INTRODUCTION

A principal role of the neuropsychologist is to assess cognition accurately and to offer an opinion as to whether the child's functioning has been affected by a developmental and/or acquired condition. Repeated assessments are frequently used to (a) estimate improvement or deterioration or (b) monitor cognitive maturation. In a forensic context, repeated assessments are also used to challenge the reliability and accuracy of opinions relating to acquired cognitive impairment.

Most books relating to clinical neuropsychology, and most test manuals, contain little if any practical information on interpreting change on single or multiple tests. This has resulted in generations of practitioners having to rely on clinical judgment or arbitrary psychometric decision rules when interpreting serial neuropsychological evaluations.

Some clinicians have no a priori methodology for how to interpret change on neuropsychological tests. Rather, they simply look at the scores (e.g., percentile ranks, scaled scores, or T scores) and speculate as to whether the change in performance seems "real" or "meaningful." Other clinicians apply an arbitrary cutoff for interpreting change, such as one standard deviation difference in performance. Accordingly, a retest score is said to have declined if it is one standard deviation (SD) lower or said to have improved if it is one SD higher than the original test score. This method for interpreting change has been used in the literature (Hermann & Wyler, 1988; Mahanna et al., 1996; Phillips & McGlone, 1995; Shaw et al., 1986). However, it is problematic because it does not account for differences in reliability among different tests, measurement error, or practice effects.

There are six main factors that complicate the interpretation of change in pediatric forensic neuropsychology: *(1)* initial level of performance; *(2)* stability; *(3)* measurement error; *(4)* practice effects; *(5)* regression to the mean; and *(6)* motivational issues. These factors and evidence-based methods for interpreting change are discussed in this chapter.

INITIAL LEVEL OF PERFORMANCE

When considering the effects of a brain injury, illness, or disease on neuropsychological test performance, it is important to properly conceptualize and explain initial level of performance. Initial levels of performance are inextricably tied to practice effects, regression to the mean, and relations among test scores. For example, baseline test scores that are in the extremely low or unusually low (i.e., "borderline") classification ranges are highly susceptible to practice effects and regression to the mean (a statistical occurrence whereby a score in one tail of a distribution is more likely to move toward the mean on retesting). Baseline test scores in the high average and superior classification ranges, in contrast, are susceptible to regression, but are somewhat less likely to show large practice effects. This is because situational factors are more likely to artificially lower, than artificially inflate, a test score. With the exception of regression-based methods for interpreting change (see following section), most methodologies for interpreting change do not account for baseline level of performance. From a practical perspective, assuming no real actual change in a person's clinical condition, very low scores are more likely to improve on retesting than average or above average scores. In some situations, this psychometric reality might lead the clinician to overestimate the degree to which a person has improved or recovered following a neurological injury.

MEASUREMENT ERROR, REGRESSION TO THE MEAN, STABILITY, AND PRACTICE EFFECTS

Measurement error can be random or systematic. It is the cumulative effect of all uncontrolled and unspecified factors on test performance. Measurement error is closely related to test reliability. Reliability relates to the consistency or stability in test scores. According to classical test theory, it has been viewed in terms of the relation between "true" scores and obtained scores. Obtained scores are believed to contain an error component, which influences both the consistency and stability of a particular score. Thus, high reliability may be viewed as the ability of a test to reflect an individual score that is minimally influenced by error (see Chapter 3 for a discussion of reliability and validity issues in pediatric forensic neuropsychology).

Reliability should not be considered a dichotomous concept; rather it falls on a continuum. One cannot say a test is reliable or unreliable, but more accurately should say it possesses a high or low degree of reliability for a specific purpose, with a specific population (Franzen, 1989, 2000). Reliability is a multidimensional psychometric construct that is evaluated through several kinds of reliability evidence, such as *(a)* consistency across test items (internal consistency), (*b*) consistency over time (test-retest reliability or test stability), and (*c*) consistency across raters (interrater reliability).

Most reliability estimates are reported in terms of correlation coefficients. These coefficients measure the degree of association between two or more variables. Common estimates of association are internal consistency, alternate forms, and test-retest coefficients. Internal consistency measures the internal structure of a test and is influenced by how consistently the test actually taps the construct it purports to measure. Internal consistency is further influenced by the nature of the construct itself. Heterogeneity in the construct is inversely related to the internal consistency of a test designed to measure it. Common measures of internal consistency include the split-half or Spearman-Brown reliability coefficient,[1] coefficient alpha (Cronbach's alpha),[2] and the Kuder—Richardson reliability coefficient.[3]

Test-retest reliability is influenced by error resulting from time and situational variables (Franzen, 1989, 2000). This reliability estimate is greatly influenced by the stability of the construct of interest. If the construct varies systematically in the same way for every individual, the resultant correlation coefficient would be unaffected. However, under most circumstances, it can be assumed that temporal, situational, and clinical factors will introduce variability into the construct being assessed. Consequently, stability estimates will be attenuated.

It is not possible for clinicians to simply view test-retest coefficients presented in test manuals or research articles and then confidently use that information to interpret change in individual cases. The test-retest coefficient provides information regarding the stability of score distributions, but it does not help us understand dispersion, regression, or practice effects.

Estimates of internal consistency reliability and test-retest reliability for the Delis-Kaplan Executive Function System (D-KEFS; Delis, Kaplan, & Kramer, 2001) are presented in Table 5.1. It is important to appreciate that the estimates of internal consistency are derived from relatively large samples of healthy children, and the estimates of stability are derived from a small sample tested over brief intervals. Notice that internal consistency estimates are not available for certain tests (i.e., those measuring processing speed), and for some tests they vary considerably across age groups. The test-retest coefficients also vary considerably from one test to another test, as illustrated in Table 5.1.

The *standard error of measurement* (SEM) is conceptually and mathematically related to, and derived from, test-retest reliability and dispersion (i.e., score variability). Theoretically, the SEM is an estimate of the probable range of obtained scores around a person's true score. We are taught to conceptualize IQ scores, for example, as falling within a range (as opposed to the Full Scale IQ being a precisely accurate estimate of a child's intelligence). This range is determined by multiplying an SEM

1. Obtained by correlating two halves of items from the same test.

2. Based on the average intercorrelation between test items.

3. Used for items with dichotomous answers (i.e., yes/no, true/false), or heterogeneous tests where split-half methods must be used.

TABLE 5.1. Internal Consistency and Test-Retest Reliability for the D-KEFS in Children and Adolescents

	Internal Consistency r_{11}	Test-Retest r_{12}
TMT 1: Visual Scanning	—	0.50
TMT 2: Number Sequencing	—	0.77
TMT 3: Letter Sequencing	—	0.57
TMT 4: Number-Letter Sequencing	—	0.20
TMT 5: Motor Speed	—	0.82
Letter Fluency	0.68–0.81	0.67
Category Fluency	0.53–0.75	0.70
Category Switching-Total Correct	0.37–0.62	0.65
Category Switching-Accuracy	0.53–0.73	0.53
Design Fluency 1: Filled Dots	—	0.66
Design Fluency 2: Empty Dots	—	0.43
Design Fluency 3: Switching	—	0.13
Color-Word: Color Naming	—	0.79
Color-Word: Word Reading	—	0.77
Color-Word: Inhibition	—	0.90
Color-Word: Inhibition/Switching	—	0.80
Sorting: Confirmed Correct Sorts	0.58–0.82	0.49
Sorting: Free Sorting Description	0.55–0.80	0.67
Sorting: Sort Recognition Description	0.62–0.74	0.56
20 Quest.: Initial Abstraction	0.72–0.87	0.62
20 Quest: Weighted Achievement	0.10–0.53	0.06
Word Context Consecutively Correct	0.47–0.71	0.58
Tower Test Achievement	0.43–0.84	0.51
Proverbs: Free Inquiry	0.68	0.90

NOTES: These data were adapted from Tables 2.1 through 2.26 in the D-KEFS Technical Manual (Delis et al., 2001). The ranges for internal consistency represent values across age groups from 8 to 19 years. The test-retest coefficients are based on 28 individuals between the ages of 8 and 19 who were tested twice separated by approximately 25 days (SD = 12.8 days).

by a z score to create a confidence interval (e.g., the 90% or 95% confidence interval). Two formulas for calculating the SEM are provided:

$$SEM = SD\sqrt{1 - r_{11}}$$ Standard deviation from time 1 multiplied by the square root of 1 minus the internal consistency coefficient

$$SEM = SD\sqrt{1 - r_{12}}$$ Standard deviation from time 1 multiplied by the square root of 1 minus the test-retest coefficient

Most test authors and publishers use internal consistency coefficients to calculate the SEM. Test-retest coefficients are usually only used when internal consistency cannot be readily calculated (e.g., test measuring processing speed, such as Coding or Symbol Search from the Wechsler tests). As seen in the formula, internal consistency coefficients, if used, will usually make the SEM smaller (i.e., less measurement error) because internal consistency coefficients are typically higher than test-retest coefficients. The SEM is also related to the amount of score variability in the normative sample. Tests with greater variability (as reflected by the SD) will have larger SEMs. Unlike the SEM, the *standard error of estimation* takes into account regression toward the mean. This estimate of measurement error will result in an asymmetric confidence interval for very high or very low scores.

The *standard error of the difference* (SE$_{diff}$) can be used to estimate measurement error relating to test-retest difference scores. As seen in the formula that follows, the SE$_{diff}$ is based on the SEM for the time 1 score and the SEM for the time 2 score. The estimated measurement error for each score is combined to estimate measurement error surrounding the test-retest difference score. The SE$_{diff}$, which will be discussed later, is the foundation for the reliable change index and methodology.

$$SE_{diff} = \sqrt{SEM_1^2 + SEM_2^2}$$ Square root of the sum of the *squared* SEMs for each testing occasion

Clinicians and researchers are familiar with practice effects noted in test manuals for many intellectual and neuropsychological tests. In test development, it is common to conduct a test-retest study using a brief retest interval (e.g., 2–12 weeks). This is done, mainly, out of convenience. The problem, of course, is that (*a*) these retest studies are not applicable to most clinical situations because the interval is too brief, and (*b*) the brief interval likely results in overestimating practice effects for clinical practice. Some examinees can actually remember the specific content of memory tests that were administered in the recent past. Examinees can also benefit from a positive carryover effect (e.g., developing better test-taking strategies), familiarity with the testing context (e.g., reduced novelty effects), reduced performance anxiety, and increased confidence related to prior exposure to testing. Accordingly, although more logistically challenging, a retest interval of 1 year would reduce a number of these effects and, more important, better approximate clinical practice. Although it is uncommon, for example, to repeat the same tests within weeks of the initial administration, it is not uncommon to administer the same tests after a year has passed.

Practice effects are a systematic source of bias in test scores. Test manuals, however, do not provide test users with very much information regarding practice effects. Part of the reason, of course, is that test-retest studies presented in test manuals often contain small healthy samples tested over brief intervals, so the practice effects might not be generalizable to clinical practice. It is important for clinicians and researchers to keep in mind the following five points regarding practice effects. First, practice effects presented in a test manual are based on a single study over a specific retest interval (usually brief). Replication of those findings would increase our confidence in their accuracy. Second, retest scores fall in a distribution (i.e., they can worsen, stay the same, improve to varying degrees). In other words, the "average" practice effect does not even apply to most people—only to a relatively small percentage of the sample. Third, practice effects vary from test to test. Fourth, most retest studies presented in test manuals do not approximate clinical practice, so the practice effects might not be accurate in a clinical context. Finally, practice effects are related to initial level of performance. From a purely theoretical standpoint, low scores are more susceptible to practice effects and regression to the mean, whereas high scores are less susceptible to practice effects, in part due to regression to the mean. Put simply, a child who obtains a very low score on the Coding subtest of the WISC-IV is theoretically more likely to obtain a higher score (i.e., show a "practice effect" and/or improved performance) on retest than a child who obtains an above average to superior score. Of course, this might also be due, in part, to situational factors in that a child who gets an unusually low score at time 1 on Coding might have done so due to a lapse of attention, other distraction, or variable effort. The relationship between level of function, regression, and practice effects is not always appreciated by clinicians and has obvious relevance for interpreting serial testing.

Examples of practice effects are provided in Figure 5.1 (WISC-IV), Figure 5.2 (Children's Memory Scale, CMS; Cohen, 1997), and Tables 5.2–5.7. Notice that some tests on the WISC-IV, such as Vocabulary and Comprehension, have very small practice effects. In contrast, Picture Completion, Block Design, Coding, Symbol Search, and Cancellation have larger practice effects. The most substantial practice effects on the CMS are on the Stories, Faces, and Word Pairs subtests. Practice effects for the D-KEFS range from nonexistent (e.g., Color-Word Reading and 20 Questions Initial Abstraction), to medium (e.g., Tower Test, Trails Number Sequencing), to fairly large (e.g., Trails Visual Scanning and Color-Word: Inhibition/Switching).

MOTIVATIONAL FACTORS

Neuropsychological test scores are greatly influenced by motivational factors (see Chapters 6 and 7 for discussions of symptom validity in children and adolescents).

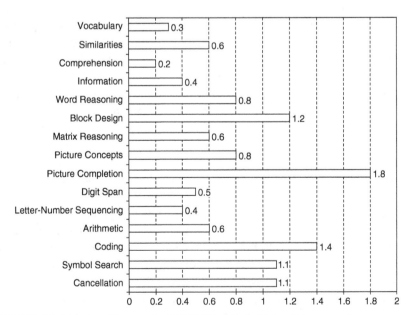

FIGURE 5.1. Practice effects on the WISC-IV expressed in scaled score units.
NOTE. These practice effects were adapted from data presented on page 40 of the WISC-IV test manual (Wechsler, 2003). The test-retest interval was 32 days (range = 13-63), and the total sample size was 243.

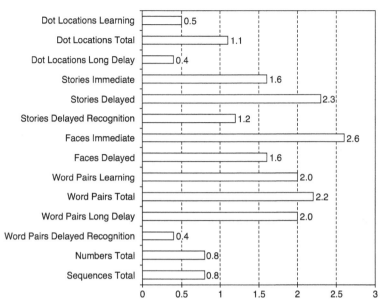

FIGURE 5.2. Practice effects on the CMS expressed in scaled score units.
NOTE: These practice effects were adapted from data presented on pages 102–103 of the CMS test manual Cohen (1997). The test-retest interval was 59.6 days (median = 65.3; SD = 29.2), and the total sample size was 125.

The accuracy of neuropsychological test results is largely dependent upon effort. Effort is a state, not a trait. Effort is variable, not constant. Effort is behavior that falls on a continuum. Some children are extremely motivated to perform well. Most of the time, children likely provide "good" or "adequate" effort for the purposes of the evaluation. Sometimes children are not motivated to perform well on testing, and the obtained results can be misinterpreted as reflecting cognitive deficits. Moreover, effort can be variable throughout an evaluation, thus accounting for "significant discrepancies" between two index scores or some isolated low test scores.

METHODS FOR INTERPRETING CHANGE

Many practitioners do not employ psychometrically sound methods for interpreting change on serial neuropsychological evaluations. Rather, they rely almost exclusively on clinical judgment. Having reviewed countless reports, many neuropsychologists seem to presuppose that cognitive test scores represent precise estimates of functioning, and that small changes in percentile ranks represent "real" changes in functioning. For example, a score going from the 10th to the 18th percentile is described as "improved" or "better," and a score going from the 82nd to the 73rd percentile is described as "declined." In forensic work, many clinicians have a tendency to refer to improved scores as reflecting recovery and declined scores as being due to measurement error (or psychological factors). The problem, of course, is that small changes in test scores are common and expected in healthy children and in children with clinical conditions that are stable. Moreover, the more tests that are administered, the more likely it is to see small, medium, and large changes in scores in the *absence of any clinically meaningful change in cognitive functioning*. In addition, it can be difficult to determine when statistical change reflects "real" or "clinical" change. Because test scores change in a statistically meaningful way does not mean that a person has improved or deteriorated in a clinically significant way. These challenges have led some researchers, such as Matarazzo, Carmody, and Jacobs (1980), to recommend certain "rules of thumb" for interpreting change. These authors suggested that a change of at least 15 points in IQ must be evident before interpreting a change as being "potentially" clinically important. In the absence of research relating to the ecological validity of change scores, practitioners have had to rely on clinical judgment for estimating meaningful improvements or declines on testing. Fortunately, slow but steady progress has been made in developing empirically based methods for interpreting change.

Regression Methods

Several research groups have used linear regression models to evaluate change on neuropsychological tests (e.g., McSweeney, Naugle, Chelune, & Luders, 1993; Salinsky, Storzbach, Dodrill, & Binder, 2001; Sawrie, Chelune, Naugle, & Luders, 1996; Sawrie, Marson, Boothe, & Harrell, 1999; Temkin, Heaton, Grant, & Dikmen, 1999). The simplest model is to use time 1 scores to predict time 2 scores (i.e., simple linear regression). If additional variables, other than the initial score, are related to the retest score, then multiple regression can be used. Multiple regression, in contrast to simple regression, involves generating an equation that includes the pretest score in addition to other relevant variables that may influence test performance. This method can account for multiple predictor or moderator variables, and control for regression to the mean (Crawford & Howell, 1998; Hermann et al., 1991).

The obvious advantage of regression models is that this approach accounts for both practice effects and regression to the mean. However, regression has certain statistical assumptions that are sometimes violated with neuropsychological test data. Homoscedasticity (similar to homogeneity of variance in analyses of variance, ANOVA) assumes an equal variation in Y's across the entire range of X's. Thus, for each score at time 1, the retest score is assumed to have a normal distribution, and the mean of this distribution is the predicted retest score (i.e., Y). Moreover, the standard deviation of Y is assumed to be the same for every value of X. Another assumption is that the mean values of Y corresponding to the various values of X fall in a straight line. Although regression is fairly robust to violations of some of its underlying assumptions, researchers should consider the nature of their data carefully, especially with regard to the assumption of linearity, prior to employing these models. McSweeney et al. (1993) recommended regression should not be used when the data for change are not normally distributed. Furthermore, measures prone to floor or ceiling effects are not amenable for use with regression methods. It is impossible to detect a decline in performance at time 2, for example, if an examinee obtains a score near the floor at time 1. Likewise, it is impossible to detect an improvement in performance if an examinee obtains a score near the ceiling at time 1.

It is important to understand the limitations of regression methods. Regression equations based on relatively small sample sizes can lead to large error terms. Regression equations from large studies,[4] therefore, are preferred. To maximize utility, sample characteristics should match populations seen clinically and predictor variables should be carefully chosen to match data that will likely be available to clinicians.

Reliable Change Methodology

The reliable change methodology, originally proposed by Jacobson and colleagues (Jacobson, Follette, & Revenstorf, 1984; Jacobson & Revenstorf, 1988; Jacobson & Truax, 1991), can be very helpful for interpreting serial testing in pediatric neuropsychology. This is a method for determining whether a change on a psychological test is reliable. That is, does the change represent a real improvement or deterioration in the patient's clinical condition—or does it simply reflect measurement error?

This method involved calculating a reliable change index (RCI). The reliable change methodology assumes that the true score of the individual remains constant from time 1 to time 2. The methodology is based on a fixed-alpha strategy, and therefore the interpretation is similar to null hypothesis testing. After the alpha level is set, the critical z score(s) are determined to mark the fixed boundaries of reliable change. For $\alpha = .05$ (two-tailed), for example, the RCI must exceed 1.96 for the change to be deemed a statistically reliable improvement or decline. A more lenient RCI of ± 1.64 ($\alpha = 0.10$, two-tailed) is also common.

The formula used by Jacobson and Truax (1991) has been debated and modified several times over the years (Hageman & Arrindell, 1993, 1999a, 1999b; Hsu, 1989, 1999; Speer, 1992; Speer & Greenbaum, 1995).[5] The reliable change "index" is a derived score from the formula, and it is expressed as a z score. Thus, reliable change index scores[6] represent discrete points on a confidence interval (CI) for measurement error surrounding test-retest difference scores.

The reliable change methodology was used extensively in clinical psychology (Jacobson, Roberts, Berns, & McGlinchey, 1999; Ogles, Lambert, & Masters, 1996), prior to being applied to clinical neuropsychology (Chelune, Naugle, Luders, Sedlak, & Awad, 1993; Heaton et al., 2001; Iverson, 1998, 1999, 2001; Temkin et al., 1999)

---

4. Particularly those equations that have been cross-validated.

5. Speer (1992) and Hsu (1989, 1999) proposed alternate reliable change formulas to correct for the effects of regression to the mean. Hageman and Arrindell (1993, 1999a, 1999b) proposed two different refinements of the methodology. The first, named RCID (for "improved difference" score), modifies the numerator substantially by accounting for regression to the mean. The second, named RC_{INDIV}, is unique in that it does not employ a fixed-alpha strategy. Instead, it uses a phi-strategy introduced by Cronbach and Gleser (1959) in which the risk of being misclassified as "improved" or "deteriorated" is set to a maximum allowable value (e.g., 5%).

6. The original formula for calculating the reliable change index has not been not included because it has been modified several times and it yields a standard z score, which is less clinically useful than creating reliable change confidence intervals.

and sports neuropsychology (Barr & McCrea, 2001; Hinton-Bayre, Geffen, Geffen, McFarland, & Friis, 1999; Iverson, Lovell, & Collins, 2003). In its modern form, the reliable change methodology allows the clinician to estimate measurement error surrounding test-retest difference scores by creating confidence intervals for these difference scores. Specifically, the standard error of the difference (SE_{diff}) is used to create a confidence interval for the baseline-retest difference score. This methodology can be used for any test. Proper calculation simply requires knowing the standard deviation from test and retest, and the test-retest correlation coefficient. The steps for calculating the SE_{diff} are as follows:

1. $SEM_1 = SD\sqrt{1 - r_{12}}$ Standard deviation from time 1 multiplied by the square root of 1 minus the test-retest coefficient
2. $SEM_2 = SD\sqrt{1 - r_{12}}$ Standard deviation from time 2 multiplied by the square root of 1 minus the test-retest coefficient
3. $SE_{diff} = \sqrt{SEM_1^2 + SEM_2^2}$ Square root of the sum of the *squared* SEMs for each testing occasion
4. Reliable change confidence intervals = the SE_{diff} is multiplied by the following z scores: ±1.04 (70% CI), ±1.28 (80% CI), ±1.64 (90% CI), and ±1.96 (95% CI).

In a practical way, the reliable change methodology allows the practitioner to reduce the impact of measurement error on test interpretation. *Ideally, to represent clinically significant improvement, the change score should be statistically reliable. However, statistically reliable change does not guarantee a clinically meaningful change.* Thus, the reliable change methodology is used to supplement clinical judgment. Reliable change is used to determine whether there has been improvement or deterioration in functioning that exceeds the probable range of measurement error.

Examples of reliable change confidence intervals are provided in Tables 5.2–5.7. These tables provide the clinician with information relating to the probable range of measurement error in the test-retest samples presented in test manuals. Some important points to keep in mind when interpreting these tables are as follows:

- Notice that for the Reynolds Intellectual Assessment Scales (RIAS; Reynolds and Kamphaus, 2003), Odd-Item Out the SDs are small for 5–8-year-olds (e.g., the SD for time 2 = 5.98, when Odd-Item Out is normed with a mean of 50 and an SD of 10). Thus, the estimate of reliable change for this age group on this test is comparatively small (see Table 5.2).
- Notice that for 6–7-year-olds the SD for time 2 for WISC-IV Cancellation is 1.9 (Cancellation is normed with a mean of 10 and an SD of 3.) Thus, WISC-IV Cancellation will have a smaller band of test-retest measurement error than some of the other subtests (see Table 5.3).
- For the 8–9-year-olds the WISC-IV Verbal Comprehension Index (VCI) has a smaller confidence interval for measurement error than the WISC-IV Perceptual Reasoning Index (PRI). This is not because

TABLE 5.2. Estimating Reliable Change for the Reynolds Intellectual Assessment Scales (RIAS) in Healthy Children

3–4-Year-Olds	SD_1	SD_2	r_{12}	SEM_1	SEM_2	SE_{diff}	.70 CI	.80 CI	.90 CI
Guess What	12.76	13.25	0.82	5.41	5.62	7.80	8.12	9.99	12.80
Verbal Reasoning	12.91	12.53	0.77	6.19	6.01	8.63	8.97	11.04	14.15
Odd Item Out	11.54	12.48	0.71	6.21	6.72	9.15	9.52	11.72	15.01
What's Missing	12.04	13.10	0.84	4.82	5.24	7.12	7.40	9.11	11.67
Verbal Memory	11.82	9.78	0.71	6.37	5.27	8.26	8.59	10.57	13.55
Nonverbal Memory	10.10	10.55	0.87	3.64	3.80	5.27	5.48	6.74	8.64
Verbal Intelligence Index	17.69	17.10	0.87	6.38	6.17	8.87	9.23	11.35	14.55
Nonverbal Intelligence Index	16.38	15.39	0.85	6.34	5.96	8.70	9.05	11.14	14.28
Composite Intelligence Index	14.39	17.17	0.75	7.20	8.59	11.20	11.65	14.34	18.37
Composite Memory Index	10.29	13.57	0.82	4.37	5.76	7.23	7.51	9.25	11.85
Reynolds Intellectual Screening Test	13.43	15.24	0.84	5.37	6.10	8.13	8.45	10.40	13.33
5–8-Year-Olds	SD_1	SD_2	r_{12}	SEM_1	SEM_2	SE_{diff}	.70 CI	.80 CI	.90 CI
Guess What	9.73	8.73	0.81	4.24	3.81	5.70	5.93	7.29	9.34
Verbal Reasoning	9.77	10.18	0.69	5.44	5.67	7.86	8.17	10.06	12.88
Odd Item Out	7.93	5.98	0.79	3.63	2.74	4.55	4.73	5.83	7.46
What's Missing	13.42	16.55	0.80	6.00	7.40	9.53	9.91	12.20	15.63
Verbal Memory	10.49	8.62	0.74	5.35	4.40	6.92	7.20	8.86	11.35
Nonverbal Memory	10.04	11.75	0.81	4.38	5.12	6.74	7.01	8.62	11.05
Verbal Intelligence Index	14.69	15.95	0.87	5.30	5.75	7.82	8.13	10.01	12.82
Nonverbal Intelligence Index	15.51	16.85	0.80	6.94	7.54	10.24	10.65	13.11	16.80
Composite Intelligence Index	16.39	17.94	0.89	5.44	5.95	8.06	8.38	10.32	13.22
Composite Memory Index	16.17	13.15	0.77	7.75	6.31	10.00	10.40	12.79	16.39
Reynolds Intellectual Screening Test	12.82	12.94	0.74	6.54	6.60	9.29	9.66	11.89	15.23
9–12-Year-Olds	SD_1	SD_2	r_{12}	SEM_1	SEM_2	SE_{diff}	.70 CI	.80 CI	.90 CI
Guess What	9.70	8.63	0.80	4.34	3.86	5.81	6.04	7.43	9.52
Verbal Reasoning	11.96	12.39	0.78	5.61	5.81	8.08	8.40	10.34	13.25
Odd Item Out	11.20	3.96	0.74	5.71	2.02	6.06	6.30	7.75	9.93
What's Missing	12.97	14.77	0.77	6.22	7.08	9.43	9.80	12.07	15.46
Verbal Memory	9.17	9.93	0.72	4.85	7.82	9.20	9.57	11.78	15.09

(Continued)

TABLE 5.2. (Continued)

Nonverbal Memory	7.07	7.15	0.66	4.12	5.79	7.11	7.39	9.10	11.66
Verbal Intelligence Index	18.99	15.69	0.87	6.85	2.58	7.32	7.61	9.36	12.00
Nonverbal Intelligence Index	16.56	16.90	0.95	3.70	3.51	5.10	5.31	6.53	8.37
Composite Intelligence Index	17.26	18.53	0.97	2.99	2.93	4.18	4.35	5.36	6.86
Composite Memory Index	11.01	10.01	0.84	4.40	7.41	8.62	8.97	11.04	14.14
Reynolds Intellectual Screening Test	16.26	11.07	0.91	4.88	3.32	5.90	6.14	7.55	9.68

NOTES: The test-retest coefficients and SDs were adapted from tables 5.8–5.10 on pages 82–83 of Reynolds and Kamphaus (2003). The test-retest interval was 21 days (range = 9–39). Sample sizes were: 3–4 = 33, 5–8 = 22, and 9–12 = 16.

TABLE 5.3. Estimating Reliable Change on the WISC-IV in Healthy Children (Ages 6–11)

Age: 6–7 Years	SD_1	SD_2	r_{12}	SEM_1	SEM_2	SE_{diff}	.70 CI	.80 CI	.90 CI
VCI	11.30	10.80	0.85	4.38	4.18	6.05	6.30	7.75	9.93
PRI	13.50	14.10	0.81	5.88	6.15	8.51	8.85	10.89	13.95
WMI	14.60	14.20	0.90	4.62	4.49	6.44	6.70	8.24	10.56
PSI	13.90	16.10	0.84	5.56	6.44	8.51	8.85	10.89	13.95
FSIQ	13.00	13.80	0.89	4.31	4.58	6.29	6.54	8.05	10.31
Block Design	2.80	2.50	0.74	1.43	1.27	1.91	1.99	2.45	3.14
Similarities	2.40	2.10	0.73	1.25	1.09	1.66	1.72	2.12	2.72
Digit Span	3.00	2.70	0.88	1.04	0.94	1.40	1.45	1.79	2.29
Picture Concepts	2.80	2.80	0.67	1.61	1.61	2.27	2.37	2.91	3.73
Coding	3.10	3.40	0.74	1.58	1.73	2.35	2.44	3.00	3.85
Vocabulary	2.60	2.40	0.76	1.27	1.18	1.73	1.80	2.22	2.84
Letter-Number	2.80	2.90	0.81	1.22	1.26	1.76	1.83	2.25	2.88
Matrix Reasoning	2.80	3.10	0.77	1.34	1.49	2.00	2.08	2.56	3.29
Comprehension	2.50	2.60	0.74	1.27	1.33	1.84	1.91	2.35	3.02
Symbol Search	3.10	3.30	0.80	1.39	1.48	2.02	2.11	2.59	3.32
Picture Completion	3.00	3.50	0.78	1.41	1.64	2.16	2.25	2.77	3.55
Cancellation	2.90	1.90	0.79	1.33	0.87	1.59	1.65	2.03	2.61
Information	2.50	2.80	0.74	1.27	1.43	1.91	1.99	2.45	3.14
Arithmetic	2.70	2.60	0.69	1.50	1.45	2.09	2.17	2.67	3.42
Word Reasoning	2.40	2.40	0.65	1.42	1.42	2.01	2.09	2.57	3.29

TABLE 5.3. (Continued)

Age: 8–9 Years	SD$_1$	SD$_2$	r$_{12}$	SEM$_1$	SEM$_2$	SE$_{diff}$	.70 CI	.80 CI	.90 CI
VCI	9.70	9.80	0.84	3.88	3.92	5.52	5.74	7.06	9.05
PRI	12.60	13.70	0.85	4.88	5.31	7.21	7.50	9.23	11.82
WMI	11.80	10.80	0.74	6.02	5.51	8.16	8.48	10.44	13.38
PSI	12.40	14.60	0.79	5.68	6.69	8.78	9.13	11.24	14.40
FSIQ	11.20	11.60	0.85	4.34	4.49	6.24	6.49	7.99	10.24
Block Design	3.10	2.70	0.81	1.35	1.18	1.79	1.86	2.29	2.94
Similarities	2.40	2.20	0.73	1.25	1.14	1.69	1.76	2.17	2.77
Digit Span	2.30	2.20	0.61	1.44	1.37	1.99	2.07	2.54	3.26
Picture Concepts	2.80	2.90	0.73	1.45	1.51	2.09	2.18	2.68	3.44
Coding	2.60	3.10	0.77	1.25	1.49	1.94	2.02	2.48	3.18
Vocabulary	2.20	2.20	0.83	0.91	0.91	1.28	1.33	1.64	2.10
Letter-Number	2.70	2.50	0.79	1.24	1.15	1.69	1.75	2.16	2.77
Matrix									
Reasoning	2.10	2.60	0.75	1.05	1.30	1.67	1.74	2.14	2.74
Comprehension	2.00	2.20	0.64	1.20	1.32	1.78	1.86	2.28	2.93
Symbol Search	2.30	2.60	0.69	1.28	1.45	1.93	2.01	2.47	3.17
Picture									
Completion	3.10	3.20	0.84	1.24	1.28	1.78	1.85	2.28	2.92
Cancellation	2.90	3.20	0.69	1.61	1.78	2.40	2.50	3.08	3.94
Information	2.20	1.90	0.78	1.03	0.89	1.36	1.42	1.75	2.24
Arithmetic	2.50	2.20	0.47	1.82	1.60	2.42	2.52	3.10	3.98
Word Reasoning	2.20	2.20	0.77	1.06	1.06	1.49	1.55	1.91	2.45
Age: 10–11 Years	**SD$_1$**	**SD$_2$**	**r$_{12}$**	**SEM$_1$**	**SEM$_2$**	**SE$_{diff}$**	**.70 CI**	**.80 CI**	**.90 CI**
VCI	11.20	12.00	0.88	3.88	4.16	5.69	5.91	7.28	9.33
PRI	11.30	11.80	0.87	4.07	4.25	5.89	6.13	7.54	9.66
WMI	13.40	13.70	0.84	5.36	5.48	7.67	7.97	9.81	12.57
PSI	12.10	15.30	0.80	5.41	6.84	8.72	9.07	11.17	14.31
FSIQ	10.40	11.10	0.86	3.89	4.15	5.69	5.92	7.28	9.33
Block Design	2.20	2.40	0.73	1.14	1.25	1.69	1.76	2.17	2.77
Similarities	2.90	2.60	0.87	1.05	0.94	1.40	1.46	1.80	2.30
Digit Span	2.90	3.00	0.82	1.23	1.27	1.77	1.84	2.27	2.90
Picture Concepts	2.80	3.00	0.82	1.19	1.27	1.74	1.81	2.23	2.86
Coding	2.70	3.30	0.87	0.97	1.19	1.54	1.60	1.97	2.52
Vocabulary	2.00	2.30	0.83	0.82	0.95	1.26	1.31	1.61	2.06
Letter-Number	2.40	2.60	0.74	1.22	1.33	1.80	1.88	2.31	2.96
Matrix									
Reasoning	2.20	2.10	0.85	0.85	0.81	1.18	1.23	1.51	1.93
Comprehension	2.20	2.40	0.55	1.48	1.61	2.18	2.27	2.80	3.58
Symbol Search	2.20	2.80	0.62	1.36	1.73	2.20	2.28	2.81	3.60

(Continued)

TABLE 5.3. (Continued)

Picture Completion	2.50	2.40	0.79	1.15	1.10	1.59	1.65	2.03	2.60
Cancellation	3.00	3.50	0.86	1.12	1.31	1.72	1.79	2.21	2.83
Information	2.50	2.50	0.91	0.75	0.75	1.06	1.10	1.36	1.74
Arithmetic	3.40	2.70	0.84	1.36	1.08	1.74	1.81	2.22	2.85
Word Reasoning	2.60	2.80	0.74	1.33	1.43	1.95	2.03	2.49	3.20

NOTES: The test-retest coefficients and SDs were adapted from tables on pages 40–41 of Wechsler (2003). The test-retest interval was 32 days (range = 13–63), and the total sample size was 243.

the WISC-IV VCI has a higher correlation coefficient than the WISC-IV PRI. This difference is because of the large SDs for time 1 and time 2 for WISC-IV PRI (see Table 5.3).

- For 12–13-year-olds, notice that the WISC-IV Symbol Search (r_{12} = .57) and WISC-IV Cancellation (r_{12} = .78) have comparable estimates of measurement error, despite the fact that WISC-IV Cancellation has a considerably higher test-retest correlation coefficient. This is because the dispersions (SDs) of scores differ (i.e., WISC-IV Symbol Search has less dispersion) (see Table 5.4).

- The confidence intervals for change vary greatly across the CMS Indexes. For example, for adolescents (13–16-year-olds), changes of 11 to 20 points are necessary to be considered statistically reliable at the 80% confidence interval. Without taking into account practice effects, an adolescent's CMS Attention/Concentration Index would need to change by 11 points and CMS Visual Immediate Index by 18 points to be considered a statistically reliable change (see Table 5.5).

- The 80% confidence interval for change on the D-KEFS varies from 2 to 5 scaled score points (see Table 5.6). Notice that the D-KEFS Trail Making Number-Letter Sequencing subtest needs to change by 5 points to be considered statistically reliable at the 80% confidence interval. In other words, if a child's score went from the 9th percentile to the 50th percentile, this would *not* be considered a statistically reliable change at the 80% confidence interval.

- For age 16, the SDs for California Verbal Learning Test, Children's Version (CVLT-C) List A Trials 1–5 are 6.15 and 10.94, respectively (see Table 5.7). The original formula for the reliable change index used only the SD for time 1, and many authors have used this original formula. In this case, the confidence interval for measurement error would be considerably smaller if that original formula was used because the proper formula uses the SD from test and retest (and the retest SD is much larger).

TABLE 5.4. Estimating Reliable Change on the WISC-IV in Healthy Adolescents (Ages 12–16)

Age: 12–13 Years	SD_1	SD_2	r_{12}	SEM_1	SEM_2	SE_{diff}	.70 CI	.80 CI	.90 CI
VCI	12.80	12.20	0.91	3.84	3.66	5.30	5.52	6.79	8.70
PRI	13.20	13.60	0.86	4.94	5.09	7.09	7.38	9.08	11.63
WMI	13.30	13.60	0.89	4.41	4.51	6.31	6.56	8.08	10.35
PSI	11.20	13.10	0.73	5.82	6.81	8.96	9.31	11.46	14.69
FSIQ	11.10	11.60	0.92	3.14	3.28	4.54	4.72	5.81	7.45
Block Design	3.20	3.40	0.84	1.28	1.36	1.87	1.94	2.39	3.06
Similarities	2.40	2.40	0.86	0.90	0.90	1.27	1.32	1.63	2.08
Digit Span	3.00	2.90	0.85	1.16	1.12	1.62	1.68	2.07	2.65
Picture Concepts	2.70	2.40	0.66	1.57	1.40	2.11	2.19	2.70	3.45
Coding	2.40	2.70	0.79	1.10	1.24	1.66	1.72	2.12	2.71
Vocabulary	2.30	2.50	0.88	0.80	0.87	1.18	1.22	1.51	1.93
Letter-Number	2.40	2.30	0.72	1.27	1.22	1.76	1.83	2.25	2.88
Matrix Reasoning	2.50	2.60	0.71	1.35	1.40	1.94	2.02	2.49	3.19
Comprehension	3.20	2.90	0.80	1.43	1.30	1.93	2.01	2.47	3.17
Symbol Search	2.10	2.30	0.57	1.38	1.51	2.04	2.12	2.61	3.35
Picture Completion	2.90	2.80	0.83	1.20	1.15	1.66	1.73	2.13	2.73
Cancellation	3.20	3.30	0.78	1.50	1.55	2.16	2.24	2.76	3.54
Information	2.60	2.40	0.80	1.16	1.07	1.58	1.65	2.03	2.60
Arithmetic	2.30	2.60	0.79	1.05	1.19	1.59	1.65	2.04	2.61
Word Reasoning	2.80	2.60	0.72	1.48	1.38	2.02	2.10	2.59	3.32
Age: 14–16 Years	SD_1	SD_2	r_{12}	SEM_1	SEM_2	SE_{diff}	.70 CI	.80 CI	.90 CI
VCI	12.00	13.10	0.93	3.17	3.47	4.70	4.89	6.02	7.71
PRI	14.20	15.70	0.87	5.12	5.66	7.63	7.94	9.77	12.52
WMI	12.70	13.70	0.82	5.39	5.81	7.93	8.24	10.14	13.00
PSI	13.20	15.80	0.80	5.90	7.07	9.21	9.58	11.79	15.10
FSIQ	12.60	14.10	0.90	3.98	4.46	5.98	6.22	7.65	9.81
Block Design	3.30	3.20	0.88	1.14	1.11	1.59	1.66	2.04	2.61
Similarities	2.80	2.90	0.82	1.19	1.23	1.71	1.78	2.19	2.80
Digit Span	2.90	2.70	0.81	1.26	1.18	1.73	1.80	2.21	2.83
Picture Concepts	2.40	2.80	0.62	1.48	1.73	2.27	2.36	2.91	3.73
Coding	2.90	3.00	0.86	1.09	1.12	1.56	1.62	2.00	2.56
Vocabulary	2.30	2.60	0.91	0.69	0.78	1.04	1.08	1.33	1.71
Letter-Number	2.20	2.60	0.64	1.32	1.56	2.04	2.13	2.62	3.35
Matrix Reasoning	2.90	3.10	0.77	1.39	1.49	2.04	2.12	2.61	3.34
Comprehension	2.60	2.20	0.82	1.10	0.93	1.44	1.50	1.85	2.37
Symbol Search	2.50	2.90	0.68	1.41	1.64	2.17	2.25	2.77	3.55
Picture Completion	2.80	3.20	0.85	1.08	1.24	1.65	1.71	2.11	2.70
Cancellation	2.90	3.10	0.76	1.42	1.52	2.08	2.16	2.66	3.41
Information	2.60	2.80	0.88	0.90	0.97	1.32	1.38	1.69	2.17
Arithmetic	3.00	2.40	0.84	1.20	0.96	1.54	1.60	1.97	2.52
Word Reasoning	2.70	2.80	0.83	1.11	1.15	1.60	1.67	2.05	2.63

NOTES: The test-retest coefficients and SDs were adapted from tables on page 42 of Wechsler (2003). The test-retest interval was 32 days (range = 13–63), and the total sample size was 243.

TABLE 5.5. Estimating Reliable Change on the Children's Memory Scale in Healthy Children

5–8-Year-Olds	SD_1	SD_2	r_{12}	SEM_1	SEM_2	SE_{diff}	.70 CI	.80 CI	.90 CI
Visual Immediate	13.40	14.70	0.66	7.81	8.57	11.60	12.06	14.85	19.02
Visual Delayed	12.50	14.50	0.66	7.29	8.45	11.16	11.61	14.29	18.31
Verbal Immediate	16.60	18.20	0.87	5.99	6.56	8.88	9.24	11.37	14.57
Verbal Delayed	16.20	15.60	0.63	9.85	9.49	13.68	14.23	17.51	22.44
General Memory	17.30	16.60	0.85	6.70	6.43	9.29	9.66	11.89	15.23
Attention/ Concentration	15.60	14.40	0.84	6.24	5.76	8.49	8.83	10.87	13.93
Learning	14.10	14.30	0.78	6.61	6.71	9.42	9.80	12.06	15.45
Delayed Recognition	15.30	17.00	0.57	10.03	11.15	15.00	15.60	19.20	24.60

9–12-Year-Olds	SD_1	SD_2	r_{12}	SEM_1	SEM_2	SE_{diff}	.70 CI	.80 CI	.90 CI
Visual Immediate	12.10	14.40	0.65	7.16	8.52	11.13	11.57	14.24	18.25
Visual Delayed	12.30	13.00	0.61	7.68	8.12	11.18	11.62	14.31	18.33
Verbal Immediate	16.50	18.30	0.82	7.00	7.76	10.45	10.87	13.38	17.14
Verbal Delayed	15.70	18.40	0.79	7.65	8.43	11.39	11.84	14.58	18.67
General Memory	16.10	15.40	0.86	6.02	5.76	8.34	8.67	10.67	13.67
Attention/ Concentration	14.50	16.60	0.88	5.02	5.75	7.64	7.94	9.77	12.52
Learning	15.10	15.90	0.67	8.67	9.13	12.60	13.10	16.12	20.66
Delayed Recognition	14.70	16.80	0.57	9.64	11.02	14.64	15.22	18.74	24.01

13–16-Year-Olds	SD_1	SD_2	r_{12}	SEM_1	SEM_2	SE_{diff}	.70 CI	.80 CI	.90 CI
Visual Immediate	10.80	12.20	0.26	9.29	10.49	14.02	14.58	17.94	22.99
Visual Delayed	14.80	12.60	0.40	11.46	9.76	15.06	15.66	19.27	24.69
Verbal Immediate	18.00	17.20	0.85	6.97	6.66	9.64	10.03	12.34	15.81
Verbal Delayed	19.00	17.90	0.87	6.85	6.45	9.41	9.79	12.05	15.44
General Memory	17.70	15.80	0.86	6.62	6.70	9.42	9.80	12.06	15.45
Attention/ Concentration	16.50	16.10	0.86	6.17	5.91	8.55	8.89	10.94	14.02
Learning	12.60	14.80	0.78	5.91	7.55	9.59	9.97	12.27	15.73
Delayed Recognition	14.50	16.80	0.56	9.62	9.82	13.74	14.29	17.59	22.54

NOTE: The test-retest interval was 59.6 days (median = 65.3; SD = 29.2), and the total sample size was 125.

SOURCE: The test-retest coefficients and SDs were produced with permission of the publisher. *Children's Memory Scale*® *(CMS)*. Copyright © 1997 NCS Pearson, Inc. Reproduced with permission. All rights reserved. *"Children's Memory Scale"* is a trademark, in the US and/or other countries, of Pearson Education, Inc. or its affiliates(s).

TABLE 5.6. Estimating Reliable Change on the D-KEFS in Healthy Children and Adolescents

Ages 8–19	SD_1	SD_2	r_{12}	SEM_1	SEM_2	SE_{diff}	.70 CI	.80 CI	.90 CI	Practice Effect
TMT 1: Visual Scanning	2.84	1.65	0.50	2.01	1.17	2.32	2.42	2.97	3.81	2.00
TMT 2: Number Sequencing	2.85	1.99	0.77	1.37	0.95	1.67	1.73	2.13	2.73	1.00
TMT 3: Letter Sequencing	3.19	2.69	0.57	2.09	1.76	2.74	2.85	3.50	4.49	1.71
TMT 4: Number-Letter Sequencing	2.93	3.05	0.20	2.62	2.73	3.78	3.93	4.84	6.20	1.14
TMT 5: Motor Speed	2.71	2.55	0.82	1.15	1.08	1.58	1.64	2.02	2.59	0.36
Letter Fluency	2.61	2.86	0.67	1.50	1.64	2.22	2.31	2.85	3.65	0.75
Category Fluency	2.52	3.00	0.70	1.38	1.64	2.15	2.23	2.75	3.52	0.96
Category Switching-Total Correct	2.86	2.32	0.65	1.69	1.37	2.18	2.27	2.79	3.57	1.29
Category Switching-Accuracy	2.77	3.15	0.53	1.90	2.16	2.88	2.99	3.68	4.72	0.71
Design Fluency 1: Filled Dots	2.74	3.19	0.66	1.60	1.86	2.45	2.55	3.14	4.02	1.54
Design Fluency 2: Empty Dots	3.38	3.10	0.43	2.55	2.34	3.46	3.60	4.43	5.68	1.75
Design Fluency 3: Switching	2.56	2.81	0.13	2.39	2.62	3.55	3.69	4.54	5.81	2.22
Color-Word: Color Naming	2.43	2.76	0.79	1.11	1.26	1.69	1.75	2.16	2.76	1.08
Color-Word: Word Reading	2.82	3.60	0.77	1.35	1.73	2.19	2.28	2.81	3.60	0.00
Color-Word: Inhibition	3.01	2.78	0.90	0.95	0.88	1.30	1.35	1.66	2.12	1.47
Color-Word: Inhibition/Switching	2.94	3.25	0.80	1.31	1.45	1.96	2.04	2.51	3.21	1.82
Sorting: Confirmed Correct Sorts	1.63	2.34	0.49	1.16	1.67	2.04	2.12	2.61	3.34	1.45
Sorting: Free Sorting Description	1.57	2.48	0.67	0.90	1.42	1.69	1.75	2.16	2.77	1.66
Sorting: Sort Recognition Description	2.95	2.77	0.56	1.96	1.84	2.68	2.79	3.44	4.40	1.59
20 Quest.: Initial Abstraction	2.34	2.63	0.62	1.44	1.62	2.17	2.26	2.78	3.56	-0.03
20 Quest: Weighted Achievement	2.84	2.87	0.06	2.75	2.78	3.91	4.07	5.01	6.42	0.80
Word Context Consecutively Correct	2.74	3.10	0.58	1.78	2.01	2.68	2.79	3.43	4.40	1.68
Tower Test Achievement	3.14	2.80	0.51	2.20	1.96	2.94	3.06	3.77	4.83	1.08
Proverbs: Free Inquiry	3.29	2.50	0.90	1.04	0.79	1.31	1.36	1.67	2.14	1.50

NOTES: These data were adapted from Tables 2.1 through 2.26 in the D-KEFS Technical Manual (Delis et al., 2001). The ranges for internal consistency represent values across age groups from 8 to 19 years. The test-retest coefficients are based on 28 individuals between the ages of 8 and 19 who were tested twice separated by approximately 25 days (SD = 12.8 days).

TABLE 5.7. Estimating Reliable Change on the CVLT-C in Healthy Children

CVLT-C	SD_1	SD_2	r_{12}	SEM_1	SEM_2	SE_{diff}	.70 CI	.80 CI	.90 CI	Practice Effect
Age 8 (N = 35)										
List A										
Trials 1–5	9.55	9.09	0.73	4.96	4.72	6.85	7.12	8.77	11.24	5.85
Short Delay										
Free Recall	2.04	2.37	0.40	1.58	1.84	2.42	2.52	3.10	3.97	1.41
Long Delay										
Free Recall	2.30	2.59	0.59	1.47	1.66	2.22	2.31	2.84	3.64	1.20
Age 12 (N = 40)										
List A										
Trials 1–5	7.19	8.92	0.73	3.74	4.63	5.95	6.19	7.62	9.76	5.83
Short Delay										
Free Recall	2.44	2.62	0.77	1.17	1.26	1.72	1.79	2.20	2.82	2.35
Long Delay										
Free Recall	2.32	2.54	0.62	1.43	1.57	2.12	2.21	2.71	3.48	1.53
Age 16 (N = 31)										
List A										
Trials 1–5	6.15	10.94	0.61	3.84	6.83	7.84	8.15	10.03	12.85	9.41
Short Delay										
Free Recall	2.09	1.91	0.48	1.51	1.38	2.04	2.12	2.61	3.35	1.91
Long Delay										
Free Recall	1.90	1.87	0.60	1.20	1.18	1.69	1.75	2.16	2.77	1.60

NOTES: List A Trials 1–5 change estimates are for T scores. The delayed recall change estimates are for raw scores. Median Retest Interval = 28 days, range = 10–42. Data adapted from pages 88–90 of the test manual (Delis, Kramer, Kaplan, & Ober, 1994).

There are several clinical and methodological challenges related to the best practice application of the reliable change methodology. The clinician and researcher should be aware of the issues summarized in the following sections.

REAL CHANGE VERSUS RELIABLE CHANGE

It is possible for a child to experience a "real" improvement or decline in functioning that is not considered statistically reliable. Without question, a child could improve in processing speed and memory, between 1 month and 6 months following a severe traumatic brain injury (TBI), and this may or may not be considered a reliable change when the confidence intervals for measurement error surrounding test-retest difference scores are applied. For example, the child with a severe TBI might reliably improve on measures of processing speed and memory but still score in the extremely low range. Our tests have limitations, and there is a constant need to balance sensitivity and specificity. If we do not account for measurement error, or we restrict our confidence intervals too much, we are very likely to overinterpret change scores. We are likely to assume "real" change has occurred when it has not. If we rigidly apply the 90% or 95% confidence interval for change to every test, we will invariably fail to identify change in some children. Thus, reliable change estimates are meant to augment, not replace, clinical judgment.

SAMPLE CHARACTERISTICS AND GENERALIZABILITY

With few exceptions, reliable change confidence intervals are calculated for healthy subjects who participated in the standardization and validation of the test. Sample sizes are usually quite small. With small samples, it is more likely that a few subjects could influence the magnitude of the test-retest correlation coefficient. If the goal is to track change following TBI, we typically do not know whether a sample of TBI patients would have similar test-retest coefficients and dispersion estimates (i.e., SDs from time 1 and time 2); thus, we do not know the accuracy of the confidence intervals for measurement error in clinical samples.

DIFFERENT FORMULAS

The formula for calculating the SE_{diff} uses the SEM for baseline *and* retest, whereas many past studies have used an "estimated" SE_{diff} by simply multiplying the squared baseline SEM by two (i.e., $\sqrt{2SEM_1^2}$). The estimated SE_{diff} averages the spread (i.e., SD) of scores from baseline, as opposed to considering the spread of scores from baseline and retest in the calculation of the SEM. Mathematically, it is clear that the implications for the computed SE_{diff} are negligible if the test and retest SDs are very similar. If they differ, however, the SE_{diff} will be affected. Accordingly, some researchers have argued that this estimated SE_{diff} should only be used when retest data are not available (Hageman & Arrindell, 1993; Iverson, 1998, 2001).

DIFFERENT CORRELATION COEFFICIENTS

There is no universal agreement on which correlation coefficient to use in the formula (i.e., internal consistency versus test-retest reliability, or corrected versus uncorrected stability coefficients). In general, internal consistency coefficients tend to be greater than test-retest coefficients, so using internal consistency will usually result in a smaller estimated range of test-retest measurement error. Moreover, conceptually, the test-retest coefficient makes more sense to use in the formula because the clinical inference relates to test-retest difference scores, not the reliability of a single test score. Moreover, some test manuals present actual and "corrected" test-retest correlations. Either coefficient can be used. For the examples in this chapter, I have always used the actual coefficient.

REGRESSION TO THE MEAN

The reliable change methodology, as applied in clinical neuropsychology, does not account for regression to the mean. In general, examinees who score very low or very high on a test at baseline are theoretically more likely to score somewhat better or worse, respectively, at retest due to regression to the mean. This is one of the reasons why the reliable change methodology is less accurate when applied to examinees who score unusually low or unusually high at baseline.

PRACTICE EFFECTS

In its original form, the reliable change methodology assumed no practice effects. This, of course, has since been corrected by including the average practice effect in the calculations of confidence intervals (Chelune, 2003; Chelune et al., 1993). This approach has obvious advantages when practice effects are expected. Among other things, it has improved the accuracy in detecting a decline in functioning. However, correcting for the average practice effect can introduce other sources of error. First, adding a constant (group average) term for the practice effect does not take into account the range of practice effects that are actually present in a sample of people tested twice. Some people will have lower scores, some will stay the same, and some will improve, to varying degrees, at retest. In fact, only a small percentage of the sample may actually improve by the average practice effect. This prompted a recommendation to correct for practice *only* when 75% or more of the sample showed at least some improvement on the test score (Iverson & Green, 2001). This recommendation, however, has not adequately corrected the problem. Second, most test-retest studies presented in test manuals use very brief retest intervals (e.g., 2–6 weeks), with some notable exceptions (Woodcock, McGrew, & Mather, 2001). Therefore, practice effects are likely to be overestimated because of the brief retest interval. Finally, test-retest studies typically are conducted with healthy subjects in normative samples. Test-retest coefficients and practice effects in clinical groups might be different.

CONSIDERING CHANGE ON A BATTERY OF TESTS

Unfortunately, our psychometric methodologies for interpreting test results are almost exclusively univariate (e.g., based on the bell curve) or bivariate (e.g., based on the distribution, such as discrepancy scores). Yet clinical practice requires a multivariate approach to analyzing and interpreting test data (i.e., interpretation of multiple test scores simultaneously). On average, for example, only 5% of healthy children will obtain a CMS Index score of 76 or lower when considering each index in isolation. However, when considering all six of the primary memory index scores, 22.4% of healthy children will obtain one or more very low index scores (Brooks, Iverson, Sherman, & Holdnack, 2009). In other words, the more tests that are administered, the more likely it is for a healthy, intact child to obtain some very low scores (see Chapter 4 for a discussion on the prevalence of low scores across test batteries in children). Similarly, our estimates of reliable change apply to a single distribution of change scores. It might be uncommon, when considering one test in isolation, for there to be a large change in test scores. However, when considering a large battery of tests administered twice, it is statistically likely that healthy intact children will show a small number of large changes in test scores. This area certainly warrants future research.

CONCLUSIONS

Determining whether there has been change in performance on neuropsychological tests is a complicated process, involving a series of steps and thorough understanding of a number of psychometric concepts. The practitioner must consider carefully the potential influences of (a) initial level of performance, (b) practice effects, *(c)* regression to the mean, *(d)* measurement error, *(e)* motivational factors, and *(f)* cognitive development. One of the most important factors to consider when interpreting test-retest differences is level of baseline (time 1) performance. The effects of practice and regression vary in relation to time 1 test scores. Low scores are likely to improve due to situational factors, practice, and regression; and high scores are less likely to improve due to practice and, in contrast, more likely to worsen due to regression and situational factors. Following is a summary of considerations for interpreting change:

- Scores are not exact estimates of functioning or ability—all contain measurement error and some contain substantial measurement error.
- Variability on neuropsychological testing within a single session may be common. That is to say, the intertest variability usually increases as more tests are given.
- Test-retest variability may be due to measurement error, situational factors, and practice effects. Unusual fluctuations in test performances may occur, may be difficult to interpret, and may not reflect true changes in cognitive functioning.
- Regarding serial neuropsychological testing, high scores are likely to be lower and low scores are likely to be higher upon retesting. If confidence intervals for test-retest difference scores were created only for baseline performances that fall in the average range, these confidence intervals would be narrower than if all subjects are included.
- As a general rule, statistically reliable change is a necessary precursor for inferring clinically meaningful change. Reliable change alone, however, does not mean that clinically meaningful change has indeed occurred.

DIRECTIONS FOR FUTURE RESEARCH

An important future direction in pediatric neuropsychology is to create test-retest normative databases for healthy children and clinical samples evaluated over clinically relevant retest intervals (e.g., 1 year). Sample sizes in excess of 200 will be necessary to adequately study change in high versus low scoring children. Different statistical methodologies likely will prove more or less effective for conceptualizing change in persons with low, average, or high baseline levels of performance. If large databases become available (e.g., more than 500 subjects), then the raw test-retest score distributions can be examined to determine the normal range for test-retest difference scores at various levels of baseline performance.

The real-world significance of statistically reliable change is an important issue that has not been systematically investigated. Is reliable change, for example, related to a functional or diagnostic change? Alternatively, are reliable changes common among certain clinical populations (due to inherent heterogeneity), though not necessarily clinically significant? Much additional research is needed to determine the ecological validity of change in neuropsychological test performance.

An obvious next step for advancing knowledge regarding the interpretation of change is to determine the base rates of reliable change scores across a battery of tests. At present, our ability to interpret change is based on a single test score, which is antithetical to clinical practice. In contrast, it is paramount that we investigate how common it is to show two or more, or five or more, reliable changes in performance in healthy children and children with stable clinical conditions. Although methodologically challenging, this will ultimately enhance clinicians' ability to interpret change in mainstream clinical practice.

Much research is needed to enhance the reliability, validity, and accuracy of serial assessments in pediatric neuropsychology. At present, interpreting change is largely an idiosyncratic process, which is poorly informed by empirical data. Hopefully, this chapter is a small step in the direction of promoting a more evidence-based approach to estimating change in cognitive functioning of children.

REFERENCES

Barr, W. B., & McCrea, M. (2001). Sensitivity and specificity of standardized neurocognitive testing immediately following sports concussion. *Journal of the International Neuropsychological Society, 7*(6), 693–702.

Brooks, B. L., Iverson, G. L., Sherman, E. M., & Holdnack, J. A. (2009). Healthy children and adolescents obtain some low scores across a battery of memory tests. *Journal of the International Neuropsychological Society, 15*(4), 613–617.

Chelune, G. J. (2003). Assessing reliable neuropsychological change. In R. D. Franklin (Ed.), *Prediction in forensic and neuropsychology: Sound statistical practices* (pp. 65–88). Mahwah, NJ: Erlbaum.

Chelune, G. J., Naugle, R. I., Luders, H., Sedlak, J., & Awad, I. A. (1993). Individual change after epilepsy surgery: Practice effects and base-rate information. *Neuropsychology, 7*, 41–52.

Cohen, M. (1997). *Children's Memory Scale*. San Antonio, TX: The Psychological Corporation.

Crawford, J. R., & Howell, D. C. (1998). Regression equations in clinical neuropsychology: An evaluation of statistical methods for comparing predicted and obtained scores. *Journal of Clinical and Experimental Neuropsychology, 20*(5), 755–762.

Cronbach, L. J., & Gleser, G. C. (1959). Interpretation of reliability and validity coefficients: Remarks on a paper by Lord. *Journal of Educational Psychology, 50*, 230–237.

Delis, D. C., Kaplan, E., & Kramer, J. H. (2001). *The Delis Kaplan Executive Function System: Technical manual*. San Antonio, TX: The Psychological Corporation.

Delis, D., Kramer, J., Kaplan, E., & Ober, B. A. (1994). *California Verbal Learning Test - Children's Version*. San Antonio, TX: The Psychological Corporation.

Franzen, M. D. (1989). *Reliability and validity in neuropsychological assessment*. New York: Plenum Press.

Franzen, M. D. (2000). *Reliability and validity in neuropsychological assessment* (2nd ed.). New York: Kluwer Academic/Plenum Press.

Hageman, W. J., & Arrindell, W. A. (1993). A further refinement of the reliable change (RC) index by improving the pre-post difference score: Introducing RCID. *Behavior Research and Therapy, 31*(7), 693–700.

Hageman, W. J., & Arrindell, W. A. (1999a). Clinically significant and practical! Enhancing precision does make a difference. Reply to McGlinchey and Jacobson, Hsu, and Speer. *Behavior Research and Therapy*, 37(12), 1219–1233.

Hageman, W. J., & Arrindell, W. A. (1999b). Establishing clinically significant change: Increment of precision and the distinction between individual and group level of analysis. *Behavior Research and Therapy*, 37(12), 1169–1193.

Heaton, R. K., Temkin, N. R., Dikmen, S. S., Avitable, N., Taylor, M. J., Marcotte, T. D., & Grant, I. (2001). Detecting change: A comparison of three neuropsychological methods using normal and clinical samples. *Archives of Clinical Neuropsychology*, 16, 75–91.

Hermann, B. P., & Wyler, A. R. (1988). Neuropsychological outcome of anterior temporal lobectomy. *Journal of Epilepsy*, 1, 35–45.

Hermann, B. P., Wyler, A. R., VanderZwagg, R., LeBailey, R. K., Whitman, S., Somes, G., & Ward, J. (1991). Predictors of neuropsychological change following anterior temporal lobectomy: Role of regression toward the mean. *Journal of Epilepsy*, 4, 139–148.

Hinton-Bayre, A. D., Geffen, G. M., Geffen, L. B., McFarland, K. A., & Friis, P. (1999). Concussion in contact sports: reliable change indices of impairment and recovery. *Journal of Clinical and Experimental Neuropsychology*, 21(1), 70–86.

Hsu, L. M. (1989). Reliable changes on psychotherapy: Taking into account regression toward the mean. *Behavioral Assessment*, 11, 459–467.

Hsu, L. M. (1999). A comparison of three methods of identifying reliable and clinically significant client changes: Commentary on Hageman and Arrindell. *Behavior Research and Therapy*, 37, 1195–1202.

Iverson, G. L. (1998). Interpretation of Mini-Mental State Examination scores in community-dwelling elderly and geriatric neuropsychiatry patients. *International Journal of Geriatric Psychiatry*, 13(10), 661–666.

Iverson, G. L. (1999). Interpreting change on the WAIS-III/WMS-III in persons with traumatic brain injuries. *Journal of Cognitive Rehabilitation, July/August*, 16–20.

Iverson, G. L. (2001). Interpreting change on the WAIS-III/WMS-III in clinical samples. *Archives of Clinical Neuropsychology*, 16, 183–191.

Iverson, G. L., & Green, P. (2001). Measuring improvement or decline on the WAIS-R in inpatient psychiatry. *Psychological Reports*, 89(2), 457–462.

Iverson, G. L., Lovell, M. R., & Collins, M. W. (2003). Interpreting change on ImPACT following sport concussion. *The Clinical Neuropsychologist*, 17(4), 460–467.

Jacobson, N. S., Follette, W. C., & Revenstorf, D. (1984). Psychotherapy outcome research: Methods for reporting variability and evaluating clinical significance. *Behavior Therapy*, 15, 336–352.

Jacobson, N. S., & Revenstorf, D. (1988). Statistics for assessing the clinical significance of psychotherapy issues: Issues, problems, and new developments. *Behavioral Assessment*, 10, 133–145.

Jacobson, N. S., Roberts, L. J., Berns, S. B., & McGlinchey, J. B. (1999). Methods for defining and determining the clinical significance of treatment effects: Description, application, and alternatives. *Journal of Consulting and Clinical Psychology*, 67(3), 300–307.

Jacobson, N. S., & Truax, P. (1991). Clinical significance: A statistical approach to defining meaningful change in psychotherapy research. *Journal of Consulting and Clinical Psychology*, 59(1), 12–19.

Mahanna, E. P., Blumenthal, J. A., White, W. D., Croughwell, N. D., Clancy, C. P., Smith, L. R., & Newman, M. F. (1996). Defining neuropsychological dysfunction after coronary artery bypass grafting. *Annals of Thoracic Surgery*, 61(5), 1342–1347.

Matarazzo, J. D., Carmody, T. P., & Jacobs, L. D. (1980). Test-retest reliability and stability of the WAIS: A literature review with implications for clinical practice. *Journal of Clinical and Experimental Neuropsychology, 2*(2), 89–105.

McSweeney, A. J., Naugle, R. I., Chelune, G. J., & Luders, H. (1993). "T scores for change": An illustration of a regression approach to depicting change in clinical neuropsychology. *Clinical Neuropsychologist, 7*, 300–312.

Ogles, B. M., Lambert, M. J., & Masters, K. S. (1996). *Assessing outcome in clinical practice.* Boston, MA: Allyn and Bacon.

Phillips, N. A., & McGlone, J. (1995). Grouped data do not tell the whole story: individual analysis of cognitive change after temporal lobectomy. *Journal of Clinical and Experimental Neuropsychology, 17*(5), 713–724.

Reynolds, C. R., & Kamphaus, R. W. (2003). *Reynolds Intellectual Assessment Scales and Reynolds Intellectual Screening Test professional manual.* Lutz, FL: Psychological Assessment Resources.

Salinsky, M. C., Storzbach, D., Dodrill, C. B., & Binder, L. M. (2001). Test-retest bias, reliability, and regression equations for neuropsychological measures repeated over a 12–16-week period. *Journal of the International Neuropsychological Society, 7*(5), 597–605.

Sawrie, S. M., Chelune, G. J., Naugle, R. I., & Luders, H. O. (1996). Empirical methods for assessing meaningful neuropsychological change following epilepsy surgery. *Journal of the International Neuropsychological Society, 2*(6), 556–564.

Sawrie, S. M., Marson, D. C., Boothe, A. L., & Harrell, L. E. (1999). A method for assessing clinically relevant individual cognitive change in older adult populations. *Journals of Gerontology. Series B, Psychological Sciences and Social Sciences, 54*(2), P116–124.

Shaw, P. J., Bates, D., Cartlidge, N. E., French, J. M., Heaviside, D., Julian, D. G., & Shaw, D. A. (1986). Early intellectual dysfunction following coronary bypass surgery. *The Quarterly Journal of Medicine, 58*(225), 59–68.

Speer, D. C. (1992). Clinically significant change: Jacobson and Truax (1991) revisited. *Journal of Consulting and Clinical Psychology, 60*(3), 402–408.

Speer, D. C., & Greenbaum, P. E. (1995). Five methods for computing significant individual client change and improvement rates: Support for an individual growth curve approach. *Journal of Consulting and Clinical Psychology, 63*(6), 1044–1048.

Temkin, N. R., Heaton, R. K., Grant, I., & Dikmen, S. S. (1999). Detecting significant change in neuropsychological test performance: A comparison of four models. *Journal of the International Neuropsychological Society, 5*(4), 357–369.

Wechsler, D. (2003). *Wechsler Intelligence Scale for Children - Fourth Edition: Technical and interpretive manual.* San Antonio, TX: Psychological Corporation.

Woodcock, R. W., McGrew, K. S., & Mather, N. (2001). *Woodcock-Johnson III Tests of Cognitive Abilities.* Itasca, IL: Riverside Publishing.

Chapter 6

Differential Diagnosis of Malingering and Related Clinical Presentations

DANIEL J. SLICK
ELISABETH M. S. SHERMAN

INTRODUCTION

Every year in North America, thousands of litigating or otherwise compensation-seeking children, adolescents, and adults undergo third-party neuropsychological assessments. Among the adults in this population, malingering is far from rare; survey data indicate that 20%–40% of compensation-seeking adults are thought to be feigning some type of neuropsychological problem or impairment (Mittenberg, Patton, Canyock, & Condit, 2002; Sharland & Gfeller, 2007; Slick, Tan, Strauss, & Hultsch, 2004). Although the rate of malingering among minors is almost certainly nontrivial as well, no good estimates are currently available—an indication of the general dearth of research on pediatric malingering. Fortunately for clinicians, researchers have finally begun to focus in earnest on the problem of pediatric malingering, and it now appears likely that the current void in our understanding of this phenomenon will have shrunken substantially by the end of this decade.

This chapter addresses malingering and related clinical presentations in children and adolescents (i.e., minors), primarily in the context of independent neuropsychological assessment of compensation-seeking individuals. The focus is first on critical concepts, constructs, and definitions; and then on differential diagnosis, with issues of neurocognitive and psychosocial development addressed where relevant. Specific psychometric tests and assessment methods can be found in Chapter 7.

DEFINITION AND CONCEPTUAL ASPECTS OF MALINGERING

The first papers on the forced-choice method for assessing the validity of sensory deficits appeared in major psychology journals in the 1970s (Pankratz, Fausti, &

Peed, 1975; Pankratz, 1979).[1] During the following decade, neuropsychologists began to adapt the forced-choice method for use in evaluating the validity of cognitive complaints (Binder & Pankratz, 1987; Hiscock, 1989). Prior to this, malingering was a relatively obscure subject of study within neuropsychology and not a phenomenon of interest or concern for many clinicians. However, these early studies helped catalyze an explosive growth in research on malingering that was driven in large part by the increasing involvement of neuropsychologists in forensic and medicolegal fields where the issue of malingering looms large. A significant problem faced by researchers and clinicians in the 1980s and 1990s was the lack of an adequate functional definition and associated diagnostic criteria for malingering. In an attempt to meet this need, a definition and detailed diagnostic criteria for malingering was developed by Slick, Sherman, and Iverson (1999). They defined *malingered neurocognitive dysfunction* (MND) as:

> the volitional exaggeration or fabrication of cognitive dysfunction for the purpose of obtaining substantial material gain, or avoiding or escaping formal duty or responsibility. Substantial material gain includes money, goods, or services of nontrivial value (e.g., financial compensation for personal injury). Formal duties are actions that people are legally obligated to perform (e.g., prison, military, or public service, or child support payments or other financial obligations). Formal responsibilities are those that involve accountability or liability in legal proceedings (e.g., competency to stand trial) (pg. 552).

More recently, some additional conceptual aspects of malingering were further elaborated by Slick, Tan, Sherman, and Strauss (2010). They proposed that four dimensions of an examinee's behavior need to be considered when contemplating a diagnosis of malingering. These are as follows:

1. Volition/awareness
2. Level of effort
3. Immediate goal
4. Long-term goal.

In this framework, a diagnosis of malingering requires evidence that an examinee *(1)* consciously chooses *(2)* to expend at least some meaningful amount of effort *(3)* toward a short-term goal of feigning deficits that is in turn directed *(4)* toward a long-term goal of obtaining a substantial personal gain or avoiding/ escaping from a substantial personal duty or obligation. Of course, when it comes to translating theory to application, the devil is always in the details, particularly with respect to how one defines and assesses constructs such as volition and goal-directedness. These continue to be the most controversial and complicated issues, as detailed in the sections that follow.

---

1. Forced-choice symptom validity testing, though new to psychology in the mid 1970s, was initially developed by physicians in the late 1950s for assessment of conversion disorder and malingering (e.g., Brady & Lind, 1961).

Primary Versus Secondary Gain

Primary gain is the immediate relief from guilt, anxiety, tension, internal conflicts, or other unpleasant psychological states that a person derives directly from engaging in a particular behavior. It is the core explanatory mechanism of conversion disorder, in which a severe emotional conflict is unconsciously converted into feigned sensorimotor symptoms such as blindness or paralysis in order to relieve otherwise unbearable anxiety. In contrast, *secondary gains* are any external advantages or benefits that a person obtains from engaging in a particular behavior. Following an injury or during an illness, people often receive external psychosocial or material benefits. These can be highly rewarding and may thus encourage the exaggeration of symptoms and/or the maintenance of a sick or injured role via feigning of ongoing symptoms during and after recovery. The prospect of obtaining secondary gains may also encourage the outright fabrication of additional symptoms and in some cases entire illness or injuries. In all of these cases, feigning behaviors are motivated by and directed toward secondary gains.

Primary gain is often associated with unconscious psychological processes and nonvolitional behaviors (e.g., conversion disorder), while secondary gain is associated with conscious psychological processes and volitional behavior (e.g., malingering). However, these associations do not always hold. For example, factitious disorder is characterized by conscious and volitional feigning that provides primary gains. Furthermore, primary gain and secondary gain are not mutually exclusive; both may be sought and obtained from feigning symptoms. That is, symptom exaggeration or fabrication may be driven in part by a need to resolve or find relief from internal emotional conflicts, but at the same time it may also be consciously and/or unconsciously motivated by and directed toward attainment of external rewards such as financial compensation.

Psychosocial Versus Material-Legal Secondary Gains

For purposes of differential diagnosis, secondary gains can be divided into two principal types: *psychosocial secondary gains* are the interpersonal, social, and associated minor material benefits or reinforcements that a person seeks and/or obtains from feigning symptoms of illness or injury. This includes both positive psychosocial reinforcement such as attention, affection, and gifts from others and also escape from or avoidance of unpleasant or aversive psychosocial situations or obligations such as interpersonal conflicts, schoolwork, and household chores. For example, consider the following case: A young child becomes seriously ill and as a result her parents become more attentive and emotionally involved. In addition, they argue among themselves much less in her presence. The changes in her parents' behavior have both positive and negative reinforcement value with respect to being ill.[2] As her illness resolves, the girl begins to fear the loss of these secondary gains and as a result attempts to maintain the sick role by feigning symptoms.

---

2. These may be counterbalanced by psychosocial secondary losses, such as reduced affiliation with friends, as discussed in more detail later in this chapter.

In contrast to psychosocial secondary gains, *material-legal secondary gains* include substantial tangible material benefits such as financial settlements or worker's compensation awards. Material-legal secondary gains can also take the form of escape from or avoidance of onerous or aversive *formal* duties, responsibilities, and obligations, such as criminal responsibility and military service. The distinction between psychosocial and material-legal secondary gains is critical to differential diagnosis in cases of feigned deficits; it is the latter type of goal and motivation that defines malingering and separates it from other diagnoses. Feigning may often be directed toward *both* psychosocial and material-legal secondary gains, and in such cases dual or multiple diagnoses will need to be considered.

Secondary Losses

Secondary losses are just the opposite of secondary gains; they are any external disadvantages, detriments or other types of aversive or negative consequences that a person receives as a result of engaging in a particular behavior. As with secondary gains, one can distinguish between psychosocial and material-legal secondary losses, and this distinction has the same diagnostic implications. Feigned symptoms may result in both secondary gains and secondary losses. For example, consider the case of an adolescent who sustains a mild traumatic brain injury in a motor vehicle accident and as a result experiences some bona-fide neurocognitive symptoms for which he receives increased attention and affection from family members and a reduction in household chores. At the same time, he also becomes aware of the prospect of a substantial material-legal secondary gain in the form of a personal injury settlement. To maintain these gains, he feigns ongoing symptoms after recovering from his injury. Over time, the adolescent's family members become increasingly frustrated with his persisting "symptoms" and begin to become openly unsupportive, at which point his feigning begins to incur psychosocial secondary losses. However, he persists with feigning symptoms until he receives a settlement. In this case, a psychosocial secondary loss is incurred in order to obtain a material-legal secondary gain. In many cases, individuals may incur substantial material-legal secondary losses in pursuit of material-legal secondary gains. For example, feigning disabilities may result in substantial reductions in income for extended periods of time, but these are willingly accepted in return for an anticipated financial payoff that exceeds any losses incurred. In most pediatric cases, this particular type of trade-off will be of lesser concern to a minor who contemplates malingering.

Secondary losses associated with persisting symptoms of illness or injury may sometimes appear to outweigh secondary gains. However, this does not necessarily rule out the possibility of feigning, as there is considerable individual variability with respect to the reinforcement value of various psychosocial and material gains and losses, and in some cases even the positive/negative valence (i.e., gain vs. loss) of specific outcomes.

Redefining Effort: Non-Compliance Detection Measures

Effort can be defined in terms of amount of exertion or expenditure of energy; a higher level of effort implies a greater degree of exertion than a lower level of effort.

All behaviors require the expenditure of some energy and are thus to some degree effortful; the act of answering a question on a test requires some effort regardless of whether a correct answer is given. Effort may be a very important determinant of test performance, but it is by no means the *only* determinant. Many other factors influence test performance, not the least of which are the goals toward which individuals direct their effort.

Some expenditure of effort is invariably required to feign deficits, and the level of effort expended may vary greatly between individuals. Consider two examinees that deliberately feign cognitive deficits in order to obtain financial compensation. The first examinee spends a substantial amount of time and energy (i.e., effort) researching brain injury sequelae and assessment methods, and then expends considerable additional effort on the application of a complex feigning strategy during a neuropsychological assessment. In contrast, the second examinee conducts no research ahead of time and then employs a very simple and undemanding feigning strategy during an assessment. The first examinee may stand a better chance of successfully feigning brain injury than the second one, but both are malingering. Any level of effort that is expended toward feigning deficits for purposes of obtaining material-legal secondary gain or avoiding material-legal secondary loss constitutes malingering. Malingering is defined by the *goal to which effort is directed* and not the level of effort expended.

Unfortunately, with respect to malingering, the distinction between level of effort and the goals toward which effort is directed often appears to be poorly appreciated. In particular, the term "effort" is frequently misapplied and misused with respect to characterization of both neuropsychological tests and the constructs that they measure. Despite the fact that no neuropsychological tests measure effort directly or uniquely, it is very common to see forced-choice symptom validity tests referred to as "effort tests" or "tests of effort." Scores below cutoffs on such measures are likewise often interpreted as indicative of "low effort" or "poor effort," when in fact this may not be the case at all. Rather, to the extent that such scores actually reflect effort, it is entirely possible that low scores actually signify a *greater* level of effort than high scores. When examinees approach assessment with the intention of feigning cognitive impairment, this alters the fundamental nature and difficulty of the tests administered. In addition to the normal cognitive demands of test-taking, feigning examinees may simultaneously engage in a variety of additional cognitive activities, such as consciously keeping a specific feigning strategy in mind, monitoring and assessing item difficulty, deciding when to make errors, deciding what type of errors to make, inhibiting correct responses, monitoring their performance over time in order to maintain a target error rate, and monitoring the examiner's reactions for clues about the believability of their feigning performance. In addition, they may also engage in extra-test behaviors such as feigning frustration and distress. Given the additional cognitive demands inherent to malingering, it is possible that some malingerers expend greater effort in feigning deficits than is required for adequate compliance with the assessment. It is thus incorrect to automatically conclude that low scores on symptom validity tests or indices are indicative of low or poor effort, when in fact just the opposite may be true. A more accurate conclusion or statement would be that such data are indicative of *misdirected* or *maldirected* effort. In most cases, an even better approach would be to dispense with use of the term "effort" entirely and instead frame test results in terms of evidence of compliance or non-compliance with test instructions.

The distinction between level of effort and the goals toward which effort is directed can be further elaborated in a continuum of compliance framework as is shown in the Figure 6.1. The figure shows level of compliance as a function of level of effort for two groups: deficit-feigning and non-deficit-feigning individuals— holding all other factors equal and assuming no other threats to validity of test results. The area shaded with vertical lines corresponds to the level of validity of test results. Regardless of group (i.e., goal or intention), any examinee who does not expend any effort is noncompliant. Feigning examinees are noncompliant regardless of how much effort they expend. In contrast, compliance increases as a function of effort for nonfeigners. As compliance increases, so too does validity of test results. The relationship between effort and compliance is mediated by goals and intentions. Regardless of intentions, low effort will always translate into low compliance and low validity, while high effort is only associated with high compliance when examinees follow instructions.

Put another way, examinees are compliant to the extent that they exert effort toward producing the highest or best possible score in full accordance with the specific directions they are given for each test (e.g., attending well to stimuli during presentation and telling the examiner everything they can remember on a memory test). Conversely, examinees are noncompliant to the extent that they exert less than maximal effort and/or they do not follow test directions (e.g., failing to attend to

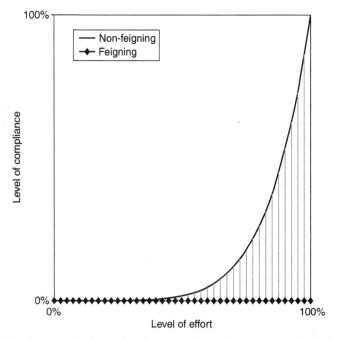

FIGURE 6.1. Conceptual relationships between effort and compliance. Shaded area under the curve denotes level of validity of test findings.

stimuli and not telling the examiner everything that they can remember). Examinees who put forth minimal effort are substantially noncompliant, but so too are examinees who direct *maximal effort* toward any goal other than obtaining the best possible scores. Tests that are designed to inform the differential diagnosis of malingering are usually sensitive to both forms of noncompliance and can therefore be referred to in general as *noncompliance detection measures*, rather than measures of effort. Such tests should not be referred to as measures of compliance because a passing score does not necessarily indicate that an examinee was compliant on any other measures. This designation can be extended to validity scales on self-report measures, as these are designed to detect noncompliance with directions to respond carefully and honestly.

Volition

Volition refers to the degree to which a behavior is both conscious *and* deliberate. That is, both conditions must be sufficiently met for a behavior to be considered fully volitional. Many neurocognitive processes and behaviors are not easily if at all accessible to direct conscious awareness and control. For example, people blink many times a day reflexively and without any conscious awareness. At other times, they may become aware of reflexive blinking, as when a foreign body enters their eye. However, in both cases, the blinking is nonvolitional. In contrast, people may consciously blink (or *not* blink) at a specific moment, such as in response to a request by an examining clinician. This, of course, is a volitional behavior. A last point of contrast is blepharospasm, a neurological condition characterized by frequent uncontrolled spasmic or twitch-like blinking. In such cases, individuals are usually consciously aware of involuntary blinking, but they may eventually habituate to it, resulting in diminished awareness.

Volition entails a subjective sense of free will, choice, and control over one's behavior. The volitionality of the behavior of others can never be determined directly, but instead must be inferred from evidence such as statements that they make. As with other subjective experiences such as pain, the assessment of volition is fraught with difficulties relating to quantification and interindividual comparisons. In addition, the construct of volition is open to interpretation and attendant debate with respect to certain behaviors and contexts, such as consciously directed and purposeful behavior that occurs in response to extreme coercion (e.g., threats of physical harm), hallucinations, or delusions. Lastly, there is the issue of whether the volitionality of behavior is an all-or-nothing attribute. Can a person be only partially aware of his or her own behavior or have only a partial sense of free will and choice with respect to a given behavior? These issues can become extremely complicated in the context of neuropsychological assessment.

With respect to malingering, the volitionality of specific behaviors is inferred from ruling out other nonvolitional causes (Slick et al., 1999). In more extreme cases, such as below chance performance on forced-choice measures, the assumption is that an examinee cannot inhibit a correct response and substitute an incorrect one during individual neuropsychological testing without any conscious awareness of doing so. However, as noted earlier, the issue of personal responsibility must be considered separately from the issue of volitionality in the differential diagnostic of malingering.

DIAGNOSTIC CRITERIA FOR MALINGERING

Along with a formal definition, Slick et al. (1999) provide a detailed set of diagnostic criteria for malingered neurocognitive dysfunction. The MND criteria have proven relatively popular among academic neuropsychologists, insofar as can be gauged by citation frequency and the number of research papers that have adopted them as a standard. They have also been adapted for use in other fields, such as the assessment of malingered pain-related disability (Bianchini, Greve, & Glynn, 2005). Despite this, no survey data have been published concerning clinical adoption and use, and so it is difficult to gauge the impact, if any, that the MND criteria have had on clinical practice.

The years since the MND criteria were published have been marked by substantial advancements in assessment methods and further developments in conceptual models of malingering. This progress has in turn prompted a number of critiques and suggestions for changes and revisions to the Slick et al. MND criteria. By far the most in-depth, thoughtful, and detailed critical analysis to date is that of Larrabee, Greiffenstein, Greve, and Bianchini (2007). One of the more important issues raised by Larrabee et al. is that the Slick et al. criteria employ a relatively crude, nonactuarial method of aggregating indicators for determining diagnostic certainty rather than more sophisticated actuarial methods for evaluating evidence such as logistic regression and advanced Bayesian analyses. Although it would certainly be preferable to dispense with crude categories of diagnostic confidence (i.e., possible, probable, and definite) in favor of actuarial procedures that would produce valid individual estimates of the probability of malingering, we lack assessment methods that would permit such an approach in many cases.

Another significant issue noted by Larrabee et al. is that with respect to evidentiary weight and diagnostic utility, research does not support a fundamental distinction between objective test data and self-report data. That is, validity indices from questionnaires such as the MMPI–2 may in some cases have diagnostic utility that is equal or superior to objective performance-based measures. Larrabee et al. raise a number of other important issues with respect to possible improvements to the Slick et al. MND criteria, but a detailed review of them is beyond the scope of this chapter.[3]

UPDATES AND REVISIONS TO THE SLICK ET AL.
(1999) MND CRITERIA

In light of developments in assessment methods and conceptual and pragmatic issues that have been raised, it is clear that the MND criteria need to be updated and

3. The chapter by Larrabee et al. (2007), and indeed the entire book from which it comes (Larrabee, 2007), is essential reading for any neuropsychologist who conducts medicolegal or forensic assessments.

revised. The most critical aspects that must be addressed are *(1)* criteria for definite malingering; *(2)* exclusionary criteria; and *(3)* the diagnostic utility of self-report data and objective evidence of exaggeration or fabrication of psychological symptoms. Potential revisions to the MND criteria that address these issues are described next.

Compelling Inconsistencies as a Criterion of Definite Malingering

Bianchini, Greve, and Glynn (2005) proposed that *compelling inconsistencies*—examinee-reported symptoms that are unambiguously incompatible with or contradicted by examinee behaviors—usually should be considered pathognomonic of malingering. For example, a litigating examinee reports that he can no longer read *at all* since his head injury, but he is later observed reading; or a litigating examinee who reports that since being struck by a car, she is always too afraid to cross streets by herself, but she is later observed crossing a street alone without any hesitation or apparent distress. In the context of potential material-legal secondary gain for feigned impairment, and in the absence of any other reasonable explanation, such patent contradictions between self-reported and observed abilities can be considered prima facie evidence of definite malingering. In addition to direct observation, surveillance video or reliable collateral reports that are sufficiently unambiguous and reliable could also be used to establish that an examinee's self-reported symptoms are unequivocally contradicted by his or her behavior.

High Posterior Probabilities as a Criterion for Definite Malingering

Advances in psychometrics and test development, particularly with respect to methods for combining numeric data, have led to the derivation of increasingly accurate posterior probabilities (e.g., Larrabee, 2008), the probative value of which needs to be formally addressed by any diagnostic criteria for MND. More specifically, given a reasonable choice of prior probability and a well-validated process for deriving posterior probabilities that is applicable to an examinee, it is reasonable to consider very high positive predictive values of feigning (e.g., $\geq .95$) as diagnostically equivalent to below chance SVT performance (i.e., indicative of definite malingering).[4] The data used for deriving posterior probabilities need not necessarily be limited to objective test scores but can also include any other reliable numerical data such as scores from self-report measures; demographic characteristics such as age, gender, and socioeconomic status (SES); and neurological data such as Glasgow Coma Scale scores, length of posttraumatic amnesia, and positive radiological findings.

---

4. In this context, positive predictive power (PPP), a type of Bayesian posterior probability, refers to the estimated probability of malingering associated with a given index score. It is calculated from the estimated sensitivity and specificity of an index and the estimated base rate of malingering. While the calculations involved are usually trivial, many factors significantly influence the accuracy and meaning of PPP values, and these must be well understood for valid interpretations. Mossman (2003) provides a good introduction to this topic.

Elimination of Exclusionary Criteria in Favor of a Diagnosis of Secondary Malingering

In the Slick et al. MND criteria, a diagnosis of malingering is excluded when feigning is fully accounted for by bona-fide psychiatric, neurological, or neurodevelopmental syndromes or conditions. Thus, an examinee who consciously and deliberately exaggerates or fabricates neuropsychological dysfunction in an attempt to obtain a substantial material gain as a result of bona fide impairment of reasoning, judgment, or other cognitive faculties (e.g., in response to command hallucinations) is *not* given a diagnosis of malingering. Unfortunately this exclusionary criterion raises some thorny issues with respect to what to label feigning behaviors in such cases. In addition, it may create unnecessary confusion by implying that persons with psychiatric illnesses, neurological injuries or disorders, and also children are incapable of malingering. One solution to this problem is to eliminate this exclusion and instead apply a diagnosis of *secondary malingering*. That is, a person who meets criteria for malingering but whose feigning behaviors are thought to primarily arise from legitimate cognitive/psychiatric dysfunction would be given a diagnosis of secondary malingering (e.g., malingering secondary to severe dysexecutive syndrome). This is a particularly important issue in pediatric settings because younger children have a limited capacity to understand the moral/ethical nature or social/legal implications of feigning impairment. As a result, there is a lower limit (with considerable individual variability) to the age at which malingering can be diagnosed.

The Utility of Self-Report Data and Evidence of Feigned Psychological Dysfunction

As noted earlier, some types of self-report data—as exemplified by compelling inconsistencies and posterior probabilities derived from scores on self-report measures—must be given greater weight in a revised set of diagnostic criteria for malingering. A comprehensive set of diagnostic criteria applicable to neuropsychological assessment should also fully account for cases of malingering that primarily or exclusively involve exaggerated or fabricated psychological dysfunction. This may necessitate development of additional criteria for the application of specifiers such as *cognitive* malingering, *psychological* malingering and *mixed cognitive/psychological* malingering. Given these considerations, a more apt nomenclature for a revised set of diagnostic criteria would be *malingered neuropsychological dysfunction*. See Table 6.1 for a proposed framework for these diagnostic criteria.

DIFFERENTIAL DIAGNOSIS

When confronted with evidence of symptom exaggeration or fabrication, a number of diagnoses and/or explanatory constructs may need to be considered. These are listed in Table 6.2. Malingering has already been discussed in detail. The other diagnoses and constructs are covered next.

TABLE 6.1. Proposed Diagnostic Criteria for Malingered Neuropsychological Dysfunction (MND): A revision and extension of the Slick et al. (1999) criteria for Malingered Neurocognitive Dysfunction

Primary MND

Definite

1. Presence of a substantial external incentive [Criterion A]
2. One or more very strong indicators of exaggeration/fabrication of neuropsychological problems or deficits [Criteria B1-B3]
3. Behaviors meeting necessary criteria are not substantially accounted for by psychiatric, neurological, or developmental factors

Probable

1. Presence of a substantial external incentive [Criterion A]
2. Three or more indicators of possible exaggeration/fabrication of neuropsychological problems or deficits [C1-C7]

Secondary MND (definite and probable)

Criteria for definite or probable MND are otherwise met, but there are compelling grounds to believe that at the time of assessment the examinee did not have the cognitive capacity to understand the moral/ethical/legal implications of his or her behavior, and/or was unable to control his or her behavior, *secondary* to immaturity (i.e., in childhood) or bona fide developmental, psychiatric or neurological disorders or injuries.

MND by Proxy (definite and probable)

Criteria for definite or probable MND are otherwise met, but there are compelling grounds to believe that a *vulnerable* examinee acted primarily under the guidance, direction, influence, or control of another individual. Examinees may be vulnerable to the influence of others by virtue of immaturity, neurodevelopmental and cognitive disabilities, and psychiatric illness, or by perceived inability to escape or avoid substantial coercion such as threats of physical harm for failure to behave as directed.

Specific Criteria

A. Clear and substantial external incentive
B. Very strong indicators of exaggeration/fabrication of neuropsychological problems or deficits
   B1. Below chance performance ($\leq .05$) on one or more forced choice measures
   B2. High posterior probability ($\geq .95$ that performance is substantially below actual ability level) on one or more well-validated psychometric indices
   B3. Self-reported symptoms are unambiguously incompatible with or directly contradicted by directly observed behavior and/or test performance
C. Possible indicators of exaggeration/fabrication of neuropsychological problems or deficits
   C1. Data from one or more well-validated psychometric measures, while not sufficient to meet Criterion B1 are on balance more consistent with non-compliance than compliance
   C2. Marked and implausible discrepancy between test performance and level of function expected based on developmental and medical history

(Continued)

TABLE 6.1. (Continued)

C3. Marked and implausible discrepancy between test performance and directly observed behavior and capabilities

C4. Marked and implausible discrepancy between test performance and reliable collateral reports concerning behavior and capabilities

C5. Marked and implausible discrepancy between self-reported and documented history, consistent with exaggeration of preinjury level of function and capabilities, minimization or pre-existing injuries or neuropsychological problems, and/or exaggeration of the severity of new injuries

C6. Marked and implausible discrepancy between self-reported symptoms and level of function expected based on developmental and medical history

C7. Marked and implausible discrepancy between self-reported symptoms and information obtained from reliable collateral informants.

Malingering by Proxy

First described by Lu and Boone in 2002, malingering by proxy (MBP) applies to cases in which minors meet criteria for malingering primarily as a result of the deliberate influence or control of an adult. In personal injury litigation contexts, MBP applies to cases in which *(1)* a minor plaintiff is induced to feign neuropsychological problems or deficits by one or more adults; *(2)* who do so as part of an attempt to increase the settlement awarded to the minor. The adults in question do not have to be parents or guardians; an adult sibling or other adult relative may take on such a role. The adult in the MBP relationship may stand to benefit directly or indirectly in some material way from the minor's malingering, but this is not required for a diagnosis. Rather, a diagnosis of malingering by proxy only requires that the child's exaggeration or fabrication of symptoms is primarily directed toward obtaining rewards and/or avoiding punishments meted out by a parent or other adult, rather than being directly

TABLE 6.2. Diagnoses and Constructs That May Need to Be Considered in Cases of Exaggerated or Fabricated Neuropsychological Dysfunction

- Malingering
- Malingering by proxy
- Secondary malingering[*]
- Conversion disorder
- Dissociative amnesia
- Factitious disorder
- Factitious disorder by proxy
- Adjustment problem/disorder with specious symptoms[*]
- Cogniform condition/disorder
- Neurocognitive hypochondriasis
- Stereotype threat
- Oppositional-defiant presentations

[*]Proposed diagnosis.

motivated by material gains from a positive litigation outcome. Rewards for malingering may include anything of psychological or material value to the child, including encouragement and praise, desired objects, participation in rewarding activities, extra privileges, and of course, money. Punishment or negative consequences for failing to malinger may include disapproval, withholding of affection, loss of objects, activities and privileges, and physical violence. A child's behavior may sometimes be influenced or controlled by both promises of rewards for success and threats of punishment for failure. In adults, malingering in response to threats by others has been referred to as coerced malingering (Slick et al., in press). However, for minors, this behavior more properly falls within the construct of malingering by proxy.

In practice, it is often difficult if not impossible to determine that any particular case meets criteria for MBP. Barring outright admission, one will rarely have at hand any strong or direct evidence bearing on the degree to which a child's behavior is deliberately being influenced or controlled by a parent or other adult. However, a number of findings may suggest MBP. Among these are signs that an adult who is in a position to influence the child appears to be deliberately engaging in activities that could negatively skew the assessment results. For example, a parent may exaggerate a child's preinjury abilities; minimize preinjury problems; exaggerate postinjury deficits; report unusual, bizarre, or illogical symptoms; or report symptoms and symptom histories that are inconsistent with injury type and severity. For this reason, it is very useful to compare parent reports against school and medical records. Other indicators of attempts to negatively bias the assessment are observations of prompts, directions, or encouragement of the child to report or demonstrate "symptoms."

When a child who exaggerates or fabricates neuropsychological dysfunction is found to have inadequate mental capacity to fully appreciate the nature and consequences of his or her behaviors, then a diagnosis of either MBP or malingering secondary to developmental limitations will need to be considered. Of course, it may be difficult to determine with any confidence what a child is capable of understanding and whether feigning is volitional. In such cases, one will have to consider what a child of the same age and similar neurological history would likely be able to appreciate about his or her situation.

With respect to other possible exclusions, MBP should not be diagnosed when a child feigns cognitive dysfunction because he or she mistakenly believes it will please or help others or when a child erroneously believes that someone wants or expects him or her to do so. For example, a child who is repeatedly exposed to comments from a parent concerning the need for a large settlement or the need for the plaintiff to be punished may infer from this that he or she should feign deficits to ensure the desired outcome, even if the parent never wanted or intended for the child to malinger. Feigning deficits in these circumstances can be considered a type of secondary malingering, particularly if the child is not capable of appreciating the potential ramifications of his or her behavior.

Secondary Malingering

A person who otherwise meets criteria for probable or definite malingering, but whose feigning behaviors primarily arise from legitimate cognitive/psychiatric dysfunction would be given a diagnosis of *secondary malingering* (SM). This diagnosis is applicable to cases in which examinees are unable to fully comprehend the nature, implications, and consequences of their behavior, and/or examinee behavior is influenced by symptoms of illness such as command hallucinations or delusions (e.g., malingering secondary to thought disorder). Similarly, a diagnosis of secondary malingering is applicable to individuals who meet criteria for malingering but are deemed unable to fully appreciate the nature and consequences of their actions because of limited neurocognitive development. This diagnosis will usually need to be considered whenever young children and persons with significant developmental disabilities feign neuropsychological impairment.

Conversion Disorder and Dissociative Amnesia

The *Diagnostic and Statistical Manual of Mental Disorders, Fourth Edition* (*DSM-IV*; APA, 2000) defines conversion disorder as nonvolitional feigning of *sensory or motor deficits* arising from unconscious psychological conflicts and processes. That is, the feigning of illness, in and of itself, provides gratification or relief from anxiety and intrapsychic conflict. Symptom feigning in conversion disorder is exclusively limited to sensory or motor deficits, and so it should not be considered in the differential diagnosis of feigned cognitive deficits (but see Boone & Lu, 1999 for a different perspective). There is ongoing debate regarding the viability of conversion disorder as a diagnosis (c.f., Miller, 1999; Turner, 1999), but it appears that it will be retained substantially intact in the *DSM-V*. According to the *DSM-IV*, conversion symptoms in children under 10 years of age are usually limited to gait problems and seizures, but there is little good evidence to back up this assertion. In fact, no really good epidemiological data on pediatric or adult conversion disorder in North America are available, and the incidence and prevalence rates that have been published vary considerably (from 11 to 500 per 100,000 in the general population, and from 1% to 14% of medical/surgical inpatients, according to the *DSM-IV*). In general, conversion disorder is thought to be more common among women than men, but it is unknown whether this is the case in children. No data whatsoever are available specifically concerning the prevalence of conversion disorder among compensation-seeking children and adolescents seen for third-party neuropsychological assessment.

The only *DSM-IV* diagnosis that specifically includes fabrication of cognitive deficits is dissociative amnesia. This is characterized by an inability to recall important autobiographical information, typically of a traumatic nature. Individuals may present with circumscribed amnesia for specific events, time periods, or types of information. In some cases, they may present with dense amnesia encompassing their entire past and continuing into the present. Other types of fabricated cognitive complaints or symptoms are not usually seen, or they are usually trivial when present. This differentiates dissociative amnesia from the broader spectrum of complaints and symptoms often seen in many bona-fide neurological conditions and also many malingering cases. As with conversion disorder, fabrication of impairment is not volitional, but rather arises from unconscious psychological conflicts and processes and provides primary gain. That is, the act of feigning of amnesia in and of itself provides relief from internal conflicts, tension, and anxiety. Similarities in the *DSM-IV* definitions of conversion disorder and dissociative amnesia would seem to suggest that the latter should also not be diagnosed whenever an individual obtains or stands to obtain secondary gains from feigning impairment, but this is not the case. Therefore, dissociative amnesia may sometimes need to be considered in the differential diagnosis of feigned *amnesia* in compensation-seeking cases.

Epidemiological data on dissociative amnesia are extremely limited; no good studies of prevalence or incidence among children and adolescents in North America are available. In general, dissociative amnesia is considered a rare disorder and it is likely that few neuropsychologists will encounter it in clinical practice. It will very rarely need to be considered in the differential diagnosis of feigned cognitive impairment in litigation cases. However, dissociative amnesia is sometimes claimed as a defense in criminal cases and so may be encountered by neuropsychologists who work in this area.

Factitious Disorder

The *DSM-IV* (APA, 2000) defines factitious disorder as the intentional production of physical or psychological signs or symptoms, the motivation for which is assumption of the sick role. A factitious presentation may include fabrication of subjective complaints, falsification of objective signs, self-inflicted conditions, exaggeration or exacerbation of preexisting general medical conditions, or any combination thereof. Unlike conversion disorder, there is no restriction on the types of symptoms that are feigned in factitious disorder and thus neuropsychological complaints may well be part of the presentation. External incentives for assuming a sick role (i.e., secondary gain) must be absent and the individual is usually unaware of the motivation behind his or her factitious behaviors. This definition of factious disorder implies that factious behaviors provide some type of primary gain. That is, the feigning of illness, in and of itself, provides gratification or relief from anxiety and intrapsychic conflict and is thus the primary motivation for factitious behaviors. Factitious behaviors are not directed toward attainment of secondary gains and any external reinforcement for assuming a sick role that the factitious patient receives is incidental. Onset is usually in early adulthood, often after predisposed individuals have been exposed to hospitalization or severe illnesses in themselves or others, and is typically precipitated by some type of loss, rejection, or abandonment. Factitious disorder is infrequently seen in children and adolescents; estimates of prevalence in psychiatric and general medical settings range from 0.3% to 0.8% (Ehrlich et al., 2008). No data are available on the prevalence of factitious disorder among compensation-seeking children and adolescents seen for third-party neuropsychological assessment.

Because factious disorder cannot be diagnosed when external incentives are present, malingering and factitious disorder are mutually exclusive, at least insofar as *DSM-IV* nosology is concerned. However, the automatic exclusion of factitious disorder in cases where external incentives are present is incompatible with the view that most, if not all behaviors are a product of both internal psychological processes and external contingencies. It has been argued that persons with factitious disorders do in fact enter the civil litigation system in some numbers, and are often misdiagnosed as malingerers (Eisendrath, 1996). This is but one of a number of substantial criticisms that have been raised about the *DSM-IV* model of factitious disorder (c.f., Bass & Halligan, 2007; Turner, 2006).

Factitious Disorder by Proxy

According to Rosenberg (1987), factitious disorder by proxy (FDP; also known as Munchausen syndrome by proxy) is defined as *(1)* an illness in a child that is simulated or induced by a parent or someone acting *in loco parentis*, *(2)* repeated and persistent presentation of the child for medical assessment and care, often resulting in multiple unnecessary medical procedures, *(3)* denial of knowledge by the perpetrator as to the etiology of the child's illness, and *(4)* abatement of the child's acute symptoms and signs when he or she is separated from the perpetrator. As with factitious disorder, the motive for the perpetrator's behavior in FDP is an internal psychological need to assume the sick role by proxy (i.e., the manifestation of symptoms in the child provides the adult with primary gain), and external incentives for the perpetrator's behavior are either not present or are incidental. Therefore, FDP and malingering (or malingering by proxy) are mutually exclusive.

According to a recent review by Shaw, Dayal, Hartman, and Demaso (2008), FDP is a rare disorder with an estimated annual incidence of 0.4 to 2 per 100,000. It is seen in children of all ages, but it is more commonly seen in preadolescents, assumedly because younger children are easier to manipulate. Although rare, FDP should be seriously considered whenever there are indications of possible occurrence because it is a potentially life-threatening condition. Mortality rates of 10% are commonly reported, and rates in excess of 25% are reported in cases of poisoning. Roughly half the children who are victims of FDP also have bona-fide medical conditions, which often complicate the process of differential diagnosis.

Adjustment Problem/Disorder with Specious Symptoms

From both clinical and medical-legal standpoints, it is important to distinguish, if possible, between the feigning of symptoms for material-legal secondary gain and the feigning of symptoms for psychosocial secondary gain. The first type of feigning is consistent with malingering, but there is currently no adequate diagnostic category for the second type. Therefore, we propose a new diagnosis, *adjustment problem/disorder with specious symptoms* (APSS/ADSS), for application to cases in which a person exaggerates or fabricates symptoms in order to obtain psychosocial secondary gains, rather than material-legal secondary gains. In APSS and ADSS, the feigning of symptoms is primarily directed toward *(1)* obtaining and maintaining psychological benefits such as increased attention, affection, and support from others; *(2)* managing problematic interpersonal relationships (e.g., controlling others); and/or *(3)* escaping from aversive interpersonal situations or avoiding informal obligations such as household chores or schoolwork. Use of the specifier "problem" or "disorder" depends on the severity of the presentation. Situational symptom feigning in response to a specific interpersonal need or dilemma would fall within the APSS end of the spectrum. In contrast, a severe, deeply entrenched, and pervasive condition in which a person's life revolves around the sick role as a means of obtaining psychosocial reinforcement and managing interpersonal relationships would fall within the ADSS end of the spectrum.

The following is an example of APSS in a pediatric neuropsychology setting seen by one of the authors: A highly talented high school athlete with a long-standing history of learning difficulties and test anxiety sustained a concussion during the course of a game. Thereafter he suffered from a number of typical concussion symptoms, including headaches, photophobia, nausea, and forgetfulness. He was subsequently held out of competition and was also excused from most academic activities and requirements. After 3 months, he successfully returned to play without recurrence of symptoms during practice or games, or any decline in athletic performance. However, he continued to complain of marked postconcussion symptoms whenever he attempted to engage in any academic activities such as reading and studying, and as a result he continued to be excused from most academic activities and requirements. Concerns about persisting postconcussion symptoms prompted referral to a neurologist, who found nothing untoward on examination and subsequently referred the young man for neuropsychological assessment. At the neuropsychological assessment, he complained of severe headaches, rapidly brought on by most cognitive activities, and also significant difficulties with attention, learning, and memory. Obvious problems of the kind reported were not apparent during the assessment, but he nevertheless obtained extremely low scores on most measures of attention and memory, consistent with a severe brain injury rather than a concussion. He also obtained a below chance score on a forced-choice noncompliance detection measure. When he later met with the neuropsychologist to go over the assessment results, he was informed that his test results were invalid, and after some discussion, he admitted to feigning symptoms to avoid academic demands. A face-saving way was found to share the assessment results with his parents and school. He was referred for psychotherapy for test anxiety to improve his academic coping abilities, and he was put on a graduated schedule for return to regular academic work with accommodations for learning difficulties and test anxiety. Over time, he was able to successfully resume a full academic schedule and workload. Because the feigning in this case was situational (i.e., restricted to academic settings) and time limited, rather than a global, long-standing and entrenched personality feature, it falls within the *problem* (APSS) rather than *disorder* (ADSS) category of severity.

An APSS/ADSS diagnosis may be relatively clear cut in cases where examinees do not stand to obtain any material-legal secondary gains for feigning symptoms. However, in medical-legal assessments it is not at all unusual to encounter examinees whose feigning appears to be motivated by both psychosocial and material-legal secondary gains (e.g., increased attention and support from family members and a financial settlement). In such cases, both APSS/ADSS and malingering may be diagnosed as appropriate.

Cogniform Disorder and Cogniform Condition

As noted previously, apart from dissociative amnesia, *unconsciously* feigned cognitive deficits do not fit within any *DSM-IV* diagnoses. In response to this, Delis and

Wetter (2007) proposed two new diagnoses, cogniform disorder and cogniform condition. These diagnoses were created to "encompass cases of excessive cognitive complaints and inadequate test-taking effort in the absence of sufficient evidence to diagnose malingering" (p. 589). Cogniform disorder is the more severe and pervasive form of the two diagnoses and is characterized by excessive cognitive symptoms affecting many activities of daily life. More specifically, cogniform disorder is defined as follows: (1) a pattern of cognitive complaints or low scores on psychometric cognitive tests that cannot be fully explained by a neurological, mental disorder, medical condition, effects of a psychoactive substance, or other factors known to affect cognitive functioning such as fatigue; accompanied by (2) significant manifestations of cognitive dysfunction in widespread areas of everyday life. The essential features of cogniform condition are the same as those of cogniform disorder, except that individuals do not present with significant manifestations of cognitive dysfunction in widespread areas of everyday life.

As proposed, symptoms of cogniform disorder/condition can include symptom validity test failure and other test-based and behavioral evidence of noncompliance. It may also be diagnosed in cases where material-legal secondary gains are present, if there is insufficient evidence of conscious intent to deceive. In such cases the specifier "with evidence of external incentive" is to be applied. However, no specific criteria are provided for determining that there is insufficient evidence of a conscious intent to deceive, and this raises particularly difficult problems in cases of symptom validity test failure in the context of material-legal secondary gain. In contrast, the Slick et al. MND criteria define forced-choice symptom validity test failure as prima-facie evidence of a volitional effort to deceive,[5] and in the context of material-legal secondary gain, this is considered evidence of definite malingering. The significant conflict between criteria for cogniform disorder/condition and criteria for MND, along with other problematic aspects of the proposed cogniform diagnoses, raises significant concerns about validity and applicability (Binder, 2007; Boone, 2007; Larrabee, 2007b). Until such time as these issues are resolved, a cogniform diagnosis should not normally be considered in cases where an examinee meets criteria for probable or definite malingering.

Neurocognitive Hypochondriasis

Boone (2009) has recently proposed a new diagnosis, neurocognitive hypochondriasis (NH), which is defined by the presence of a fixed belief in neurologically based cognitive impairment, in the absence of any objective impairment. NH is characterized by hypervigilance to minor cognitive difficulties and failures, which are then attributed to neurological injury or illness. According to Boone, NH typically develops in the context of other psychiatric/adjustment problems and problematic interpersonal relationships, and it is often precipitated by a real illness or injury.

---

5. However, malingering is not diagnosed if such efforts are entirely symptomatic of neurological, psychiatric, or developmental disorders; see also the discussion of secondary malingering in this chapter.

Because a diagnosis of NH can only be made when there is no objective evidence of impairment (e.g., abnormal test scores), it will infrequently be on the differential diagnosis list for malingering, as it is unusual to find compensation-seeking cases where exaggeration is limited to self-report and all test scores fall within the normal range. Nevertheless, it is not unusual to see some hypochondriacal features such as hypervigilance and misattribution in compensation-seeking examinees, particularly among those with more mild injuries who have been led to believe that they have more serious and/or permanent brain injuries. This may be especially problematic in younger children because they are more susceptible to suggestion. Although NH will infrequently be on the differential diagnosis list for malingering, any hypochondriacal tendencies should be noted if they are present.

Stereotype/Diagnosis Threat

Stereotype threat is defined as expectancy-based modulation of test performance (Kit, Tuokko, & Mateer, 2008; Steele, 1997; Suhr & Gunstad, 2002, 2005). This differentiates it from neuropsychological hypochondriasis in which beliefs do not negatively affect performance on objective measures. For example, Levy (1996) demonstrated that older adults' performance on cognitive tests can be affected by priming with positive and negative stereotypes about aging. Suhr and Gunstad (2002, 2005) demonstrated a similar effect, which they termed "diagnosis threat" in young adults who had suffered mild head injuries. They found that neuropsychological test performance was worse among individuals who were informed about the potential effects of head injury on cognition in comparison to those who were not reminded of their head injury history. Given the greater susceptibility of younger children to suggestion, it is conceivable that injury-based expectations may sometimes negatively impact their performance on cognitive tests. However, the expectancy effects that have been found in research are relatively small, and in the absence of any compelling research data that indicate otherwise, there is no reason to believe such effects could substantially account for findings consistent with probable or definite malingering in compensation-seeking cases. Therefore, stereotype/diagnosis threat would not usually be considered in the differential diagnosis of probable or definite malingering.

Oppositional-Defiant Presentations

Children and adolescents sometimes approach neuropsychological assessment in an oppositional-defiant manner. The degree of oppositionality can range from subtle/mild to blatant/extreme. At the milder end of the oppositional-defiant (OD) spectrum are behaviors such as negative comments about the examiner and assessment, minimal responses, refusal to guess, and other signs of lack of engagement, motivation, and mental exertion. At the opposite end of the OD spectrum are more extreme behaviors such as outright test refusal, nonsensical responses, and incompatible activities like looking away from or playing with test materials. In the majority of more extreme cases, there are documented prior histories of OD behaviors and/or formal oppositional-defiant disorder diagnoses. Less severe OD behaviors are often situational (i.e., the child is unhappy about being tested) rather than symptomatic of more pervasive or serious clinical conditions. OD behaviors will always have implications for the validity of assessment results, but the diagnostic significance of such presentations may be more complex in compensation-seeking cases. In such cases, marked OD behaviors will often have the same implications as in regular clinical assessments (i.e., a situational response to assessment or symptomatic of a more serious clinical condition), but they may occasionally constitute a naïve attempt to feign impairment, particularly in cases where there is no documented history of such problems. Alternatively, OD behaviors may sometimes be a way for a child or adolescent who presents with exaggerated or fabricated complaints to avoid the challenge of feigning impairment on tests—along with the possibility of getting caught and the associated consequences.

MALINGERING VERSUS BONA-FIDE IMPAIRMENT

There is some tendency to equate malingering and related diagnoses such as factitious disorder with complete fabrication of *all* symptoms. However, there is no inherent contradiction in concluding that an examinee most probably has bona-fide neuropsychological problems or deficits but is nevertheless also very likely exaggerating or fabricating symptoms over and above whatever deficits he or she has. All of the differential diagnoses considered in this chapter can co-occur with bona-fide brain injuries and real neuropsychological problems or deficits. When there is evidence of feigning, it is always good practice to consider the possibility that an examinee suppressed his or her performance on only a subset of tests from a test battery, and more generally, whether exaggeration or fabrication is limited to specific deficits or more global impairment. In such cases, clinicians must rely on reliable elements of case history such as objective medical records to estimate the likelihood and, if possible, the nature and extent of any bona-fide dysfunction or deficits.

SUMMARY AND CONCLUDING THOUGHTS

Pediatric malingering is as yet an understudied phenomenon and much about it remains unknown. However, with due consideration for developmental factors and appropriate revisions to reflect advances in the field, a definition and set of diagnostic criteria that were developed primarily with adults in mind (i.e., Slick et al. 1999) can be applied to compensation-seeking children. In particular, a distinction between *primary* and *secondary* malingering should be considered in many pediatric cases—and some adult cases as well.

Whenever malingering is suspected, no matter how strongly, it is always necessary to carefully consider any alternate or complimentary diagnoses that might be applicable. In pediatric cases, secondary malingering and malingering by proxy will often need to be considered in the differential diagnosis. In addition, it is not at all unusual to find evidence of strong hypochondriacal and specious components to an examinee's presentation. In many cases, the possibility of coexisting bona-fide dysfunction or impairment will often have to be considered, especially when documented injuries are more severe. In such cases, all relevant aspects of an examinee's presentation should be noted as contributing or coexisting factors, even when a diagnosis of probable or definite malingering is warranted. In such instances, it is usually difficult, if not impossible, to parse out and assign any meaningful weight to the relative contributions of the different etiologies. While there has been some promising research and conceptual development in this area, much more will be required to build a fully integrated and internally consistent differential diagnostic nosology. Until such time, the process of arriving at a differential diagnosis or multiple diagnoses will continue to be more difficult than need be.

Finally, pediatric malingering is a relatively new area of focus in neuropsychology and also one that raises some unique and at times extremely vexing clinical, ethical, legal, and moral issues and challenges. This sometimes leads to substantial differences in opinions and clinical approaches that can become quite contentious. Nevertheless, we hope this chapter stimulates open and collegial discussion and much needed further research.

ACKNOWLEDGMENTS

We are extremely grateful to Dr. Kevin Bianchini for his very thoughtful and insightful review of an early draft of this chapter.

REFERENCES

American Psychiatric Association. (2000). *Diagnostic and statistical manual of mental disorders* (4th ed., text rev.). Arlington, VA: Author.

Bass, C., & Halligan, P. W. (2007). Illness related deception: social or psychiatric problem? *Journal of the Royal Society of Medicine, 100*, 81–84.

Bianchini, K. J., Greve, K. W., & Glynn, G. (2005). On the diagnosis of malingered pain-related disability: Lessons from cognitive malingering research. *The Spine Journal, 5*, 404–417.

Binder, L. M. (2007). Comment on "Cogniform disorder and cogniform condition: Proposed diagnoses for excessive cognitive symptoms." *Archives of Clinical Neuropsychology, 22*(6), 681–682.

Binder, L. M., & Pankratz, L. (1987). Neuropsychological evidence of a factitious memory complaint. *Journal of Clinical and Experimental Neuropsychology, 9*(2), 167–171.

Boone, K. B. (2007). Commentary on "Cogniform disorder and cogniform condition: Proposed diagnoses for excessive cognitive symptoms" by Dean C. Delis and Spencer R. Wetter. *Archives of Clinical Neuropsychology, 22*(6), 675–679.

Boone, K. B. (2009). Fixed belief in cognitive dysfunction despite normal neuropsychological scores: Neurocognitive hypochondriasis? *The Clinical Neuropsychologist, 23*(6), 1016–1036.

Boone, K., & Lu, P. (1999). Impact of somatoform symptomatology on credibility of cognitive performance. *Clinical Neuropsychologist, 13*(4), 414–419.

Brady, J. P., & Lind, D. L. (1961). Experimental analysis of hysterical blindness. *Archives of General Psychiatry, 4*, 331–339.

Delis, D. C., & Wetter, S. R. (2007). Cogniform disorder and cogniform condition: Proposed diagnoses for excessive cognitive symptoms. *Archives of Clinical Neuropsychology, 22*(5), 589–604.

Eisendrath, S. J. (1996). When Munchausen becomes malingering: Factitious disorders that penetrate the legal system. *Bulletin of the American Academy of Psychiatry and Law, 24*(4), 471–481.

Ehrlich, S., Pfeiffer, E., Salbach, H., Lenz, K., & Lehmkuhl, U. (2008). Factitious disorder in children and adolescents: A retrospective study. *Psychosomatics, 49,* 392–398.

Hiscock, M. (1989). Refining the forced-choice method for the detection of malingering. *Journal of Clinical and Experimental Neuropsychology, 11*(6), 967–974.

Kit, K. A., Tuokko, H. A., & Mateer, C. A. (2007). A review of the stereotype threat literature and its application in a neurological population. *Neuropsychology Review, 18*(2), 132–148.

Larrabee, G. (Ed.). (2007a). *Assessment of malingered neuropsychological deficits.* New York: Oxford University Press.

Larrabee, G. J. (2007b). Commentary on Delis and Wetter, "Cogniform disorder and cogniform condition: Proposed diagnoses for excessive cognitive symptoms." *Archives of Clinical Neuropsychology, 22*(6), 683–687.

Larrabee, G. J. (2008). Aggregation across multiple indicators improves the detection of malingering: Relationship to likelihood ratios. *Clinical Neuropsychologist, 22*(4), 666–679.

Larrabee, G. J., Greiffenstein, M. F., Greve, K. W., & Bianchini, K. J. (2007). Refining diagnostic criteria for malingering. In G. J. Larrabee, (Ed.), *Assessment of malingered neuropsychological deficits* (pp. 334–371). New York: Oxford University Press.

Levy, B. (1996). Improving memory in old age through implicit self-stereotyping. *Journal of Personality and Social Psychology, 71*(6), 1092–1107.

Lu, P., & Boone, K. (2002). Suspect cognitive symptoms in a 9-year-old child: Malingering by proxy? *Clinical Neuropsychologist, 16*(1), 90–96.

Miller, E. (1999). Conversion hysteria: Is it a viable concept? *Cognitive Neuropsychiatry, 4*(3), 181–191.

Mittenberg, W., Patton, C., Canyock, E. M., & Condit, D. (2002, February). *A national survey of symptom exaggeration and malingering baserates.* Poster presented at the Annual Meeting of the International Neuropsychological Society, Toronto, Canada.

Mossman, D. (2003). Daubert, cognitive malingering, and test accuracy. *Law and Human Behavior, 27,* 229–249.

Pankratz, L. (1979). Symptom validity testing and symptom retraining: Procedures for the assessment and treatment of functional sensory deficits. *Journal of Consulting and Clinical Psychology, 47*(2), 409–410.

Pankratz, L., Fausti, S. A., & Peed, S. (1975). A forced-choice technique to evaluate deafness in the hysterical or malingering patient. *Journal of Consulting and Clinical Psychology, 43,* 421–422.

Sharland, M. J., & Gfeller, J. D. (2007). A survey of neuropsychologists' beliefs and practices with respect to the assessment of effort. *Archives of Clinical Neuropsychology, 22*(2), 213–223.

Shaw, R., Dayal, S., Hartman, J. K., & DeMaso, D. (2008). Factitious disorder by proxy: Pediatric condition falsification. *Harvard Review of Psychiatry, 16*(4), 215–224.

Slick, D. J., Tan, J. E., Sherman, E. M. S., & Strauss, E. (2010). Malingering and Related Conditions in Pediatric Populations. In A. S. Davis, (Ed.), *Handbook of pediatric neuropsychology* (pp. 454–470). New York: Oxford University Press.

Slick, D. J., Tan, J. E., Strauss, E., & Hultsch, D. (2004). Detecting malingering: A survey of experts' practices. *Archives of Clinical Neuropsychology, 19*(4), 465–473.

Slick, D. J., Sherman, E., & Iverson, G. (1999). Diagnostic criteria for malingered neurocognitive dysfunction: Proposed standards for clinical practice and research. *Clinical Neuropsychologist*, 13(4), 545–561.

Steele, C. (1997). A threat in the air: How stereotypes shape intellectual identity and performance. *American Psychologist*, 52(6), 613–629.

Suhr, J., & Gunstad, J. (2002). "Diagnosis threat": The effect of negative expectations on cognitive performance in head injury. *Journal of Clinical and Experimental Neuropsychology*, 24(4), 448–457.

Suhr, J., & Gunstad, J. (2005). Further exploration of the effect of "diagnosis threat" on cognitive performance in individuals with mild head injury. *Journal of the International Neuropsychological Society*, 11(1), 23–29.

Turner, M. (1999). Malingering, hysteria, and the factitious disorders. *Cognitive Neuropsychiatry*, 4(3), 193–201.

Turner, M. A. (2006). Factitious disorders: Reformulating the DSM–IV criteria. *Psychosomatics*, 47, 23–32.

Chapter 7

Overview of Tests and Techniques to Detect Negative Response Bias in Children

MICHAEL W. KIRKWOOD

INTRODUCTION

Neuropsychological test interpretation rests upon the assumption that the examinee responded in a nonbiased fashion during the exam. If an individual provides noncredible effort or exaggerates or feigns symptoms, the resulting data will represent an inaccurate representation of the person's true abilities or difficulties (see also Chapter 6). Reliance on such data can lead to a host of problems, including interpretive errors, inaccurate diagnostic and etiologic conclusions, mischaracterization of brain–behavior relationships, ineffective treatment recommendations, and inappropriate use of limited health care and educational resources. The current chapter will highlight developmental psychology studies relevant to understanding when children are capable of deception and provide an overview of medical and neuropsychological cases establishing that children can feign and exaggerate physical, psychiatric, and cognitive symptoms. Lastly, the tests and techniques available to the pediatric neuropsychologist to help detect negative response bias will be reviewed.

DEVELOPMENTAL CAPACITY FOR DECEPTION

Although youth have been assumed historically to be less capable of deception than adults, acts of deception in childhood are not uncommon, even in normative populations (Newton, Reddy, & Bull, 2000; Stouthamer-Loeber & Loeber, 1986; Wilson, Smith, & Ross, 2003). Developmental psychology studies indicate that the ability to make factually untrue statements is in place by 2 to 3 years of age for most children, even though concealment techniques remain unsophisticated at this age (Newton et al., 2000; Talwar & Lee, 2002). During these early years, the use of deception is driven primarily by a desire to avoid situation-specific punishment or negative emotional states such as guilt or shame after a misdeed, rather than preplanned attempts to instill false beliefs in others (Polak & Harris, 1999; Talwar, Gordon, & Lee, 2007). The capacity to intentionally deceive and maintain that consistent false belief over time is thought to develop by 7 or 8 years in most children (Johnson, 1997; Talwar et al., 2007). Throughout later childhood and into adolescence, more advanced skills that can lend credibility to deceptive acts continue to emerge (e.g., the capacity to hold multiple disparate beliefs in mind, the ability to convey a consistent semantic message, greater appreciation of others' perspectives).

EVIDENCE OF PEDIATRIC FEIGNING, EXAGGERATION, AND NONCREDIBLE PERFORMANCE

Despite the capacity of school-age children to deceive, relatively little scientific attention has focused on how frequently feigning and exaggeration occur during health care evaluations. A number of mostly case reports have, however, documented clearly that medical and neuropsychological noncredible presentations do occur, varying widely in the nature and severity of the symptomatology, evaluative context, and underlying reason for the distortion. Table 7.1 provides a framework for differentiating the psychiatric conditions most relevant to medically unexplained symptomatology, even if this *Diagnostic and Statistical Manual* (*DSM*)-based nosology dependent upon dichotomizing conscious and unconscious processes and internal and external incentives has been convincingly criticized (e.g., Boone, 2007).

Cases From the Medical and Psychiatric Literature

Factitious disorder by proxy (or Munchausen syndrome by proxy) refers to intentional illness-producing behavior similar to adult factitious disorder but with a caregiver using the child as a proxy for his/her own psychological gain. The term *malingering by proxy* has been used when the incentive for the symptom production is clear external gain for the caregiver, rather than psychological benefit. In most of these cases, children are viewed as passive instruments that parents manipulate as a form of abuse to meet their own needs. However, several cases have been described in which the child has been known to take a more active role in the illness falsification.

TABLE 7.1. Differentiation of Relevant Psychiatric Conditions by Presumed Responsible Person, Underlying Motivation, and Incentive

Condition	Person Driving Symptom Production	Motivation	Incentive
Malingering by proxy	Caregiver	Conscious	External gain
Malingering	Child	Conscious	External gain
Factitious disorder by proxy	Caregiver	Conscious	Psychological
Factitious disorder	Child	Conscious	Psychological
Somatoform disorders (e.g., somatization disorder, conversion disorder)	Child	Unconscious	Psychological

For example, Croft and Jervis (1989) report a case of factitious disorder by proxy in which a 4-year-old boy was trained by his mother to simulate seizures by falling off his chair, shivering, and flickering his eyes. His presentation was convincing enough that he was diagnosed with epilepsy and treated with an antiepileptic drug before it was discovered that he was feigning the events. In a case of malingering by proxy, Stutts, Hickey, and Kasdan (2003) describe a 13-year-old boy who was coached by a parent to feign hand immobility with the hope of obtaining a legal settlement. His medical history included 43 emergency room visits, 9 hospital admissions, 20 X-ray films, and 52 laboratory evaluations. Despite videotape surveillance showing the boy to have a full range of motion, he held his right upper extremity in a fixed position during all medical evaluations, suggesting that he was actively involved in the injury simulation.

Children are also well known to present to health care providers with medically unexplained symptoms when parents are not thought to be overtly driving the behavior. Most commonly, youth present with a single or a few unexplained physical symptoms (e.g., stomachache, headache) that are transient, coincide with a known psychosocial stressor, and are presumably produced unintentionally. Rates of more serious and disabling somatization are low in early childhood but may approach 5% to 10% by the teenage years (Lieb, Pfister, Mastaler, & Wittchen, 2000; Offord et al., 1987). Conversion disorders occur in children as well, with the most common presentations involving disturbances in motor function, sensory symptoms, nonepileptic seizures, and respiratory problems (Kozlowska et al., 2007). Although conversion disorder is considered a low-incidence condition, nonepileptic seizures (i.e., "psychogenic seizures") are not uncommon, occurring in roughly 10% of pediatric epilepsy patients (Kutluay, Selwa, Minecan, Edwards, & Beydoun, 2010; Wood, Haque, Weinstock, & Miller, 2004).

In addition to the presumed unconscious production of symptoms in somatoform presentations, children also knowingly feign health-related problems. The most comprehensive review of intentional illness production in children was provided by Libow (2000). She reviewed the world literature for the previous 30 years and found 42 cases in which the child was thought to have intentionally deceived physicians without parental involvement and with the primary motivation to adopt the sick role, consistent with factitious disorder. The majority of the cases were females who had early experience with the medical world, either through chronic illness or after a bona fide, if minor, episode of illness. The most frequently induced conditions included fever, diabetic ketoacidosis, purpura, and infections. The production of the symptoms ranged from the fairly benign such as warming a thermometer and putting blood from a superficial wound into a urine specimen to the more dangerous such as deliberately ingesting steroids and manipulating insulin to an extent that a subtotal pancreatectomy was conducted.

Cases of pediatric malingering in which the child is attempting to achieve a clear external goal with the illness falsification have been reported as well. Conti (2004) described several cases of likely malingered attention-deficit/hyperactivity disorder (ADHD), including one teenage boy who learned about ADHD on the Internet, feigned the symptoms, secured a stimulant medication, and in turn sold and traded the medication to other teenagers. Peebles, Sabella, Franco, and Goldfarb (2005) also describe two cases of malingering: a 14-year-old girl who applied makeup to her face to look like a rash to get out of school and a 13-year-old who applied menstrual blood to old surgical wounds to get out of school. Greenfield (1987) additionally reported on a 14-year-old girl who malingered psychosis to extricate herself from an aversive foster-care living arrangement.

Cases From the Neuropsychological Literature

During pediatric neuropsychological evaluation specifically, a number of case studies have also documented that children can feign and exaggerate cognitive impairment. One of the most detailed descriptions of a child feigning was provided by Lu and Boone (2002), who reported on a 9-year-old boy whose family was involved in litigation after he was struck by a motor vehicle and sustained a moderate traumatic brain injury (TBI). During the independent neuropsychological exam, the youngster failed multiple symptom validity tests (SVTs) and displayed a noncredible performance pattern on standard cognitive measures. Because the plan to deceive was thought to have originated from his parents, not the child, the results were characterized as a case of malingering by proxy. McCaffrey and Lynch (2009) described another case of malingering by proxy in a 13-year-old girl referred by an attorney because of questions about neurobehavioral changes following a motor vehicle-related TBI. In a case of Munchausen by proxy first identified through neuropsychological evaluation, Heubrock (2001) described a mother who induced multiple developmental and learning problems in a young girl through unnecessary isolation at home, hospitalization, and treatment procedures.

Cases of noncredible deficits during neuropsychological evaluation have also been documented when the parents are not known to have been involved directly in the deception. Flaro and Boone (2009) reported on a 16-year-old male with a history of multiple mild head injuries who feigned cognitive symptoms to evade responsibility for criminally violent behavior. Flaro, Green, and Blaskewitz (2007) described a similar case of a 12-year-old boy faced with criminal charges who provided invalid data in an attempt to secure a less restrictive psychiatric placement. Flaro et al. (2007) additionally described a clinically referred 7-year-old boy who, for unspecified reasons, provided suboptimal effort on one day but valid effort on the next, resulting in a 28-point increase on IQ testing. In a forensic context, Henry (2005) described a case of an 8-year-old boy who also for unknown reasons scored far below chance on SVTs and produced an implausible neuropsychological protocol.

A number of neuropsychological case series studies have also documented instances of children providing noncredible effort. When Donders (2005) examined the performance of 100 general pediatric patients on the Test of Memory Malingering (TOMM; Tombaugh, 1996), he found two boys with a history of noncompliant behavior who were thought to be putting forth insufficient effort. MacAllister, Nakhutina, Bender, Karantzoulis, and Carlson (2009) reported that 2 out of 60 pediatric epilepsy patients performed poorly on the TOMM because of effort-related problems, rather than seizure-related impairment. Similarly, in a study by Carone (2008) that included 38 children with moderate–severe TBI and other types of serious neurological dysfunction, 2 children were thought to have failed the Medical Symptom Validity Test (MSVT; Green, 2004) because of non-credible effort.

Higher rates of negative response bias have been found in two additional pediatric neuropsychological studies. In a largely nonlitigating mild TBI sample of 193 children and adolescents referred exclusively for clinical neuropsychological evaluation, 17% of the patients failed the MSVT (Kirkwood & Kirk, 2010). Although no identified pediatric studies have examined the base rate of response bias during independent forensic or educational evaluations, Chafetz, Abrahams, and Kohlmaier (2007) examined the frequency of SVT failure in a clear secondary gain context. They administered a stand-alone SVT as part of a determination evaluation for U.S. Social Security Disability benefits. The TOMM was administered to 96 children and the MSVT to 27 children, with failure rates of 28% and 37%, respectively.

The importance of work attempting to identify abuse in those seeking child-related compensation is highlighted by additional reports in the scientific literature (e.g., Cassar, Hales, Longhurst, & Weiss, 1996), as well as by well-publicized cases in the popular press. One of the most egregious instances of recent child-related fraud was the case of Rosie Costello, who admitted in U.S. District Court to coaching her children to fake mental retardation and physical disability beginning when they were in the preschool to early elementary years (Clarridge, 2007). The motivation for the malingering was to collect Social Security benefits on behalf of her children, which Ms. Costello had done for approximately two decades. The mother and a son were sentenced to federal prison, with the mother ordered to pay back the nearly $290,000 that she had been awarded over the years.

TESTS AND TECHNIQUES TO DETECT NEGATIVE RESPONSE BIAS

The aforementioned review suggests that children can and do feign deficits and exaggerate medical and neuropsychological symptomatology for varying reasons and across varying contexts. Given the limits of subjective clinical judgment in identifying negative response bias, adult-based research into symptom validity testing has grown exponentially over the last two decades, with recent survey data indicating that the majority of neuropsychologists now incorporate objective SVTs into their evaluations (Sharland & Gfeller, 2007). Position statements by both the National Academy of Neuropsychology (Bush et al., 2005) and the American Academy of Clinical Neuropsychology (Heilbronner, Sweet, Morgan, Larrabee, & Millis, 2009) essentially suggest that a decision *not* to use SVTs is only rarely justifiable, especially during forensic evaluations. Though given much less scientific attention, relying on objective tools to identify response bias in children is no less important, because subjective judgment alone is unlikely to be consistently effective (Faust, Hart, & Guilmette, 1988; Faust, Hart, Guilmette, & Arkes, 1988).

The two primary objective methods to evaluate the validity of an individual's neuropsychological performance are stand-alone performance-based SVTs and embedded indices derived from conventional tests. The validity of self-report data is measured primarily by scales designed to detect symptom exaggeration or "faking bad." In adult populations, an extensive body of evidence supports each of these approaches, with a multitude of well-validated tests and techniques available (Boone, 2007; Larrabee, 2007). Research investigating the appropriateness and utility of SVT use in children is comparatively sparse, although pediatric normative data and independent studies exist for several stand-alone performance-based tests. Much less pediatric research has focused on embedded indicators and self-report validity scales.

Stand-Alone Performance-Based Symptom Validity Tests

Table 7.2 provides a brief description of all identified stand-alone SVTs that have at least some support for use in children. Table 7.3 provides strength of empirical evidence estimates for the tests and the approximate age at which studies suggest developmental effects may be minimal or no longer apparent. Of note, research into SVTs in children is less than a decade old. As might be expected for a burgeoning but still initial area of investigation, many of the existing studies are methodologically imperfect (Rohling, 2004). Thus, the current classification of the empirical support and suggested age ranges should be considered preliminary, noticeably weaker at present than the evidence supporting SVT use with adults.

Several SVTs have been investigated in only one identified pediatric study. Although these tests may have utility in children, the supporting work will only be reviewed briefly here because of the limited data available. Martin, Haut, Stainbrook, and Franzen (1995) described a study in which the Dot Counting Test (DCT; Lezak, 1983; Rey, 1941) and 21-Item Test (Iverson, 1998) were administered to 299 clinical patients aged 9 through 17 years. Children in the 9- to 11-year-old age group performed worse than the teenage groups, but by age 12 years, performance was at adult levels on both tests. Similar findings were obtained by Courtney, Dinkins, Allen, and Kuroski (2003) when they administered the Computerized Assessment of Response Bias (CARB; Allen, Conder, Green & Cox, 1997) to 111 mixed pediatric patients aged 6 to 17 years referred because of academic and/or neurobehavioral problems. CARB performance was found to correlate with both IQ and age. Children younger than age 10 years performed significantly worse than older children, but by age 11, performance was consistently at adult levels. Rienstra, Spaan, and Schmand (2010) recently examined performance on both the Amsterdam Short-Term Memory Test (ASTM; Schmand & Lindeboom, 2004) and the Word Completion Memory Test (WCMT; Hilsabeck & LeCompte, 1997) in a sample of 48 typically developing Dutch children aged 7 through 12 years. Ten percent of the children failed the ASTM (all of whom were younger than 9 years), and 35% failed the WCMT using cutoffs recommended for adults, with mean scores for both tests significantly lower than those found for healthy adults. Green, Flaro, Brockhaus, and Montijo (in press) describe data from Green's Nonverbal Medical Symptom Validity Test (NV-MSVT; Green, 2008) derived from 217 pediatric patients in Canada. The children were tested clinically and had a wide variety of medical, psychiatric, and developmental diagnoses.

TABLE 7.2. Description of Stand-Alone Symptom Validity Tests Investigated in Pediatric Populations

	Nature of Task	Examinee Response	Approximate Administration Time (min)	Description
Amsterdam Short-Term Memory Test (ASTM)	Word recognition	Oral	15	Examinee reads five stimulus words from a common semantic category (e.g., clothing) and is then asked to recognize three of the words in a forced-choice format
Computerized Assessment of Response Bias (CARB)	Number recognition	Computerized	15	Examinee presented with five-digit numbers and then asked to choose number in forced-choice format
Dot Counting Test (DCT)	Dot counting	Oral	10	Examinee counts the number of dots on six individually presented cards in both grouped and ungrouped formats
Fifteen-Item Test (FIT)	Letter, number, shape recall	Drawing	5	Examinee shown 15 items and asked to draw items from memory
Medical Symptom Validity Test (MSVT)	Word recognition	Computerized	5	Examinee shown a list of semantically related words and asked to choose words in forced-choice format
Nonverbal Medical Symptom Validity Test (NV-MSVT)	Object recognition	Computerized	5	Examinee shown pictures of common objects and asked to choose objects in forced-choice format
Test of Memory Malingering (TOMM)	Object recognition	Oral	15	Examinee shown pictures of common objects and asked to choose objects in forced-choice format
21-Item Test	Word recognition	Oral	5	Examinee reads a list of words and is then asked to freely recall and then recognize in forced-choice format
Word Completion Memory Test (WCMT)	Word stem completion	Written	25	Examinee copies and rates words read aloud for pleasantness and then completes word stems with words on and not on the list
Word Memory Test (WMT)	Word recognition	Computerized	15	Examinee is shown a list of semantically related words and is asked to choose words in forced-choice format

TABLE 7.3. Strength of Empirical Evidence Estimates for Stand-Alone Symptom Validity Tests Investigated in Pediatric Populations

| | Strength of Evidence for Use in Children | | | | Age Effects Minimal by |
	Community Samples	Clinical Samples	Secondary Gain Samples	Simulation Samples	
Amsterdam Short-Term Memory Test (ASTM)	+	—	—	—	≥ 10 years
Computerized Assessment of Response Bias (CARB)	—	+	—	—	≥ 11 years
Dot Counting Test (DCT)	—	+	—	—	≥ 12 years
Fifteen-Item Test (FIT)	+	+	—	—	≥ 11 or 12 years
Medical Symptom Validity Test (MSVT)	+	++	+	++	≥ 8 years or ≥ third grade reading level
Nonverbal Medical Symptom Validity Test (NV-MSVT)	—	+	—	—	≥ 7 years
Test of Memory Malingering (TOMM)	++	++	+	+	≥ 5 or 6 years
21-Item Test	–	+	–	–	≥ 12 years
Word Memory Test (WMT)	+	++	–	+	≥ 11 years or ≥ 3rd grade reading level

NOTE: ++, adequate evidence base; +, modest evidence base; —, no or conflicting evidence.

Ninety-one percent of the children passed the NV-MSVT effort subtests, with 4% of the patients who failed reportedly displaying an overall performance profile consistent with poor effort.

Several additional stand-alone SVTs have received more empirical attention in children including the Test of Memory Malingering (TOMM; Tombaugh, 1996), Green's Word Memory Test (WMT; Green, 2003, 2005), Green's Medical Symptom Validity Test (MSVT; Green, 2004), and the Rey Fifteen Item Test (FIT; Rey, 1964). These tests will be reviewed in detail later in this chapter. For heuristic value, discussion of the available empirical studies will be organized by the type of sample primarily studied: *(1)* community-based children, *(2)* clinical patients, *(3)* examinees seen in a secondary gain context, and *(4)* simulators. In actuality, many of the studies relied on mixed samples of convenience without well-specified inclusion and exclusionary criteria, so there may be known or unknown overlap in the types of patients included in each group.

TEST OF MEMORY MALINGERING

Description

The Test of Memory Malingering (TOMM) is a 50-item forced-choice visual recognition test designed by Tombaugh (1996) to detect individuals who exaggerate
or fake memory impairment. The test kit can be ordered from Multi-Health Systems (800-456-3003; http://www.mhs.com). The TOMM includes two learning
trials, two recognition trials, and an optional retention trial. On each learning trial,
the examinee is presented with 50 line drawings one at a time for 3 seconds.
Examinees are then asked to choose the correct drawing from a pair consisting of
the target and a foil, during the two recognition trials and after a 15-minute delay
during the optional retention trial. Examiner feedback regarding the correctness of
the response is provided after each item.

Normative Data

Tombaugh (1996) first investigated the TOMM in primarily adult samples of community-dwelling individuals and clinical patients. The community samples included
a small group of 16- and 17-year-olds, although the exact number of patients below
18 years was not reported. These studies suggested that individuals who provided
adequate effort earned perfect or near perfect scores on Trial 2, whereas those
instructed to feign impairment performed below the cutoff scores.

Empirical Studies

The TOMM has been investigated in child samples more than any other SVT.
Table 7.4 presents the mean scores, standard deviations, and percentage of children
performing above the recommended cutoff score available in published studies.
The first pediatric study to use the TOMM was conducted by Constantinou and
McCaffrey (2003) and included children aged 5 through 12 years, recruited from
general school populations in Cyprus ($n = 61$) and New York ($n = 67$). All children
in New York passed the TOMM using the recommended adult cutoffs and all but
two children from Cyprus passed. The nine children with significant medical or psychiatric disorders in both samples passed. TOMM performance was not influenced
by age, educational level, culture, or gender. Rienstra et al. (2010) also investigated
TOMM performance in their community sample of 48 Dutch children aged 7
through 12 years. All children passed the TOMM, with every child earning a perfect
score on Trial 2.

Several studies have also investigated TOMM performance in clinical populations. As mentioned, Donders (2005) evaluated TOMM performance in a sample
of mixed clinical patients aged 6 through 16 years. Performance was above adult
cutoffs for 97 of the children, with 2 patients who failed considered true positives
and 1 patient who failed considered a potential false positive. Performance on Trial 2
did not vary with gender, ethnicity, parental occupation, independent memory
test performance, or length of coma. Performance on Trial 2 covaried with age,
accounted for by slightly lower performance in the youngest children (6–8 years).
In another clinical study, MacAllister and colleagues (2009) investigated TOMM
performance in 60 patients with epilepsy aged 6 through 17 years. Fifty-four of the
children (90%) passed the TOMM, with two of the failures said to be accurately

TABLE 7.4. Test of Memory Malingering (TOMM) Mean Scores, Standard Deviations, and Percentage Passing in Pediatric Studies

Source	Population	N	Age Range	Mean Age (SD)	Trial 1 Mean (SD)	Trial 2 Mean (SD)	% Passing
Constantinou & McCaffrey (2003)	Cyprus community	61	5–12	8.4 (2.1)	46.8 (3.4)	49.5 (1.7)	97%
Constantinou & McCaffrey (2003)	U.S. community	67	5–12	7.9 (2.0)	45.9 (3.7)	49.9 (0.3)	100%
Rienstra et al. (2010)	Netherlands community	48	7–12	9.9 (1.6)	—	50.0 (0.0)	100%
Donders (2005)	U.S. clinical mixed–cases passing TOMM	97	6–16	11.9 (3.4)	46.5 (4.2)	49.7 (0.72)	97%[*]
MacAllister et al. (2009)	U.S. clinical epilepsy	60	6–17	~13.0 (~3.5)	43.5 (6.6)	47.5 (4.8)	90%
Gast & Hart (2010)	U.S. juvenile court system	107	12–17	15.4 (1.4)	46.7 (3.4)	49.7 (0.9)	99%
Chafetz (2008)	U.S. Social Security Disability applicants	80	6–16	10.8 (2.4)	38.2 (5.5)	40.6 (2.4)	72%[**]
Nagle et al. (2006)	U.S. simulation controls	17	6–12	~8.6 (~2.9)	—	49.7 (0.8)	100%
Blaskewitz et al. (2008)	Germany simulation controls	51	6–11	8.9 (1.0)	—	49.8 (0.9)	100%
Gunn et al. (2010)	Australia simulation controls	50	6–11	~8.7 (~1.8)	46.6 (3.2)	49.2 (1.3)	98%

[*]Based on the entire sample of 100 children.
[**]Based on the entire sample of 96 children administered the TOMM reported in Chafetz et al. (2007).

identifying suboptimal effort and four of the failures thought to be false positives. Estimated IQ varied widely (M = 86.2, SD = 20.2). Of the 11 patients with intellectual disability (ID), 7 passed the TOMM. The four patients who had IQ estimates below 50 passed the TOMM. In the entire sample, TOMM scores were unrelated to age, though there was a significant correlation between Trial 2 scores and IQ. Gast and Hart (2010) investigated TOMM performance in 107 males aged 12 through 17 years who were involved in the U.S. juvenile court system. Only one youth failed the TOMM. All 13 adolescents whose IQ fell in the range of ID passed.

Performance on Trial 1 and 2 did not covary with age, educational level, lifetime adjudications, or IQ.

Chafetz et al. (2007) is the only identified TOMM study focused on a sample with a clear external incentive to perform poorly. The TOMM was administered to 96 child claimants for U.S. Social Security Disability benefits. In this secondary gain context, failure rates were considerably higher than in other pediatric studies, with 28% of the sample performing below the actuarial cutoff and 23% scoring at chance levels or below.

Several studies have also investigated TOMM performance using simulation designs in which subjects are experimentally assigned to put forth optimal or suboptimal effort. Nagle, Everhart, Durham, McCammon, and Walker (2006) assigned 35 typically developing children aged 6 through 12 years to a group instructed to do their best or a group instructed to fake impairment from a brain injury. Consistent with expectations, the optimal effort group performed comparably to adults on Trial 2. Counter to hypotheses, all but one of the children instructed to feign also performed comparably to adults and no differently from the group told to do their best. Blaskewitz, Merten, and Kathmann (2008) also conducted a simulation study with 70 typically developing German children aged 6 to 11 years. One group ($n = 51$) was instructed to perform optimally and the other ($n = 19$) was told to make some mistakes but not to do everything wrong. All children in the control group passed the TOMM. In the experimental condition, 68% of the children were correctly identified by TOMM performance. Gunn, Batchelor, and Jones (2010) conducted another simulation study in a group of school children from Australia aged 6 through 11 years. Fifty of the children were assigned to the control condition and forty children were instructed to simulate memory impairment. One of the fifty children in the control group failed the TOMM. Thirty-eight of the forty children in the experimental malingering group were correctly identified, resulting in 95% sensitivity and 98% specificity.

Summary Comments

The TOMM has a number of strengths. The test stimuli consist of simple pictures of common objects, so they can be used with young and language-impaired children. The stimulus books are also small and easily transportable, allowing them to be used readily in a variety of inpatient and outpatient settings. More independent empirical work has focused on the TOMM than any other SVT and strongly suggests that it is appropriate for children 5 or 6 years old and older across a variety of settings, patient populations, and cultures. Though performance may be affected slightly by age or IQ, the vast majority of school-age children score above recommended adult cutoffs. The MacAllister et al. (2009) study indicates that caution is needed when interpreting failing scores for those with significant cognitive or neurological impairment, although, of note, many individuals with IQs in the range of ID have been found to perform above adult cutoffs on the TOMM. Drawbacks for the test include the length of administration time, as it can take at least 20 to 30 minutes to complete for children who are slow to respond. Though failure is likely to be highly specific in all but the most impaired children, questions about sensitivity are raised by both the Nagle et al. (2006) and Blaskewitz et al. (2008) simulation studies, not unlike findings from certain studies with adults (Green, 2007).

WORD MEMORY TEST

Description

Green's Word Memory Test (WMT) for Windows is a forced-choice verbal memory test that was designed to evaluate both effort and memory (Green, 2005). The test is available in approximately 10 different languages and can be ordered from its developer and publisher, Dr. Paul Green (866–463-6968; http://www.wordmemorytest. com). The WMT involves the computerized presentation of 20 semantically related word pairs (e.g., pig-bacon) over two trials. Examinees are then asked to choose the correct word from pairs consisting of the target and a foil, during Immediate Recognition (IR) and Delayed Recognition (DR) conditions. These scores, along with the consistency of response during IR and DR, comprise the effort indices. After each IR and DR response, examinees receive auditory and visual feedback. Examinees are then asked to recognize or recall the words during several additional subtests intended to measure verbal memory rather than effort, including a multiple-choice task, paired-associate subtest, a delayed free recall subtest, and another free recall subtest after a further delay. When a patient scores below the specified effort cutoffs, profile analysis is recommended. Such analysis is predicated on the idea that the primary effort subtests are easier than the other subtests intended to tap memory ability. Decision rules have been created to help examiners determine when a profile may suggest severe cognitive impairment, rather than poor effort, as described in a revision to the manual (Green, 2005) and in more recent publications (Green et al., in press; Green, Flaro, & Courtney, 2009).

Normative Data

As part of the development of the WMT, the test was administered by Dr. Lloyd Flaro to clinical pediatric patients from Canada who had a wide variety of medical, psychiatric, and developmental diagnoses. These data have been presented in several places, including the test manual, computer program, and select scientific publications (Green & Flaro, 2003; Green et al., in press; Green et al., 2009). As reported in Green et al. (in press), as of December 2008, 380 children with a third grade reading level or higher had been tested on the WMT. Of these patients, 10% failed using the recommended actuarial cutoffs and 5% failed displaying a profile consistent with what is seen in those who display suboptimal effort. Of the 38 children who were administered the WMT and had less than a third grade reading level, 26% failed.

Empirical Studies

Four identified studies have focused on the WMT: one involving typically developing children, two involving clinical populations, and one using a simulation design. Table 7.5 presents the mean WMT effort scores, standard deviations, and percentage of children performing above the recommended cutoff scores available in published studies.

Rienstra and colleagues (2010) investigated WMT performance in their sample of 48 typically developing Dutch children. When compared to the performance of healthy adults, the children's WMT scores were significantly lower, although all children passed using recommended adult cutoffs. Courtney, Dinkins, Allen, and Kuroski (2003) administered the WMT to their 111 mixed clinical pediatric patients.

TABLE 7.5. Mean Word Memory Test (WMT) Effort Scores, Standard Deviations, and Percentage Passing in Pediatric Studies

Source	Population	N	Age Range	Mean Age (SD)	IR % Mean (SD)	DR % Mean (SD)	CNS %	% Passing
Green et al. (in press)	Canada clinical mixed ≥ third grade reading level	380	—	13.4 (2.7)	95.9 (5.7)	95.9 (7.0)	93.8 (7.7)	89%
Courtney et al. (2003)	U.S. clinical mixed–younger group	55	6–9	8.5 (1.2)	Average effort scores 74.2 (18.8)			—
Courtney et al. (2003)	U.S. clinical mixed–older group	56	10–17	13.4 (2.0)	Average effort scores 93.4 (10.4)			—
Gunn et al. (2010)*	Australia simulation controls	50	6–11	~8.7 (~1.8)	90.6 (7.6)	95.3 (6.1)	—	98%

NOTE: *Oral version used.

No relation was found between IQ and performance on the effort subtests, whereas age was positively related to performance. Children younger than age 10 years were found to perform significantly worse on the WMT than older children. Once children reached age 11, performance was consistently at adult levels. Green and Flaro (2003) examined WMT performance in 135 Canadian children aged 7 to 18 years referred for clinical evaluation. Fourteen percent of the children failed the WMT, with evidence presented that at least some of these children likely failed because of fluctuations in effort rather than ability-based deficits. Performance was found to be unrelated to IQ. In contrast to the Courtney et al. study, Green and Flaro found WMT performance to be related to reading level rather than age. Those children with second grade reading level or below scored worse than the other children, but once children could read at a third grade level, their performance was comparable to adults, regardless of age.

The Gunn et al. (2010) simulation study included an oral version of the WMT administered to a group of school children from Australia. Age, IQ, and reading ability were not related to the DR trial. Oral vocabulary and reading did account for a small, significant amount of variance on the IR trial. One of the fifty children in the control group failed the WMT. Thirty-six of the forty children in the experimental malingering group were correctly identified, resulting in 90% sensitivity and 98% specificity for this oral version of the WMT.

Summary Comments

The WMT has a number of strengths, including an extensive literature in adults demonstrating its sensitivity and specificity. Administration, scoring, and data storage are automated and computerized, so they are particularly quick and easy. The availability of the stimuli in multiple languages is a plus. Normative data and empirical studies suggest that the vast majority of clinical patients who are older than age 10 years or who can read at a third grade level should be able to pass using adult cutoffs. Because the test requires reading and more administration time than certain other SVTs (e.g., MSVT), it can be expected to have less utility in younger or very impaired children or when testing time is limited. Though adult-based studies suggest that it is likely to be quite sensitive to poor effort, further independent work examining sensitivity in child samples will be necessary. Additional independent work is also necessary to examine specificity in pediatric patients who have significant learning, attentional, and neurological impairment. The proposed profile analysis is unique among SVTs and could be a clear added benefit in allowing examiners to differentiate failure resulting from true impairment from that resulting from noncredible effort; further study will be required to establish the classification accuracy of such analysis in child samples.

MEDICAL SYMPTOM VALIDITY TEST

Description
Green's Medical Symptom Validity Test (MSVT) for Windows is a forced-choice verbal memory test that was designed to evaluate effort and memory in both adults and children (Green, 2004). The test is available in approximately 10 languages and can be ordered from its developer and publisher, Dr. Paul Green (866-463-6968; http://www.wordmemorytest.com). It is similar in design to the WMT but shorter and easier, taking only about 5 minutes to administer. It involves the computerized presentation of 10 semantically related word pairs (e.g., school-book) over two trials. Examinees are then asked to choose the correct word from pairs consisting of the target and a foil, during Immediate Recognition (IR) and Delayed Recognition (DR) conditions. After each response, examinees receive auditory and visual feedback. Examinees are then asked to recall the words during paired associate (PA) and free recall (FR) conditions. The primary effort indices are IR, DR, and consistency of response (CNS) during these subtests. Like the WMT, when a patient scores below the specified cutoffs on the MSVT, profile analysis is recommended, with decision rules available designed to help identify severe neurological impairment, rather than noncredible effort (Green et al., in press; Green et al., 2009).

Normative Data
As part of the development of the MSVT, the test was administered by colleagues of the publisher who work with children. These data have been presented in several places, including the test manual, computer program, and select scientific publications (Green et al., in press; Green et al., 2009). The two primary datasets are from Dr. Lloyd Flaro and Dr. John Courtney. Dr. Flaro administered the MSVT to 55 healthy Canadian children without psychiatric or neurological illness aged 8 through 11 years (and one 7-year-old). Out of the 55 children, 53 passed the easy MSVT subtests, with no age/grade effect found on the primary effort subtests. Dr. Courtney's data are from 82 healthy Brazilian children asked to do their best and 27 healthy Brazilian children asked to simulate memory impairment. In the children

asked to try their best, 80 out of 82 cases passed the effort subtests. All 27 simulators failed the effort subtests. Dr. Flaro has also administered the MSVT to clinical pediatric patients with a wide variety of medical, psychiatric, and developmental diagnoses. As reported in Green et al. (in press), as of December 2008, 265 children with a third grade reading level or higher had been administered the MSVT. Of these patients, 5% failed using the recommended actuarial cutoffs and 3% failed with a poor effort profile. Of the 46 children who were administered the MSVT and had less than a third grade reading level, 19.5% failed the MSVT.

Empirical Studies

Four identified pediatric studies have focused on the MSVT: two with clinical populations, one in a secondary gain context, and one using a simulation design. Table 7.6 presents the mean MSVT effort scores, standard deviations, and percentage

TABLE 7.6. Mean Medical Symptom Validity Test (MSVT) Effort Scores, Standard Deviations, and Percentage Passing in Pediatric Studies

Source	Population	N	Age Range	Mean Age (SD)	IR % Mean (SD)	DR % Mean (SD)	CNS % Mean (SD)	% Passing
Green et al. (2009)	Canada community	56	7–11	9.2 (1.7)	98.6 (3.8)	98.6 (3.0)	97.6 (5.4)	96%
Green et al. (2009)	Brazil community young	36	6–10	8.7 (1.4)	95 (5)	99 (3)	94 (8)	98%
Green et al. (2009)	Brazil community old	34	11–15	12.4 (1.3)	96 (4)	100 (2)	96 (4)	
Green et al. (in press)	Canada clinical mixed ≥ third grade reading level	265	—	13.6 (2.9)	98.8 (3.7)	98.0 (4.3)	97.3 (5.8)	95%
Carone (2008)	U.S. clinical mixed	38	—	11.8 (3.1)	98.6 (3.7)	97.6 (6.3)	96.7 (9.0)	95%
Kirkwood & Kirk (2010)	U.S. clinical mild TBI	193	8–17	14.5 (2.4)	95.5 (5.3)	93.6 (5.4)	93.9 (4.8)	83%
Chafetz (2008)	U.S. Social Security Disability applicants	25	6–16	11.36 (2.6)	86.4 (8.0)	84.2 (9.9)	87.8 (9.1)	63%*
Blaskewitz et al. (2008)	Germany simulation controls	51	6–11	8.9 (1.0)	98.6 (2.5)	99.6 (1.2)	98.2 (3.6)	98%

NOTE: *Based on the entire sample of 27 children administered the MSVT reported in Chafetz et al. (2007). TBI = traumatic brain injury.

of children performing above the recommended cutoff scores available in published studies.

The Carone (2008) study compared performance of 38 children with moderate/severe TBI or other significant neurological or developmental problems with 67 adults who had sustained a mild TBI. Whereas only 5% of the children failed the MSVT, 21% of the adults did. The two children who failed the MSVT were deemed to be accurately identified as exerting noncredible effort. The Kirkwood and Kirk (2010) study also investigated MSVT performance in a clinical sample of 193 mild TBI pediatric patients. Seventeen percent of the sample failed the MSVT. Three patients who failed did not display other evidence of suboptimal effort and so were considered possible false positives. There were also three possible false negatives, in which the MSVT was passed but the patient was determined to be putting forth noncredible effort during other aspects of the exam.

The Chafetz et al. (2007) study that focused on individuals seeking Social Security Disability compensation is the only identified study with the MSVT that has included a sample with a clear incentive to perform poorly. The authors administered the MSVT to 27 children under a nonstandardized administration procedure (i.e., the examiner read the directions and the stimuli to the claimants as they were presented on the computer screen, instead of allowing the examinees to read on their own). Thirty-seven percent of the children failed the MSVT based on recommended cutoffs, with 19% scoring at chance levels or below.

The Blaskewitz et al. (2008) study with 70 typically developing German children was the only independent simulation study to include the MSVT. All but one child in the control group instructed to give good effort passed the MSVT. The one child who failed was in second grade and scored right at the recommended cutoff for poor effort. In the experimental suboptimal condition, 90% of the children were correctly identified by the MSVT, better than the 68% identified by the TOMM.

Summary Comments

One of the MSVT's clear strengths is its brief administration time, which makes it an ideal screening test for suboptimal effort. Like the WMT, administration, scoring, and data storage are automated and computerized, so they are particularly quick and easy. The availability of the stimuli in multiple languages is a plus as well. Normative data and a growing body of independent work suggest that the vast majority of children who can read at a third grade level or higher can pass using adult cutoffs. The Blaskewitz et al. (2008) study also suggests that the test may be more sensitive than the TOMM in the detection of poor effort. Because it requires reading, it will generally be inappropriate for children in the earliest of school years or who are very impaired. Further independent research is also necessary to examine sensitivity compared with other well-validated measures and to examine specificity in pediatric patients with significant learning, attentional, and neurological impairment. As is the case for the WMT, the proposed profile analysis could be a clear added benefit in allowing examiners to differentiate failure resulting from true impairment from that resulting from poor effort; further work will be required to establish the classification utility of such analysis in children.

Rey Fifteen-Item Test

Description

The Fifteen-Item Test (FIT) was developed originally by Rey (1964) to detect memory feigning and has since been adapted by a number of authors (e.g., Boone, Salazar, Lu, Warner-Chacon, & Razani, 2002; Lezak, 1983). The test is not copyrighted and can be created simply from available descriptions (e.g., Strauss, Sherman, & Spreen, 2006). It consists of 15 items that are arranged in three columns by five rows, which examinees are shown for 10 seconds before being asked to draw the items from memory. Because of item redundancy (e.g., ABC, abc), the examinee needs to recall only a few ideas rather than 15 independent items.

Normative Data

No child normative data were provided originally.

Empirical Studies

Three pediatric studies have included administration of the FIT: one with typically developing children, one with a clinical population, and one using a simulation design. Table 7.7 presents the mean FIT scores, standard deviations, and percentage of children performing above the recommended cutoff score available in published studies.

In the Constantinou and McCaffrey (2003) study described previously, the authors administered the FIT along with the TOMM to community child samples from Cyprus and New York. Performance on the FIT at both sites correlated significantly with age and educational level. Above about age 10 years, performance was nearly errorless, though the sample sizes in the older age range were quite small. In a study with a diverse clinical population, Martin and colleagues (1995) administered a modified FIT to 299 mixed pediatric patients. Children in the 9- to 11-year-old age group performed worse than the teenage groups, but by age 12 years, performance was said to rise to adult levels. The FIT has also been used in one study with simulators. In the Blaskewitz et al. (2008) simulation study, the FIT was administered to 70 typically developing German children. No child in the entire control group scored below the established cutoffs for adults. In the experimental

TABLE 7.7. Mean Rey Fifteen Item Test (FIT) Scores, Standard Deviations, and Percentage Passing in Pediatric Studies

Source	Population	N	Age Range	Mean Age (SD)	Test Mean (SD)	% Passing
Constantinou & McCaffrey (2003)	Cyprus community	61	5–12	8.4 (2.1)	10.8 (4.7)	—
Constantinou & McCaffrey (2003)	U.S. community	67	5–12	7.9 (2.0)	10.8 (4.3)	—
Blaskewitz et al. (2008)	Germany simulation controls	51	6–11	8.9 (1.0)	12.6 (2.2)	100%

suboptimal effort condition, only 10% of the children failed the FIT, suggesting very low sensitivity.

Summary Comments

The FIT has been historically one of the most frequently used SVTs by neuropsychologists, presumably because of its ease of administration and minimal cost. Nonetheless, in adults, it appears to be sensitive to genuine cognitive dysfunction and fairly insensitive to malingering (Strauss, Sherman, & Spreen, 2006). Similarly, extant studies in children suggest that it needs to be used with caution by pediatric practitioners, because performance appears correlated significantly with age below about age 11 or 12 years. Although it may be appropriate to use with older children, the Blaskewitz et al. (2008) data suggest that traditional cutoff scores may be rather insensitive to feigning.

Embedded Indicators

The value of embedded indices to detect negative response bias is well established in adult populations, as they are time efficient, resistant to coaching, and allow for more continuous monitoring of effort than stand-alone SVTs. In contrast to the rapidly growing body of literature focused on stand-alone measures in children, only a modest amount of work has focused on the utility of embedded indices in pediatric populations.

Digit Span performance from the Wechsler instruments is one of the most thoroughly investigated of all embedded indicators in adults and includes examination of raw scores, age-corrected scale scores (ACSS), and a variety of derived scores. The most popular of the derived scores is the Reliable Digit Span (RDS), introduced by Greiffenstein, Baker, and Gola (1994). RDS is calculated by summing the longest string of digits repeated without error over two trials under both forward and backward conditions. Two identified pediatric studies have examined RDS as an indicator of noncredible effort. In the previously discussed Blaskewitz et al. (2008) simulation study with German children, 90% of the children in the feigning condition were identified using adult RDS cutoffs; however, 59% of the matched controls performed below this cutoff as well, supporting the sensible idea that RDS cutoffs for adults are unlikely to be appropriate for young children. Unfortunately, the authors did not publish the classification statistics for lower RDS cutoff scores or for other Digit Span scores.

In recent analyses using an updated version of the mild TBI dataset described in Kirkwood and Kirk (2010), we examined the sensitivity and specificity of both RDS and ACSS in the detection of noncredible effort. The sample consisted of 274 mild TBI clinical patients aged 8 through 16 years (Kirkwood, Hargrave, & Kirk, 2011). Fourteen percent of the sample failed both the MSVT and TOMM, which was used as the criterion for poor effort. An RDS ≤ 7 cutoff had an unacceptably high false-positive rate (31%). However, an RDS cutoff of ≤ 6 resulted in 51% sensitivity and 92% specificity, comparable to the classification statistics from many adult RDS studies. An ACSS cutoff of ≤ 5 also resulted in sensitivity of 51%, with even better specificity at 96%. The findings suggest that scores from Wechsler Digit Span may be only moderately sensitive, but that they are likely to have utility in identifying subop-timal effort in older children and adolescents, at least in those who are relatively high functioning.

McKinzey, Prieler, and Raven (2003) examined the value of the Raven's Standard Progressive Matrices in detecting feigned impairment. They administered the test under standard instructions to 44 typically developing Austrian children aged 7 through 17 years. The participants were then asked to take the test again, instructed the second time to do as badly on the test as possible without being detected. Using a formula developed originally for adults to detect suboptimal effort resulted in a false-positive rate of 7% but an unacceptably high false-negative rate of 64%. The authors subsequently used item difficulty analyses to create a three-item scale using a floor effect strategy, with the modified formula resulting in 95% sensitivity and 95% specificity.

The most sophisticated pediatric work focused on embedded indices comes from Chafetz and colleagues (Chafetz, 2008; Chafetz et al., 2007). In the context of conducting psychological consultative examinations with adult and child claimants for U.S. Social Security Disability benefits, Chafetz developed a rating scale that relied on data collected routinely as part of the exam. The rating scale is now referred to as the Symptom Validity Scale (SVS) for Low Functioning Individuals. The item content and scoring instructions are shown in Table 7.8 with permission of the author (M. Chafetz, personal communication, August 29, 2010). The scale has been validated against the TOMM and MSVT (Chafetz, 2008; Chafetz et al., 2007), with reasonable classification statistics found for different cutoff scores across a variety of effort levels (e.g., below chance and below actuarial criteria for the respective SVT).

Self-Report Validity Indices

In adult neuropsychological populations, a number of self-report instruments have demonstrated good value in detecting symptom feigning or exaggeration across multiple domains. The Minnesota Multiphasic Personality Inventory-2 (MMPI-2) has garnered the bulk of the investigative attention and has strong support in not only identifying individuals who exaggerate psychiatric symptoms but also those who feign or exaggerate cognitive, health, and injury-related concerns (Larrabee, 2007).

Numerous pediatric self-report instruments include validity scales designed to detect symptom exaggeration. Commonly used measures in pediatric neurop-sychological evaluations that contain a "fake bad" scale include general personal-ity instruments such as the MMPI-Adolescent (Infrequency Scale), Personality Inventory for Youth (PIY; Dissimulation Scale), and Behavior Assessment Sys-tem for Children-Second Edition (BASC-2; F Index), as well as domain and disorder specific scales such as the Behavior Rating Inventory of Executive Function–Self-Report (Negativity Scale) and Trauma Symptom Checklist for Children (Hyperresponse Scale). Each of these scales has solid normative data and at least adequate psychometric properties. However, to date, very little research has focused on the utility of the validity indices in particular.

TABLE 7.8. Chafetz's Symptom Validity Scale (SVS) for Low-Functioning Individuals

1. Three simple arithmetic (one each)	0	1	2	3
2. Three simple sequences (one each)	0	1	2	3
3. Does not know president/picks wrong one from list	0	1	2	
4. Misses personal information (age, birthday)	0	1	2	
5. Ganser-like answers (0, 2, 3, >3)	0	1	2	3
6. WISC/WAIS–misses items before start	0	1	2	3
7. WISC/WAIS–Low Average Scaled Scores (>2, 1, 0)	0	1	2	
8. WISC/WAIS–Reliable Digit Span (<7, <6)	0	1	2	
9. WISC/WAIS–Coding (0, 2, >2 errors)	0	1	2	
10. Any highly improbable response (e.g., ball = triangle)	0		2	
11. Claims improbable pathology (e.g., seeing ghosts)	0		2	

NOTES: Instructions for scoring: *(1)* Score a point for each arithmetic item missed (Mental Status [MS] exam); *(2)* One point for each sequence missed (MS exam); *(3)* One point for not knowing current U.S. President; two points for missing from list (MS exam); *(4)* One point for misstating a personal item; two for a second misstatement (MS exam); *(5)* One point for at least two Ganser-like answers; 2 points for three answers; 3 points for more (MS and Wechsler); *(6)* A point for each subtest in which an item (or more) is missed before the start point (up to three subtests) (Wechsler); *(7)* If have at least two Low Average scaled scores on Wechsler (Scaled Score = 6+), score is 0; one Low Average score = 1 point; none = 2 points; *(8)* Reliable Digit Span score <7 = 1 point; <6 = 2 points; *(9)* two coding errors = 1 point; >2 errors = 2 points; *(10)* and *(11)* can occur anywhere in the exam. There may also be some overlap where answers count toward multiple ratings (e.g., stating there are "11" months in a year gives a point for #6 and 2 points on #10 and counts toward a Ganser-like error; stating that 3 + 4 = "53" gives a point on #1 and 2 points on #10).

SOURCE: Adapted from Chafetz et al. (2007).

A few studies have provided initial support for the MMPI-A in identifying feigned psychopathology (Baer, Kroll, Rinaldo, & Ballenger, 1999; Lucio, Duran, Graham, & Ben-Porath, 2002; Rogers, Hinds, Sewell, 1996; Stein, Graham, & Williams, 1995). One study also provided support for the PIY Dissimulation Scale in identifying feigned emotional distress and psychosis (Wrobel, Lachar, Wrobel, Morgan, & Gruber, 1999). All of these studies have focused on simulators, so the value of the scales to detect negative response bias in real-world patients remains largely unknown. Moreover, none of the studies were conducted with individuals presenting for neuropsychological evaluation, so their applicability to patients who may be more likely to present with exaggerated physical or cognitive complaints than psychiatric problems is uncertain.

In a recent project using an updated version of the mild TBI dataset described in Kirkwood and Kirk (2010), we examined the base rate of "fake bad" elevations in real-world pediatric patients administered the BASC-2 Self-Report of Personality and the MSVT during a neuropsychological evaluation. The sample consisted of 274 mild TBI patients aged 8 through 17 years (Kirk, Kirkwood, & Hutaff-Lee, 2010).

Only 7 of the 274 patients (2.5%) fell in the "Caution" or "Extreme Caution" range on the BASC-2 F Index. Of the 50 patients who failed the MSVT, only 3 were identified by the F Index. One additional patient who failed the MSVT was identified by the Response Pattern Index. Though further analysis will be required, these data suggest that sole reliance on the BASC-2 self-report validity indices may substantially underestimate the number of children who display noncredible presentations following TBI. Very little overlap in this sample was found between patients identified by the self-report validity indices and patients failing a performance-based SVT, which contrasts with findings from a number of adult validity scales (e.g., MMPI-2 Fake Bad Scale; Strauss, Sherman, & Spreen, 2006).

CONCLUSION AND FUTURE RESEARCH DIRECTIONS

That children feign, exaggerate, or exert suboptimal effort at times is probably unsurprising to most pediatric professionals, but that they do so during neuropsychological exam has been given relatively limited scientific attention over the years. One possible reason for this lack of attention is that noncredible presentations in children might occur only very rarely, so that there are simply few cases to draw from. On the other hand, as has been suggested previously (Lu & Boone, 2002), the sparse literature could also reflect a failure by pediatric neuropsychologists to systematically examine negative response bias in their evaluations and/or an inadequacy of the methods that have been used historically. The work reviewed here suggests that noncredible effort is apt to occur more frequently than previously recognized, even if it occurs less often than in comparable adult samples. Based on research with adult populations and existing pediatric work, it would seem that certain conditions (e.g., mild TBI) and circumstances (e.g., financial incentive) serve to increase the risk of children displaying negative response bias, though this will require further empirical study to confirm.

At this point, the number of SVTs that have demonstrated utility in children pales in comparison to those available to the adult practitioner. Even so, pediatric neuropsychologists now have sufficient data to support the use of several stand-alone SVTs with school-age children, including the TOMM, WMT, and MSVT. Of course, performance on any SVT depends in part on the particular demands of the task and can vary for a multitude of reasons, including true cognitive impairment and temporary fluctuations in arousal, attention, emotional state, and effort. Determining whether a child is responding more broadly in a biased fashion not only requires careful examination of SVT performance but also a solid understanding of the natural history of the presenting condition; scrutiny of the child's developmental, medical, educational, and environmental background; and thorough consideration of the consistency and neuropsychological plausibility of the behavioral, self-report, and test data.

The motivation to feign or exaggerate is typically complex and can include both conscious and unconscious processes and attempts to obtain external incentives and/or to fulfill internal psychological needs (Boone, 2007). In children, the motivations underlying noncredible performance are apt to be quite diverse, even in clinical populations (Kirkwood, Kirk, Blaha, & Wilson, 2010). In forensic settings, motivations are likely to be even more challenging to discern, with some children likely feigning in an attempt to seek indirect approval or attention from family members and others acting more directly to achieve an external incentive, either on their own accord or after explicit coaching. Regardless of whether a practitioner fully appreciates why a child fails an SVT, such performance should raise questions about the reliability and validity of all collected data, particularly if there is not a reasonable explanation for the results (e.g., well-documented genuine impairment). Although more work will be required to understand the implications of SVT failure in children, one pediatric study (Kirkwood, Yeates, Randolph, & Kirk, 2011) and multiple adult studies (Constantinou, Bauer, Ashendorf, Fisher, & McCaffrey, 2005; Green, Rohling, Lees-Haley, & Allen, 2001; Lange, Iverson, Brooks, & Rennison, 2010) suggest that poor performance on even a single SVT is associated with a significant decrement in scores across multiple neuropsychological domains.

Future work is also needed to demonstrate the base rate of pediatric suboptimal effort and SVT classification statistics across child samples ranging more widely in ability level, presenting condition, and evaluative context. The introduction of new developmentally grounded SVTs is also in order, to establish a more complete armamentarium of child-specific measures similar to that which is available to adult providers. To supplement the information gleaned from stand-alone SVTs, investigators will also need to focus on demonstrating the worth of intrinsic indices that can be derived from conventional ability tests, as "effort" is a continuous variable that should ideally be monitored repeatedly throughout a pediatric evaluation, not just at one or two distinct time points. Finally, as the focus of research to date has been on suboptimal cognitive effort almost exclusively, a separate line of study needs to focus on validating pediatric methods to detect exaggerated psychiatric and health-related symptoms in neuropsychological patients, to more fully capture the multifaceted nature of biased responding. Tools to evaluate the credibility of self-report data will be especially valuable when assessing patients with disorders in which subjective symptoms play a defining role in the diagnostic process, such as mild TBI and ADHD.

REFERENCES

Allen, L. M., Conder, R. L., Green, P., & Cox, D. R. (1997). *Manual for the Computerized Assessment of Response Bias.* Durham, NC: CogniSyst, Inc.

Baer, R. A., Kroll, L. S., Rinaldo, J., & Ballenger, J. (1999). Detecting and discriminating between random responding and over-reporting on the MMPI-A. *Journal of Personality Assessment, 72,* 308–320.

Blaskewitz, N., Merten, T., & Kathmann, N. (2008). Performance of children on symptom validity tests: TOMM, MSVT, and FIT. *Archives of Clinical Neuropsychology, 23,* 379–391.

Boone, K. B. (2007). *Assessment of feigned cognitive impairment: A neuropsychological perspective.* New York: The Guilford Press.

Boone, K. B., Salazar, X., Lu, P., Warner-Chacon, K., & Razani, J. (2002). The Rey 15-Item Recognition Trial: A technique to enhance sensitivity of the Rey 15-Item Memorization Test. *Journal of Clinical and Experimental Neuropsychology, 24,* 561–573.

Bush, S. S., Ruff, R. M., Tröster, A. I., Barth, J. T., Koffler, S. P., Pliskin, N. H., . . . Silver, C. H. (2005). Symptom validity assessment: practice issues and medical necessity NAN policy & planning committee. *Archives of Clinical Neuropsychology, 20,* 419–426.

Carone, D. A. (2008). Children with moderate/severe brain damage/dysfunction out-perform adults with mild-to-no brain damage on the Medical Symptom Validity Test. *Brain Injury, 22,* 960–971.

Cassar, J. R., Hales, E. S., Longhurst, J. G., & Weiss, G. S. (1996). Can disability benefits make children sicker? *Journal of the American Academy of Child & Adolescent Psychiatry, 35,* 701–702.

Chafetz, M. D. (2008). Malingering on the Social Security disability consultative exam: Predictors and base rates. *The Clinical Neuropsychologist, 22,* 529–546.

Chafetz, M. D., Abrahams, J. P., & Kohlmaier, J. (2007). Malingering on the Social Security disability consultative exam: A new rating scale. *Archives of Clinical Neuropsychology, 22,* 1–14.

Clarridge, C. (2007, May 17). Mother gets 3 years for faking kids' disabilities. *The Seattle Times.* Retrieved July 11, 2010, from http://seattletimes.nwsource.com/html/localnews/2003711379_webfraud17m.html.

Constantinou, M., Bauer, L., Ashendorf, L., Fisher, J. M., & McCaffrey, R. J. (2005). Is poor performance on recognition memory effort measures indicative of generalized poor performance on neuropsychological tests? *Archives of Clinical Neuropsychology, 20,* 191–198.

Constantinou, M., & McCaffrey, R. J. (2003). Using the TOMM for evaluating children's effort to perform optimally on neuropsychological measures. *Child Neuropsychology, 9,* 81–90.

Conti, R. P. (2004). Malingered ADHD in adolescents diagnosed with conduct disorder: A brief note. *Psychological Reports, 94,* 987–988.

Courtney, J. C., Dinkins, J. P., Allen, L. M., 3rd, & Kuroski, K. (2003). Age related effects in children taking the Computerized Assessment of Response Bias and Word Memory Test. *Child Neuropsychology, 9,* 109–116.

Croft, R. D., & Jervis, M. (1989). Munchausen's syndrome in a 4 year old. *Archives of Disease in Childhood, 64,* 740–741.

Donders, J. (2005). Performance on the Test of Memory Malingering in a mixed pediatric sample. *Child Neuropsychology, 11,* 221–227.

Faust, D., Hart, K., & Guilmette, T. J. (1988). Pediatric malingering: The capacity of children to fake believable deficits on neuropsychological testing. *Journal of Consulting and Clinical Psychology, 56,* 578–582.

Faust, D., Hart, K. J., Guilmette, T. J., & Arkes, H. R. (1988). Neuropsychologists' capacity to detect adolescent malingerers. *Professional Psychology: Research and Practice, 19,* 508–515.

Flaro, L., & Boone, K. (2009). Using objective effort measures to detect noncredible cognitive test performance in children and adolescents. In J. E. Morgan & J. J. Sweet (Eds.), *Neuropsychology of malingering casebook* (pp. 369–376). New York: Psychology Press.

Flaro, L., Green. P., & Blaskewitz, N. (2007). Die bedeutung der beschwerdenvalidierung im kindesalter. [The importance of symptom validity testing in children: WMT & MSVT]. *Praxis der Rechtspsychologie, 17,* 125–139.

Gast, J., & Hart, K. J. (2010). The performance of juvenile offenders on the Test of Memory Malingering. *Journal of Forensic Psychology Practice, 10,* 53–68.

Green, P. (2003, revised 2005). *Manual for the Word Memory Test.* Edmonton, AB: Green's Publishing.

Green, P. (2004). *Manual for the Medical Symptom Validity Test*. Edmonton, AB: Green's Publishing.

Green, P. (2007). Spoiled for choice: Making comparisons between forced-choice effort tests. In K. B. Boone (Ed.), *Assessment of feigned cognitive impairment* (pp. 50–77). New York: The Guilford Press.

Green, P. (2008). *Manual for the Nonverbal Medical Symptom Validity Test*. Edmonton, AB: Green's Publishing.

Green, P., & Flaro, L. (2003). Word Memory Test performance in children. *Child Neuropsychology, 9*, 189–207.

Green, P., Flaro, L., Brockhaus, R., & Montijo, J. (in press). Performance on the WMT, MSVT, & NV-MSVT in children with developmental disabilities and in adults with mild traumatic brain injury. In C. R. Reynolds & A. Horton (Eds.), *Detection of malingering during head injury litigation* (2nd ed.). New York: Plenum Press.

Green, P., Flaro, L., & Courtney, J. (2009). Examining false positives on the Word Memory Test in adults with mild traumatic brain injury. *Brain Injury, 23*, 741–50.

Green, P., Rohling, M., Lees-Haley, P., & Allen, L. M. (2001). Effort has a greater effect on test scores than severe brain injury in compensation claimants. *Brain Injury, 15*, 1045–1060.

Greenfield, D. (1987). Feigned psychosis in a 14-year-old girl. *Hospital and Community Psychiatry, 38*, 73–75.

Greiffenstein, M. F., Baker, W. J., & Gola, T. (1994). Validation of malingered amnesia measures with a large clinical sample. *Psychological Assessment, 6*, 218–224.

Gunn, D., Batchelor, J., & Jones, M. (2010). Detection of simulated memory impairment in 6- to 11-year-old children. *Child Neuropsychology, 16*, 105–118.

Heilbronner, R. L., Sweet, J. J., Morgan, J. E., Larrabee, G. J., & Millis, S. R. (2009). American Academy of Clinical Neuropsychology Consensus Conference Statement on the neuropsychological assessment of effort, response bias, and malingering. *The Clinical Neuropsychologist, 23*, 1093–1129.

Henry, G. K. (2005). Childhood malingering: Faking neuropsychological impairment in an 8-year-old. In R. L. Heilbronner (Ed.), *Forensic neuropsychology casebook* (pp. 205–217). New York: The Guilford Press.

Heubrock, D. (2001). Munchhausen by proxy syndrome in clinical child neuropsychology: A case presenting with neuropsychological symptoms. *Child Neuropsychology, 7*, 273–285.

Hilsabeck, R. C., & LeCompte, D. C. (1997). *Word Completion Memory Test (WCMT)*. Durham, NC: CogniSyst, Inc.

Iverson, G. L. (1998). *21-Item Test research manual*. Vancouver, BC: Author.

Johnson, E. A. (1997). Children's understanding of epistemic conduct in self-deception and other false beliefs stories. *Child Development, 68*, 1117–1132.

Kirk, J. W., Kirkwood, M. W., & Hutaff-Lee, C. F. (2010). Utility of the Self-Report Behavior Assessment System for Children, Second Edition validity indicators in identifying suboptimal effort after pediatric mild traumatic brain injury [Abstract]. *The Clinical Neuropsychologist, 4*, 627.

Kirkwood, M. W., Hargrave, D., & Kirk, J. W. (2011). The value of the WISC-IV Digit Span subtest in detecting noncredible performance during pediatric neuropsychological exam. *Archives of Clinical Neuropsychology, 26*, 377–384.

Kirkwood, M. W., & Kirk, J. W. (2010). The base rate of suboptimal effort in a pediatric mild TBI sample: Performance on the Medical Symptom Validity Test. *The Clinical Neuropsychologist, 24*, 860–872.

Kirkwood, M. W., Kirk, J. W., Blaha, R. Z., & Wilson, P. E. (2010). Noncredible effort during pediatric neuropsychological exam: A case series and literature review. *Child Neuropsychology, 16,* 604–618.

Kirkwood, M. W., Yeates, K. O., Randolph, C., & Kirk, J. W. (2011). The implications of symptom validity test failure for ability-based test performance in a pediatric sample. *Psychological Assessment.* Advance online publication. doi: 10.1037/a0024628.

Kozlowska, K., Nunn, K. P., Rose, D., Morris, A., Ouvrier, R. A., & Varghese, J. (2007). Conversion disorder in Australian pediatric practice. *Journal of the American Academy of Child and Adolescent Psychiatry, 46,* 68–75.

Kutluay, E., Selwa, L., Minecan, D., Edwards, J., & Beydoun, A. (2010). Nonepileptic paroxysmal events in a pediatric population. *Epilepsy and Behavior, 17,* 272–275.

Lange, R. T., Iverson, G. L., Brooks, B. L., & Rennison, L. A. (2010). Influence of poor effort on self-reported symptoms and neurocognitive test performance following mild traumatic brain injury. *Journal of Clinical and Experimental Neuropsychology, 32,* 961–972.

Larrabee, G. J. (2007). *Assessment of malingered neuropsychological deficits.* New York: Oxford University Press.

Lezak, M. D. (1983). *Neuropsychological assessment.* New York: Oxford University Press.

Libow, J. A. (2000). Child and adolescent illness falsification. *Pediatrics, 105,* 336–342.

Lieb, R., Pfister, H., Mastaler, M., & Wittchen, H. U. (2000). Somatoform syndrome and disorders in a representative population sample of adolescents and young adults: Prevalence, comorbidity and impairments. *Acta Psychiatrica Scandinavica, 101,* 194–208.

Lu, P. H., & Boone, K. B. (2002). Suspect cognitive symptoms in a 9-year-old child: malingering by proxy? *Clinical Neuropsychology, 16,* 90–96.

Lucio, E., Duran, C., Graham, J. R., & Ben-Porath, Y. S. (2002). Identifying faking bad on the Minnesota Multiphasic Personality Inventory-Adolescent with Mexican adolescents. *Assessment, 9,* 62–69.

MacAllister, W. S., Nakhutina, L., Bender, H. A., Karantzoulis, S., & Carlson, C. (2009). Assessing effort during neuropsychological evaluation with the TOMM in children and adolescents with epilepsy. *Child Neuropsychology, 15,* 521–531.

Martin, R. C., Haut, J. S., Stainbrook, T., & Franzen, M. D. (1995). Preliminary normative data for objective measures to detect malingered neuropsychological deficits in a population of adolescent patients [Abstract]. *Archives of Clinical Neuropsychology, 10,* 364–365.

McCaffrey, R. J., & Lynch, J. K. (2009). Malingering following documented brain injury: Neuropsychological evaluation of children in a forensic setting. In J. E. Morgan & J. J. Sweet (Eds.), *Neuropsychology of malingering casebook* (pp. 377–385). New York: Psychology Press.

McKinzey, R. K., Prieler, J., & Raven, J. (2003). Detection of children's malingering on Raven's Standard Progressive Matrices. *British Journal of Clinical Psychology, 42,* 95–99.

Nagle, A. M., Everhart, D. E., Durham, T. W., McCammon, S. L., & Walker, M. (2006). Deception strategies in children: Examination of forced choice recognition and verbal learning and memory techniques. *Archives of Clinical Neuropsychology, 21,* 777–785.

Newton, P., Reddy, V., & Bull, R. (2000). Children's everyday deception and performance on false-belief tasks. *British Journal of Developmental Psychology, 18,* 297–317.

Offord, D. R., Boyle, B. H., Szatmari, P., Rae-Grant, N. L., Links, P. S., Cadman, D. T., . . . Byrne, C. (1987). Ontario child health study II. Six-month prevalence of disorder and rates of service utilization. *Archives of General Psychiatry, 44,* 833–836.

Peebles, R., Sabella, C., Franco, K., & Goldfarb, J. (2005). Factitious disorder and malingering in adolescent girls: Case series and literature review. *Clinical Pediatrics, 44,* 237–243.

Polak, A., & Harris, P. L. (1999). Deception by young children following noncompliance. *Developmental Psychology, 35*, 561–568.

Rey, A. (1941). L' examen psychologique dans les cas d'encephalopathie traumatique. *Archives de Psychologie, 28*, 286–340.

Rey, A. (1964). *L'examen clinique en psychologie*. Paris: Presses Universitaires de France.

Rienstra, A., Spaan, P. E., & Schmand, B. (2010). Validation of symptom validity tests using a "child-model" of adult cognitive impairments. *Archives of Clinical Neuropsychology, 25*, 371–382.

Rohling, M. L. (2004). Who do they think they're kidding: Review of the use of symptom validity tests with children. *Division of Clinical Neuropsychology Newsletter, 22*, (1), 21–26.

Rogers, R., Hinds, J. D., & Sewell, K. W. (1996). Feigning psychopathology among adolescent offenders: Validation of the SIRS, MMPI-A, and SIMS. *Journal of Personality Assessment, 67*, 244–257.

Schmand, B., & Lindeboom, J. (2004). *Amsterdam Short-Term Memory Test*. Leiden, The Netherlands: Pits Test Publishers.

Sharland, M. J., & Gfeller, J. D. (2007). A survey of neuropsychologists' beliefs and practices with respect to the assessment of effort. *Archives of Clinical Neuropsychology, 22*, 213–223.

Stein, L. A. R., Graham, J. R., & Williams, C. L. (1995). Detecting fake-bad MMPI-A profiles. *Journal of Personality Assessment, 65*, 415–427.

Stouthamer-Loeber, M., & Loeber, R. (1986). Boys who lie. *Journal of Abnormal Child Psychology, 14*, 551–564.

Strauss, E., Sherman, E. M. S., & Spreen, O. (2006). *A compendium of neuropsychological tests: Administration, norms, and commentary* (3rd ed.). New York: Oxford University Press.

Stutts, J. T., Hickey, S. E., & Kasdan, M. L. (2003). Malingering by proxy: A form of pediatric condition falsification. *Developmental and Behavioral Pediatrics, 24*, 276–278.

Talwar, V., Gordon, H., & Lee, K. (2007). Lying in the elementary school: Verbal deception and its relation to second-order belief understanding. *Developmental Psychology, 43*, 804–810.

Talwar, V., & Lee, K. (2002). Development of lying to conceal a transgression: Children's control of expressive behavior during verbal deception. *International Journal of Behavioral Development, 26*, 436–444.

Tombaugh, T. N. (1996). *Test of Memory Malingering (TOMM)*. North Tonawanda, NY: Multi Health Systems.

Wilson, A. E., Smith, M. D., & Ross, H. D. (2003). The nature and effects of young children's lies. *Social Development, 12*, 21–45.

Wood, B. L., Haque, S., Weinstock, S., & Miller, B. D. (2004). Pediatric stress-related seizures: Conceptualization, evaluation, and treatment of nonepileptic seizures in children and adolescents. *Current Opinion in Pediatrics, 16*, 523–531.

Wrobel, T. A., Lachar, D., Wrobel, N. H., Morgan, S. T., & Gruber, C. P. (1999). Performance of the Personality Inventory for Youth validity scales. *Assessment, 6*, 367–380.

Chapter 8

Forensic Issues in Neuropsychological Assessment: Culture and Language

DANIELLE N. LANDWHER
ANTOLIN M. LLORENTE

INTRODUCTION

Clinical neuropsychology has a long-standing history of involvement in the legal setting (e.g., McMahon & Satz, 1981), yet never before in the history of the field has it been asked to play a greater role in forensic cases with a concomitant growth in related research (Larrabee, 2005; Sweet, King, Malina, Bergman, & Simmons, 2002). In fact, in a recent survey of neuropsychologists, increase in forensic work exhibited an explosion in practice involvement relative to past surveys (Sweet, Nelson, & Moberg, 2006). Although this increase can be attributed to adult cases predominantly, a similar trend has been noted in pediatric cases. As the number of pediatric forensic cases continues to expand and include more diverse groups of children, important factors that are not typically associated with traditional neuropsychological variables will play a major role. In fact, the outcome of all neuropsychological assessments, including pediatric forensic neuropsychological evaluations, is moderated by demographic variables. For example, the age of the child is relevant across various dimensions, including age of the child at the time of injury, time since injury onset as it relates to injury recovery and maturation, and age at the time of assessment. Aside from age, two other critical demographic moderating variables play a major role and merit close attention in pediatric forensic neuropsychological cases, namely the child's cultural and linguistic background. This chapter succinctly attempts to address the impact of cultural and linguistic variables from theoretical and applied perspectives, buttressing and underscoring the importance of considering these factors during the course of pediatric forensic neuropsychological evaluations.

PEDIATRIC FORENSIC NEUROPSYCHOLOGY: THEORETICAL FOUNDATIONS ASSOCIATED WITH CULTURE

Childhood as a Cultural Construct

With regard to the psychosocial-historical development of the child, Vygotsky's (1934/1978) work highlights the notion that culture is a phenomenon inextricably intertwined to neurobiology. In his principle of "extracortical organization of complex mental functions," Vygotsky emphasized that the course of a child's development is shaped by his or her culture. In support of Vygotsky's principle, emerging research has demonstrated that an individual's experiences and environment impact the brain's anatomy (c.f., Elbert, Pantev, Wienbruch, Rockstroh, & Taub, 1995; Bates, Thal, Finlay, & Clancy, 2003).

From a cultural perspective, the definition of "childhood" as a construct is inherently related to forensic pediatric neuropsychology. According to Kessen (1979, pg. 815), ". . . the child is essentially and eternally a cultural invention and . . . the variety of the child's definition is not the removable error of an incomplete science." Given its cultural roots, is it possible then to define childhood beyond the scope of its cultural boundaries? Candelaria and Llorente (2009) offer numerous examples of broad differences in demarcating childhood based on physiological, psychological, social, and legal variables, emphasizing that definitions of childhood vary significantly and are usually context dependent. In other words, the nature of the "object" or the "subject" under investigation in pediatric forensic neuropsychology, the child is, as Candelaria and Llorente (2009) noted, formed and forged within the crucible of society in which the child develops (c.f., Wartofsky, 1983).

Based on the argument that all citizens within a particular nation are held accountable to their respective legal systems, at first glance one might argue that the technical definition of childhood falls under the purview of the law. However, closer scrutiny of the legal definition of childhood, as noted by Candelaria and Llorente (2009), demonstrates that this definition varies from jurisdiction to jurisdiction. However, a child's culture defines the legal definition of childhood, which further complicates its very definition. Moreover, the definition of childhood in the legal arena bears weight in pediatric forensic neuropsychological evaluations. For example, the age at which an individual may be considered an emancipated minor varies depending on the state in which one resides, and this may impact whether a clinician is able to evaluate a child in a forensic evaluation involving civil litigation without the permission of a legal guardian.

Nevertheless, laws governing children's actions and the consequences of their actions reflect important cultural mores with significant implications for pediatric forensic neuropsychology. One dramatic example that illuminates cultural perspectives on childhood, albeit from the criminal arena, involves the age at which a defendant can be sentenced to death in the United States. In particular, the landmark case of *Thompson v. Oklahoma* merits attention. In this 1988 U.S. Supreme Court case, the very definition of childhood was challenged, and the presiding district attorney filed for and was granted a statutory petition to have Thompson tried as an adult, despite the fact that the defendant was a " 'child' by matter of Oklahoma law." This ruling was then overturned by the Supreme Court, citing a violation of the

Eighth Amendment. Thompson's death sentence was deemed "cruel and unusual punishment" based on the Fourteenth Amendment, which prohibits the execution of persons less than 16 years of age at the time of their offenses. Subsequently in 1989, two Supreme Court cases occurred in which the death penalty was affirmed and upheld for two minors, ages 16 and 17 years old (*Stanford v. Kentucky*, 1989; *Wilkins v. Missouri*, 1989). In both of these cases, minors were tried as adults, found guilty of murder, and subsequently sentenced to death for their crimes. Notably, the discrepancies among rulings in three different court cases highlight the interpretive variability of the term "childhood" between and among state jurisdictions as well as between Supreme Court Justices. How can such variability be objectively explained? Perhaps cultural differences and their powerful influences on the nature of and expectations for conduct in childhood may be one of the answers to such a difficult question. Ultimately, citizens, including children, are bound to laws that govern society, and culture plays a major role in establishing those laws. In the same vein, the culture in which a child grows and develops bears a major influence not only on the child's personality and behavior, but it also impacts brain anatomy and function and the very definition of childhood.

Culture and the Brain

As we enter the 21st Century, modern research provides technologically advanced mileposts about potential relationships between culture and the brain. Mediated by genetics, such research bridges the gap between culture and the child's brain. For example, normal language development coincides with the transmission of culture through songs, narratives, and other verbal means. Language development also relies upon genetics, as highlighted by Lai and colleagues (2001). In this regard, Lai et al. (2001) discovered a mutation in a gene (forkhead box P_2) that led to speech and language abnormalities, suggesting that this particular gene plays a key role in normal language development, including grammar skills and other linguistic markers. Similarly, discovery of mirror neurons in the premotor cortex and inferior parietal cortex offers an example of how culture may actually impact the child's brain and how it develops (c.f., Kohler et al., 2002). Believed to represent the brain's mechanism of imitation, mirror neurons respond to action or observation of an action by reflecting the observation of another's action onto the brain itself, as if the observer were performing the original action. Mirror neurons serve to mediate interactions between one's biology and the environment (or more aptly, culture) by facilitating the process by which one models behavior or learns from the environment. For example, the process by which children learn to assimilate complex cultural variables is thought to involve mirror neurons (c.f., Candelaria & Llorente, 2009).

Although modern, technologically advanced neuroscientific research supports the notion that culture is able to impact brain functions, such findings are not novel and essentially uphold previous conclusions from extant anthropological research. In particular, the work of Franz Boas (1911/1938) revealed during the early 1900s that culture (e.g., dance) impacted the brain. In his research, Boas demonstrated that even specific motor characteristics (e.g., walking) were inextricably related to cultural factors (Boas, 1911/1938; Kuper, 1999).

In essence, as Ardila (2005) has aptly noted, "culture is in the brain." At its foundation, culture reflects a set of unifying beliefs, behavior, ideas, and values within a society. Ardila (2005) suggests that, at minimal, culture may be defined as "*the specific way of living of a human group*" (p. 185). In this way, culture may be described as encompassing the foundational tenets by which individuals, including children, are expected to conduct themselves. Eventually, culture becomes ingrained in an individual, often unbeknownst to him or her.

As Llorente (2008) has highlighted, "culture" is often, yet inappropriately, used interchangeably with the term "ethnicity" given the similarities between the concepts; both are learned and flexible. Even some definitions of ethnicity utilize culture as a synonym, as in Jalali's (1988) definition of ethnicity as "the culture of [a] people [that] is thus critical for values, attitudes, perceptions, needs, and modes of expression, behavior, and identity" (p. 10). These similarities might lead one to question how culture differs from ethnicity. While culture represents the ways of conducting oneself within society, the parameters of ethnicity lie within an individual. For example, many ethnicities can exist within any given culture. Whereas culture develops from symbolic elements which come to define a group of individuals, one's ethnicity stems from the process by which an individual adopts specific characteristics from his or her culture over time. As such, ethnicity reflects a defining element of an individual based on his or her ancestry, language, geography, history, religion, rituals, and values (Applebaum, 1987).

Interestingly, the concept of "ethnic minority" varies depending on the country (and therein, the culture) of reference. Hays (2001) cites the example of definitional differences for "ethnic minorities" between people of Indigenous or Aboriginal heritage in the United States and Canada. When Native Americans in the United States rallied together with African, Asian, and Latino Americans during the equal rights movement as a representative ethnic minority, Aboriginal people in Canada distinguished themselves from identification as an ethnic minority, because the term there explicitly refers to groups of people with a history of immigration to Canada. Furthermore, individuals within a specific ethnic group can vary in the degree of affiliation and association with that particular ethnicity. As such, "two individuals who belong to the same group may differ widely on their identification with the group and their commitment to it" (Phinney, 1996, p. 923).

Take the case of Hispanics as an example; the term "Hispanic" refers to a very heterogeneous group of people, encompassing individuals from various countries across the world. Although the term intends to refer to ethnicity, it often has been misused. Frequently, the label "Hispanic" is mistakenly used as a racial category. As indicated by Harris and Llorente (2005), the use of this label to describe an individual fails to "capture the unique attributes" of that person, sometimes including his or her racial identity. Ries, Potter, and Llorente (2008) offer an interesting example of such misuse with a comparison between a Mexican American born and raised in the United States and a Mexican immigrant born and raised in Mexico with Aboriginal ancestors. While both may be considered "Hispanic," applying this label does not adequately reflect the various distinguishing features of each individual. Moreover, Hispanics may (or may not) share a common language, but they represent a vastly heterogeneous group that traces their origins from countries such as Mexico, Puerto Rico, Cuba, the Dominican Republic, Argentina, Columbia, Spain, Honduras, and Panama (Echemendia, 2004).

On the other hand, race is a sociohistorical or political term used to categorize people by their physical features. The concept of race assumes that people can be differentiated by these physical characteristics, such as skin color or facial features. The use of the term "race" can also be misleading, because it is highly unlikely that people can be differentiated according to physical features, given the course of migrations, explorations, and invasions of lands throughout history (Schwartz, 2001). As such, perhaps the proper definition of race is the genetic attributes of an individual, which are assumed to have a biological origin. While race may or may not be a central aspect of an individual's identity (Hays, 2001), clinicians must keep in mind that racial identity in and of itself cannot offer clinical information about a person's educational level, culture, religion, or other demographic characteristics. Nevertheless, there remains little doubt today that culture influences the anatomy of a child's brain and the underlying behaviors, posing a significant impact in the forensic arena.

PEDIATRIC FORENSIC NEUROPSYCHOLOGY: THEORETICAL FOUNDATIONS ASSOCIATED WITH LANGUAGE

Cultural factors modulate biologically based responses and behavior, including the biological predisposition of infants to develop a language (e.g., Bates, Thal, Finlay, & Clancy, 2003; Chomsky, 1991), and the specific language that infants and young children eventually learn heavily depends on their culture. Nevertheless, these findings support the fact that everyday brain functions derive from cultural influences, such as using an abacus to count, can lead to culture-based brain differences. Such influences impact the anatomy of the brain and underscore the need to take linguistic variables into consideration when evaluating neurocognitive functioning during the course of pediatric forensic assessments.

To scientifically illustrate the impact of language on the human brain, Tang and colleagues (2006) revealed differences in functional magnetic resonance imaging (fMRI) between native Chinese and English speakers on tasks which evaluated foundational arithmetic skills and targeted the brain's occipitoparietal region. The native English speakers demonstrated increased left perisylvian activity, while the native Chinese speakers showed increased activity in the premotor cortex. Tang et al. (2006) proposed that these differences directly related to the greater demand on visuospatial skills within the Chinese language. They cited a relative advantage for Chinese speakers who learned to effectively utilize an abacus for counting, compared to the less effective English speaker's method of processing number symbols. Moreover, this anatomical difference may explain why Chinese-speaking children often perform better than their English-speaking counterparts on mathematics tests (Cantlon & Brannon, 2006).

An individual's language background also bears weight on neuropsychological test performance. In a subtle example, Mok, Tsang, Lee, and Llorente (2008) studied the effect of language background on two different trail making tests with Chinese dominant, English dominant, and Chinese-English bilingual groups of children.

The study results showed that the Chinese dominant group outperformed both the English dominant and Chinese-English bilingual groups on measures of speed and executive functions using the Children's Color Trails Test 1 & 2 (Llorente, Williams, D'Elia, & Satz, 2003). The authors concluded that language background exerts an impact on performance during trail making tests. In another study documenting the effects of language spoken in the home, reliable discrepancies in test performance between individuals with similar as well as different ethnic backgrounds were documented, even after accounting for variability derived from demographic factors such as age, education, gender, and income (Brickman, Cabo, & Manly, 2006).

Although the majority of research investigating the effects of language background has been conducted with adults, research with pediatric populations has also demonstrated that language background impacts neuropsychological test performance. In the study by Harris and Llorente (2005), language spoken in the home was the only variable able to completely account for differences in the performance on the Wechsler Intelligence Scale for Children, Fourth Edition (WISC-IV; Wechsler, 2003) of Hispanic children who spoke either English or Spanish at home when compared with the "White" sample. Therefore, language can significantly alter test results and their interpretations.

While a thorough review of this topic is beyond the scope of this chapter, one proposed reason for such differences in test performance involves the ways in which immigration patterns impact the composition of normative samples and thus affect representativeness of certain demographic or cultural variables in any given normative group (Llorente, Ponton, Taussig, & Satz, 1999; Llorente, Taussig, Perez, & Satz, 2000). Thus, patterns in immigration can have implications for comparisons between group and individual test performance, and consequently, immigration can moderate the utility of data obtained during the neuropsychological evaluation (Harris & Llorente, 2005; Rey, Feldman, Rivas-Vazquez, Levin, & Benton, 1999). In other words, individual neuropsychological test performance may vary depending on the representativeness of a particular client's ethnic standing within the normative sample.

Bilingualism

Complex linguistic abilities, such as bilingualism, reflect additional factors for consideration in forensic pediatric neuropsychology. Bilingualism involves the ability to speak two (or more, in the case of multilingualism) languages. However, bilingualism is more complex than merely monolingual skills in two languages; rather, the development of a second language directly relates to the bilingual individual's need to communicate in different contexts, with different individuals, and for specific purposes (Casas, Calamia, & Tranel, 2008). Notably, individuals who admit to speaking multiple languages often vary greatly in their fluency and competency in each. Encompassing linguistic, communicative, and sociocultural aspects (Garratt & Kelly, 2008) bilingualism can range from the individual who has expertise in his or her native tongue and near-native knowledge in another language, to someone who has only basic conversational ability in his or her second language.

Early studies considering the relationship between bilingualism and test performance emphasized bilingualism's negative effects on cognition. For example,

Barke and Williams (1938) asserted that the introduction of a second language inhibited continued development in the first language. To the contrary, contemporary research indicates that bilingualism can be advantageous to cognitive functioning. Specifically, Garratt and Kelly (2008) reviewed research that indicated a bilingual advantage when compared to monolinguals in the following cognitive domains: development of reading skills, metalinguistic ability, phonological awareness, concept formation, divergent thinking skills, symbolic development, working memory, attention, and impulse control. Despite these promising findings, bilingual normative data to which a clinician might compare his or her client are scarce, if not nonexistent.

Research investigating the proposed reasons behind the differences in test performance between bilinguals and monolinguals implicate two competing cognitive mechanisms: competition or interference between languages and the reduced frequency of language-specific use (Mindt et al., 2008). The former mechanism explains the process by which a bilingual individual inhibits use of one language in order to more effectively use a second language. Typically, the dominant language is more readily accessible and its use must be suppressed during nondominant language use (Mindt et al., 2008). The latter mechanism is based on the notion that, because bilinguals have two languages at their disposal, their use of words within each language is less frequent. Words which are used less frequently have fewer established connections between neurons required for effective retrieval. Both principles ultimately impact a bilingual individual's proficiency in the languages they use.

Notably, not all speakers of a given language have the same level of mastery over the languages that they speak. Distinguishing between different levels of language mastery, Cummins (1979, 1981) described a range in proficiency that varied from basic "surface fluency" to more cognitively complex levels of language processing. "Surface fluency" is a term used to describe basic interpersonal communication skills. However, one's surface fluency can often be misleading, because interpersonal situations offer the language-user contextual cues that facilitate comprehension and thus may lead one to overestimate a language user's level of proficiency.

During the clinical interview, neuropsychologists are predisposed to overestimating a client's language proficiency, given the interpersonal context in which the interview occurs.

In fact, Cummins (1979) indicates that becoming proficient in a second language takes a significant amount of time before it is acquired on a deep, structural level within the brain. Within the testing situation, a lack of context combined with the demand on one's cognitive ability requires that the examinee possess significantly more proficiency than what is required in basic social interactions. Accordingly, the neuropsychologist would be making an egregious error to assume level of language proficiency based solely on observation of communication skills.

CULTURE, LANGUAGE, AND APPLIED PEDIATRIC FORENSIC NEUROPSYCHOLOGY

While culture may be manifest implicitly, albeit sometimes covertly in the legal system, it underlies child development. Hence, emphasis on cultural issues is vital to conducting an effective pediatric forensic neuropsychological evaluation and to the science of pediatric forensic neuropsychology. A similar argument can be made for the importance of linguistic variables. Accordingly, how can neuropsychologists accurately interpret test performance without considering ethnicity, linguistic development, bilingualism, and other cultural and language-moderated variables, and other demographic variables? This issue is particularly important and complicated from an applied standpoint, because where children are concerned, the literature describing the impact of culture and ethnicity on test performance is sparse. Byrd, Arentoft, Scheiner, Westerveld, and Baron (2008) offer a review of 10 empirical studies depicting the current state of multicultural neuropsychological assessment specific to children. These authors found that while some test measures are sensitive to the child's ethnicity (i.e., the Peabody Picture Vocabulary Test, Third Edition; Restrepo et al., 2006), there is no parsimonious link between one's ethnic minority group and patterns in test performance due to a more complex array of variables at play with children (i.e., development). Therefore, several applied factors associated with culture and language that require attention during the course of forensic pediatric neuropsychological evaluations are presented next.

The first issue is associated with the epidemiology of pediatric trauma, a key reason for children to undergo pediatric forensic neuropsychological evaluation. In this regard, brain trauma and other acquired brain diseases have varying representation in different ethnicities and cultures. For example, the Centers for Disease Control and Prevention (CDC) conducted an investigation in 1999 that studied causes of traumatic brain injury (TBI) across different ethnic groups, including adolescents throughout the United States (CDC, 1999; Ries, Potter, & Llorente, 2008). Results revealed equivalent rates of death attributed to TBI as a consequence of transportation accidents for Caucasian and African American groups. However, African Americans had a greater risk of death subsequent to TBI due to firearm injuries when compared to the Caucasian group. Despite the fact that it is difficult to accept this association, it is critical to underscore that ethnicity is associated with the typology of certain traumatic injuries during childhood that can sometimes lead to forensic evaluations.

In addition, other demographic variables, such as parental education, quality of parental and the child's education, and socioeconomic status, can impact the nature and outcome of a pediatric forensic neuropsychological evaluation; see Chapter 4 for further evidence. These variables often interact, overlap, and are inextricably related. Therefore, conclusions drawn about test performance without due consideration of these important mediating and moderating variables may be based on false premises. As Brickman, Cabo, and Manly (2006) indicate, socioeconomic status affects access to resources, such as health care and adequate nutrition, which in turn impacts brain development and functioning. In another example, given that socioeconomic status is often intertwined with race, the naïve neuropsychologist may notice differences in performance that seem to be based on racial group but can be accounted for by other demographic variables. Thus, despite documented racial differences in performance, it is inaccurate to directly attribute such differences to race or ethnicity (Brickman, Cabo, & Manly, 2006).

Level of acculturation also impacts neuropsychological test performance (Coffey, Marmol, Schock, & Adams, 2005), and it is defined as the process by which an individual, minority group, or society conforms to and integrates foreign cultural traits and values into their own culture. Acculturation is bidirectional; while the individual is changed through the process of immersion in the foreign culture, the culture of the society itself is also altered as a result of the acculturation of immigrating populations. Many variables can influence the degree of acculturation that occurs in any given situation, including age at migration and geographic location (Portes & Rumbaut, 1990). For example, Cuban children living in Miami may be able to live and function in the community with minimal adoption of the dominant U.S. culture. On the other hand, Cuban children who immigrate to South Dakota may undergo extensive acculturation and ultimately become proficient in English, partially the result of requirements imposed by the child's environment (e.g., limited number of Spanish-speaking individuals in South Dakota).

During a pediatric forensic neuropsychological evaluation, level of acculturation is critical to assess prior to selecting a test battery and commencing the evaluation. Furthermore, measurement of a patient's level of acculturation is vital to the validity of an evaluation, as it informs the clinician of the best matter in which to approach the testing process, including which language and measures to use during the assessment. Depending on a client's level of acculturation, the clinician will tailor the evaluation for the individual or choose to refer a client to another clinician with expertise in that particular person's culture and/or dominant language. For example, the interested reader is referred to Ostrosky-Solis and Oberg's (2006) introduction to an important special issue of a prominent journal that reviews similarities and differences in performance on various tests across languages and cultures. For information specific to the Hispanic population, the reader may review the work of Llorente (2008) and Marin and Marin (1991). During the clinical interview, the neuropsychologist must gather information that will inform him or her as to the best way to proceed, including test selection and whether the client needs a referral to a more appropriate professional. To determine how to proceed, the neuropsychologist must inquire about the demographic characteristics of the client and obtain a thorough understanding of the referral reasons. Equally important is the collection and review of collateral sources of information. This information can include the patient's own verbal report, past personal and family history, and cross-informant reports (Llorente, 2008). Gaining informants' perspectives on the referral questions is also essential to understanding and preparing for an effective evaluation. Specifically, the neuropsychologist would benefit from learning the client's level of education in the United States and elsewhere, the length of time the client lived in the country, what language(s) are primarily spoken at home, whether the client participated in English as a Second Language classes in school, and specifically how bilingual the client is. Does he or she write in only one language, but speaks both? If the client speaks multiple languages, which one does he or she prefer?

While subjective information obtained through the clinical interview is vital to an evaluation, the clinician should also conduct a formal assessment of acculturation. Making judgments about acculturation and linguistic skills solely from simple conversational interactions during the clinical interview is egregious. Fortunately, objective measures of these variables have been developed to assist the neuropsychologist in making important decisions about minority clients. Formal acculturation scales can tap into the client's preferred language across a variety of settings, including home, leisure time, and more formal language use. Remarkably, such acculturation scales are effective in predicting generational cohort and degree of acculturation (Marin, Sabogal, Marin, & Otero-Sabogal, 1984). For example, the acculturation scale developed by Marin et al. (1984) can be reliably used with the Hispanic population and encompasses seven simple questions to which the client responds. These acculturation scales take into consideration variables that include the timing of immigration, generational differences in migration, ethnic identification, and length of U.S. residence (Franco, 1983; Marin et al., 1984; Suinn, Richard-Figueroa, Lew, & Vigil, 1987).

Although linguistic factors were discussed earlier from theoretical and empirical perspectives, several variables associated with language and applied assessment merit attention and are now reviewed. In particular, establishing a child's language dominance is essential before conducting the evaluation, given its significant impact on cognitive test performance (Harris & Llorente, 2005). This relationship can become problematic when a clinician interprets the results of an evaluation conducted in the client's nondominant language. Problems typically assumed to indicate cognitive impairments in a child may instead relate to language competency in the language used for test administration; consequently, the unaware clinician may inadvertently apply an inaccurate diagnostic label based on inaccurate interpretations of deficit test performance.

The evaluation of language in the child often necessitates that the neuropsychologist possess intricate and thorough mastery of the language spoken by the client. Given that nuances in a language can affect the standardized administration of the test, a clinician must possess knowledge of the overt and covert aspects of language functioning, including but not limited to prosodic variation, word retrieval, fluency, and comprehension. When a clinician is not fluent in the patient's native language, he or she must make an important choice before proceeding further: either refer the client to a colleague who is fluent in that language or collaborate with a bilingual clinician to complete the evaluation. Only under *extreme* circumstances should the clinician employ an interpreter to conduct a forensic pediatric neuropsychological evaluation. Alhtough many reasons could be provided to support such an evaluative posture, the reader is reminded that U.S. law depends on precedent, including forensic pediatric neuropsychological cases (see below).

As noted for the assessment of acculturation, accounting for linguistic proficiency through observation and inferences made during the clinical interview alone is insufficient. Formal measures are also essential to an effective pediatric forensic evaluation, such as the flowchart, published by Ponton and Leon-Carreon (2001), which aids the clinician in gauging language dominance and proficiency. Mindt and colleagues (2008) also offer a rubric for determining linguistic proficiency, including both subjective and objective means. They recommend that the prudent clinician begin by determining whether the client requires a bilingual examiner in order to effectively administer the tests. Obtaining a thorough history and background information, including age at which both languages were acquired, what language(s) are spoken primarily at home, and years of formal education in each language is essential. Administration of questionnaires that rate one's fluency and level of acculturation also offers subjective information about one's fluency. Furthermore, comparison of test performance on similar or identical tests administered in both languages can reveal discrepancies that may indicate language dominance. For example, Mindt et al. (2008) suggests that verbal fluency and academic achievement tests may offer insights into level of language proficiency. In addition to evaluating a minority client's linguistic skills, the neuropsychologist must also account for literacy by administering an objective reading measure. Formal assessment of literacy can also help the clinician determine the most appropriate language(s) of administration and which tests to administer.

Test Translations

Alternately, some professionals choose to conduct a translation of an existing test measure from English into a new language. However, the literal translation of test measures is wrought with problems, including the potential misinterpretation of the meaning being conveyed or an illogical, absurd use of the language. In fact, certain test measures are not appropriate for use with bilingual populations, even after a careful translation into another language. For example, the Boston Naming Test (BNT; Kaplan, Goodglass, & Weintraub, 1983) is a commonly used neuropsychological test measure assessing confrontation naming ability and boasting sensitivity to cognitive impairment. However, the BNT is also sensitive to the effects of bilingualism. Presenting an example of the differences between bilingual and monolingual performance on this measure, Gollan and colleagues (2007) offer an explanation for the discrepancy. They indicate that almost half of the BNT stimuli have Spanish-English cognate names, which are not matched for level of difficulty in Spanish, and many of which were ranked as more difficult than stimuli with noncognate names. Supported by the work of Gollan et al. (2007), it is clear that bilingualism can negatively affect an individual's BNT performance, leading to an increase in false-positive claims of naming difficulties. However, naming ability is an important component in the pediatric forensic evaluation, because this skill can be a diagnostic indicator for different types of cognitive impairment. Accordingly, efforts have been made to reduce test bias and to fairly assess this important skill. For example, Casas, Calamia, and Tranel (2008) developed and evaluated a different set of picture stimuli for bilingual speakers, proposing that these stimuli are more valid and appropriate for use with Spanish and English bilingual individuals.

A major concern with translating test measures into other languages is that professionals who conduct the translation do not have training in neuropsychology. As with any test translation, the translator's level of bilingualism and language dominance issues can affect the quality of the translation. Another concern involves false assumptions of a test's equivalence in different languages. As an example, the administration of the Digit Span subtest from the WISC leads to differences in performance for Korean-speaking and English-speaking examinees, which may be attributed to the level of difficulty of the task itself. While the test in either language requires an individual to repeat back a series of orally presented numbers in increasing spans, the level of difficulty differs depending on the language used. In English (and Spanish), the task is more difficult because there are more bisyllabic digit names for numbers 0–9 compared to Korean digit words (Kwak, 2003). Such variance in level of difficulty on this measure is also true of other languages. Consider the number "four," which has one syllable in English, compared to the Spanish "cuatro," which has two syllables. Using Baddeley and Hitch's (1974) model of working memory, there is more syllabic information in Spanish that must be held in the phonological loop, or temporary working memory storage for speech-based information, leading to differences in performance. Guidelines for the development and translation of tests into different languages call for intensive knowledge about not only the language itself but also about the culture of the people who speak it. If the test developers do not possess such in-depth knowledge, then they are urged to seek consultation with professionals who are competent in that particular culture or language (Brickman, Cabo, & Manly, 2006). A careful translation includes a thorough examination of local dialects, word usage, and frequency of use, in order to check the accuracy and appropriateness of the translated test content. Tests translated or created for use with certain populations must withstand considerable scrutiny in order to ensure their validity, reliability, and appropriateness for use with a particular population.

Using Interpreters

The use of an interpreter represents another attempt to adapt the evaluation for clients who speak another language, but this method should be avoided at all costs, but particularly in a forensic pediatric neuropsychological evaluation (Candelaria & Llorente, 2009; De Jongh, 1991; LaCalle, 1987; Llorente, 2008). According to forensic psychology and cross-cultural bodies of research, evaluations that utilize an interpreter may be invalid, unethical, and easily challenged in a court of law (LaCalle, 1987). As evidenced by the American Psychological Association's (APA) Ethical Principles and Standards, the neuropsychologist is ethically responsible for maximizing the validity of the parameters of the evaluation (APA, 2002). Thus, given the strong support from multiple, prevalent bodies of research, the use of an interpreter may represent an egregious ethical error in the course of a pediatric forensic neuropsychological evaluation.

The only situation in which the use of an interpreter during a neuropsychological evaluation would be acceptable is when the client speaks an extremely rare aboriginal or other language, and the clinician's attempts to locate and refer the client to a more appropriate neuropsychologist who speaks such a language are fruitless. Still, test results and conclusions drawn in the evaluation would be of questionable validity, and the neuropsychologist is obligated to emphasize limited confidence in test results in the written report. In the extremely rare occurrence wherein an interpreter must be used, the neuropsychologist is implored to follow certain guidelines in order to preserve the validity of the evaluation as much as possible (Llorente, 2008). Specifically, the interpretative services should be of high quality and should utilize trained professionals. Individuals with mental health training are most preferred, as they are more likely to be familiar with the parameters of the testing situation (Llorente, 2008), particularly a bilingual neuropsychology psychometrician. However, a client's family member or associate should never be utilized as an interpreter during the course of a neuropsychological evaluation (Dodd, 1983). The problems with the use of family members should be self-evident, but they deserve emphasis here. Family members do not have proper training in the ethical guidelines and proper procedures of interpretation (Byrd, Sanchez, & Manly, 2005), their own levels of acculturation and language proficiency can impact the quality of their interpretation, and their use can lead to bias, given their inevitable vested interest in the results and outcome of the evaluation.

Normative Samples

While factors like acculturation, language proficiency, and test translations directly influence the nature and outcomes of a pediatric forensic evaluation, other important variables, such as normative data, affect an evaluation in a more understated manner. Normative data are an essential component for making inferences about a child's performance; these data sets allow neuropsychologists to make comparisons between an individual and a reference group, which is assumed to provide the clinician with *representative* benchmarks for expected performance. Unfortunately, normative data in general frequently do not adequately account for diversity in demographic variables. For example, normative cohorts utilized in the development and empirical validation of the most commonly used neuropsychological tests often include only non-Hispanic "Caucasian" participants (Brickman, Cabo, & Manly, 2006; Llorente, 2008).

While it is easy to criticize test developers for their presumed lack of multicultural sensitivity, it would be next to impossible to include adequate normative data for all existing ethnic groups. This level of inclusion would require an infinite number of participants for each demographic (age, race, ethnic group, gender, hand dominance, etc.) in order to accurately stratify the test measure and fulfill each category in the normative sample with an adequate number of participants. For example, consider again the heterogeneity in the Hispanic population: while the intention of the normative data is to be comparable with population statistics, an individual who originates from Spain or Cuba and migrated to the United States may not be represented in the U.S. normative sample. Given the low rate or lack of minority representation in many neuropsychological measures, tests may be biased when administered to a client whose demographics diverge from that of the normative group. Thus, the prudent neuropsychologist should question whether the norms for a particular measure are appropriate for each individual client. Generally speaking, one must consider the period of time in which the norms were created, whether there is an adequate number of participants, and most important, whether the data were stratified to adequately represent different demographic factors such as age, gender, and preferably ethnicity not race (Brickman, Cabo, & Manly, 2006). In fact, there are significant gaps on certain demographic factors in the normative sample for one of the most well-respected and commonly used measures of intelligence. Specifically, as an example, the Wechsler Adult Intelligence Scale, Third Edition

(WAIS-III; Wechsler, 1997) does not have normative data for examinees who are Hispanic, ages 55 to 64, with greater than or equal to 16 years of education, living in the North Central region of the United States.

Reasons for such gaps in normative sample demographics may point to immigration patterns, which directly affect the representativeness of certain cultural, ethnic, or other demographic groups within the standardization of any given test. Despite this impact, immigration patterns are rarely considered during the development of a normative sample for a psychoeducational or neuropsychological instrument (Harris & Llorente, 2005). Certainly, attempts at addressing immigration patterns add a level of often unanticipated complexity to test development. For example, the authors of the Spanish version of the WISC-IV strove to adequately represent Cuban children in the normative sample by establishing a target of 9% within the sample (Wechsler, 2004). However, at that time Cubans represented only 3.5% of the total U.S. Hispanic population due to low immigration numbers circa 2002. This immigration pattern strained the data collection process (Harris & Llorente, 2005), although the target was ultimately reached with added measures taken to include this subgroup. Nevertheless, the predicted increasing diversity in the U.S. population underscores the need for neuropsychologists' thorough understanding of the dynamics between culture and patterns in test performance (Candelaria & Llorente, 2009).

Race- and Ethnicity-Specific Norms

In an attempt to better account for minority representation in normative data, "race"-specific norms have been developed for some neuropsychological tests. Given the literature citing race as a powerful correlate of test performance, researchers sought to eliminate potential variance in test performance accounted for by race and thus increase the sensitivity and specificity of neuropsychological tests. Because the goal in many neuropsychological evaluations is to accurately identify and diagnose brain dysfunction, ethnicity can potentially serve as a confounding variable that can impact test results. Ethnicity-specific normative data, then, might increase the clinician's diagnostic accuracy by accounting for factors that affect test performance, but are not directly due to brain dysfunction.

Clearly, enthicity-specific norms are not a panacea for minority representation in neuropsychological normative data sets. Even within specific groups, there exists variability in other important and influencing factors, such as cultural experiences, linguistic proficiency, and level of education. Not surprisingly, the use of race-specific norms has sparked controversy among experts in the field of neuropsychology. Brandt (2005) has asserted that race does not have significant meaning when interpreting neuropsychological test results. Furthermore, Brandt (2005) argues that race-specific normative data do not address the underlying issue of test bias. Variance in performance attributed to race may instead be accounted for by other underlying variables, such as socioeconomic status or education.

The question remains whether race-specific norms should be utilized by neuropsychologists to compare pediatric test performance to demographically similar normative groups. Brickman, Cabo, and Manly (2006) directly address this question and implore neuropsychologists to first consider the purpose of the evaluation. These authors recommend the use of race-specific norms only when the neuropsychologist has obtained a thorough history for the client, including his or her educational and cultural background. Moreover, the quality of race-specific norms is also a factor to weigh when considering their use; if the sample size is small or lacks representative stratification, the neuropsychologist should seek norms that are more applicable or have better methodology. Finally, the clinician must consider whether the race-based norms are representative of the individual client's demographics; comparison of an individual's performance to minority group norms will only be effective (and appropriate) if an individual's demographics are similar to that of the normative sample. As an example, the Wisconsin Card Sorting Test (WCST; Berg, 1948; Grant & Berg, 1948) was administered to 52 Mexican Americans as part of a study investigating whether this measure upheld claims that it was relatively culture-free, or if level of acculturation affected test performance (Coffey, Marmol, Schock, & Adams, 2005). Study authors compared the WCST scores of two groups with higher or lower levels of acculturation, and they found that the more acculturated group performed significantly better than those in the less acculturated group. Additionally, this study compared both groups' performance to both Spanish and English norms; results revealed that the study sample did not significantly differ from the available Spanish norms, but there was a significant difference in WCST performance across all test scores between the Mexican American sample and the English norms (Coffey et al., 2005).

Nonverbal Measures and "Culture-Free" Tests

To the credit of the field, attempts have been made to address the nature and impact of important mediating and moderating variables, such as culture and language, in the neuropsychological evaluation. Historically in clinical neuropsychology, it was assumed that nonverbal test measures were "culture-free" and that the effects of culture on performance could be minimized when these measures were administered to members of minority groups. However, the opposite is true; in a critical review of the literature, Rosselli and Ardila (2003) asserted that on some nonverbal measures, the impact of culture and other demographic variables (i.e., education) is paramount. As an example, these authors describe how select skills (such as drawing a map or working under the pressure of time) are not essential skills in, and therefore may be meaningless to, some cultures. Thus, it is unfair to evaluate these selective skills and make performance interpretations, given the inherent bias in a task that is not emphasized or valued within one's culture.

CULTURE AND LANGUAGE: ETHICAL ISSUES IN THE PRACTICE OF PEDIATRIC FORENSIC NEUROPSYCHOLOGY

Although Chapter 2 covers ethical issues in a more comprehensive fashion, there are several relevant points that relate to the influence of culture and language issues which deserve mention here. In fact, the most current version of the APA ethics code clearly acknowledges the influence of culture and language on the work of professional psychologists (APA, 2002). While each of the General Principles may apply to all pediatric forensic neuropsychological assessments, there are several specific Principles that address culture and language directly.

Beginning with Ethical Principle E, Respect for People's Rights and Dignity, the code mandates that psychologists be "aware of and respect cultural, individual, and role differences..." Moreover, Principle E continues, "Psychologists try to eliminate the effect on their work of biases based on those factors." Most directly related to the pediatric forensic neuropsychological evaluation, Standard 9.06 emphasizes, "When interpreting assessment results, including automated interpretations, psychologists take into account... situational, personal, linguistic, and cultural differences, which might affect psychologists' judgments or reduce the accuracy of their interpretations." Standard 2:01(b) instills, "Where scientific or professional knowledge... establishes that an understanding of factors associated with age, gender, gender identity, race, ethnicity, culture, national origin, religion, sexual orientation, disability, language, or socioeconomic status is essential for effective implementation of their services or research, psychologists have or obtain the training, experience, consultation, or supervision necessary to ensure the competence of their services, or they make appropriate referrals..." As implied by Standard 2:01(b), psychologists must be competent in the areas in which they practice. Competency begins to develop through knowledge and experience gained within professional psychology training programs; this knowledge and experience includes cultural and individual diversity (Lezak, Howieson, & Loring, 2004). Accordingly, the ethics code requires that practicing psychologists be aware of ethical issues in all aspects of pediatric forensic assessments as they apply to culturally and linguistically divergent populations.

The first step in the ethical awareness of cultural issues is sensitivity to racial, linguistic, and ethnic differences, which is obtained through thorough history-taking, education and training, and keeping the prospect of individual biases in mind (Wong, Strickland, Fletcher-Janzen, Ardila, & Reynolds, 2000). A psychologist undertaking the evaluation of a cultural and linguistic minority client must exert time and energy into obtaining as much information about the client prior to the assessment. This information, including cultural, educational, and socioeconomic background, will not only assist the neuropsychologist in determining whether and how to proceed with the evaluation, but it will also inform the neuropsychologist of the best approach to a fair, reliable, and valid assessment of a client's neuropsychological functioning. Such knowledge requires more than just identifying the client's ethnicity or race; rather, the clinician must assess how the cultural aspects of a client's identity contribute to his or her individual presentation (c.f., Brickman, Cabo, & Manly, 2006).

REFERENCES

American Psychological Association. (2002). *Ethical principles of psychologists and code of conduct.* Retrieved December 12, 2009, from http://www.apa.org/ethics/code2002.html.

Applebaum, H. (1987). *Perspectives in cultural anthropology.* Albany: State University of New York Press.

Ardila, A. (2005). Cultural values underlying psychometric cognitive testing. *Neuropsychological Review, 15*, 185–195.

Baddeley, A. D., & Hitch, G. (1974). Working memory. In G. H. Bower (Ed.), *The psychology of learning and motivation: Advances in research and theory* (Vol. 8, pp. 47–89). New York: Academic Press.

Barke, E. M., & Williams, D. E. P. (1938). A further study of the comparative intelligence of children in certain bilingual and monoglot schools in South Wales. *British Journal of Educational Psychology, 8*, 63–77.

Bates, E., Thal, D., Finlay, B., & Clancy, B. (2003). Early language development and its neural correlates. In S. Segalowitz & I. Rapin (Eds.), *Handbook of neuropsychology: Child neuropsychology* (Vol. 8, 2nd ed., pp. 109–176). Amsterdam: Elsevier.

Berg, E. A. (1948). A simple objective treatment for measuring flexibility in thinking. *Journal of General Psychology, 39*, 15–22.

Boas, F. (1911/1938). *The mind of primitive man* (Rev. ed.). New York: Free Press.

Brandt, J. (2005, February). *Neuropsychological crimes and misdemeanors*. Paper presented at the annual meeting of the International Neuropsychological Society, St. Louis, MO.

Brickman, A. M., Cabo, R., & Manly, J. J. (2006). Ethical issues in cross-cultural neuropsychology. *Applied Neuropsychology, 13*(2), 91–100.

Byrd, D. A, Arentoft, A., Scheiner, D., Westerveld, M., & Baron, I. S. (2008). State of multicultural neuropsychological assessment in children: Current research issues. *Neuropsychology Review, 18*, 214–222.

Byrd, D. A, Sanchez, D., & Manly, J. J. (2005). Neuropsychological test performance among Caribbean-born and U.S.-born African American elderly: The role of age, education, and reading level. *Journal of Clinical and Experimental Neuropsychology, 27*, 1056–1069.

Candelaria, M. A., & Llorente, A. M. (2009). The assessment of the Hispanic child. In C. R. Reynolds & E. Fletcher-Janzen (Eds.), *Handbook of clinical child neuropsychology* (pp. 401–424). New York: Springer Science + Business Media, LLC.

Cantlon, J. F., & Brannon, E. M. (2006). Adding up the effects of cultural experience on the brain. *TRENDS in Cognitive Science, 11*(1), 1–4.

Casas, R., Calamia, M., & Tranel, D. (2008). A screening test of English naming ability in bilingual Spanish/English speakers. *Journal of Clinical and Experimental Neuropsychology, 30*(8), 956–966.

Centers for Disease Control and Prevention. (1999). *Traumatic brain injury in the United States: A report to congress*. Atlanta, GA: Author.

Coffey, D. M., Marmol, L., Schock, L., & Adams, W. (2005). The influence of acculturation on the Wisconsin Card Sorting Test by Mexican Americans. *Archives of Clinical Neuropsychology, 20*, 795–803.

Chomsky, N. (1991). Linguistics and cognitive science: Problems and mysteries. In A. Kasher (Ed.), *The Chomskyan turn* (pp. 26–53). Cambridge, MA: Blackwell.

Cummins, J. (1979). Linguistic interdependence and the educational development of bilingual children. *Review of Educational Research, 49*, 222–251.

Cummins, J. (1981). The role of primary language development in promoting educational success for language minority students. In *Schooling and language minority students* (pp. 3–49). Sacramento, CA: California Department of Education.

De Jongh, E. M. (1991). Foreign language interpreters in the courtroom: The case for linguistic and cultural proficiency. *Modern Language Journal, 75*, 285–295.

Dodd, W. (1983). Do interpreters affect consultation? *Family Practice, 1*, 42–47.

Echemendia, R. J. (2004). Cultural diversity and neuropsychology: An uneasy relationship in a time of change. *Applied Neuropsychology, 11*(1), 1–3.

Elbert, T., Pantev, C., Wienbruch, C., Rochstroh, P., & Taub, E. (1995). Increased cortical representation of fingers of the left hand in string players. *Science, 270,* 305–307.

Franco, J. N. (1983). An acculturation scale for Mexican-American children. *Journal of General Psychology, 108,* 175–81.

Garratt, L. C., & Kelly, T. P. (2008). To what extent does bilingualism affect children's performance on the NEPSY? *Child Neuropsychology, 14,* 71–81.

Gollan, T. H., Fennema-Notestine, C., Montoya, R. I., & Jernigan, T. L. (2007). The bilingual effect on Boston Naming Test performance. *The Journal of the International Neuropsychological Society, 13,* 197–208.

Grant, D. A., & Berg, E. A. (1948). A behavioral analysis of the degree of reinforcement and ease of shifting to new responses in a Weigl-type card sorting problem. *Journal of Experimental Psychology, 38,* 404–411.

Harris, J. G., & Llorente, A. M. (2005). Cultural considerations in the use of the Wechsler Intelligence Scale for Children-Fourth Edition (WISC-IV). In A. Prifitera, D. H. Saklofske, & L. G. Weiss (Eds.), *WISC-IV clinical use and interpretation: Scientist- practitioner perspectives* (pp. 382–413). Burlington, MA: Elsevier Academic Press.

Hays, P. A. (2001). *Addressing cultural complexities in practice: A framework for clinicians and counselors.* Washington, DC: American Psychological Association.

Jalali, B. (1988). Ethnicity, cultural adjustment, and behavior: Implications for family therapy. In L. Comas-Diaz & E. E. H. Griffith (Eds.), *Clinical guidelines in crosscultural mental health* (pp. 9–32). New York: John Wiley & Sons.

Kaplan, E., Goodglass, H., & Weintraub, S. (1983). *Boston Naming Test* (Revised 60-item version). Philadelphia, PA: Lea & Febiger.

Kessen, W. (1979). The American child and other cultural inventions. *American Psychologist, 34*(10), 815–820.

Kohler, E., Keysers, C., Alessandra Umilta, M., Fogassi, L., Gallese, V., & Rizzolatti, G. (2002). Hearing sounds, understanding actions: Action representation in auditory mirror neurons. *Science, 297,* 846–848.

Kuper, A. (1999). *Culture: The anthropologists' account.* Cambridge, MA: Harvard University Press.

Kwak, K. (2003). South Korea. In J. Georgas, L. Weiss, F. J. R. van de Vijver, & D. H. Saklofske (Eds.), *Culture and children's intelligence: Cross cultural analysis of the WISC-III* (pp. 227–240). London: Academic Press.

LaCalle, J. (1987). Forensic psychological evaluations through an interpreter: Legal and ethical issues. *American Journal of Forensic Psychology, 5,* 29–43.

Lai, C. S., Fisher, S. E., Hurst, J. A., Vargha-Khadem, F., & Monaco, A. P. (2001). A forkhead-domain gene is mutated in a severe speech and language disorder. *Nature, 413,* 519–523.

Larrabee, G. J. (Ed.). (2005). *Forensic neuropsychology: A scientific approach.* New York: Oxford University Press.

Lezak, M. D., Howieson, D. B., & Loring, D. W. (2004). *Neuropsychological assessment* (4th ed.). New York: Oxford University Press.

Llorente, A. M. (2008). *Principles of neuropsychological assessment with Hispanics: Theoretical foundations and clinical practice.* New York: Springer.

Llorente, A. M., Ponton, M. O., Taussig, I. M., & Satz, P. (1999). Patterns of American immigration and their influence on the acquisition of neuropsychological norms for Hispanics. *Archives of Clinical Neuropsychology, 14,* 603–614.

Llorente, A. M., Taussig, I. M., Perez, L., & Satz, P. (2000). Trends in American immigration: Influences on neuropsychological assessment and inferences with ethnic-minority populations. In E. Fletcher-Janzen, T. Strickland, & C. R. Reynolds (Eds.), *Handbook of cross-cultural neuropsychology* (pp. 345–359). New York: Kluwer Academic/Plenum Publishers.

Llorente, A. M., Williams, J., D'Elia, L., Satz, P. (2003). *Children's Color Trails Test Manual.* Odessa, FL: Psychological Assessment Resources.

Marin, G., & Marin, B. V. (1991). *Research with Hispanic populations.* Newbury Park, CA: Sage.

Marin, G., Sabogal, F., Marin, B., & Otero-Sabogal, R. (1984). Development of a short acculturation scale for Hispanics. *Hispanic Journal of Behavioral Sciences, 9,* 183–205.

McMahon, E., & Satz, P. (1981). Clinical neuropsychology: Some forensic applications. In S. Filskov & T. Boll (Eds.), *Handbook of clinical neuropsychology* (pp. 686–701). New York: Wiley.

Mindt, M. R., Arentoft, A., Germano, K. K., D'Aquila, E., Scheiner, D., Pizzirusso, M., . . . Gollan, T. H. (2008). Neuropsychological, cognitive, and theoretical considerations for evaluation of bilingual individuals. *Neuropsychology Review, 18*(3), 255–268.

Mok, N., Tsang, L., Lee, T., & Llorente, A. (2008). The impact of language on the equivalence of trail making tests: Findings from three pediatric cohorts with different language dominance. *Applied Neuropsychology, 15*(2), 123–130.

Ostrosky-Solis, F., & Oberg, G. (2006). Neuropsychological functions across the world— common and different features: From digit span to moral judgment. *International Journal of Psychology, 41*(5), 321–323.

Phinney, J. S. (1996). When we talk about American ethnic groups, what do we mean? *American Psychologist, 51,* 918–927.

Ponton, M. O., & Leon-Carreon, J. (Eds.). (2001). *Neuropsychology and the Hispanic patient.* Mahwah, NJ: Erlbaum.

Portes, A., & Rumbaut, R. G. (1990). *Immigrant America: A portrait.* Los Angeles: University of California Press.

Restrepo, M. A., Schwanenflugel, P. J., Blake, J., Neuharth-Pritchett, S., Cramer, S. E., & Ruston, H. P. (2006). Performance on the PPVT-III and the EVT: Applicability of the measures with African-American and European American preschool children. *Language, Speech, and Hearing Services in Schools, 37*(1), 17–27.

Rey, G. J., Feldman, E., Rivas-Vazquez, R., Levin, B. E., & Benton, A. (1999). Neuropsychological test development for Hispanics. *Archives of Clinical Neuropsychology, 14,* 593–601.

Ries, J. K., Potter, B., & Llorente, A. M. (2008). Rehabilitation. In A. M. Llorente (Ed.), *Principles of neuropsychological assessment with Hispanics: Theoretical foundations and clinical practice* (pp. 164–179). New York: Springer Science + Business Media.

Rosselli, M., & Ardila, A. (2003). The impact of culture and education on non-verbal neuropsychological measurements: A critical review. *Brain and Cognition, 52,* 326–333.

Schwartz, R. S. (2001). Racial profiling in medical research. *New England Journal of Medicine, 344,* 1392–1393.

Stanford v. Kentucky, 492 U.S. 361. (1989).

Sweet, J. J., King, J. H., Malina, A. C., Bergman, M. A., & Simmons, A. (2002). Documenting the prominence of forensic neuropsychology at national meetings and in relevant professional journals from 1990–2000. *The Clinical Neuropsychologist, 16*(4), 481–94.

Sweet, J. J., Nelson, N. W., & Moberg, P. J. (2006). The TCN/AACN 2005 "Salary Survey": Professional practices, beliefs, and incomes of U.S. Neuropsychologists. *The Clinical Neuropsychologist, 20*(3), 325–364.

Suinn, R. M., Richard-Figueroa, K., Len, S., & Vigil, P. (1987). The Suinn-Law Asian Self-Identity Acculturation Scale: An initial report. *Educational and Psychological Measurement, 6*, 103–112.

Tang, Y., Zhang, W., Chen, K., Feng, S., Ji, Y., Shen, J., . . . Liu, Y. (2006). Arithmetic processing in the brain shaped by cultures. *Proceedings of the National Academy of Sciences USA, 103*(28), 10775–10780.

Thompson v. Oklahoma. 487 U.S. 815 (1988).

Thompson v. State. 724 P.2d 780 (Okl.Cr. 1986).

Vygotsky, L. S. (1934/1978). *Mind in society: The development of higher psychological processes,* 163. Cambridge, MA: Harvard University Press.

Wartofsky, M. (1983). The child's construction of the world and the world construction of the child: From historical epistemology to historical psychology. In F. S. Kessel & A. W. Sigel (Eds.), *The child and other cultural inventions* (pp. 188–215). New York: Praeger.

Wechsler, D. (1997). *Wechsler Adult Intelligence Scale-Third Edition administration and scoring manual.* San Antonio, TX: The Psychological Corporation.

Wechsler, D. (2003). *Manual for the Wechsler Intelligence Scale for Children-Fourth Edition.* San Antonio, TX: The Psychological Corporation.

Wechsler, D. (2004). *Manual for the WISC-IV Spanish: Wechsler Intelligence Scale for Children-Fourth Edition–Spanish.* San Antonio, TX: The Psychological Corporation.

Wilkins v Missouri. 492 U.S. 361 (1989). State v Wilkins. 736 SW 2d 409 (Mo. 1987).

Wong, T. M., Strickland, T., Fletcher-Janzen, E., Ardila, A., & Reynolds, C. R. (2000). Theoretical and practice issues in neuropsychological assessment and treatment of culturally dissimilar patients. In E. Fletcher-Janzen, T. Strickland, & C. R. Reynolds (Eds.), *Handbook of cross-cultural neuropsychology* (pp. 3–18). New York: Kluwer Academic/Plenum Publishers.

Chapter 9

Interpretive Confounds in the Independent Pediatric Neuropsychological Evaluation

JACOBUS DONDERS

INTRODUCTION

Pediatric neuropsychologists are often asked to offer opinions in civil litigation about matters pertaining to cause and effect when behavioral or cognitive deficits are alleged or identified. This is seldom a simple matter, as there are a host of potentially confounding factors that may blur the apparent line between event X and symptom Y. This chapter will review some of the variables that need to be considered routinely in the context of independent pediatric neuropsychological evaluations. These will include base rates, premorbid history, and comorbid conditions. Finally, a case study will be presented to illustrate the way some of these factors can be considered in a pragmatic manner.

BASE RATES

Base rates have to do with how common a symptom or level of performance is in a population. Just because a particular complaint is reported, that does not necessarily make it indicative of pathology. For example, headaches are a common complaint in children with brain tumors, but the fact that a child has a headache is not diagnostic of a brain tumor. First of all, that complaint is not specific to brain tumors, as it is also seen in a host of other conditions, such as in sinusitis. Second, and perhaps more important, there are plenty of children who have headaches in the absence of any known intracranial pathology. In other words, headaches have a fairly high base rate in the population at large (Fox, Lees-Haley, Earnest, & Dolezal-Wood, 1995). Base rates can confound the interpretation of neuropsychological data in a number of ways. Knowledge of and consideration of base rates can, however, improve diagnostic accuracy.

Base Rates and Impairment

Interpretation of pediatric neuropsychological test data typically includes, among other things, consideration of the level of performance across a range of measures, with reference to published norms. However, the definition of "impairment" is not uniformly agreed upon. One practitioner may consider scores that are more than 1 standard deviation below the population mean (i.e., below the 16th percentile) to be impaired, whereas another one may use a more conservative criterion, such as scores below the 5th percentile. If both practitioners were to consider the data from the same 100 pediatric patients, there would be 11 children on whom they would disagree about the presence or absence of impairment; that is, about 1 in 10. Given the suboptimal state of norms for many pediatric neuropsychological tests (Baron, 2004), this can be problematic. In general, a more liberal criterion for impairment is associated with an increased risk for false-positive errors (i.e., diagnosing a problem where none exists), whereas a more conservative criterion is associated with an increased risk for false-negative errors (i.e., missing a problem where one does exist).

There is no golden rule with regard to which diagnostic error is more important to avoid when it comes to decisions about impairment. For example, if one were to do a blood test to screen newborns for HIV, it could reasonably be argued that false-negative errors should be avoided at all costs. However, there are other situations where false-positive errors may be much more damaging. An example would be in a jury deliberation of an older adolescent who is accused of murder and who may face the death penalty, if convicted. Thus, it is important for the pediatric neuropsychologist to consider the context of the independent evaluation, as well as the relative costs of misdiagnosing the presence or absence of impairment. In general, the legal system tends to emphasize the need to protect the public against false positives, whereas the practice of medicine is more geared toward the avoidance of false negatives. Although these considerations are not mutually exclusive, the pediatric neuropsychologist needs to have a clear awareness of the risks and consequences of both false-positive and false-negative errors.

Base Rates and Predictive Values

A related problem is the influence of base rates on the degree of confidence that the pediatric neuropsychologist can have in the interpretation of specific test scores, even if there were general agreement about the definition of impairment. This is where it is helpful to have an understanding of the difference between sensitivity, specificity, and predictive values. The sensitivity of a test refers to the proportion of all children with a condition who are correctly identified by the test as having that condition. Specificity refers to the proportion of all children without the condition in question who are correctly identified by the test as not having that condition. A commonly used mnemonic in this context is that of the difference between "spin" and "snout" (Smith, Ivnik, & Lucas, 2008; Straus, Richardson, Glasziou, & Haynes, 2005). When specificity is high, a positive test result tends to rule in the condition (SPpIN), whereas when sensitivity is high, a negative test result tends to rule out the condition (SNnOUT). However, both sensitivity and specificity apply to situations where the presence or absence of a condition is known. In contrast, in the context of an independent pediatric neuropsychological evaluation, the presence or absence of a condition or impairment is often in dispute. Furthermore, the pediatric neuropsychologist does not have a large sample to deal with, but an n of 1. Instead of considering group proportions, this practitioner must decide on the basis of his or her test data whether there is evidence for impairment in that particular case. As such, it is important to know the predictive values of the test(s) being used.

The positive predictive value of a test refers to the proportion of the children with "positive" test results (i.e., scores deemed to reflect impairment) who indeed have a true condition or problem. The negative predictive value of a test refers to the proportion of the children with "negative" test results (i.e., scores deemed to reflect normal performance) who truly do not have the condition or problem of interest. It is very important for the pediatric neuropsychologist to understand that, whereas sensitivity and specificity are independent of the base rate of the condition under consideration, positive and negative predictive values can be strongly influenced by base rates. The following example may illustrate this.

Let us assume that two consecutive series of 100 children each are obtained from two different pediatric clinics, and all children were evaluated for the possibility of attention-deficit/hyperactivity disorder (ADHD). The neuropsychological test to evaluate for ADHD yields a binary diagnosis: either the child has ADHD or the child does not. Table 9.1 presents the data from these two clinics. In clinic A, the base rate of ADHD is 36% (30 + 6), whereas in clinic B, it is 12% (10 + 2). The sensitivity of the diagnostic test is unaffected by this change in base rate: 83% in both clinic A (30/[30 +6]) and clinic B (10/[10 + 2]). Similarly, the specificities are 84% in clinic A (54/[54 + 10]) and clinic B (74/[74 + 14]). However, the predictive values change drastically with the variation in base rate.

The positive predictive value of the neuropsychological test in clinic A is acceptable at 75% (30/[30 + 10]) and its negative predictive value is excellent at 90% (54/[54 + 6]). However, with the considerably lower base rate of ADHD in clinic B, the positive predictive value plummets to 42% (10/[10 + 14]), whereas the negative predictive value actually improves slightly to 97% (74/[74 + 2]). In fact, the pediatric neuropsychologist in clinic B would more often be correct if he or she simply concluded that none of the children had ADHD, regardless of the result of the neuropsychological test. This is because the base rate of the condition in clinic B is so low that the false-positive rate, defined as 1 – specificity, is greater at 16% than the base

TABLE 9.1. Influence of Base Rates on Predictive Values

Clinic A	Children With ADHD	Children Without ADHD
Test index suggests ADHD	30	10
Test index suggests no ADHD	6	54
Clinic B	Children With ADHD	Children Without ADHD
Test index suggests ADHD	10	14
Test index suggests no ADHD	2	74

ADHD, Attention-Deficit/Hyperactivity Disorder.

rate of 12%. In general, whenever the base rate of a condition is <50%, psychometric tests are helpful only when they have a combined false-positive and false error rate that is less than the actual base rate (Gouvier, 1999).

It could be argued that the neuropsychologist may not necessarily know the exact base rate of each condition in his or her clinic. However, there are general sources of information that can be used to estimate this. For example, there are plenty of data that suggest that the vast majority of school-age children with an uncomplicated mild head injury will be asymptomatic at approximately 3 months post injury (Babikian & Asarnow, 2009; McCrea, 2008), so the base rate of persistent sequelae at such a time point or later will be relatively low. The setting in which the evaluation is conducted may also influence this. For example, data obtained from consecutive emergency room admissions will be associated with a lower prevalence of problems at 3 months post injury than a selective sample of children referred to a specialty clinic for the treatment of traumatic brain injury (TBI). In either case, an informed estimate of the base rate of the condition may help to improve diagnostic classification accuracy.

Some practitioners might be a bit annoyed by the need to consider statistical concepts like positive and negative predictive values. However, it has been shown that even preschool children are capable of using information about base rates to guide their interpretations of events (Sobel & Munro, 2009; Sobel, Tenenbaum, & Gopnik, 2004). Thus, there seems to be little excuse for not having a working knowledge of these concepts, especially not in a medicolegal context where it is the responsibility of the pediatric neuropsychologist to provide the trier of fact with the most accurate representation of the data.

Base Rates and Statistical Significance

Manuals for many pediatric psychological or neuropsychological tests now include information about the degree to which discrepancies between specific scores are statistically significant, and these are sometimes broken down further by the direction of the discrepancy. However, it is important to appreciate that statistical significance does not necessarily mean clinical significance. For example, a discrepancy of 13 points between Verbal Comprehension (VC) and Perceptual Reasoning (PR) is statistically significant at $p < .05$ at any age in the standardization sample of the Wechsler Intelligence Scale for Children—Fourth Edition (WISC–IV; Wechsler, 2004). However, a discrepancy of that magnitude or greater also occurs in about a third of the same standardization sample (with 18% having VC < PR, and almost 15% having VC > PR); in other words, it is hardly unusual and not necessarily indicative of pathology. This is a good example of where consideration of the base rate of specific discrepancies may be more informative than routine acceptance of statistical significance levels. Such interpretation should be tempered further by realization that discrepancy scores, in general, tend to have limited reliability (Crawford, Sutherland, & Garthwaite, 2008).

Recent research has also demonstrated that the majority of presumably normal children will have at least one or two scores in the "impaired" range on a test with multiple indexes (Brooks, Iverson, Sherman, & Holdnack, 2009). If one just gives enough tests, it is almost inevitable that a few of the obtained scores are going to fall below average (see Chapter 4). Multiple comparisons within the same data set augment this problem. For example, in a study of the base rate of discrepancies on the California Verbal Learning Test—Children's Version (CVLT-C; Delis, Kramer, Kaplan, & Ober, 1994), where four separate, direction-specific discrepancies were each defined as unusual if they occurred in less than approximately 10% of the standardization sample, no less than one-third of the same standardization sample had at least one such "unusual" discrepancy (Donders, 1999).

A related issue is that even if it can be demonstrated that a specific phenomenon occurs at a relatively greater rate in a particular clinical diagnostic group than in the general population, that does not make it a "signature" phenomenon. For example, it has been demonstrated that children with TBI had a statistically significantly higher rate of large ($\leq$–1.5 SD) proactive interference effects on the CVLT–C than children in the standardization sample (21% vs. 11%; Donders & Minnema, 2004). However, this was clearly only a relative risk, as the majority (79%) of the same children with TBI did not demonstrate such a proactive interference effect. Similarly, Hack and colleagues (2009) reported that, when compared at the age of 8 years to children who were born with normal birth weight, children with a history of extremely low birth had a more than two-fold increased risk for having at least one of several behavioral disorders, including ADHD, generalized anxiety disorder, major depressive disorder, and/or autistic disorder. Again, this appeared to be a relative risk, as the majority of the children with extremely low birth weight (more than two-thirds) did not meet *Diagnostic and Statistical Manual of Mental Disorders, Fourth Edition (DSM–IV)* criteria for any such disorder at age 8 years. There are multiple ways of quantifying relative risk, such as odds ratios and likelihood ratios, of which a full discussion falls outside the scope of this chapter. The reader is referred to Bland and Altman (2000), Deeks and Altman (2004), and Grimes and Schulz (2005) for further details.

Base Rates of Pathology

A final consideration of base rates concerns knowledge about how common specific disorders are in the general population, and how such estimates vary with the method used to screen or diagnose the disorder, the severity of the scoring criteria, and the taxonomy that they are designed to operationalize. For example, Costello, Egger, and Angold (2005) reported that the median prevalence estimate of functionally impairing psychiatric disorders in children and adolescents is 12%, but that the range of such estimates is wide, between 3% and 18%. Other studies have suggested that at any specific time point, approximately 1 out of every 10 children will have a psychiatric disorder that causes sufficient distress or social impairment to warrant treatment, but that when considered across the entire period between childhood and adolescence, about 1 in 3 children will have at least one brief period of psychiatric impairment (Costello, Mustillo, Erkanli, Keeler, & Angold, 2003; Ford, Goodman, & Meltzer, 2003). Furthermore, prevalence rates tend to be affected by factors such as age and gender. For example, alcohol abuse is much more common in teenagers than in toddlers, and learning disabilities are more often diagnosed in boys than girls.

There is also mounting evidence that many lifetime psychiatric disorders have origins in childhood or adolescence, and that even in preschoolers, the base rates of the most common psychiatric disorders, as well as the comorbidities between them, are similar to those seen later in childhood (Egger & Angold, 2006). This is an important consideration, especially in independent pediatric neuropsychological evaluations where a particular disorder is often diagnosed many years after a specific event, be that exposure to toxins or a motor vehicle accident. Retrospective attribution is likely tempting in such cases but may not always be justified. Before concluding that a TBI, sustained at age 4, "must" be responsible for the mood disorder that is now objectively present at age 12, it would behoove the practitioner to consider the base rate of the specific mood disorder in the general population, the severity of the original injury, the family psychiatric history (see later discussion), and the occurrence of other intervening variables over the 8 years between injury and assessment.

Just because cerebral dysfunction can be suggested by neuropsychological tests that does not necessarily mean that the dysfunction was recently acquired. For example, structural and functional neuroimaging studies have strongly suggested prefrontal involvement in children with bipolar disorder, in the absence of any known toxic exposure or other environmental abnormalities (Pavuluri, Birmaher, & Naylor, 2005). Similarly, chronic stress such as associated with child abuse and/or neglect can lead to structural abnormalities in the brain, even in the absence of significant head trauma (De Bellis & Kuchibhatla, 2006; Jackowski, de Araujo, de Lacerda, Mari Jde, & Kaufman, 2009). The pediatric neuropsychologist must be aware of these issues within the context of independent neuropsychological evaluations. Consideration of the premorbid history of the child and family is an important next consideration.

PREMORBID HISTORY

No pediatric neuropsychological assessment is complete without a thorough history and review of relevant records (Beers, Hammond, & Ryan, 2006). Although an exhaustive discussion of all the issues that should be covered during an interview and records review is beyond the scope of this chapter, a number of specific issues that often come up in the context of independent pediatric neuropsychological evaluations will be emphasized. These include the prior developmental, academic, and family histories.

Developmental History

Acquired brain injury often does not occur in a vacuum. For example, a child with a long-standing history of spina bifida myelomeningocele and shunted hydrocephalus who sustains a penetrating head injury at the age of 10 years can reasonably be considered to have had a considerably lessened degree of cognitive or cerebral reserve to start with, and he or she can therefore be expected to be at increased risk for poor outcomes after the subsequent injury (Dennis, Yeates, Taylor, & Fletcher, 2007). Similarly, a child who gets exposed to lead-based paint residue between the ages of 2 and 3 years is likely to have grown up in poverty, which is known to be associated with increased risks for prior adversities such as limited prenatal health care, suboptimal nutrition, poor parental education, and so on—all of which can contribute to poor cerebral and cognitive development (Jurewicz & Hanke, 2008; Lipina & Colombo, 2009). Furthermore, many of such children do not receive adequate follow-up, which further compounds their disadvantage (Kemper, Cohn, Fant, & Dombkowski, 2005; Kemper, Cohn, Fant, Dombkowski, & Hudson, 2005).

Another important consideration is that children who incur TBI are not necessarily a representative sample of the general population. For example, children with a history of treatment with methylphenidate are almost two times more likely to sustain a traumatic injury, even after controlling for demographic variables, than children without such a history (Brehaut, Miller, Raina, & McGrail, 2003).

A good independent pediatric neuropsychological evaluation will not only consider obvious prior medical conditions and family circumstances but also prior child development. Several studies have indicated that children with worse premorbid behavioral and adaptive functioning have more persistent adaptive and behavioral deficits after severe TBI (Catroppa, Anderson, Morse, Haritou, & Rosenfeld, 2008; Fay et al., 2009). Furthermore, children with worse premorbid attention problems tend to demonstrate greater vulnerability to the impact of severe TBI on postinjury measures of attention than children without such prior problems (Yeates et al., 2005). In many of these kinds of studies, measures of premorbid functioning were obtained through retrospective parent ratings, shortly after hospitalization. This kind of information is rarely available in medicolegal cases because it is not routinely collected as part of standard clinical care, outside of research projects. However, careful review of premorbid medical records can still be informative. For example, a pediatrician's notes will often comment on attainment of developmental milestones, and they will most likely document when a particular medication (e.g., a stimulant for treatment of ADHD) was first prescribed. If the latter was prior to the accident in question that was allegedly associated with a TBI, this should raise some questions for the pediatric neuropsychologist to address during the interview as part of the independent evaluation (see Chapter 12).

In some cases, prior medical records may not be sufficiently clear or complete. For example, a child may have had difficulties with concentration or impulse control, but these kinds of concerns were not brought to the attention of the primary care physician, either because the parents did not consider the associated behaviors as problematic as did school professionals, or because they did not want to use stimulant medications. In this context, it is important to realize that severe TBI can result in "secondary" ADHD (i.e., the development of ADHD symptoms in the absence of such symptoms prior to injury) that is essentially indistinguishable from long-standing ADHD on formal psychometric tests of attention (Slomine et al., 2005). Postinjury parental ratings of children's daily executive functioning are also affected by both premorbid history of ADHD and the presence of a diffuse intracranial lesion as the result of TBI, but the influence of the former history tends to be relatively more pronounced (Donders, DenBraber, & Vos, 2010).

To illustrate the importance of premorbid developmental history, Figure 9.1 presents data that were selected from the latter study, according to the following criteria: Group 1 included 20 children with TBI that was associated with both coma of at least 24 hours and positive findings on neuroimaging, but who did not have any premorbid

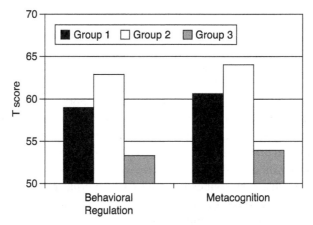

FIGURE 9.1. Parental ratings on the Behavior Rating Inventory of Executive Function. Group 1 includes 20 children with traumatic brain injury (TBI), including coma of at least 24 hours and positive findings on neuroimaging, but negative for premorbid history of attention-deficit/hyperactivity disorder (ADHD), learning disability, or psychiatric treatment; Group 2 includes 15 children with TBI, no prolonged coma or intracranial findings on neuroimgaging, but positive for premorbid history of treatment for ADHD; and Group 3 includes 24 children with TBI, no prolonged coma, intracranial findings on neuroimaging, or premorbid complicating histories.

history of ADHD, learning disability, or psychiatric treatment; Group 2 included 15 children with TBI that was associated with neither prolonged coma nor intracranial findings on neuroimgaging but who did have a known premorbid history of treatment for ADHD; and Group 3 included 24 children with TBI that was not associated with either prolonged coma or intracranial findings on neuroimaging and who also did not have premorbid complicating histories. The children's daily functioning after the TBI was rated by their parents on the Behavior Rating Inventory of Executive Function (BRIEF; Gioia, Isquith, Guy, & Kenworthy, 2000). As can be seen in Figure 9.1, Group 2 had the highest postinjury parent ratings on this instrument (i.e., reflective of worse pathology), and Group 3 the lowest, with Group 1 taking an intermediate position. Thus, a premorbid history of ADHD in children with mild, uncomplicated TBI yielded slightly worse postinjury parental ratings of daily executive functioning than did severe TBI in the absence of a prior history of ADHD.

These findings indicate that psychometric variables obtained post TBI, when considered in isolation, may not necessarily or exclusively reflect injury-related phenomena. This is why, especially with school-age children, review of the prior academic history and of the associated records is essential in the context of the independent pediatric neuropsychological evaluation.

Academic History

It has been well established that premorbid cognitive level of functioning has a significant impact on children's adaptive as well as cognitive abilities after TBI (Arroyos-Jurado, Paulsen, Merrell, Lindgren, & Max, 2000). Lower level of preinjury adaptive functioning has also been identified as risk factor for post-TBI personality change as well as secondary ADHD (Max et al., 2005; Max et al., 2006). However, in the context of an independent pediatric neuropsychological evaluation, the question often comes up to what degree a known or suspected premorbid condition has affected the neurobehavioral functioning of the child post incident; that is, after the lead exposure, car accident, or other event that allegedly caused brain compromise. Review of premorbid academic records is nothing but short of essential in order to answer this question. Several studies have shown that, when *only* postinjury neuropsychological test scores were considered, children with moderate–severe TBI who had a documented premorbid history of ADHD, depression, or learning disability were virtually indistinguishable from children with similar injury severity and from similar demographic backgrounds but without premorbid psychiatric or special education histories (Donders & Strom, 1997, 2000). It was only when a comparison was made between premorbid and postinjury psychometric data that it became apparent that there was a statistically significant decline from premorbid functioning in the group with the prior complicating histories, as evidenced by a median drop of 10–12 points (depending on the sample) in Full Scale IQ.

Formal premorbid IQ scores are often included in the individual education plan of children with prior special education histories, but children without such prior histories most often do not have prior assessment data. This actually affords the pediatric neuropsychologist a paradoxical advantage when evaluating children with preexisting cognitive or emotional dysfunction. However, this advantage can only be materialized when the premorbid school records are considered as a routine part of the evaluation. In cases where formal prior IQ scores are not available, review of such records can still be informative with regard to issues such as attendance, discipline problems, and overall achievement on nationally standardized tests such as the PLAN or PSAT or, for high school juniors and seniors, the ACT or SAT.

Methods have also been developed to estimate premorbid intelligence in children on the basis of demographic variables, sometimes supplemented with current subtest scores from the WISC–IV (e.g., Schoenberg, Lange, Brickell, & Saklofske, 2007), with subsequent attempt at validation in clinical samples like children with TBI (Schoenberg, Lange, Saklofske, Suarez, & Brickell, 2008). A relative strength of these actuarial algorithms is that they do not include WISC–IV subtests like Coding or Symbol Search, which happen to be the only ones that are actually sensitive to severity of TBI (Donders & Janke, 2008) and therefore would not be appropriate to use on a postinjury basis to estimate premorbid functioning. However, it needs to be realized that such algorithms should be used with considerable caution because the resulting estimates are associated with fairly large standard errors of estimation; 8–9 points not being uncommon (Schoenberg et al., 2008). This would result in 90% confidence intervals that are often close to a standard deviation (i.e., 13–16 points) in either direction of the actual estimate. Failure to appreciate this wide margin of error would seriously hamper the accuracy of the conclusions in independent pediatric neuropsychological evaluations.

Family History

Several studies of children with pediatric TBI have demonstrated that a dysfunctional pre-injury family environment as well as premorbid psychosocial disadvantage can adversely affect children's neurobehavioral recovery from such injuries (Anderson, Morse, Catroppa, Haritou, & Rosenfeld, 2004; Taylor et al., 2002; Wassenberg, Max, Lindgren, & Schatz, 2004; Yeates et al., 1997). Similarly, effects of lead exposure on neurobehavioral outcome may be especially detrimental to children from socioeconomically disadvantaged backgrounds (Dilworth-Bart & Moore, 2006; Ris, Dietrich, Succop, Berger, & Bornschein, 2004). In contrast, genetic factors appear to be relatively less predictive of cognitive development in impoverished than in affluent families (Turkheimer, Haley, Waldron, D'Onofrio, & Gottesman, 2003). This does not mean that every child who comes from lower socioeconomic strata, or whose parents had a hotly contested divorce within a year prior to injury or exposure, is going to have a poor outcome, but failure to consider the potential impact of these variables can contribute to diagnostic errors in the context of the independent pediatric neuropsychological evaluation. This is why a thorough interview and history are so important.

Obtaining information about biological family psychiatric history is of crucial relevance. Having a first-degree biological parent with a serious mental illness is known to be associated with a significantly increased risk for the development of a variety of psychiatric illnesses in children. For example, children with a mother with schizophrenia are known to be about five times more likely to develop this disease than children without such a family history (Arendt, Mortensen, Rosenberg, Pedersen, & Waltoft, 2008). Family psychiatric risk may be particularly relevant with younger children. For example, compared to adolescents with late onset, persons with childhood-onset bipolar disorder have significantly higher percentages of a positive first-degree family history of a wide range of disorders, ranging from anxiety to depression to substance dependence (Rende et al., 2007). For other common childhood psychiatric conditions, like ADHD, a biological family history of the same condition is strongly predictive of persistence of the disorder into adolescence (Biederman, 2005) or, in the case of a major depressive episodes, recurrences (Wickramaratne, Greenwald, & Weissman, 2000).

The postevent family environment is another potentially powerful contributor to child outcomes, and this has been studied extensively in the field of pediatric TBI. Greater levels of family stress as well as suboptimal coping styles have been identified as risk factors for poor neurobehavioral outcomes in children with TBI (Anderson et al., 2006; Kinsella, Ong, Murtagh, Prior, & Sawyer, 1999; Sesma, Slomine, Ding, & McCarthy, 2008; Taylor et al., 1999). In addition, parents often experience considerable burden, and the way they cope with this can affect postinjury family functioning (Wade et al., 2001; Wade et al., 2004). Unfortunately, measures of family functioning are not routinely included in pediatric neuropsychological evaluations. However, several widely used, psychometrically sound, standardized measures of the emotional and behavioral adjustment of older children allow for the formal evaluation of various aspects of family dysfunction, from both the child's and the parent's point of view. Examples include the Personality Inventory for Children–Second Edition (Lachar & Gruber, 2001) and the Personality Inventory for Youth (Lachar & Gruber, 1995). Another option for the pediatric neuropsychologist evaluating younger children is to try to obtain standardized ratings about children's daily functioning from both the parent and the school teacher (e.g., with the BRIEF).

All of these instruments also include validity checks for overreporting of problems, which is an important consideration in the independent pediatric neuropsychological evaluation. Obtaining standardized input from several independent sources about children's daily functioning is likely to increase the accuracy of the diagnostic process.

A final consideration with regard to family history is the influence of other psychosocial stressors that occurred around the same time as the original event that caused the brain compromise, or during the period between that event and the time of the neuropsychological evaluation. Although children and adolescents do sometimes show a remarkable degree of resilience to common family transitions (Ruchena, Prior, Sanson, & Smart, 2005), they are vulnerable to the effects of more significant traumatic stressors such as parental death (Saldinger, Cain, & Porterfield, 2003) or military deployment (Lincoln, Swift, & Shorteno-Fraser, 2008). Witnessing domestic abuse is also associated with a significantly increased risk for psychological maladjustment in children (Gewirtz & Medhanie, 2008). Children who experience bereavement as the result of the death of a sibling or parent in the same accident in which they got injured may also experience significant adjustment difficulties, even if they have absolutely no recollection of the traumatic event and do not have subjective reexperiences of the event (Donders, 1993). A careful review of such potentially complicating psychosocial stressors should be a routine part of any independent pediatric neuropsychological evaluation.

COMORBID CONDITIONS

Even when the premorbid psychosocial history is fairly unremarkable, children may still have other complicating conditions that are causally related to the event that brought them to the attention of the pediatric neuropsychologist. Such comorbid factors can potentially affect the level of performance during cognitive tests or change the priorities for intervention. Although a full review of all the physical complications and adjustment reactions that children may have to acquired brain injury is outside the scope of this chapter, two specific conditions will be emphasized: pain and posttraumatic stress disorder.

It is conceivable that pain might be a potential source of significant distraction during a neuropsychological evaluation and that this might deflate some cognitive test scores. However, this issue has received surprisingly little attention in the pediatric literature, despite the fact that widespread pain has a prevalence of between 8% and 15% between the ages of 10 and 16 years in the general population (Mikkelsson et al., 2008). Haverkamp, Hönscheid, and Müller-Sinik (2002) reported that children with migraine did not do worse than sibling controls on a test of general cognitive ability, but they did not administer more specific neuropsychological tests. In addition, the children were not evaluated during an acute migraine episode, and no correlations between subjective pain intensity and performance level were explored. It is also important to realize that the effects of pain on children's cognitive performance may go beyond the acute subjective experience but can be confounded, especially in chronic conditions like sickle cell disease, by the impact of fatigue, absenteeism due to numerous medical appointments, and side effects of prescription medications

(Bonner, Gustafson, Schumacher, & Thompson, 1999). In addition, sleep disturbance is common in a variety of pediatric conditions and can be associated with neuropsychological impairment (Beebe, 2006).

There have been several studies in adult and geriatric samples that have suggested that greater self-reported pain is associated with lower scores on tests of executive functioning, complex attention, or memory (Dick, Verrier, Harker, & Rashiq, 2008; Oosterman, de Vries, Dijkerman, de Haan, & Scherder, 2009; Sjögren, Christrup, Petersen, & Hojsted, 2005; Weiner, Rudy, Morrow, Slaboda, & Lieber, 2006). On the other hand, there is evidence that at least some of this impact may be influenced by depressive symptoms (Scherder et al., 2008). There is also concern about the influence of motivation and secondary gain in adult populations with alleged pain (Greve, Etherton, Ord, Bianchini, & Curtis, 2009). Furthermore, it has been suggested that performing a cognitively demanding task may actually facilitate distraction from pain (Veldhuijzen, Kenemans, de Bruin, Olivier, & Volkerts, 2006). Again, the vast majority of this research has been conducted in adult samples, and there is a clear need for more empirical investigation into the effect of pain on cognition in children. Meanwhile, statements about the impact of pain on pediatric neuropsychological test results need to be made with caution.

Another potentially complicating comorbid condition is posttraumatic stress disorder (PTSD). This condition can be seen especially in the acute stage after motor vehicle accidents, particularly when there was minimal loss of consciousness associated with a mild TBI (Gerring et al., 2002; Mather, Tate, & Hannan, 2003). In children with trauma-related intracranial findings, greater orbitofrontal involvement tends to be associated with a decreased risk for PTSD, whereas temporal lobe compromise may increase this risk (Vasa et al., 2004). This is an important consideration because temporal lobe integrity is also known to be important for successful memory test performance after pediatric TBI (Salorio et al., 2005). Furthermore, PTSD in and by itself has been related to poor performance on tests of attention and executive functioning in children (Beers & De Bellis, 2002; Moradi, Doost, Taghavi, Yule, & Dalgleish, 1999). Thus, careful exploration of the possibility of confounding PTSD is an important consideration in the independent pediatric neuropsychological evaluation.

CASE STUDY

The following case may illustrate the way some of the aforementioned confounds can be addressed in the context of an independent pediatric neuropsychological evaluation. This adolescent was originally seen at the request of defense counsel in the context of civil litigation, but the information is presented with permission from the plaintiff's counsel. Some characteristics have been modified slightly in order to protect confidentiality.

Jane Doe was seen for neuropsychological evaluation at the age of 16 years for question of encephalopathy associated with lead exposure due to paint residue ingestion. Available medical records revealed an uncomplicated pregnancy and delivery, with attainment of developmental milestones, including independent walking, talking in short sentences, and potty training, at normal intervals; all prior to the age of 3 years. Between the ages of 3½ and 5 years, she had a consistent series of more than a half dozen elevated blood lead levels, ranging from 18 to 34 μg/dl. Although there is debate in the literature about the significance of low lead levels such as <10 μg/dl, there is general consensus that values >20 μg/dl are associated with a significantly increased risk for cognitive compromise (Dietrich, 2010). There was no known or reported family psychiatric history. A significant confounding factor was that, at the age of 8 years, Jane was struck as a pedestrian by a motor vehicle. Although there was no prolonged loss of consciousness, head computed tomography (CT) did reveal a left frontal hemorrhagic cerebral contusion. None of the available records reflected any follow-up for this apparent TBI.

At the time of the neuropsychological evaluation, Jane was about to start the 10th grade, reportedly having completed much of her prior schooling with special education support. School records were initially not available at the time of this evaluation. Semi-structured interview did not yield evidence for any mood concerns. Table 9.2 presents a summary of some of the key data from the neuropsychological assessment.

Inspection of Table 9.2 suggests good effort (TOMM). Levels of psychometric intelligence (WASI) and academic achievement (WRAT–4) were in the borderline range. A Full Scale IQ at almost 2 standard deviations below the mean appeared to be a bit lower than "just" the range of expectation for a child who had grown up in poverty, with the latter effect to have been estimated at a median of about two-thirds of a standard deviation, although with considerable variability (McLoyd, 1998). However, there were relatively more significant deficits on tests of learning/memory (CVLT–C), attention and speed of processing (Trail Making), and executive functioning (WCST). Importantly, assessment of sensorimotor skills (Grooved Pegboard)

TABLE 9.2. Neuropsychological Test Results for Jane Doe

Test	Result
TOMM, Trial 1 (% correct)	96
TOMM, Trial 2 (% correct)	100
WASI, Verbal IQ	68
WASI, Performance IQ	79
WASI, Full Scale IQ	71
WRAT–4, Sentence Comprehension	74
WRAT–4, Math Computation	72
CVLT–C, List A1–5	54
WCST, Total Errors	57
Trail Making, Part A	67
Trail Making, Part B	50
Grooved Pegboard, right hand	55
Grooved Pegboard, left hand	90

NOTES: All test results in standard scores (M = 100, SD = 15) except where otherwise indicated. CVLT–C, California Verbal Learning Test—Children's Version; TOMM, Test of Memory Malingering; WASI, Wechsler Abbreviated Scale of Intelligence; WCST, Wisconsin Card Sorting Test; WRAT–4, Wide Range Achievement Test–Fourth Edition.

revealed a selective impairment with the right hand, which could be consistent with the location of the focal injury associated with her TBI.

It was concluded that Jane had cognitive compromise in higher level cognitive skills that were likely beyond what could reasonably be expected on the basis of poverty and that it was possible that her early history of lead exposure had contributed to this. However, it was also made clear that without review of the pre- and post-TBI academic records, no firm conclusion could be reached about the effect from the TBI, later in childhood.

School records were eventually made available. These included a school psychological evaluation that was completed at the age of 7 years; that is, after the lead exposure, but before the TBI. At that time, Jane's Verbal IQ was 65 and her Performance IQ was 79. Another school psychological evaluation had been done 2 years later, at the age of 9 years; that is, almost a year after the TBI. At that time, the corresponding scores were 67 and 80. Unfortunately, more specific neuropsychological tests were not performed, either before or after the TBI, and the school psychologist did not administer on either occasion the Processing Speed subtests. Nevertheless, review of these records demonstrated that Jane's IQ scores were already below average prior to the TBI, remained stable after that, and were similar in pattern to results obtained about 8 years later, at the age of 16 years. The final conclusion was that Jane's history of early lead exposure probably contributed to her general cognitive limitations, but that a further exacerbation in selective areas as the result from her TBI was strongly suspected.

CONCLUSION

There are many factors that can play a confounding role in independent pediatric neuropsychological evaluations, even when the examiner is aware of his or her own personal biases and even when the selection of test instruments is based on evidence of reliability and validity. A good understanding of the impact of base rates on diagnostic accuracy, a comprehensive review of both the child's and the family's pre- and postevent history, and a careful consideration of possible comorbid conditions, are all absolutely essential. Specific goals for future research include the elucidation of the impact of physical factors like pain, fatigue, sleep disturbance, and medication side effects on pediatric neuropsychological test results, and the longer term predictive accuracy of such psychometric findings, beyond the first few years post assessment.

REFERENCES

Anderson, V. A., Catroppa, C., Dudgeon, P., Morse, S. A., Haritou, F., & Rosenfeld, J. V. (2006). Understanding predictors of functional recovery and outcome 30 months following early childhood head injury. *Neuropsychology, 20*(1), 42–57.

Anderson, V. A., Morse, S. A., Catroppa, C., Haritou, F., & Rosenfeld, J. V. (2004). Thirty month outcome from early childhood head injury: a prospective analysis of neurobehavioural recovery. *Brain, 127*(12), 2608–2620.

Arendt, M., Mortensen, P. B., Rosenberg, R., Pedersen, C. B., & Waltoft, B. L. (2008). Familial predisposition for psychiatric disorder: comparison of subjects treated for cannabis-induced psychosis and schizophrenia. *Archives of General Psychiatry, 65*(11), 1269–1274.

Arroyos-Jurado, E., Paulsen, J. S., Merrell, K. W., Lindgren, S. D., & Max, J. E. (2000). Traumatic brain injury in school-age children: Academic and social outcome. *Journal of School Psychology, 38,* 571–587.

Babikian, T., & Asarnow, R. (2009). Neurocognitive outcomes and recovery after pediatric TBI: Meta-analytic review of the literature. *Neuropsychology, 23*(3), 283–296.

Baron, I. S. (2004). *Neuropsychological evaluation of the child.* New York: Oxford University Press.

Beebe, D. W. (2006). Neurobehavioral morbidity associated with disordered breathing during sleep in children: A comprehensive review. *Sleep, 29*(9), 1115–1134.

Beers, S. R., & De Bellis, M. D. (2002). Neuropsychological function in children with maltreatment-related posttraumatic stress disorder. *American Journal of Psychiatry, 159*(3), 483–486.

Beers, S. R., Hammond, K., & Ryan, C. M. (2006). General assessment issues for a pediatric population. In P. J. Snyder, P. D. Nussbaum, & D. L. Robins (Eds.), *Clinical neuropsychology: A pocket handbook for assessment* (pp. 123–154). Washington, DC: American Psychological Association.

Biederman, J. (2005). Attention-deficit/hyperactivity disorder: A selective overview. *Biological Psychiatry, 57*(11), 1215–1220.

Bland, J. M., & Altman, D. G. (2000). Statistics notes. The odds ratio. *British Medical Journal, 320*(7247), 1468.

Bonner, M. J., Gustafson, K. E., Schumacher, E., & Thompson, R. J. (1999). The impact of sickle cell disease on cognitive functioning and learning. *School Psychology Review, 28,* 182–193.

Brehaut, J. C., Miller, A., Raina, P., & McGrail, K. M. (2003). Childhood behavior disorders and injuries among children and youth: A population-based study. *Pediatrics, 111*(2), 262–269.

Brooks, B. L., Iverson, G. L., Sherman, E. M. S., & Holdnack, J. A. (2009). Healthy children and adolescents obtain some low scores across a battery of memory tests. *Journal of the International Neuropsychological Society, 15*(4), 613–617.

Catroppa, C., Anderson, V. A., Morse, S. A., Haritou, F., & Rosenfeld, J. V. (2008). Outcome and predictors of functional recovery 5 years following pediatric traumatic brain injury (TBI). *Journal of Pediatric Psychology, 33*(7), 707–718.

Costello, E. J., Egger, H., & Angold, A. (2005). 10-year research update review: The epidemiology of child and adolescent psychiatric disorders: I. Methods and public health burden. *Journal of the American Academy of Child and Adolescent Psychiatry, 44*(10), 972–986.

Costello, E. J., Mustillo, S., Erkanli, A., Keeler, G., & Angold, A. (2003). Prevalence and development of psychiatric disorders in childhood and adolescence. *Archives of General Psychiatry, 60*(8), 837–844.

Crawford, J. R., Sutherland, D., & Garthwaite, P. H. (2008). On the reliability and standard errors of measurement of contrast measures from the D-KEFS. *Journal of the International Neuropsychological Society, 14*(6), 1069–1073.

De Bellis, M. D., & Kuchibhatla, M. (2006). Cerebellar volumes in pediatric maltreatment-related posttraumatic stress disorder. *Biological Psychiatry, 60*(7), 697–703.

Deeks, J. J., & Altman, D. G. (2004). Diagnostic tests 4: Likelihood ratios. *British Medical Journal, 329*(7458), 168–169.

Delis, D. C., Kramer, J. H., Kaplan, E., & Ober, B. A. (1994). *California Verbal Learning Test-Children's Version.* San Antonio, TX: Psychological Corporation.

Dennis, M., Yeates, K. O., Taylor, H. G., & Fletcher, J. M. (2007). Brain reserve capacity, cognitive reserve capacity, and age-based functional plasticity after congenital and acquired brain injury in children. In S. Y. (Ed.), *Cognitive reserve: Theory and applications* (pp. 53–83). New York: Taylor & Francis.

Dick, B. D., Verrier, M. J., Harker, K. T., & Rashiq, S. (2008). Disruption of cognitive function in fibromyalgia syndrome. *Pain, 139*(3), 610–616.

Dietrich, K. N. (2010). Environmental toxicants. In K. O. Yeates, M. D. Ris, H. G. Taylor, & B. F. Pennington (Eds.), *Pediatric neuropsychology: Research, theory, and practice* (2nd ed., pp. 211–264). New York: Guilford Press.

Dilworth-Bart, J. E., & Moore, C. F. (2006). Mercy mercy me: Social injustice and the prevention of environmental pollutant exposures among ethnic minority and poor children. *Child Development, 77*(2), 247–265.

Donders, J. (1993). Bereavement and mourning in pediatric rehabilitation settings. *Death Studies, 17*(6), 517–527.

Donders, J. (1999). Performance discrepancies on the California Verbal Learning Test-Children's Version in the standardization sample. *Journal of the International Neuropsychological Society, 5*(1), 26–31.

Donders, J., DenBraber, D., & Vos, L. (2010). Construct and criterion validity of the Behavior Rating Inventory of Executive Function (BRIEF) in children referred for neuropsychological assessment after pediatric traumatic brain injury. *Journal of Neuropsychology, 4,* 197–209.

Donders, J., & Janke, K. (2008). Criterion validity of the Wechsler Intelligence Scale for Children-Fourth Edition after pediatric traumatic brain injury. *Journal of the International Neuropsychological Society, 14*(4), 651–655.

Donders, J., & Minnema, M. T. (2004). Performance discrepancies on the California Verbal Learning Test-Children's Version (CVLT-C) in children with traumatic brain injury. *Journal of the International Neuropsychological Society, 10*(4), 482–488.

Donders, J., & Strom, D. (1997). The effect of traumatic brain injury on children with learning disability. *Pediatric Rehabilitation, 1*(3), 179–184.

Donders, J., & Strom, D. (2000). Neurobehavioral recovery after pediatric head trauma: Injury, pre-injury, and post-injury issues. *Journal of Head Trauma Rehabilitation, 15*(2), 792–803.

Egger, H. L., & Angold, A. (2006). Common emotional and behavioral disorders in preschool children: Presentation, nosology, and epidemiology. *Journal of Child Psychology and Psychiatry, 47*(3–4), 313–337.

Fay, T. B., Yeates, K. O., Wade, S. L., Drotar, D., Stancin, T., & Taylor, H. G. (2009). Predicting longitudinal patterns of functional deficits in children with traumatic brain injury. *Neuropsychology, 23*(3), 271–282.

Ford, T., Goodman, R., & Meltzer, H. (2003). The British Child and Adolescent Mental Health Survey 1999: The prevalence of DSM-IV disorders. *Journal of the American Academy of Child and Adolescent Psychiatry, 42*(10), 1203–1211.

Fox, D., Lees-Haley, P., Earnest, K., & Dolezal-Wood, S. (1995). Base rates of postconcussive symptoms in health maintenance organization patients and controls. *Neuropsychology, 9,* 606–611.

Gerring, J. P., Slomine, B., Vasa, R. A., Grados, M., Chen, A., Rising, W., ... Ernst, M. (2002). Clinical predictors of posttraumatic stress disorder after closed head injury in children. *Journal of the American Academy of Child and Adolescent Psychiatry, 41*(2), 157–165.

Gewirtz, A. H., & Medhanie, A. (2008). Proximity and risk in children's witnessing of intimate partner violence incidents. *Journal of Emotional Abuse, 8*, 67–82.

Gioia, G. A., Isquith, P. K., Guy, S. C., & Kenworthy, L. (2000). Behavior rating inventory of executive function. *Child Neuropsychology, 6*(3), 235–238.

Gouvier, W. D. (1999). Base rates and clinical decision making in neuropsychology. In J. Sweet (Ed.), *Forensic neuropsychology: Fundamentals and practice* (pp. 23–37). Lisse, The Netherlands: Swets & Zeitlinger.

Greve, K. W., Etherton, J. L., Ord, J., Bianchini, K. J., & Curtis, K. L. (2009). Detecting malingered pain-related disability: Classification accuracy of the test of memory malingering. *Clinical Neuropsychology, 23*(7), 1250–1271.

Grimes, D. A., & Schulz, K. (2005). Epidemiology 3: Refining clinical diagnosis with likelihood ratios. *Lancet, 365*, 1500–1505.

Hack, M., Taylor, H. G., Schluchter, M., Andreias, L., Drotar, D., & Klein, N. (2009). Behavioral outcomes of extremely low birth weight children at age 8 years. *Journal of Developmental & Behavioral Pediatrics, 30*(2), 122–130.

Haverkamp, F., Honscheid, A., & Muller-Sinik, K. (2002). Cognitive development in children with migraine and their healthy unaffected siblings. *Headache, 42*(8), 776–779.

Jackowski, A. P., de Araujo, C. M., de Lacerda, A. L., Mari Jde, J., & Kaufman, J. (2009). Neurostructural imaging findings in children with post-traumatic stress disorder: Brief review. *Psychiatry and Clinical Neuroscience, 63*(1), 1–8.

Jurewicz, J., & Hanke, W. (2008). Prenatal and childhood exposure to pesticides and neurobehavioral development: Review of epidemiological studies. *International Journal of Occupational Medicine and Environmental Health, 21*, 121–132.

Kemper, A. R., Cohn, L. M., Fant, K. E., & Dombkowski, K. J. (2005). Blood lead testing among Medicaid-enrolled children in Michigan. *Archives of Pediatric and Adolescent Medicine, 159*(7), 646–650.

Kemper, A. R., Cohn, L. M., Fant, K. E., Dombkowski, K. J., & Hudson, S. R. (2005). Follow-up testing among children with elevated screening blood lead levels. *Journal of the American Medical Association, 293*(18), 2232–2237.

Kinsella, G., Ong, B., Murtagh, D., Prior, M., & Sawyer, M. (1999). The role of the family for behavioral outcome in children and adolescents following traumatic brain injury. *Journal of Consulting and Clinical Psychology, 67*, 116–123.

Lachar, D., & Gruber, C. (1995). *Personality Inventory for Youth.* Los Angeles: Western Psychological Services.

Lachar, D., & Gruber, C. (2001). *Personality Inventory for Children-Second edition.* Los Angeles: Western Psychological Services.

Lincoln, A., Swift, E., & Shorteno-Fraser, M. (2008). Psychological adjustment and treatment of children and families with parents deployed in military combat. *Journal of Clinical Psychology, 64*(8), 984–992.

Lipina, S. J., & Colombo, J. A. (2009). *Poverty and the brain: An approach from cognitive psychology and neuroscience.* Washington, DC: American Psychological Association.

Mather, F. J., Tate, R. L., & Hannan, T. J. (2003). Post-traumatic stress disorder in children following road traffic accidents: A comparison of those with and without mild traumatic brain injury. *Brain Injury, 17*(12), 1077–1087.

Max, J. E., Levin, H. S., Schachar, R. J., Landis, J., Saunders, A. E., Ewing-Cobbs, L., . . . Dennis, M. (2006). Predictors of personality change due to traumatic brain injury in children and adolescents six to twenty-four months after injury. *Journal of Neuropsychiatry and Clinical Neuroscience, 18*(1), 21–32.

Max, J. E., Schachar, R. J., Levin, H. S., Ewing-Cobbs, L., Chapman, S. B., Dennis, M., . . . Landis, J. (2005). Predictors of secondary attention-deficit/hyperactivity disorder in children and adolescents 6 to 24 months after traumatic brain injury. *Journal of the American Academy of Child and Adolescent Psychiatry, 44*(10), 1041–1049.

McCrea, M. A. (2008). *Mild traumatic brain injury and postconcussion syndrome.* New York: Oxford.

McLoyd, V. C. (1998). Socioeconomic disadvantage and child development. *American Psychology, 53*(2), 185–204.

Mikkelsson, M., El-Metwally, A., Kautiainen, H., Auvinen, A., Macfarlane, G. J., & Salminen, J. J. (2008). Onset, prognosis and risk factors for widespread pain in school-children: A prospective 4-year follow-up study. *Pain, 138*(3), 681–687.

Moradi, A. R., Doost, H. T., Taghavi, M. R., Yule, W., & Dalgleish, T. (1999). Everyday memory deficits in children and adolescents with PTSD: Performance on the Rivermead Behavioural Memory Test. *Journal of Child Psychology and Psychiatry, 40*(3), 357–361.

Oosterman, J. M., de Vries, K., Dijkerman, H. C., de Haan, E. H., & Scherder, E. J. (2009). Exploring the relationship between cognition and self-reported pain in residents of homes for the elderly. *International Psychogeriatrics, 21*(1), 157–163.

Pavuluri, M. N., Birmaher, B., & Naylor, M. W. (2005). Pediatric bipolar disorder: A review of the past 10 years. *Journal of the American Academy of Child and Adolescent Psychiatry, 44*(9), 846–871.

Rende, R., Birmaher, B., Axelson, D., Strober, M., Gill, M. K., Valeri, S., . . . Keller, M. (2007). Childhood-onset bipolar disorder: Evidence for increased familial loading of psychiatric illness. *Journal of the American Academy of Child and Adolescent Psychiatry, 46*(2), 197–204.

Ris, M. D., Dietrich, K. N., Succop, P. A., Berger, O. G., & Bornschein, R. L. (2004). Early exposure to lead and neuropsychological outcome in adolescence. *Journal of the International Neuropsychological Society, 10*(2), 261–270.

Ruchena, E., Prior, M., Sanson, A., & Smart, D. (2005). A longitudinal study of adolescent adjustment following family transitions. *Journal of Child Psychology and Psychiatry, 46,* 353–363.

Saldinger, A., Cain, A., & Porterfield, K. (2003). Managing traumatic stress in children anticipating parental death. *Psychiatry, 66*(2), 168–181.

Salorio, C. F., Slomine, B. S., Grados, M. A., Vasa, R. A., Christensen, J. R., & Gerring, J. P. (2005). Neuroanatomic correlates of CVLT-C performance following pediatric traumatic brain injury. *Journal of the International Neuropsychological Society, 11*(6), 686–696.

Scherder, E. J., Eggermont, L., Plooij, B., Oudshoorn, J., Vuijk, P. J., Pickering, G., . . . Oosterman, J. (2008). Relationship between chronic pain and cognition in cognitively intact older persons and in patients with Alzheimer's disease. The need to control for mood. *Gerontology, 54*(1), 50–58.

Schoenberg, M. R., Lange, R. T., Brickell, T. A., & Saklofske, D. H. (2007). Estimating premorbid general cognitive functioning for children and adolescents using the American Wechsler Intelligence Scale for Children-Fourth Edition: demographic and current performance approaches. *Journal of Child Neurology, 22*(4), 379–388.

Schoenberg, M. R., Lange, R. T., Saklofske, D. H., Suarez, M., & Brickell, T. A. (2008). Validation of the Child Premorbid Intelligence Estimate method to predict premorbid Wechsler Intelligence Scale for Children-Fourth Edition Full Scale IQ among children with brain injury. *Psychological Assessment, 20*(4), 377–384.

Sesma, H. W., Slomine, B. S., Ding, R., & McCarthy, M. L. (2008). Executive functioning in the first year after pediatric traumatic brain injury. *Pediatrics, 121*(6), e1686–e1695.

Sjögren, P., Christrup, L. L., Petersen, M. A., & Hojsted, J. (2005). Neuropsychological assessment of chronic non-malignant pain patients treated in a multidisciplinary pain centre. *European Journal of Pain, 9*(4), 453–462.

Slomine, B. S., Salorio, C. F., Grados, M. A., Vasa, R. A., Christensen, J. R., & Gerring, J. P. (2005). Differences in attention, executive functioning, and memory in children with and without ADHD after severe traumatic brain injury. *Journal of the International Neuropsychological Society, 11*(5), 645–653.

Smith, G. E., Ivnik, R. J., & Lucas, J. (2008). Assessment techniques: Tests, test batteries, norms and methodological approaches. In J. E. Morgan & J. H. Ricker (Eds.), *Textbook of clinical neuropsychology* (pp. 38–57). New York: Taylor & Francis.

Sobel, D. M., & Munro, S. E. (2009). Domain generality and specificity in children's causal inference about ambiguous data. *Developmental Psychology, 45*(2), 511–524.

Sobel, D. M., Tenenbaum, J. B., & Gopnik, A. (2004). Children's causal inferences from indirect evidence: Backwards blocking and Bayesian reasoning in preschoolers. *Cognitive Science, 28*, 303–333.

Straus, S. E., Richardson, W. S., Glasziou, P., & Haynes, R. B. (2005). *Evidence-based medicine: How to practice and teach EBM.* New York: Elsevier.

Taylor, H. G., Yeates, K. O., Wade, S. L., Drotar, D., Klein, S. K., & Stancin, T. (1999). Influences on first-year recovery from traumatic brain injury in children. *Neuropsychology, 13*(1), 76–89.

Taylor, H. G., Yeates, K. O., Wade, S. L., Drotar, D., Stancin, T., & Minich, N. (2002). A prospective study of short- and long-term outcomes after traumatic brain injury in children: Behavior and achievement. *Neuropsychology, 16*(1), 15–27.

Turkheimer, E., Haley, A., Waldron, M., D'Onofrio, B., & Gottesman, II (2003). Socioeconomic status modifies heritability of IQ in young children. *Psychological Science, 14*(6), 623–628.

Vasa, R. A., Grados, M., Slomine, B., Herskovits, E. H., Thompson, R. E., Salorio, C., . . . Gerring, J. P. (2004). Neuroimaging correlates of anxiety after pediatric traumatic brain injury. *Biological Psychiatry, 55*(3), 208–216.

Veldhuijzen, D. S., Kenemans, J. L., de Bruin, C. M., Olivier, B., & Volkerts, E. R. (2006). Pain and attention: Attentional disruption or distraction? *Journal of Pain, 7*(1), 11–20.

Wade, S. L., Borawski, E. A., Taylor, H. G., Drotar, D., Yeates, K. O., & Stancin, T. (2001). The relationship of caregiver coping to family outcomes during the initial year following pediatric traumatic injury. *Journal of Consulting and Clinical Psychology, 69*(3), 406–415.

Wade, S. L., Stancin, T., Taylor, H. G., Drotar, D., Yeates, K. O., & Minich, N. M. (2004). Interpersonal stressors and resources as predictors of parental adaptation following pediatric traumatic injury. *Journal of Consulting and Clinical Psychology, 72*(5), 776–784.

Wassenberg, R., Max, J. E., Lindgren, S. D., & Schatz, A. (2004). Sustained attention in children and adolescents after traumatic brain injury: Relation to severity of injury, adaptive functioning, ADHD and social background. *Brain Injury, 18*(8), 751–764.

Wechsler, D. (2004). *Wechsler Intelligence Scale for Children—Fourth Edition.* San Antonio, TX: Harcourt Assessment.

Weiner, D. K., Rudy, T. E., Morrow, L., Slaboda, J., & Lieber, S. (2006). The relationship between pain, neuropsychological performance, and physical function in community-dwelling older adults with chronic low back pain. *Pain Medicine, 7*(1), 60–70.

Wickramaratne, P. J., Greenwald, S., & Weissman, M. M. (2000). Psychiatric disorders in the relatives of probands with prepubertal-onset or adolescent-onset major depression. *Journal of the American Academy of Child and Adolescent Psychiatry, 39*(11), 1396–1405.

Yeates, K. O., Armstrong, K., Janusz, J., Taylor, H. G., Wade, S., Stancin, T., & Drotar, D. (2005). Long-term attention problems in children with traumatic brain injury. *Journal of the American Academy of Child and Adolescent Psychiatry, 44*(6), 574–584.

Yeates, K. O., Taylor, H. G., Drotar, D., Wade, S. L., Klein, S., Stancin, T., & Schatschneider, C. (1997). Preinjury family environment as a determinant of recovery from traumatic brain injuries in school-age children. *Journal of the International Neuropsychological Society, 3*(6), 617–630.

PART TWO

Applied Clinical Issues in Pediatric Forensic Neuropsychology

Chapter 10

Independent Neuropsychological Evaluation of Children With Mild Traumatic Brain Injury

GERARD A. GIOIA
CHRISTOPHER G. VAUGHAN
PETER K. ISQUITH

INTRODUCTION

Forensic neuropsychological evaluation with children and adolescents, hereafter referred to as simply "children," who have sustained a mild traumatic brain injury (TBI) presents the clinician with a number of challenges in providing an evidence-based examination (see Chapter 11 for a discussion of moderate to severe TBI). The evaluation requires an assessment of the child's history, including preinjury risk factors and injury characteristics, as well as the child's current neurocognitive, symptom, and social-emotional status, all in the context of change from preinjury (baseline) function. In this chapter, we provide injury definitions and known epidemiology, and we summarize current knowledge of the neuropathology of mild TBI, neurocognitive deficits, symptom profiles (and associated functional and behavioral outcomes), and factors that modify recovery. Postinjury recovery is discussed in terms of short-term (including acute [0–3 days] and postacute [3 days to 3 months]) and long-term (>3 months) outcomes (Kirkwood et al., 2008). While a forensic evaluation is more likely to occur in the long-term phase, understanding the earlier phases and the typical course of signs and symptoms of mild TBI provides key information to guide the evaluation process. The reader must recognize that knowledge regarding this injury continues to rapidly evolve, and one must keep abreast of new developments to incorporate recent findings into his or her clinical evaluation.

Prior to 1983, scant attention was paid to mild TBI in children because it was presumed that it was a temporary condition and recovery would be swift without any permanent concerns. Boll (1983) famously challenged the notion that all children with mild TBI recover fully and quickly with the contention that "Mild head injury is a quiet disorder. It is common, typically bloodless and without call for significant medical intervention. It seems even more quiet because the noise it does make (its symptoms) is often attributed to other causes. Nevertheless the disruption in coping capacity and attendant breakdown in usual behavioral patterns causes more psychosocial and academic-economic hardship than have begun to be appreciated" (p. 74). Since Boll's call to alarm in 1983, there has been considerable study and characterization regarding the impact of mild TBI in children.

It is important to appreciate that long-term effects of mild TBI can be a complex matter. While there has been considerable attention paid to this question, the different methodologies and populations can make the integration of this body of work challenging. Literature on mild TBI primarily contains four basic types of studies on recovery outcomes: (1) symptom-based reports of neurobehavioral outcomes; (2) cross-sectional, and more recently, postacute and longitudinal studies (>1–3 months post injury up to over 20 years), using traditional broad neuropsychological test batteries (e.g., IQ, memory, language, attention, academic achievement); (3) neuroimaging studies using newer methods; and (4) studies of sports-related injuries tracking longitudinal recovery with recently developed focused test batteries designed to be sensitive to the effects of mild TBI. The reader is directed to reviews of this literature for a more in-depth examination of recovery outcomes (Babikian & Asarnow, 2009; Carroll et al., 2004a; Ellemberg, Henry, Macciocchi, Guskiewicz, & Broglio, 2009; McKinlay, 2009; Satz et al., 1997). It is notable that very little empirical work has been conducted with preschool children while relatively more research has been conducted with school-age children and a greater amount with adolescents.

To frame the forensic neuropsychological evaluation of children with mild TBI, we present a set of four basic assumptions:

1. Most children, adolescents, and young adults recover fully from a mild TBI within 3 months (Collins, Lovell, Iverson, Ide, & Maroon, 2006; Iverson, 2006; McCrea, 2008).

2. Most forensic evaluations of children with mild TBI will take place following the acute or early postacute stage. The child seen for a forensic evaluation, therefore, likely has a question of persistent sequelae.

3. As a mild TBI with persistent sequelae is a relatively low-frequency event, its evaluation will require assessment of factors that complicate recovery, including an atypical injury (e.g., more significant, or complicated, injury), premorbid disabilities, poor early identification with little or no treatment, possible exacerbation or reinjury, or other issues contributing to prolonged recovery.

4. To understand the reasons for persisting dysfunction, the neuropsychological evaluation will necessarily be comprehensive to examine potential contributing factors.

The foci of the neuropsychological evaluation is three-fold: (1) identify abnormal areas of neuropsychological functioning, (2) establish whether these abnormalities are significantly greater than preinjury functioning and likely related to the injury, and (3) define the persisting effects on the child's life. Clinicians must approach the evaluation with knowledge of the specific nature of this injury and the neuropsychological domains that current evidence indicates will likely exhibit persisting problems. The evaluation is, therefore, constructed to capture these key functional domains in addition to defining the important historical factors that contextualize the neuropsychological profile.

DEFINITIONS

Establishing a singular definition of mild TBI has continued to challenge the field (Blostein & Jones, 2003). There is agreement, however, that a new classification system of TBI is needed, as the simple designation of mild, moderate, and severe classically based on the Glasgow Coma Scale (GCS; Teasdale & Jennett, 1974) falls woefully short in describing the complex and diverse spectrum of injury to the brain (Saatman et al., 2008). Even within the mild TBI category, there are a number of definitions (e.g., American Congress of Rehabilitation Medicine, 1993; Concussion in Sport Group, 2008, McCrory et al., 2009; World Health Organization Collaborating Centre Task Force on Mild TBI, Borg et al., 2004) and a variety of terms are routinely used by health care professionals to describe this injury, including concussion, mild traumatic brain injury, mild closed head injury, and minor head trauma, some with different inherent connotations (DeMatteo et al., 2010). Most definitions concur that mild TBI is the result of a blunt impact with sudden acceleration, deceleration, or rotation of the head accompanied by a GCS of 13–15, any alteration in mental state, and the presence of postinjury signs and/or symptoms.

Within the "mild" category of TBI, there is a range of severity and pathology, including those with and without structural findings—that is, "complicated" versus "uncomplicated" mild TBI (Williams, Levin, & Eisenberg, 1990). Furthermore, many definitions of "concussion" imply that there is no permanent or structural damage to the brain, yet this may reflect limitations of current clinical neuroimaging techniques (Bigler, 2008; McCrory et al., 2009). More sophisticated brain imaging techniques used thus far primarily in research have begun to yield heretofore undetected structural findings and possible biomarkers of mild TBI (Ellemberg et al., 2009). Thus, for those with persistent postconcussion symptoms, underlying structural pathology ultimately may be discovered with more advanced imaging methods (Bigler, 2008).

A broad range of recovery times is evident following the injury from minutes and hours to weeks, months, and beyond (Collins et al., 2006). The presence of persistent symptoms following mild TBI is often referred to as postconcussive syndrome (PCS), although it is not without its controversies (Bigler, 2008; Ruff, 2009). The term *persistent postconcussive syndrome* has also been used if the symptoms last more than 3 months, although this is not a formal diagnostic entity (Iverson, 2006; Satz et al., 1999). For the purposes of this chapter, PCS is operationally defined as symptoms that persist beyond 3 months following a mild TBI or concussion, indicating more chronic sequelae.

EPIDEMIOLOGY

As the definition, severity, and outcomes of mild TBI vary widely, understandably so do incidence estimates. Mild TBI is estimated to account for up to 90% of all brain injuries (Cassidy, Carroll, Cote, Holm, & Nygren, 2004; McCrea, 2008). Recent annual incidence estimates specific to sports- and recreation-related TBI in the United States by the Centers for Disease Control and Prevention (CDC) suggest that up to 3.8 million children and adults sustain a concussion each year (Langlois, Rutland-Brown, & Wald, 2006). Even this figure may be an underestimate given the challenges in identifying mild TBI, particularly in younger children (Gioia, Collins, & Isquith, 2008; Williamson & Goodman, 2006). Varying definitions and multiple pathways to diagnosis (e.g., emergency department visits, pediatrics office contacts, school or sports team–associated individuals such as coaches and trainers, or no treatment at all) may interfere with detecting the full scope of the problem via traditional surveillance methods and underestimate the incidence of mild TBI in children (NCIPC, 2003). The need remains for better incidence and prevalence estimates, definitions, and injury classification.

PATHOPHYSIOLOGY, NEUROLOGICAL FINDINGS, AND IMAGING

Knowledge of the pathophysiology of mild TBI has increased significantly over the past decade due to the greater availability of sophisticated research neuroimaging methods (Bigler, 2008) and animal models (Greisbach, Gomez-Pinella, & Hovda, 2007). Giza and Hovda (2001) used animal models to describe the temporary neurometabolic dysfunction associated with a complex pathophysiological process involving ionic shifts, altered metabolism, impaired connectivity, and changes in neurotransmission. Following the biomechanical forces to the brain, there is a rapid release of neurotransmitters such as glutamate accompanied by unregulated ionic fluxes through the efflux of potassium and influx of calcium in cells. This ultimately leads to neuronal depolarization and changes in glucose metabolism as well as altered cerebral blood flow and impaired axonal function. This model of neurometabolic dysfunction in mild TBI is attractive in its description of the dysfunction, but there are as yet limitations in its direct application to humans. More recent advanced neuroimaging methods, however, have improved our understanding of the neuronal dysfunction in human mild TBI, including functional magnetic resonance imaging (fMRI), electroencephalography (EEG) and event-related potentials (ERPs), proton magnetic resonance spectroscopy (H-MRS), and diffusion tensor imaging (DTI). Several recent reviews are available for a more in-depth examination of the issues (see Bigler, 2008; Davis, Iverson, Guskiewicz, Ptito, & Johnston, 2009; DiFiori & Giza, 2010; Ellemberg et al., 2009; Jantzen, 2010). We briefly summarize these findings here.

Abnormal brain activation using fMRI has been associated with working memory task performance in symptomatic (Chen, Johnston, Petrides, & Ptito, 2008) and nonsymptomatic (Slobounov et al., 2010) concussed young adult athletes. Furthermore, adolescent athletes showed increased activation related to longer recovery times (Lovell et al., 2007). ERPs may differentiate adults with mild TBI from uninjured controls (Gosselin, Theriault, Leclerc, Montplaisir, & Lassonde, 2006), including those with persistent PCS (Broglio, Pontifex, O'Connor, & Hillman, 2009) and those with multiple concussions (De Beaumont, Brisson, Lassonde, & Jolicoeur, 2007). ERP also has been correlated with self-reported postconcussion symptoms (Lavoie, Dupuis, Johnston, Leclerc, & Lassonde, 2004). McCrea et al. (2010) found a significant relationship between quantitative EEG (QEEG) and both symptom report and cognitive test performance immediately following injury in high school and college football players, with QEEG abnormalities persisting in some players to 45 days post injury.

The neurometabolic dysfunction of mild TBI has also been examined using proton magnetic resonance spectroscopy (h-MRS) although its use, thus far, has been limited to children with moderate to severe TBI (e.g., Babikian et al., 2006), young adults with mild TBI (e.g., Henry, Tremblay, Boulanger, Ellemberg, & Lassonde, 2010; Vagnozzi et al., 2008), and experimental animal studies (e.g., Vagnozzi et al., 2007). Neurometabolic changes are being directly examined with respect to postconcussive symptoms (Henry et al., 2010); with metabolic recovery possibly persisting beyond subjective symptom report (Vagnozzi et al., 2008). Reduced integrity of neurotransmission following mild TBI in adults has been demonstrated with diffusion tensor imaging (DTI) (e.g., Rutgers et al., 2008). Abnormal axonal integrity (reduced fractional anisotropy and increased diffusivity) has been correlated with increased symptom report in adolescents with mild TBI (Chu et al., 2010; Wilde et al., 2008). As with h-MRS, DTI has been used more so in children with moderate and severe TBI but may hold promise for detecting otherwise unseen axonal dysfunction in mild TBI (Niogi & Mukherjee, 2010). The use of these more sensitive methods "may be critical in refining diagnosis, therapeutic intervention, and management of mild TBI" (Wilde et al., 2008, p. 954). As more advanced neuroimaging techniques reveal heretofore undetected neuropathology associated with mild TBI, the basic distinction between "complicated" and "uncomplicated" mild TBI based on traditional imaging studies (i.e., CT, MRI) may be rendered less meaningful.

RECOVERY OUTCOMES

The literature on the effects of mild TBI can be viewed in terms of the short-term time frame (within 3 months of the injury) and long-term (greater than 3 months) as the clinical question is often raised: "Are there long-term problems associated with mild TBI?" Furthermore, recovery outcomes can be classified within three general categories: neurocognitive changes; postconcussion symptoms; and social, emotional, and behavioral changes.

Short-Term Outcome

The literature on the acute effects of mild TBI is somewhat limited by inconsistent use of clinical tools for standardized evaluation and diagnosis of mild TBI in primary care and emergency care settings (Blostein & Jones, 2003), resulting in unstructured, cursory assessment of postinjury signs and symptoms with varied assessment of mental status. The focus is often on a limited set of readily identifiable and/or high-frequency symptoms such as loss of consciousness (LOC), GCS, headache, and memory loss (Kennedy et al., 2006). Postconcussion symptoms have been typically classified as physical, cognitive, and emotional (Ayr et al., 2009;

Axelrod et al., 1996) with sleep disruption also described in some classifications (Gioia et al., 2008; Pardini et al., 2004). Beyond the first several days post injury, symptom manifestation is typically a continuation of those reported in the acute phase and is important to track systematically and serially. New symptoms do not typically emerge following the acute phase, although secondary responses to the injury (e.g., mood changes or various stress responses) may emerge later in the recovery process and complicate the recovery profile.

Short-term outcomes of pediatric mild TBI have been studied with similar symptom patterns but variable recovery periods. The study of sport-related concussion, arguably a select subsample of mild TBI, describes relatively short time frames for recovery (Collins et al., 2006; Iverson et al., 2006) with most adolescent athletes recovering in less than 1 month. There may be limitations in generalizing acute outcomes in this athlete group to the general pediatric population as differences likely exist in characteristics of the athlete versus nonathlete sample and mechanisms of the injury. In addition, differences exist in the settings in which the injuries occur, availability of immediate postinjury surveillance, and early access to medical care. In contrast to the shorter recovery times in student athletes, typically measured in terms of days or weeks, studies that examine a broader group of children who sustained mild TBI report neurocognitive recovery time frames within 2 to 3 months post injury (Babikian & Asarnow, 2009; Carroll et al., 2004a). Importantly, within this time period there can be a range of recovery trajectories (Collins et al., 2006; Yeates & Taylor, 2005). Consideration of recovery outcomes simply based on group averages will obscure important individual differences in outcome (Iverson et al., 2006).

Long-Term Outcome

While the majority of children who sustain a mild TBI recover within 3 months, a minority of children experience long-term or chronic effects. In their widely cited review, Satz and colleagues (Satz et al., 1997) culled 40 studies between 1970 and 1995 that included use of control group, adequate sample size ($n > 20$), and specification of study design, patient ascertainment methods, injury severity, control methods for preinjury factors, number and timing of follow-up assessments, and domains assessed. Their review found little evidence for adverse effects on academic-psychosocial or neuropsychological outcomes in children. There were some long-term effects associated with greater injury severity though these were partially explained by preinjury risk factors. They concluded that there was little evidence of any long-term effects of mild TBI in children, but acknowledged that neither were their findings definitive nor was the null hypothesis of no long-term effects proven. An examination of the measures that were predominantly used in these early studies (e.g., general intelligence) reveals a possible insensitivity to the kinds of neurocognitive problems described in the current literature.

Recent reviews (Babikian & Asarnow 2009; McKinlay, 2009) have examined the issue of long-term effects. McKinlay (2009) noted that few studies of children with mild TBI found evidence of deficits on performance tests, including measures of academic skills (Ayr, Yeates, & Enrile, 2005), language (Barnes & Dennis, 2001), attention (Catroppa, Anderson, Morse, Haritou, & Rosenfeld, 2008), memory (Hannay & Levin, 1989), and executive function (Catroppa & Anderson, 2003). A recent series of studies by Catroppa, Anderson, and colleagues (Catroppa & Anderson, 2003, 2005; Catroppa et al., 2007) examined attention and executive function with a battery of tests in the immediate postinjury period and again at 6, 12, and 24 months post injury and found deficits in the moderate and severe TBI groups but not in the mild TBI group, though there was no control group. These studies suggest that it is at best difficult to detect attention and executive problems with performance measures in children following mild TBI.

In a rigorous meta-analysis of pediatric mild TBI outcome studies, Babikian and Asarnow (2009) examined 28 studies from 1988 to 2007 that included a control group, clearly defined mild TBI groups, performance measures of several domains of cognitive function (e.g., attention, memory, executive function), and multiple measurement time points (0–5 months, 6–23 months, 24 or more months post injury). The majority of these studies excluded children with prior neurological, psychiatric, learning, behavior, or attention problems. Overall, there were negligible to small differences between mild TBI and control groups over time for most functions, including IQ, working memory, visual immediate memory, and visual/perceptual function. There were small effects in verbal IQ and attention between groups at time 3, initially small but increasing to moderate effects by time 3 for verbal fluency, and small-to-moderate effects for processing speed at all time points. These differences were attributed primarily to effects in younger children. They concluded that the majority of children with mild TBI show few, if any, long-term deficits in the measured domains, though there may be a small percentage with persistent effects.

Most of these studies lead to the conclusion that long-term neurocognitive deficits are not commonly found in most domains following mild TBI. Yet these studies pose limitations that restrict generalization. The majority of cognitive tests used in routine clinical practice were not designed to be sensitive to the effects of mild TBI. Measures designed to detect cognitive dysfunction secondary to mild TBI (e.g., computerized measures with alternate forms for repeated assessment) have become widely available only recently. Most computerized measures to date, however, were developed for adolescents and adults, not younger children, and are not part of the standard neuropsychology toolkit. Another issue that may limit generalizability of mTBI studies is the exclusion of participants with preexisting behavioral, attentional, learning, or psychiatric difficulties or with prior neurological injury, including prior mild TBI. Studies that exclude children with such risk factors can focus more on the effects of the injury itself free from the confounding effects of prior risks. At the same time, it may be that children with such prior risk factors are more vulnerable to mild TBI and may have a different recovery course. For example, cognitive ability (i.e., cognitive reserve) has a protective influence on outcome following mild TBI, with children of lower cognitive functioning showing more adverse outcomes (Fay et al., 2010). Finally, studies that combine the small number of subjects with persistent postconcussion symptoms with the larger number who do not experience symptoms are unlikely to detect group differences (Kent & Hayward, 2007). They argue that it is difficult to detect persistent symptoms or cognitive deficits in the small number of persistently symptomatic individuals when studied in the context of the much larger group of asymptomatic individuals. The few extant studies that directly compare symptomatic with asymptomatic individuals with mild TBI find important cognitive differences (Collie, Makdissi, Maruff, Bennell, & McCrory, 2006; Iverson, Gaetz, Lovell, & Collins, 2004), supporting the need to examine these groups separately.

In a series of studies of postconcussion symptoms in children designed to address several methodological concerns, Yeates, Taylor, and colleagues (Taylor et al., 2010; Yeates & Taylor, 2005; Yeates et al., 2009) reported on a large group of children with well-defined mild TBI along with an orthopedic injury (OI) control group followed from the acute stage through 1 year post injury. Yeates and Taylor (2005) found four distinct longitudinal trajectories in symptom patterns, with mild TBI more likely than the OI group to show high levels of acute symptoms that resolved (24%) or persisted (7%). Symptoms were not explained by traumatic injuries in general or by preexisting symptoms (Taylor et al., 2010). Furthermore, they demonstrated the importance of separating symptoms into domains (e.g., cognitive, somatic) rather than relying on general symptom counts, as parent ratings of somatic symptoms were initially elevated but resolved by 12 months post injury, while parent ratings of cognitive symptoms peaked at 3 months and remained elevated at 12 months. Child self-report ratings correlated well with parent ratings. Symptom ratings were related to injury factors, including presence of LOC, CT scan or MRI abnormality, need for hospitalization, and motor-vehicle injury. At the same time, higher premorbid symptoms and earlier age at injury predicted higher postinjury symptoms. This series of well-controlled studies contributes to a better understanding of both acute and late effects of mild TBI in children with known preinjury characteristics and identified risk factors.

The study group described earlier (Taylor et al., 2010) also completed computerized measures of planning and working memory while parents completed a rating scale of executive function. The study found no differences between the mild TBI and OI groups at 3 or 12 months on the neurocognitive measures, and only one small difference on the parent ratings. Unlike the results of tracking postconcussion symptoms, these findings suggest that broader executive deficits following mild TBI in children may be absent, or at least difficult to assess. Other recent evidence, however, suggests that this may be dependent on the study sample. Sesma and colleagues (Sesma, Slomine, Ding, & McCarthy, 2008) found substantial differences in parent ratings of child executive functions at 3 and 12 months post injury for children with either mild, moderate, or severe TBI versus an orthopedic injury control group. Effects were related to injury severity and moderated by preinjury and family variables. It may be that the participant ascertainment for this group, namely at least a one-night hospital stay, resulted in a selection bias toward more severe brain injuries even among the large group of children considered to have "mild" TBI.

Changes in emotional, behavioral, and social functioning in the long-term following mild TBI in children has received some attention with mixed findings. Several studies that relied on informant (e.g., parent, teacher reports of everyday behavior) reported no greater risk for behavior problems following mild TBI

(Fletcher, Ewing-Cobbs, Miner, Levin, & Eisenberg, 1990; Kinsella, Ong, Murtagh, Prior, & Sawyer, 1999), others reported greater behavior problems but attributed them to noninjury factors (e.g., premorbid problems) (Asarnow et al., 1995; Ponsford et al., 1999), while still others excluded children with preexisting behavior problems and attributed increased problems to the mild TBI (Bijur, Haslum, & Golding, 1990; Hawley, 2003; McKinlay, Dalrymple-Alford, Horwood, & Fergusson, 2002). Other studies have taken a psychiatric diagnostic approach, examining the incidence of clinically diagnosable psychiatric conditions following mild TBI. For example, McKinlay and colleagues (2009) followed a birth cohort who had sustained a mild TBI prior to age 5 years longitudinally and found a higher risk for attention-deficit/ hyperactivity disorder (ADHD), conduct disorder, and oppositional defiant disorder in adolescence that was not explained by preinjury behavior. Other studies, however, have found few diagnosable attention problems following mild TBI relative to higher frequency of diagnosis in severe TBI (Max et al., 2004).

Factors Modifying Recovery Outcome

A variety of injury- and non-injury-related variables may be associated with long-term outcome and should be considered in the evaluation. Understanding the contribution of these factors provides the clinician with hypotheses to explain persisting dysfunction. In general, severity of the injury within the mild TBI category has been shown to be associated with outcome (Hessen, Nestvold, & Sundet, 2006) with more severe injury characteristics (e.g., "complicated" mild TBI) resulting in higher risk for long-term neuropsychological dysfunction (Fay et al., 2010; Taylor et al., 2010). Age at injury likely plays a role in time to recovery (Babikian & Asarnow, 2009; McKinlay et al., 2002) as high school athletes may require longer time to recover than collegiate and professional athletes (Field, Lovell, Collins, & Maroon, 2003; Moser, Schatz, & Jordan, 2005; Pellman, Lovell, Viano, & Casson, 2006) and younger children may recover more slowly than older children (McKinlay et al., 2002). Collins and colleagues (2006) report at least 25% of high school football players taking up to 4 weeks to reach recovery criteria, well beyond what is reported for older athletes. Additional factors have been reported as possible modifiers of recovery outcome with each of them increasing the likelihood of prolonged recovery, including premorbid learning and behavioral status (Collins, Lovell, & McKeag, 1999; Light et al., 1998; Massagli et al., 2004; Ponsford et al., 1999), history of chronic headaches (Mihalik et al., 2005), and history of previous concussions (Collins et al., 2002; Iverson et al., 2006; Ponsford et al., 1999; Swaine et al., 2007). The family expectations and functioning (Anderson, Catroppa, Morse, Haritou, & Rosenfeld, 2001; Hawley, Ward, Magnay, & Long, 2003) and type of postinjury activity management (Comper, Bisschop, Carnide, & Tricco, 2005; Majerske et al., 2008; Ponsford et al., 2001) have also been associated with recovery outcomes. Finally, although still in an early stage of research, genetic vulnerability may also be a contributing factor to length of recovery (Liberman, Stewart, Wesnes, & Troncoso, 2002; Teasdale, Murray, & Nicoll, 2005). Iverson (2005) reported that injury-related variables accounted for more variance in the initial postinjury presentation and non-injury-related variables more in subsequent periods.

While most studies conclude that the majority of children are at low risk for persisting postconcussion problems, more recent conceptualizations employing the "cognitive reserve" model suggest that it may be the child *with* these premorbid disorders that is at higher risk and should be directly studied. The basic concept here is that the child with these premorbid issues has fewer degrees of freedom to support a faster recovery. Fay et al. (2010) posited that postconcussive symptom presentation in children may be associated with cognitive reserve capacity. They found children of lower cognitive ability with complicated mild TBI were more prone to cognitive symptoms across time and to high levels of postconcussion symptoms in the acute period (Fay et al., 2010).

CLINICAL EVALUATION

Given that multiple factors can potentially modify recovery outcomes, they must be considered in the clinical evaluation as possible contributors to an atypical recovery pattern. When symptoms and/or cognitive deficits persist beyond the typical 3-month recovery period, the evaluation should broaden to include assessment of injury characteristics, a comprehensive history of premorbid and postinjury risk factors and corrective factors, the child's current neurocognitive functioning, a detailed assessment of postconcussion symptoms, family factors, level of postinjury management, and examination of associated behavioral, social, and emotional functioning. The primary goal of clinical evaluation is to differentiate and document injury-related symptoms from noninjury characteristics. The evaluation explores problems across a broad range of functional domains in the context of family, school, or other environmental factors that facilitate or impede recovery. The evaluation should assess the child's functioning beyond the testing session to understand how the neuropsychological/symptom profile affects school, social/recreational, and sports activities (Camiolo Reddy, Collins, & Gioia, 2008).

The forensic neuropsychological evaluation is less likely to occur within the first several weeks following injury, yet it is important to appreciate the early postinjury evaluations to inform the clinician about the course of recovery. Table 10.1 delineates the evaluation goals, data sources, and potential types of measurement instruments for assessment in the short- and long-term postinjury phases. Immediately post injury, early identification is emphasized (roadside, field side, emergency department, physician office) using such tools as the Acute Concussion Evaluation (ACE) (CDC, 2007; Gioia et al., 2008) or the Standardized Assessment of Concussion (SAC) (McCrea et al., 1998). Key early postinjury signs and symptoms are the focus of these assessments with the question of change from baseline functioning to establish presence or absence of injury. Clinical evaluation early post injury is typically quite narrowly focused with the goal of identifying symptoms and neurocognitive dysfunction to initiate early management. Direct assessment of neurocognitive functioning in the first several days post injury is infrequent, as many medical settings do not have neuropsychological assessment services available on demand. Brief neurocognitive assessment, when available, should focus on attention, working memory, new learning, memory storage and retrieval, and speed of

TABLE 10.1. Phase-Specific Mild Traumatic Brain Injury Evaluation Goals, Data Sources, and Tools

Phase	Evaluation Goal	Data Sources	Evaluation Tools
Short term (<3 months)	Identify symptoms and neurocognitive dysfunction, monitor recovery process, symptom management, guide return to school and physical activity *Primary Question:* Are there changes from baseline functioning that establish presence or absence of injury?	1. Injury definition and characteristics, postconcussion symptoms 2. History: Previous mild traumatic brain injury, medical, neurological, developmental, learning/school, psychiatric 3. Testing: narrow focus	1. Standardized postinjury signs and symptom inventory 2. Focused neuropsychological functions: attention, working memory, new learning, memory storage and retrieval, and speed of processing
Long term (>3 months)	Differentiate and document injury-related symptoms and dysfunction from noninjury characteristics *Primary Question:* Are there areas of neuropsychological function that show persisting change from baseline, and what factors contribute to their persistence?	Above plus: 1. Comprehensive history of pre- and postinjury risk and protective factors, neuroimaging findings, exacerbating events/conditions, reinjury, adherence to postinjury treatment/management 2. Detailed assessment of postconcussion symptoms, family factors, examination of associated behavioral, social, and emotional functioning 3. Testing: broad focus	1. Postinjury signs and symptom inventory 2. Comprehensive, broad-based neuropsychological functions: attention, memory, cognitive speed; intellectual functioning; executive functions; language; visual-spatial processes 3. Social-emotional-behavioral functioning, including effort and motivational factors 4. Family factors 5. School performance 6. Possible neuroimaging, other medical evaluation (e.g., headache, sleep)

processing together with standardized assessment of the four categories of symptoms (Gioia, Isquith, Schneider, & Vaughan, 2009).

Postacute clinical evaluation (within the first 3 months) consists of serial focused standardized assessments of postconcussion symptoms and neurocognitive functioning, each of which do not necessarily recover within the same time frame (Fazio, Lovell, Pardini, & Collins, 2007; Iverson et al., 2006), reinforcing the point that each measures distinct aspects of recovery and should be included in the postacute phase evaluation. The clinical goals of the evaluation in the postacute stage are to monitor the recovery process, actively manage symptoms, and guide gradual return to school and play/sports decisions. While the forensic evaluator may become involved at this point, a comprehensive neuropsychological evaluation typically is not necessary at this stage.

The neuropsychological evaluation for persisting dysfunction is necessarily more comprehensive and broad based than the focused evaluation that occurs shortly after the injury. The evaluation first broadly assesses the child's profile of neuropsychological strengths and weaknesses, including the standard domains of functioning (e.g., Baron, 2004). To understand the reasons for persisting dysfunction, the evaluation examines factors that can complicate recovery, including an atypical injury (e.g., more significant, or complicated, injury), premorbid risk factors (e.g., medical, psychiatric, developmental, learning disabilities), poor early identification, incomplete treatment, exacerbation or reinjury, or other issues contributing to prolonged recovery. Examining direct and indirect evidence for suboptimal effort and atypical informant reporting (e.g., effort tests, embedded test measures of effort, highly variable response styles, and atypical symptoms or symptom severity) are also strongly recommended (see Chapters 6 and 7). A comprehensive evaluation therefore taps the neuropsychological domains typically affected by the injury as well as defining preinjury and postinjury factors that contribute to the persisting effects on the child's life. The broad-based neuropsychological evaluation of the child with persisting dysfunction includes an assessment of a variety of factors, including preinjury characteristics, injury characteristics, neurocognitive functioning, postconcussion symptoms, and social-emotional functioning. We discuss these areas next.

Assessment of Preinjury Characteristics

It is critical to obtain a good clinical history of preinjury functioning from the patient, family, and teachers accompanied by any available documentation in the medical and school records. A thorough developmental history, medical/neurological history (including personal/family history of chronic headaches), school history, and psychiatric history (including sleep disorders, anxiety, depression) provides essential information about the child's preinjury functioning, risk factors such as premorbid learning; attentional, psychiatric, or behavioral disorders; familial risks for the same; and family environment. In addition, to explore the possibility of cumulative effects, the clinician should gather a detailed history of previous brain injuries, including age at injury, injury characteristics, and length of symptoms and neurocognitive dysfunction.

Injury Characteristics

Defining the acute injury factors is important to frame the severity and possible risks of the injury. Elements to include are a description of the injury and the types of forces involved, mechanism of injury, location of the blow (direct or indirect), evidence of alteration of conscious and/or confusion, presence of retrograde and anterograde amnesia, seizure activity, early signs and symptoms, and radiological findings. Postinjury signs such as retrograde amnesia or confusion can be important because they have been shown to be predictive of later neurocognitive dysfunction and protracted symptom resolution (Lovell et al., 2003).

Neurocognitive Functions

The specific neurocognitive domains that have demonstrated greater sensitivity to the effects of mild TBI—attention/concentration, working memory, speed of processing, and learning/memory, and the executive functions (Babikian & Asarnow, 2009; Catroppa et al., 2007; Schatz, Pardini, Lovell, Collins, & Podell, 2006)—should provide a focus for the evaluation. Two basic approaches to post-acute neuropsychological testing are common: paper-and-pencil and computerized measures, each method having its strengths and limitations. Paper-and-pencil-based tests have demonstrated appropriate sensitivity to the effects of concussion (Echemendia & Julian, 2001; McCrea et al., 2005). They pose psychometric limitations, however, making them less ideal for serial assessment in that many of these tests lack equivalent alternative forms, are susceptible to interrater biases, and show significant practice effects (Collie, Darby, & Maruff, 2001). They may also be less able to detect the subtle changes in reaction time and processing speed (Maroon et al., 2000).

Computer-administered tests have gained greater attention (Collie & Maruff, 2003; Lovell, 2008), allowing for alternate randomized forms and serial tracking of recovery with limited or known practice effects. They can be more easily parameterized to increase sensitivity to mild cognitive dysfunction, incorporating precise reaction time to the hundredth of a second (McCrory, Makdissi, Davis, & Collie, 2005). Computer-based measures, however, have the disadvantage of constrained response options—for example, allowing only recognition memory responses versus free-recall format.

Postconcussion Symptoms

A thorough assessment of postconcussion symptoms is an essential component of the evaluation. The four symptom types—physical, cognitive, emotional, and sleep-related—should be fully explored in terms of their presence, severity, and change over time. Symptoms typically encompass a combination of somatic (e.g., headache, dizziness, fatigue, sensitivity to light and noise), cognitive (e.g., difficulty concentrating, trouble remembering), emotional (e.g., irritability), and sleep-related (e.g., difficulty falling asleep) changes from preinjury functioning (Iverson, Lovell, & Collins, 2003; Schatz et al., 2006). It is most useful to track symptoms from the onset of injury to the time of the evaluation in order to understand the rate of recovery and assess the degree and type of impact that the injury is having on the child's life. This assessment should include collecting structured symptom ratings from the parents and the injured child (Gioia et al., 2009).

Standardized assessment of symptoms and neurocognitive function provide separate yet complementary information (Lovell et al., 2003). For example, Fazio et al. (2007) report a group of concussed but asymptomatic athletes who demonstrated poorer neurocognitive test performance than control subjects within the first several days post injury, indicating incomplete recovery and underscoring the unique contributions of neurocognitive testing and symptom reports. The validity of parent and child reports of subjective and nonspecific postconcussive symptoms may at times be challenged, in part, as reflecting premorbid difficulties or other noninjury factors (Hawley et al., 2003; Light et al., 1998). It is important to assess the presence and degree of preinjury factors and their contribution to current postinjury presentation.

Social-Emotional Functioning

Social, emotional, and behavioral functioning can be assessed using standardized broadband instruments. Tools that look at everyday functioning in terms of symptom reports (i.e., depression, anxiety, somatic concerns, atypical behaviors, etc.) and adaptive functioning provide data from parents, teachers, and sometimes the child that can be compared to normative expectations. Several standard behavior rating scales have been used in studies to evaluate preinjury and postinjury functioning, and they tend to capture problems in more severe or complicated TBI but less so in uncomplicated mild TBI over the long term (Satz et al., 1997). A thorough screening utilizing a standardized instrument completed by multiple informants (i.e., parents and teachers) is an important way to assess preinjury baseline functioning as well as the impact of the injury on the child's functioning via repeat assessment. Interviewing the child, reviewing grade reports and transcripts, and talking to teachers or other care providers all are valuable clinical means of assessing the scope and impact of the injury.

Deviation From Baseline

The challenge in the clinical evaluation of mild TBI, particularly in the forensic setting, is to distinguish change from preinjury functioning. As is noted in other chapters, normal developmental change in the child must be factored in as well. The nature of the postinjury neuropsychological evaluation is largely about detecting functional change from the individual's typical preinjury baseline, requiring measures with appropriate psychometric properties that can detect change reliably. The examiner must have familiarity with reliable change concepts, as well as an understanding of these properties with the particular measures chosen for the evaluation.

How does one determine that the child's neuropsychological functioning has or has not returned to its "normal" baseline? Preinjury baseline data may be available for comparison. In a small number of cases, baseline data may come from prior evaluations if the child was evaluated for educational purposes. Baseline data are also increasingly available from preseason assessments for the students involved in sports. The baseline assessment model posits that capturing neurocognitive functioning preinjury serves as a specific benchmark against which postinjury functioning can be compared using reliable change metrics to identify the likelihood of clinically significant differences in performance and symptoms. In the majority of situations, however, no baseline test data are available, requiring other strategies for estimation of preinjury functioning. One strategy for estimating return to baseline functioning involves serial tracking of cognitive performance and symptom reports to establish improvements in functioning, or a recovery curve. It is essential to assess change in the child's everyday functioning across environments, including home and school, across behavioral, social, and academic domains via parent, teacher, and self-report.

Case Example: Keira

Keira is an otherwise healthy 15-year-old high school sophomore with no reported developmental, familial, or medical risk factors who had a history of good grades in a competitive school. She sustained two concussive injuries over the past year. Recall that the goals for the acute/postacute evaluations include identifying symptoms and neurocognitive dysfunction, monitoring recovery process, providing symptom management, and guiding return to school and physical activity. The primary question to be address in these evaluations is: Are there changes from Keira's baseline (preinjury) functioning that establish presence or absence of injury?

Keira has always been involved in sports, and her high school requires preseason baseline cognitive testing designed to be sensitive to cognitive effects of mild TBI. This increasingly common practice provided a baseline of cognitive functioning and symptom reports with which postinjury performance could be compared. Her first injury occurred during her freshman year when she was in a motor vehicle collision while a belted passenger in a friend's car. There was no loss of consciousness and no retrograde or anterograde amnesia reported. She was seen in the emergency department and computed tomography (CT) scan was normal with no evidence of hemorrhage. She was evaluated within a week following this injury and her performance on a narrow battery of traditional paper-and-pencil neuropsychological tests and on the computer-administered battery revealed mildly slowed speed of processing, reduced working memory, and mild difficulty with new learning for a word list. She and her parents reported symptoms including dizziness, fatigue, and headaches. With Keira's and her parents' permission, her coach and school guidance staff were contacted and informed of the difficulty and connection between the mild TBI, fatigue, and poor concentration as well as further risks should she continue to engage in contact sports until symptom-free. Given that her school had a concussion management program in place and staff were familiar with management strategies for students with concussion symptoms, Keira's workload was temporarily reduced, particularly for homework, and she was allowed to leave class and lie down in the health office when she felt fatigued and unable to concentrate. Keira used the school accommodations for 1 month before returning to her normal routine. Self-report of symptoms fully resolved by 2 months post injury, and neurocognitive performance returned to preinjury baseline levels.

Eleven months after her first mild TBI/concussion, and after several months of sports participation, Keira sustained a second mild TBI during a basketball game. She was elbowed in the right temporal region of the head, fell to the floor, and struck the back of her head hard on the floor. Injury characteristics included no loss of consciousness but brief (approximately 30 seconds) of anterograde amnesia. Cognitive assessment 1 week post injury was remarkable for slowed speed of processing but otherwise at baseline levels. Keira's symptom report and that of her parents on structured postconcussion symptom inventories included complaints of fatigue and trouble concentrating that were interfering with ability to complete schoolwork. Her school expectations were again modified, though Keira only needed reduced workload for 2 weeks. One month after the injury, Keira reported no symptoms and neurocognitive test performance was at expected baseline levels. She again completed a graduated return to play protocol without symptom return and was cleared for return to sports and other activities.

Three months after her second concussion, Keira was referred by her parents' attorney for neuropsychological evaluation as part of a civil suit alleging injuries sustained in the motor vehicle collision now 14 months earlier. The goal of this type of evaluation differs from the earlier two: Differentiate and document injury-related symptoms and dysfunction from noninjury characteristics. Additionally, the primary question for the evaluation has a different focus: Are there areas of neuropsychological function that show persisting change from baseline, and what factors contribute to their persistence?

The suit was prompted by ongoing difficulties completing schoolwork in a timely fashion since the injury with dropping grades, which her parents believed began at the time of her first injury. Mood and sleep problems were also reported, with delayed sleep onset (as late as 1 AM) and significant fatigue during the day. Keira recently expressed feeling depressed and having thoughts of self-harm to her peers who were concerned enough about her safety to contact the school psychologist. A school-based mental health screening did not find evidence of a diagnosable mood disorder. Keira also exhibited some behavior changes since the collision, with greater irritability than previously seen and one incident where she ran away from home for several hours after a disagreement with her parents. Keira denied additional stressors, although her parents reported that social stressors, including dating, recently increased in high school. All parties denied substance use in Keira.

At the time of the evaluation, symptom report on a postconcussion symptom inventory included fatigue, irritability, sadness, difficulty with concentration, feeling mentally slowed down, and disrupted sleep. These symptoms were much higher than reported on the initial postinjury assessment following the first injury, now almost 14 months prior to the present evaluation. Performance on a comprehensive neuropsychological evaluation and on the computer-administered measure documented mild weaknesses in speed of processing in the context of average overall cognitive functioning, average academic skills, and no other problematic areas of functioning. Thus, Keira's academic difficulties appeared to be beyond expectation given formal test findings.

Careful exploration of preinjury academic functioning revealed that, while Keira had always obtained good grades (As and Bs) in middle school and into high school, she needed to spend a substantial amount of time on homework in order to achieve at this level. Her scores on statewide assessments were average, but somewhat below expectation for students at her academically competitive school. This suggests that the etiology of Keira's academic struggles is likely multifactorial and unlikely entirely explained by her initial mild TBI. Following each injury, Keira demonstrated return to baseline levels of functioning both symptomatically and cognitively. Neurological evaluation did not identify a structural injury, suggesting that her injury was uncomplicated, although the absence of findings on standard clinical imaging does not rule out more subtle pathology.

While a direct causal relationship between the original mild TBI sustained in the collision and current symptoms is difficult to establish, her injuries may have had an indirect effect on her current concerns. For individuals who sustain concussions or even orthopedic injuries, the resulting disruption to everyday functioning, including participation in enjoyable activities (e.g., sports, school, and social life), can cause depression and the perception of cognitive problems. Keira's sleep schedule is also a potential contributing factor, because she does not get sufficient rest. Her resulting fatigue may also contribute to reported distractibility and reduced cognitive efficiency. It is therefore likely that Keira's frustrations, restricted sleep, and resulting fatigue play a role in adversely affecting her everyday functioning. The most parsimonious explanation for her current difficulties is likely a combination of preinjury factors (average intellectual abilities, average academic skill), environmental factors (rigorous and academically demanding setting, increased social and academic stressors), comorbid issues (sleep disturbance, mood issues), and the complicating factor of the second injury.

In terms of treatment, the primary targets were addressing Keira's mood symptoms and poor sleep habits in order to reduce fatigue. Additionally, the evaluation findings were discussed with Keira's parents, noting that she is an individual of average ability and average academic skill who has been attempting to achieve high grades in very competitive, often honors, classes, requiring inordinate amounts of study and a likely setup for anxiety and stress. Consideration of a more appropriate academic program was recommended. Following treatment for depression and adolescent adjustment issues and with a sleep hygiene program to increase sleep and reduce fatigue during the day, a clearer picture of any possible persistent postconcussion effects may emerge. Regardless of etiology, without intervention for the mood and fatigue problems, Keira continues to be at significant risk for a variety of difficulties related to emotional functioning and academic performance.

SUMMARY

Mild TBI is the most common brain injury in children and is increasingly recognized as potentially problematic, requiring assessment and management early post injury and in the short term until recovery is complete. In most cases, recovery is relatively rapid, with most children showing no measurable neurocognitive deficits by a few weeks to a few months, and few symptom reports by 3 months. There are, however, a small minority of children who exhibit persisting symptoms/ neurocognitive changes. It is at this point that a forensic neuropsychological evaluation may be requested. The examiner must keep in mind three foci: (1) identify abnormal areas of neuropsychological functioning, (2) establish whether these abnormalities are significantly greater than preinjury functioning and likely related to the injury, and (3) define the persisting effects on the child's life. Accompanying these evaluation foci must be a solid understanding of the nature of a mild TBI and the current evidence supporting or refuting likely persisting neuropsychological dysfunction. A broadband approach to the evaluation of a child with a mild TBI is, therefore, essential, including direct neurocognitive testing, structured and quantitative assessment of postconcussion symptoms, and effects on everyday functioning. To fully examine the basis for persisting problems, the evaluation should include the following: (a) preinjury functioning of the child gathered via a thorough clinical history; (b) definition of the injury characteristics; (c) elapsed time since the injury; (d) progression of the symptoms (i.e., improvement, worsening, no change); (e) assessment of key neurocognitive domains expected to change (e.g., attention, executive function, learning, memory) and not change; (f) postinjury treatment provided and response to treatment over time; (g) other possible contributory influences, including family strengths and stresses; and (h) possible motivational factors. Incorporating the core and contributing factors associated with the persisting postinjury dysfunction into the neuropsychological evaluation will provide a more full understanding of the child's needs.

REFERENCES

American Congress of Rehabilitation Medicine. (1993). Definition of mild traumatic brain injury. Developed by the Mild Traumatic Brain Injury Committee of the Head Injury Interdisciplinary Special Interest Group of the American Congress of Rehabilitation Medicine. *Journal of Head Trauma Rehabilitation, 8,* 86–87.

Anderson, V., Catroppa, C., Morse, S., Haritou, F., & Rosenfeld, J. (2001). Outcome from mild head injury in young children: A prospective study. *Journal of Clinical and Experimental Neuropsychology, 23,* 705–717.

Asarnow, R. F., Satz, P., Light, R., Zaucha, K., Lewis, R., & McCleary, C. (1995). The UCLA study of mild closed head injury in children and adolescents. In S. H. Broman & M. E. Michel (Eds.), *Traumatic head injury in children* (pp. 117–146). New York: Oxford University Press.

Axelrod, B. N., Fox, D. D., Lees-Haley, P. R., Earnest, K., Dolezal-Wood, S., & Goldman, R. S. (1996). Latent structure of the postconcussion syndrome questionnaire. *Psychological Assessment, 8,* 422–427.

Ayr, L. K., Yeates, K. O., & Enrile, B. G. (2005). Arithmetic skills and their cognitive correlates in children with acquired and congenital brain disorder. *Journal of the International Neuropsychological Society, 11,* 249–262.

Ayr, L. K., Yeates, K. O., Taylor, H. G., & Browne, M. (2009). Dimensions of postconcussive symptoms in children with mild traumatic brain injuries. *Journal of the International Neuropsychological Society, 15*(1), 19–30.

Babikian, T., & Asarnow, R. (2009). Neurocognitive outcomes and recovery after pediatric TBI: Meta-analytic review of the literature. *Neuropsychology, 23*(3), 283–296.

Babikian, T., Freier, M. C., Ashwal, S., Riggs, M. L., Burley, T., & Holshouser, B. A., (2006). MR spectroscopy: Predicting long-term neuropsychological outcome following pediatric TBI. *Journal of Magnetic Resonance Imaging, 24*(4), 801–811.

Barnes, M. A., & Dennis, M. (2001). Knowledge-based inferencing after childhood head injury. *Brain and Language, 76*, 253–265.

Baron, I. S. (2004). *Neuropsychological evaluation of the child.* New York: Oxford University Press.

Bigler, E. D. (2008). Neuropsychology and clinical neuroscience of persistent postconcussive syndrome. *Journal of the International Neuropsychological Society, 14*, 1–22.

Bijur, P. E., Haslum, M., & Golding, J. (1990). Cognitive and behavioral sequelae of mild head injury in children. *Pediatrics, 86*, 337–344.

Blostein, P., & Jones, S. J. (2003). Identification and evaluation of patients with mild traumatic brain injury: Results of a national survey of level I trauma centers. *Journal of Trauma, 55*, 450–453.

Boll, T. J. (1983). Minor head injury in children: Out of sight but not out of mind. *Journal of Clinical Child Psychology, 12*, 74–80.

Borg, J., Holm, L., Cassidy, J. D., Peloso, P. M., Carroll, L. J., Von Holst, H., & Ericson, K. (2004). Diagnostic procedures in mild traumatic brain injury: Results of the WHO Collaborating Centre Task Force on mild traumatic brain injury. *Journal of Rehabilitation Medicine, 43*(Suppl), 61–75.

Broglio, S. P., Pontifex, M. B., O'Connor, P., & Hillman, C. H. (2009). The persistent effects of concussion on neuroelectric indices of attention. *Journal of Neurotrauma, 26*, 1463–1470.

Camiolo Reddy, C., Collins, M. W., & Gioia, G. A. (2008). Adolescent sports concussion. *Physical Medicine and Rehabilitation Clinics of North America, 19*, 247–269.

Carroll, L. J., Cassidy, J. D., Peloso, P. M., Borg, J., von Holst, H., Holm, L., Paniak, C., . . . WHO Collaborating Centre Task Force on Mild Traumatic Brain Injury. (2004a). Prognosis for mild traumatic brain injury: Results of the WHO collaborating centre task force on mild traumatic brain injury. *Journal of Rehabilitation Medicine, 43*, 84–105.

Cassidy, J. D., Carroll, L., Cote, P., Holm, L., & Nygren, A. (2004). Mild traumatic brain injury after traffic collisions: A population-based inception cohort study. *Journal of Rehabilitation Medicine, 36*, 15–21.

Catroppa, C., & Anderson, V. (2003). Children's attentional skills 2 years post-traumatic brain injury. *Developmental Neuropsychology, 23*, 359–373.

Catroppa, C., & Anderson, V. (2005). A prospective study of the recovery of attention from acute to 2 years following pediatric traumatic brain injury. *Journal of the International Neuropsychological Society, 11*, 84–98.

Catroppa, C., Anderson, V., Morse, S., Haritou, F., & Rosenfeld, J. (2007). Children's attentional skills 5 years post-TBI. *Journal of Pediatric Psychology, 32*, 354–369.

Catroppa, C., Anderson, V. A., Morse, S. A., Haritou, F., & Rosenfeld, J. V. (2008). Outcome and predictors of functional recovery 5 years following pediatric traumatic brain injury (TBI). *Journal of Pediatric Psychology, 33*(7), 707–718.

Centers for Disease Control and Prevention (CDC) & National Center for Injury Prevention and Control. (2007). *Heads up: Brain injury in your practice. Facts for physicians.* Atlanta (GA): CDC Retrieved from http://www.cdc.gov/ncipc/tbi/Physicians_Tool_Kit.htm.

Chen, J. K., Johnston, K. M., Petrides, M., & Ptito, A. (2008). Neural substrates of symptoms of depression following concussion in male athletes with persisting postconcussion symptoms. *Archives of General Psychiatry, 65*, 81–89.

Chu, Z., Wilde, E. A., Hunter, J. V., McCauley, S. R., Bigler, E. D., Troyanskaya, M., Yallampalli, R., Levin, H. S. (2010). Voxel-based analysis of diffusion tensor imaging in mild traumatic brain injury in adolescents. *American Journal of Neuroradiology, 31*, 340–346.

Collie, A., Darby, D., & Maruff, P. (2001). Computerized cognitive assessment of athletes with sports related head injury. *British Journal of Sports Medicine, 35*, 297–302.

Collie, A., Makdissi, M., Maruff, P., Bennell, K., & McCrory, P. (2006). Cognition in the days following concussion: Comparison of symptomatic versus asymptomatic athletes. *Journal of Neurology, Neurosurgery, and Psychiatry, 77*, 241–245.

Collie, A., & Maruff, P. (2003). Computerized cognitive assessment of concussed Australian Rules footballers. *British Journal of Sports Medicine, 37*, 2–3.

Collins, M. W., Lovell, M. R., Iverson, G. L., Cantu, R. C., Maroon, J. C., & Field, M. (2002). Cumulative effects of concussion in high school athletes. *Neurosurgery, 51*, 1175–1179.

Collins, M. W., Lovell, M. R., Iverson, G. L., Ide, T., & Maroon, J. (2006). Examining concussion rates and return to play in high school football players wearing newer helmet technology: A three year prospective cohort study. *Neurosurgery, 58*(2), 275–283.

Collins, M. W., Lovell, M. R., & McKeag, D. B. (1999). Current issues in managing sports-related concussion. *Journal of the American Medical Association, 282*, 2283–2285.

Comper, P., Bisschop, S. M., Carnide, N., & Tricco, A. (2005). A systematic review of treatments for mild traumatic brain injury. *Brain Injury, 19*(11), 863–880.

Davis, G. A., Iverson, G. L., Guskiewicz, K. M., Ptito, A., & Johnston, K. M. (2009). Contributions of neuroimaging, balance testing, electrophysiology and blood markers to the assessment of sport-related concussion. *British Journal of Sports Medicine, 43*, 36–45.

De Beaumont, L., Brisson, B., Lassonde, M., & Jolicoeur, P. (2007). Long-term electrophysological changes in athletes with a history of multiple concussions. *Brain Injury, 21*, 631–644.

DeMatteo, C. A., Hanna, S. E., Mahoney, W. J., Hollenberg, R. D., Scott, L. A., Law, M. C., ... Xu, L. (2010). "My child doesn't have a brain injury, he only has a concussion." *Pediatrics, 125*, 327–334.

DiFiori, J. P., & Giza, C. (2010). New techniques in concussion imaging. *Current Sports Medicine Reports, 9*(1), 35–39.

Echemendia, R. J., & Julian, L. J. (2001). Mild traumatic brain injury in sports: Neuropsychology's contribution to a developing field. *Neuropsychological Review, 11*, 69–88.

Ellemberg, D., Henry, L. C., Macciocchi, S. N., Guskiewicz, K. M., & Broglio, S. P. (2009). Advances in sport concussion assessment: From behavioral to brain imaging measures. *Journal of Neurotrauma, 26*, 2365–2382.

Fay, T. B., Yeates, K. O., Taylor, H. G., Bangert, B., Dietrich, A., Nuss, K., Rusin, J., & Wright, M. (2010). Cognitive reserve as a moderator of postconcussive symptoms in children with complicated and uncomplicated mild traumatic brain injury. *Journal of the International Neuropsychological Society, 16*(1), 94–105.

Fazio, V. C., Lovell, M. R., Pardini, J. E., & Collins, M. W. (2007). The relation between post concussion symptoms and neurocognitive performance in concussed athletes. *Neurorehabilitation, 22*(3), 207–216.

Field, M., Lovell, M. W., Collins, M., R., & Maroon, J. (2003). Does age play a role in recovery from sports-related concussion? A comparison of high school and collegiate athletes. *Journal of Pediatrics, 142*, 546–553.

Fletcher, J. M., Ewing-Cobbs, L., Miner, M. E., Levin, H. S. & Eisenberg, H. M. (1990). Behavioral changes after closed head injury in children. *Journal of Consulting and Clinical Psychology, 58*, 93–98.

Gioia, G. A., Collins, M. W., & Isquith, P. K. (2008). Improving identification and diagnosis of mild TBI with evidence: Psychometric support for the Acute Concussion Evaluation (ACE). *Journal of Head Trauma Rehabilitation, 23*(4), 230–242.

Gioia, G. A., Isquith, P. K., Schneider, J. C., & Vaughan, C. G. (2009). New approaches to assessment and monitoring of concussion in children. *Topics in Language Disorders, 29*(3), 266–281.

Giza, C. C., & Hovda, D. A. (2001). The neurometabolic cascade of concussion. *Journal of Athletic Training, 36*, 228–235.

Gosselin, N., Theriault, M., Leclerc, S., Montplaisir, J., & Lassonde, M. (2006). Neurophysiological anomalies in symptomatic and asymptomatic concussed athletes. *Neurosurgery, 58*, 1151–1161.

Greisbach, G. S., Gomez-Pinilla, F., & Hovda, D. A., (2007). Time window for voluntary exercise-induced increases in hippocampal neuroplasticity molecules after traumatic brain injury is severity dependent. *Journal of Neurotrauma, 24*, 1161–1171.

Hannay, H. J., & Levin, H. S. (1989). Visual continuous recognition memory in normal and closed-head-injured adolescents. *Journal of Clinical and Experimental Neuropsychology, 11*, 444–460.

Hawley, C. A. (2003). Reported problems and their resolution following mild, moderate and severe traumatic brain injury amongst children and adolescents in the UK. *Brain Injury, 17*, 105–129.

Hawley, C. A., Ward, A. B., Magnay, A. R., & Long, J. (2003). Parental stress and burden following traumatic brain injury amongst children and adolescents. *Brain Injury, 17*(1), 1–23.

Henry, L. C., Tremblay, S., Boulanger, Y., Ellemberg, D., & Lassonde, M. (2010). Neurometabolic changes in the acute phase following sports concussions correlate with symptom severity. *Journal of Neurotrauma, 27*, 65–76.

Hessen, E., Nestvold, K., & Sundet, K. (2006). Neuropsychological function in a group of patients 25 years after sustaining minor head injuries as children and adolescents. *Scandinavian Journal of Psychology, 47*, 245–251.

Iverson, G. L. (2005). Outcome from mild traumatic brain injury. *Current Opinion in Psychiatry, 18*(3), 301–317.

Iverson, G. L. (2006). Misdiagnosis of the persistent postconcussion syndrome in patients with depression. *Archives in Clinical Neuropsychology, 21*, 303–310.

Iverson, G. L., Brooks, B. L., Lovell, M. R., & Collins, M. W. (2006). Tracking neuropsychological recovery following concussion in sport. *Brain Injury, 20*, 245–252.

Iverson, G. L., Gaetz, M., Lovell, M. R., & Collins, M. W. (2004). Relation between subjective fogginess and neuropsychological testing following concussion. *Journal of the International Neuropsychological Society, 10*, 904–906.

Iverson, G. L., Lovell, M. R., & Collins, M. W. (2003). Interpreting change on ImPACT following sport concussion. *Clinical Neuropsychologist, 17*, 460–467.

Jantzen, K. J. (2010). Functional magnetic resonance imaging of mild traumatic brain injury. *Journal of Head Trauma Rehabilitation, 25*(4), 256–266.

Kennedy, R. E., Livingston, L., Marwitz, J. H., Gueck, S., Kreutzer, J. S., & Sander, A. M. (2006). Complicated mild traumatic brain injury on the inpatient rehabilitation unit: A multicenter analysis. *Journal of Head Trauma Rehabilitation, 21*, 260–271.

Kent, D. & Hayward, R. (2007). When averages hide individual differences in clinical trials. *American Scientist, 95,* 60–68.

Kinsella, G., Ong, B., Murtagh, D., Prior, M., & Sawyer, M. (1999). The role of the family for behavioral outcome in children and adolescents following traumatic brain injury. *Journal of Consulting and Clinical Psychology, 67,* 116–123.

Kirkwood, M. W., Yeates, K. O., Taylor, H. G., Randolph, C., McCrea, M., & Anderson, V. A. (2008). Management of pediatric mild traumatic brain injury: A neuropsychological review from injury through recovery. *The Clinical Neuropsychologist, 22,* 769–800.

Langlois J. A., Rutland-Brown W., & Wald, M. M., (2006). The epidemiology and impact of traumatic brain injury. *Journal of Head Trauma Rehabilitation, 21,* 375–378.

Lavoie, M. E. Dupuis, F., Johnston, K. M., Leclerc, S., & Lassonde, M. (2004). Visual p300 effects beyond symptoms in concussed college athletes. *Journal of Clinical and Experimental Neuropsychology, 26,* 55–73.

Liberman, J. N., Stewart, W. F., Wesnes, K., & Troncoso, J. (2002). Apolipoprotein E ε4 and short-term recovery from predominantly mild brain injury. *Neurology, 58*(7), 1038–1044.

Light, R., Asarnow, R. F., Satz, P., Zaucha, K., McCleary, C., & Lewis, R. (1998). Mild closed-head injury in children and adolescents: Behavior problems and academic outcomes. *Journal of Consulting and Clinical Psychology, 66,* 1023–1029.

Lovell, M. R. (2008). The neurophysiology and assessment of sports-related head injuries. *Neurologic Clinics, 26,* 45–62.

Lovell, M. R., Collins, M. W., Iverson, G. L., Field, M., Maroon, J. C., Cantu, R., Podell, K., ... Fu, F. H. (2003). Recovery from mild concussion in high school athletes. *Journal of Neurosurgery, 98*(2), 295–301.

Lovell, M. R., Pardini, J. E., Welling, J., Collins, M. W., Bakal, J., Lazar, N., Roush, R., ... Becker, J. T. (2007). Functional brain abnormalities are related to clinical recovery and time to return-to-play in athletes. *Neurosurgery, 61,* 352–360.

Majerske, C. W., Mihalik, J. P., Ren, D., Collins, M. W., Reddy, C. C., Lovell, M. R., & Wagner, A. K. (2008). Concussion in sports: Postconcussive activity levels, symptoms, and neurocognitive performance. *Journal of Athletic Training, 43*(3), 265–274.

Maroon, J. R., Lovell, M. R., Norwig, J., Podell, K., Powell, J. W., & Hartl, R. (2000). Cerebral concussion in athletes: Evaluation and neuropsychological testing. *Neurosurgery, 47,* 659–669.

Massagli, T. L., Fann, J. R., Burington, B. E., Jaffe, K. M., Katon, W. J., & Thompson, R. S. (2004). Psychiatric illness after mild traumatic brain injury in children. *Archives of Physical Medicine and Rehabilitation, 85,* 1428–1434.

Max, J. E., Lansing, A. E., Koele, S. L., Castillo, C. S., Bokura, H., Schachar, R., Collings, N., & Williams, K. E. (2004). Attention deficit hyperactivity disorder in children and adolescents following traumatic brain injury. *Developmental Neuropsychology, 25,* 159–177.

McCrea, M. (2008). *Mild traumatic brain injury and postconcussion syndrome.* New York: Oxford University Press.

McCrea, M., Barr, W. B., Guskiewicz, K., Randolph, C., Marshall, S. W., Cantu, R., ... Kelly, J. P. (2005). Standard regression-based methods for measuring recovery after sports-related concussion. *Journal of the International Neuropsychology Society, 11,* 58–69.

McCrea, M., Kelly, J., Randolph, C., Kluge, J., Bartolic, E., Finn, G., & Baxter, B. (1998). Standardized assessment of concussion (SAC): On site mental status evaluation of the athlete. *Journal of Head Trauma and Rehabilitation, 13,* 27–35.

McCrea, M., Prichep, L., Powell, M. R., Chabot, R., & Barr, W. B. (2010). Acute effects and recovery after sport-related concussion: A neurocognitive and quantitative brain electrical activity study. *Journal of Head Rehabilitation, 25*(4), 283–292.

McCrory, P., Makdissi, M., Davis, G., & Collie, A. (2005). Value of neuropsychological testing after head injuries in football. *British Journal of Sports Medicine, 39*(Suppl), 58–63.

McCrory, P., Meeuwisse, W., Johnston, K., Dvorak, J. Aubry, M., Molloy, M., & Cantu, R. (2009). Consensus statement on concussion in sport: The 3rd International Conference on Concussion in Sport held in Zurich, November 2008. *British Journal of Sports Medicine, 43*(Suppl 1), i76–84.

McKinlay, A. (2009). Controversies and outcomes associated with mild traumatic brain injury in childhood and adolescences. *Child: Care, Health and Development, 36,* 3–21.

McKinlay, A., Dalrymple-Alford, J. C., Horwood, L. J., & Fergusson, D. M. (2002). Long term psychosocial outcomes after mild head injury in early childhood. *Journal of Neurology, Neurosurgery, & Psychiatry, 73,* 281–288.

McKinlay, A., Grace, R. C., Horwood, L. J., Fergusson, D. M., & MacFarlane, M. R. (2009). Adolescent psychiatric symptoms following preschool childhood mild traumatic brain injury: Evidence from a birth cohort. *Journal of Head Trauma Rehabilitation, 24,* 221–227.

Mihalik, J. P., Stump, J., E., Collins, M. W., Lovell, M. R., Field, M., & Maroon, J. C. (2005). Posttraumatic migraine characteristics in athletes following sports-related concussion. *Journal of Neurosurgery, 102,* 850–855.

Moser, R. S., Schatz, P., & Jordan, B. D., (2005). Prolonged effects of concussion in high school atheletes. *Neurosurgery, 57,* 300–306.

National Center for Injury Prevention and Control. (NCIPC). (2003). *Report to Congress on Mild Traumatic Brain Injury in the United States: Steps to Prevent a Serious Public Health Problem.* Atlanta, GA: Centers for Disease Control and Prevention.

Niogi, S. N., & Mukherjee, P. (2010). Diffusion tensor imaging of mild traumatic brain injury. *Journal of Head Trauma Rehabilitation, 25*(4), 241–255.

Pardini, D., Stump, J., Lovell, M. R., Collins, M. W., Moritz, K., & Fu, F. (2004). The post-concussion symptom scale (PCSS): A factor analysis. *British Journal of Sports Medicine, 38,* 654–664.

Ponsford, J., Willmott, C., Rothwell, A., Cameron, P., Ayton, G., Nelms, R., Curran, C., & Ng, K. T. (1999). Cognitive and behavioral outcome following mild traumatic head injury in children. *Journal of Head Trauma Rehabilitation, 14,* 360–372.

Ponsford, J., Willmott, C., Rothwell, A., Cameron, P., Ayton, G., Nelms, R., Curran, C., & Ng, K. (2001). Impact of early intervention on outcome after mild traumatic brain injury in children. *Pediatrics, 108*(6), 1297–1303.

Pellman, E. J., Lovell, M. R., Viano, D. C., & Casson, I. R. (2006). Concussion in professional football: Recovery of NFL and High School Athletes assessed by Computerized Neuropsychological Testing-Part 12. *Neurosurgery, 58*(2), 263–274.

Ruff, R. (2009). Best practice guidelines for forensic neuropsychological examinations of patients with traumatic brain injury. *Journal of Head Trauma Rehabilitation, 24,* 131–140.

Rutgers, D. R., Toulgoat, F., Cazejust, J., Fillard, P., Lasjaunias, P., & Ducreux, D. (2008). White matter abnormalities in mild traumatic brain injury: A diffusion tensor imaging study. *American Journal of Neuroradiology, 29,* 514–519.

Saatman, K. E., Duhaime, A. C., Bullock, R., Maas, A. I., Valadka, A., & Manley, G. T., (2008). Classification of traumatic brain injury for targeted therapies. *Journal of Neurotrauma, 25,* 719–738.

Satz, P. S., Alfano, M. S., Light, R. F., Morgenstern, H. F., Zaucha, K. F., Asarnow, R. F., & Newton, S. (1999). Persistent post-concussive syndrome: A proposed methodology and literature review to determine the effects, if any, of mild head and other bodily injury. *Journal of Clinical and Experimental Neuropsychology, 21*, 620–628.

Satz, P., Zaucha, K., McCleary, C., Light, R., Asarnow, R., & Becker, D. (1997). Mild head injury in children and adolescents: A review of studies (1970–1995). *Psychological Bulletin, 122*(2), 107–131.

Schatz P., Pardini J. E., Lovell M. R., Collins, M. W., & Podell, K. (2006). Sensitivity and specificity of the ImPACT Test Battery for concussion in athletes. *Archives of Clinical Neuropsychology, 21*, 91–99.

Sesma, H. W., Slomine, B. S., Ding, R., & McCarthy, M. L. (2008). Executive functioning in the first year after pediatric traumatic brain injury. *Pediatrics, 121*(6), 1686–1695.

Slobounov, S. M., Zhang, K., Pennell, D., Ray, W., Johnson, B., & Sebastianelli, W. (2010). Functional abnormalities in normally appearing athletes following mild traumatic brain injury: a functional MRI study. *Experimental Brain Research, 202*, 341–354.

Swaine, B. R., Tremblay, C., Platt, R. W., Grimard, G., Zhang, X., & Pless, I. B. (2007). Previous head injury is a risk factor for subsequent head injury in children: A longitudinal cohort study. *Pediatrics, 119*(4), 749–758.

Taylor, H. G., Dietrich, A., Nuss, K., Wright, M., Rusin, J., Bangert, B., Minich, N., & Yeates, K. O. (2010). Post-concussive symptoms in children with mild traumatic brain injury. *Neuropsychology, 24*(2), 148–159.

Teasdale, G., & Jennett, B. (1974). Assessment of coma and impaired consciousness: A practical scale. *Lancet, 2*, 81–84.

Teasdale, G. M., Murray, G. D., & Nicoll, J. A. R. (2005). The association between APOE ε4, age and outcome after head injury: A prospective cohort study. *Brain: A Journal of Neurology, 128*(11), 2556–2561.

Vagnozzi, R., Signoretti, S., Tavazzi, B., Floris, R., Ludovici, A., Marziali, A., Tarascio, et al. (2008). Temporal window of metabolic brain vulnerabilty to concussion: A pilot ^{1}H-magnetic resonance spectroscopic study in concussed athletes-part III. *Neurosurgery, 62*(6), 1–10.

Vagnozzi, R., Tavazzi, B., Signoretti, S., Amorini, A. M., Belli, A., Cimatti, M., Delfini, R., Lazzarino, G. (2007). Temporal Window of Metabolic Brain Vulnerability to Concussions: Mitochondrial-related Impairment – Part I. *Neurosurgery, 61*, 379–389.

Wilde, E. A., McCauley, S. R., Hunter, J. V., Bigler, E. D., Chu, Z., Wang, Z. J., Hanten, G. R., . . . Levin, H. S. (2008). Diffusion tensor imaging of acute mild traumatic brain injury in adolescents. *Neurology, 70*, 949–955.

Williams, D. H., Levin H. S., & Eisenberg, H. M. (1990). Mild head injury classification. *Neurosurgery, 27*, 422–428.

Williamson, I. J., & Goodman, D. (2006). Converging evidence for the under-reporting of concussion in youth ice hockey. *British Journal of Sports Medicine, 40*, 128–132.

Wozniak, J. R., Krach, L., Ward, E., Mueller, B. A., Muetzel, R., Schnoebelen, N., Kiragu, A., Yeates, K. O., & Taylor, H. G. (2005). Neurobehavioural outcomes of mild head injury in children and adolescents. *Pediatric Rehabilitation, 8*, 5–16.

Yeates, K. O., Taylor, H. G., Rusin, J., Bangert, B., Dietrich, A., Nuss, K., Wright, M., . . . Jones, B. L. (2009). Longitudinal trajectories of postconcussive symptoms in children with mild traumatic brain injuries and their relationship to acute clinical status. *Pediatrics, 123*(3), 735–743.

Chapter 11

Independent Neuropsychological Evaluation of Children With Moderate to Severe Traumatic Brain Injury

KEITH OWEN YEATES

INTRODUCTION

Traumatic brain injury (TBI) resulting from closed-head trauma in children is a significant public health problem, associated with total annual health care costs exceeding $1 billion in the United States (Schneier, Shields, Hostetler, Xiang, & Smith, 2006). TBI is a leading cause of death and disability among youth, and it represents the most common source of acquired brain injury among children and adolescents. Because TBI often occurs in circumstances that involve potential liability (e.g., automobile collisions), it is also a major source of referrals for forensic neuropsychological evaluations. The goal of the present chapter is to provide a summary of the current state of knowledge regarding pediatric TBI and to discuss specific issues that arise in the forensic neuropsychological evaluation of children with moderate to severe TBI (see Chapter 10 for a discussion of mild TBI).

EPIDEMIOLOGY

Incidence and Prevalence

Accurate statistics regarding the incidence and prevalence of TBI in the United States are difficult to obtain. Epidemiological studies vary widely in terms of definition of injury, sources of data, data collection techniques, description of cases, and ages of the target population (Kraus, 1995). The most recent and complete data come from the Centers for Disease Control (CDC; Langlois, Rutland-Brown, & Thomas, 2006), which estimated a total of 475,000 TBIs annually for children ages 0–14, with an overall annual incidence of 799 TBIs per 100,000 population based on deaths, hospitalizations, and emergency department visits.

Incidence varies as a function of injury severity. The most common measure of injury severity is the Glasgow Coma Scale (Teasdale & Jennett, 1974), on which scores range from 3 to 15 (see Table 11.1). By convention, scores from 13 to 15 represent mild injuries (see Chapter 10), scores from 9 to 12 represent moderate injuries, and scores of 8 and less represent severe injuries. Studies using the Glasgow Coma Scale as the measure of severity have found that about 15%–25% of all TBIs fall in the moderate to severe range (Langlois et al., 2003).

Cause of Injury

The most common causes of TBI involve transportation and falls. Together, those two causes account for more than 50% of all pediatric TBI (Langlois, Rutland-Brown, & Thomas, 2006). The distribution of causes varies significantly as a function of age (Keenan & Bratton, 2006). Infants are especially likely to sustain TBI through falls,

TABLE 11.1. Glasgow Coma Scale

Category	Score	Description
Eye Opening		
None	1	Not attributable to ocular swelling.
To pain	2	Pain stimulus is applied to chest or limbs.
To speech	3	Nonspecific response to speech or shout; does not imply patient obeys command to open eyes.
Spontaneous	4	Eyes are open, but this does not imply intact awareness.
Motor Response		
No response	1	Flaccid.
Extension	2	Decerebrate posturing: Adduction, internal rotation of shoulder, and pronation of forearm.
Abnormal flexion	3	Decorticate posturing: Abnormal flexion, adduction of the shoulder.
Withdrawal	4	Normal flexor response; withdraws from pain stimulus with abduction of the shoulder.
Localizes pain	5	Pain stimulus applied to supraocular region or fingertip causes limb to remove it.
Obeys commands	6	Follows simple commands.
Verbal Response		
No response	1	No vocalization.
Incomprehensible	2	Vocalizes, but no recognizable words.
Inappropriate	3	Intelligible speech (e.g., shouting or swearing) but no sustained or coherent conversation.
Confused	4	Responds to questions in a conversational manner, but the responses indicate disorientation.
Oriented	5	Normal orientation to time, person, and place.

NOTE: Glasgow Coma Scale Score = Eye opening score + Motor response score + Verbal response score (range 3 to 15).

as well as via inflicted injuries secondary to child abuse. Young children are most likely to be injured through falls and motor vehicle collisions, either as occupants or pedestrians. In older children, sports and recreational accidents and pedestrian or bicycle collisions with motor vehicles account for an increasing proportion of TBI. Adolescents are especially likely to be injured in motor vehicle collisions.

Demographic Variation

Boys are about twice as likely to sustain TBI as girls, although the ratio varies somewhat with age (Langlois et al., 2006). Children ages 0–4 years are most likely to visit emergency departments for evaluation of TBI, with an annual incidence of about 1,100 per 100,000, suggesting that milder injuries may be especially common among younger children. In contrast, older adolescents ages 15–19 show the highest rate of hospitalizations and deaths, with a combined annual incidence of about 150 per 100,000, probably reflecting the increasing severity of TBI in that age group as a function of motor vehicle collisions.

Incidence rates also may vary as a function of race and socioeconomic status. Among children 0–9 years of age, blacks demonstrate higher rates of hospitalization and death than whites for motor-vehicle related TBI (Langlois, Rutland-Brown, & Thomas, 2005). In the United Kingdom, epidemiological data indicate that social disadvantage is a risk factor for more severe TBI (Parslow et al., 2005).

Mortality and Morbidity

Traumatic injuries are the leading cause of death among children and adolescents, and about 40% to 50% of the deaths resulting from trauma are associated with TBI (Kraus, 1995). Mortality rates are lower among children than among adolescents and adults. The CDC estimates an annual mortality rate around 4.5 per 100,000 for children 0–14 years of age, but a rate of about 24 per 100,000 for 15–19-year-olds (Langlois et al., 2006). The mortality rate is highest among children with severe injuries. Kraus (1995) found case fatality rates among hospital admissions to range from 12% to 62% for severe injuries, less than 4% for moderate injuries, and less than 1% for mild injuries.

NEUROPATHOLOGY AND PATHOPHYSIOLOGY

TBI is associated with multiple forms of neuropathology (see Table 11.2). These include overt damage to brain tissue, including both focal and diffuse lesions, as well as disruptions in brain function at a cellular level. The pathophysiology of TBI begins at the time of impact, but it continues over a period of days or weeks and perhaps even longer. Indeed, recent research indicates that the brain damage resulting from TBI arises from more complex, prolonged, and interwoven processes than was previously recognized (Farkas & Povlishock, 2007; Giza & Prins, 2006; Povlishock & Katz, 2005).

Although pathophysiological commonalities exist among all types of TBI, the immature brain responds differently to trauma than the mature brain of the adult (Giza, Mink, & Madikians, 2007). For example, children are more likely to

TABLE 11.2. Neuropathology of Traumatic Brain Injury

Type of Insult	Neuropathology
Primary	Skull fracture
	Intracranial contusions and hemorrhage
	Shear/strain injury
Secondary	Brain swelling
	Cerebral edema
	Elevated intracranial pressure
	Hypoxia-ischemia
	Mass lesions (hematoma)
Neurochemical	Excessive production of free radicals
	Excessive release of excitatory neurotransmitters
	Alterations in glucose metabolism
	Decreased cerebral blood flow
Late/delayed	White matter degeneration and cerebral atrophy
	Posttraumatic hydrocephalus
	Posttraumatic seizures

display posttraumatic brain swelling, hypoxic-ischemic insult, and diffuse, rather than focal, injuries. The biomechanical properties of the young brain may explain at least some of these differences. Compared to adults, children have a greater head-to-body ratio, less myelination, and greater relative proportion of water content and cerebral blood volume. Once children reach adolescence, TBI-related pathology begins to more closely resemble that seen in adults.

Primary and Secondary Injuries

Observable injuries resulting from closed-head trauma can be classified into two broad categories, *primary* and *secondary*. Primary injuries result directly from the trauma itself. They include skull fractures, contusions and lacerations, and mechanical injuries to nerve fibers and blood vessels. Secondary injuries arise indirectly from the trauma, and in children include brain swelling and edema, hypoxia and hypotension, increased intracranial pressure, and mass lesions.

The primary injuries that arise from closed-head trauma reflect biomechanical forces that are not fully understood in children (Margulies & Coats, 2010). Most causes of TBI in children give rise to acceleration/deceleration injuries that typically involve both translational and rotational trauma. Translational trauma can result in deformation of the skull or skull fractures, as well as contusions at the site of impact. Rotational trauma results in the tearing or bruising of blood vessels that gives rise to focal contusions or hemorrhage, as well as in shearing or straining of nerve fibers that can give rise to diffuse axonal injury.

Focal contusions are especially likely to occur in the frontal and temporal cortex, because of its proximity to the bony prominences in the anterior and middle fossa of the skull (Bigler, 2007; Wilde et al., 2005). In contrast, diffuse axonal injury appears to be most common at the boundaries between gray and white matter, and it tends to occur most often around the basal ganglia, periventricular regions, superior cerebellar peduncles, fornices, corpus callosum, and fiber tracts of the brainstem.

Medical management of TBI tends to focus not on primary injuries, but instead on the secondary injuries that arise indirectly following the initial trauma. Brain swelling and cerebral edema are two major secondary complications of TBI, and they are especially common in children (Bruce, 1995; Kochanek, 2006). They can result in decreased cerebral blood flow, increased cerebral blood volume, and increased intracranial pressure, which together can give rise to ischemic and hypoxic injury, as well as to brain herniation and death (Bruce, 1995). In contrast, mass lesions involving the accumulation of fluid, usually blood associated with contusion and hemorrhage, are less common in children than adults (Bruce, 1995).

Neurochemical and Neurometabolic Mechanisms

The mechanical forces involved in head trauma do not account for the majority of diffuse axonal injury. Instead, reactive axonal changes occur following the trauma that only gradually lead to brain damage. These reactive changes are mediated by a cascade of biochemical and metabolic reactions that take place following TBI. These neurochemical events include the overproduction of free radicals and excitatory amino acids and the disruption of normal calcium homeostasis, as well as changes in glucose metabolism and cerebral blood flow (Farkas & Povlishock, 2007; Novack, Dillon, & Jackson, 1996).

Late Effects

TBI can be associated with a variety of late effects. Severe TBI often results in a gradual and prolonged process of white matter degeneration and cortical thinning, with associated cerebral atrophy and ventricular enlargement (Ghosh et al., 2009; Merkley, 2008). In some cases, ventricular dilatation results from a disturbance in the circulation of cerebrospinal fluid and is associated with hydrocephalus. Posttraumatic hydrocephalus is relatively uncommon, though, and typically develops only after severe injuries associated with certain predisposing factors, such as subarachnoid hemorrhage (McLean et al., 1995).

Early posttraumatic seizures, defined as occurring within the first week after TBI, occur in many children and can involve focal status epilepticus (Statler, 2006). Younger children may be especially vulnerable to early posttraumatic seizures. The occurrence of seizures soon after injury does not clearly place children at risk for later epilepsy, which occurs in about 10%–20% of children with severe TBI. Posttraumatic epilepsy is more common in children with penetrating or inflicted injuries, or injuries associated with depressed skull fractures.

NEUROPSYCHOLOGICAL CONSEQUENCES

The literature on the neuropsychological consequences of pediatric TBI is extensive, and it has been the subject of several recent reviews and meta-analyses (Babikian & Asarnow, 2009; Taylor, 2010; Yeates, 2010). In general, research indicates that

TBI, especially when severe, can produce deficits in a variety of domains: alertness and orientation; corticosensory and motor skills; intellectual functioning; language and communication skills; nonverbal skills; and attention, memory, and executive functions. The following sections provide a selective overview of the existing literature and highlight recent research findings.

Alertness and Orientation

Orientation and alertness are often disturbed following TBI, particularly during the initial phase of recovery. Most children with TBI, especially those that are moderate or severe, experience a period of fluctuations in arousal, as well as disorientation, confusion, and memory loss after the injury. These changes in mental status occur during what is usually referred to as the period of posttraumatic amnesia (PTA). Various standardized measures are available to assess the presence and duration of PTA in children, such as the Children's Orientation and Amnesia Test (COAT; Ewing-Cobbs et al., 1990).

Corticosensory and Motor Skills

Children with TBI often demonstrate deficits in corticosensory and complex motor skills. Approximately 25% of children with severe injuries display deficits on tests of stereognosis, finger localization, and graphesthesia (Levin & Eisenberg, 1979). Similarly, they show deficits on many measures of fine-motor skills, especially those that are timed (Bawden, Knights, & Winogron, 1985). Disturbances in gait and gross motor skills are also common (Kuhtz-Buschbeck et al., 2003).

Intellectual Functioning

Children with TBI tend to display intellectual deficits, as measured by traditional IQ tests, and the magnitude of the deficits is related to injury severity (Chadwick et al., 1981). Early research suggested that IQ scores that reflect nonverbal skills are particularly likely to be depressed, presumably because of requirements for fluid problem-solving skills and speeded motor output. In contrast, verbal intelligence was considered less vulnerable, because its assessment depends more on previously acquired knowledge and makes few demands for speeded responses or motor control. However, more recent studies have found deficits in both nonverbal and verbal intellectual functioning (Anderson et al., 2004, 2005b; Taylor et al., 1999).

Children demonstrate significant recovery in intellectual functioning following TBI. Thus, IQ scores tend to increase over time following TBI, with the largest increases occurring among children with more severe injuries (Yeates et al., 2002). IQ scores increase most rapidly immediately after injury and tend to plateau after 1 to 2 years. Persistent deficits in IQ appear to be especially likely among children with severe TBI and those injured early in life (Anderson et al., 2004, 2005a).

Language and Communication Skills

Spontaneous mutism and expressive language deficits are common immediately after TBI (Levin et al., 1983), but overt aphasic disorders rarely persist following acute recovery. However, subtle language difficulties often persist, again most often following moderate to severe injuries. Long-term deficits have been identified in a variety of basic linguistic skills, including syntactical comprehension, sentence repetition, confrontation naming, object description, and verbal fluency (Ewing-Cobbs & Barnes, 2002). Language deficits typically improve over time, with the most improvement seen following severe TBI (Catroppa & Anderson, 2004).

Children with TBI display more pronounced difficulties with the pragmatic aspects of language, particularly narrative discourse (Dennis & Barnes, 1990). Deficits have been demonstrated in a variety of pragmatic skills, such as interpreting ambiguous sentences, making inferences, formulating sentences from individual words, and explaining figurative expressions. Studies of narrative discourse indicate that children with severe TBI use fewer words and sentences when recalling stories, and their stories contain less information, are not as well organized, and are less complete than those produced by children with milder injuries or by normal controls (Chapman et al., 2004).

Nonverbal Skills

Long-term deficits in nonverbal skills are a relatively frequent consequence of pediatric TBI, and they encompass both perceptual/spatial and constructional abilities. Deficits following head injuries have been reported on a variety of constructional tasks, including block and puzzle tasks such as the Block Design subtest on the WISC-IV and drawing tasks such as the Developmental Test of Visual-Motor Integration (Thompson et al., 1994; Yeates et al., 2002) and Rey-Osterrieth Complex Figure (Yeates et al., 2003). Children with TBI also show deficits in perceptual or spatial skills on measures that do not involve motor output (Lehnung et al., 2001).

Attention

Complaints about attention problems are very common following childhood TBI (Yeates et al., 2005). However, studies using performance-based measures of attention were relatively infrequent until the past decade. In recent years, a substantial literature has developed that documents deficits in many different aspects of attention. Early studies generally focused on continuous performance tests (e.g., Dennis et al., 1995). On such measures, children with TBI display poorer response modulation, especially in the presence of distraction, as well as slower reaction times. More recent studies have shown deficits in sustained, selective, shifting, and divided attention, particularly on more complex and timed measures (Catroppa & Anderson, 2005; Catroppa et al., 2007; Ewing-Cobbs et al., 1998b).

Memory

Childhood TBI frequently results in complaints of memory deficits (Ward et al., 2004). Deficits have been reported on a wide variety of tasks assessing explicit memory, the magnitude of which depends on injury severity (Catroppa & Anderson,

2002, 2007; Yeates et al., 1995a, 2003). Research has attempted to delineate more precisely the specific components of memory that are impaired. For instance, research using the California Verbal Learning Test suggests that deficits occur in a variety of memory components, including storage, retention, and retrieval (Roman et al., 1998; Yeates et al., 1995a).

Children with TBI may be less likely to display deficits in implicit memory, which involves demonstrations of learning or facilitation of performance in the absence of conscious recollection (Ward et al., 2002; Yeates & Enrile, 2005). In contrast, children with TBI do display deficits in prospective memory, which involves remembering to perform an intended action at some time in the future (McCauley & Levin, 2004; Ward et al., 2007).

Executive Functions

Deficits in executive functions occur frequently after childhood TBI and have been demonstrated on a variety of tasks meant to assess working memory, inhibitory control, and planning (Levin et al., 1996; Levin & Hanten, 2005). The magnitude of deficits on executive function tasks correlates with lesion volume in the frontal lobes, but not with extrafrontal lesion volume (Levin et al., 1994; Levin et al., 1997). Young children and those with severe injuries are particularly vulnerable to executive deficits following TBI (Anderson & Catroppa, 2005; Ewing-Cobbs et al., 2004b), and the deficits can persist for years after injury (Nadebaum, Anderson, & Catroppa, 2007).

Because of concerns about the ecological validity of performance-based tests of executive functions, research has also begun to focus on executive problems that children with TBI display in everyday settings (Mangeot et al., 2002; Sesma et al., 2008). Children with TBI, particularly that which is more severe, consistently are reported to demonstrate executive deficits that extend to their emotional and behavioral regulation, as well as to their working memory, cognitive flexibility, and planning skills. Moreover, these deficits have been linked to broader difficulties with social and behavioral adjustment (Ganesalingam et al., 2007).

DEVELOPMENTAL CONSIDERATIONS

The outcomes associated with childhood TBI depend on a variety of developmental factors. Research suggests that outcomes can vary along three distinct but interrelated age-related dimensions: the age of the child at the time of injury, the amount of time that has passed since the injury, and the child's age at the time of outcome assessment (Taylor & Alden, 1997).

Most studies of childhood TBI have focused on school-age children and adolescents. In these groups, age at injury has not been found to be strongly related to outcomes. In contrast, studies of preschool children suggest that injuries sustained during infancy or early childhood are associated with more persistent deficits than are injuries occurring during later childhood and adolescence (Anderson et al., 2005a; Ewing-Cobbs et al., 2006). Younger children appear to demonstrate a slower rate of change over time and more significant residual deficits than do older children with injuries of equivalent severity (Catroppa et al., 2008; Koskiniemi et al., 1995).

With regard to time since injury, children with TBI generally display a gradual recovery over the first few years after injury, with the most rapid improvement occurring soon after the injury (Yeates et al., 2002). The initial rate of recovery tends to be most rapid among children with severe TBI, although severe injuries are more likely to be associated with persistent deficits after the rate of recovery slows (Fay et al., 2009). Recent studies of outcomes 5 or more years post injury suggest that children with severe TBI rarely show any progressive deterioration in neuropsychological functioning relative to noninjured peers after their initial recovery (Cattelani et al., 1998; Jonsson, Horneman, & Emanuelson, 2004; Klonoff, Clark, & Klonoff, 1995).

Of the three age-related dimensions potentially related to outcomes, the influence of age at testing has been the focus of the least research. The effects of age at testing would be reflected in latent or delayed sequelae resulting from children's failure to meet new developmental demands following a TBI. Although such sequelae sometimes appear to occur in individual clinical cases (Baron, 2008), the demonstration of such effects is difficult in research, because it requires evidence that differences in the consequences of pediatric TBI are due specifically to age at testing, as opposed to age at injury or time since injury (Taylor & Alden, 1997).

FUNCTIONAL OUTCOMES

School Performance

Childhood TBI is frequently associated with reports of declines in school performance (Ewing-Cobbs et al., 2004a; Taylor et al., 2002) and with an increased risk of grade retention, placement in special education, and other indicators of academic difficulties (Ewing-Cobbs et al., 1998a; Taylor et al., 2003). However, the reported academic difficulties do not necessarily translate into deficits on formal achievement testing. Deficits in academic skills following TBI are most likely to be apparent in children injured at a young age (Ewing-Cobbs et al., 2004a, 2006). Children injured at a later age do not necessarily display deficits on standardized achievement tests (Taylor et al., 2002).

The academic difficulties that children with TBI face are predicted by a variety of factors, including the child's premorbid classroom performance (Catroppa & Anderson, 2007) and postinjury neuropsychological functioning (Kinsella et al., 1997; Miller & Donders, 2003), as well as the child's postinjury behavioral adjustment (Yeates & Taylor, 2006). Interestingly, the family environment moderates academic performance, such that more supportive and functional homes lessen the impact of TBI (Taylor et al., 2002). In contrast, standardized achievement testing is not always a strong predictor of academic outcomes after TBI (Yeates & Taylor, 2006).

Social Functioning

Childhood TBI often results in problems with social functioning (Yeates et al., 2007). Children with moderate to severe TBI are rated as less socially competent and lonelier than healthy children or children with injuries not involving the brain and their poor social outcomes persist over time (Bohnert, Parker, & Warschausky, 1997; Dennis et al., 2001a; Yeates et al., 2004). The poor social outcomes displayed by children with TBI may be mediated by deficits in social information processing. Following TBI, children display deficits in the understanding of emotion (Dennis et al., 1998) and mental states (Dennis et al., 2001b), as well as in social problem solving (Hanten et al., 2008; Janusz et al., 2002). Collectively, deficits in executive functions, language pragmatics, and social problem solving account for significant variance in social outcomes among children with TBI (Yeates et al., 2004). The social deficits shown by children with TBI may be linked specifically to damage to anterior brain regions. Children with frontal lobe injury in association with TBI are more likely to have problems with social discourse (Dennis et al., 2001a) and social problem solving (Hanten et al., 2008), as well as more generally with social functioning (Levin et al., 2004).

Behavioral Adjustment

Moderate to severe TBI in children increases the risk for a wide range of emotional and behavioral problems (Fletcher et al., 1990; Schwartz et al., 2003; Taylor et al., 2002). In contrast to cognitive difficulties, which often show recovery in the initial months after injury, behavioral problems are more likely to show a stable or even worsening pattern over time (Fay et al., 2009). Research on behavioral adjustment can be confounded by the high incidence of preinjury behavior problems in children with TBI. Children with mild TBI display higher rates of preinjury behavior problems than do children with no injury, but their preinjury behavioral functioning tends not to differ from that of children with injuries not involving the head (Light et al., 1998). The presence of premorbid behavior problems likely increases the risk of traumatic injuries. Indeed, children with preinjury psychiatric disorders, such as attention-deficit/hyperactivity disorder (ADHD) and anxiety disorders, are more likely to experience a head injury than are children without preinjury psychiatric disorders (Bloom et al., 2001; see also Chapter 12).

Behavioral functioning following childhood TBI does not appear to be closely related to cognitive outcomes. Fletcher and colleagues (Fletcher et al., 1990) found small and generally nonsignificant correlations between neuropsychological measures and measures of adaptive functioning and behavioral adjustment. The determinants of cognitive and behavioral outcomes also may be somewhat independent following TBI. Cognitive outcomes are related more strongly to injury-related variables, whereas behavioral outcomes are related more strongly to measures of preinjury family functioning (Yeates et al., 1997).

Psychiatric Disorder

Pediatric TBI is associated with an increased risk of psychiatric disorder (Bloom, 2001; Max, 1997). The most common psychiatric diagnoses that are identified following childhood TBI are oppositional defiant disorder (ODD; Max et al., 1998a), ADHD (Levin et al., 2007; Max et al., 2005b; Yeates et al., 2005), and organic personality syndrome (now termed "personality change due to TBI"; Max et al., 2000, 2005a). Internalizing disorders have also been documented following pediatric TBI, including obsessive-compulsive symptoms, generalized anxiety, separation anxiety, and depression (Grados et al., 2008; Luis & Mittenberg, 2002; Vasa et al., 2002). Symptoms of posttraumatic stress disorder (PTSD) are also elevated following childhood TBI, although relatively few children meet full diagnostic criteria for PTSD (Gerring et al., 2002; Levi et al., 1999).

Adaptive Functioning and Quality of Life

Moderate or severe TBI is also associated with persistent adaptive behavior deficits (e.g., poorer communication, socialization, and daily living skills) and functional limitations (Fay et al., 2009; Max et al., 1998c). More generally, children with TBI demonstrate significant declines in their overall quality of life, although the differences are more pronounced from the perspective of parents than when based on children's self-reports (McCarthy et al., 2006; Stancin et al., 2002).

Long-Term Adult Outcomes

Although the literature on long-term adult outcomes following childhood TBI is relatively sparse, the existing research clearly documents an increased risk of poor outcomes in a variety of functional outcomes. For instance, long-term survivors of severe TBI tend to display less educational attainment, lower employment and reduced occupational status, poorer socialization, increased psychiatric disorder, and reductions in functional independence and perceived quality of life as compared to normative expectations, individuals with mild TBI, and individuals with injuries not involving the head (Anderson, Brown, & Newitt, 2010; Anderson, Brown, Newitt, & Hoile, 2009; Asikainen, Kaste, & Sarna, 1996; Cattelani, Lombardi, Brianti, & Mazzucchi, 1998; Jonsson, Horneman, & Emanuelson, 2004; Klonoff, Clark, & Klonoff, 1995; Koskiniemi, Kyykka, Nybo, & Jarho, 1995; Nybo, Sainio, & Muller, 2004).

FACTORS INFLUENCING OUTCOMES

The preceding summary of the neurobehavioral outcomes of pediatric TBI is based largely on the results of group comparisons (e.g., severe TBI versus orthopedic injuries). Although the generalizations are valid, they must be tempered by the realization that children with TBI display substantial variation in outcomes, even when they are grouped according to injury severity. These individual differences in outcomes reflect a complex interplay among injury characteristics and non-injury-related influences, as well as the developmental factors described earlier.

Injury Characteristics

Injury severity is a major determinant of the consequences of TBI. Generally speaking, a dose–response relationship exists between injury severity and neuropsychological outcome, such that more severe injuries are associated with poorer outcomes. Injury severity has been assessed using a variety of clinical metrics, including level of consciousness, duration of impaired consciousness, and length of posttraumatic amnesia. Injury severity has also been assessed using a variety of specific medical indicators, including brainstem abnormalities (e.g., pupillary reactivity), seizures, and elevated intracranial pressure.

The Glasgow Coma Scale (see Table 11.1; Teasdale & Jennett, 1974) is most often used to assess level of consciousness; it not only predicts cognitive recovery and functional outcome but is also correlated with later cerebral atrophy (Ghosh et al., 2009). The motor scale on the Glasgow Coma Scale can be used to assess duration of impaired consciousness, which is usually defined as the amount of time that elapses from an injury until a child is able to follow commands consistently (i.e., the number of days during which the motor scale on the Glasgow Coma Scale falls below 6). An injury is usually considered severe when the duration of impaired consciousness lasts more than 24 hours. Duration of impaired consciousness is an indirect indicator of rate of recovery, because it reflects the speed with which a child's mental status improves acutely post injury. The length of posttraumatic amnesia, or the time that elapses from the injury until a child is oriented and displays intact memory for daily events, also indirectly reflects the child's rate of recovery. In comparative studies, duration of coma, impaired consciousness, and posttraumatic amnesia have generally been better predictors of outcome than were static measures such as the lowest postresuscitation Glasgow Coma Scale (Ewing-Cobbs et al., 1996; McDonald et al., 1994).

The classification of severity has begun to move beyond simple clinical metrics, such as the Glasgow Coma Scale, to more sophisticated indices that are linked more closely to the pathophysiology of TBI (Saatman et al., 2008). One of the major advances in assessing severity involves neuroimaging. Computed tomography (CT) is the preferred method of neuroimaging during the acute phase of TBI because it is rapidly and widely available and relatively inexpensive, and also sensitive to lesions that may necessitate neurosurgical intervention (Bigler, 2003; Poussaint & Moeller, 2002). However, magnetic resonance imaging (MRI) is superior to CT in documenting most pathology associated with TBI, particularly the subacute and chronic changes that can occur across time following TBI (Bigler, 2003; Sigmund et al., 2007).

Numerous advanced imaging procedures have been developed to assess both structural and functional brain abnormalities in childhood TBI. An extensive review of these methods is beyond the scope of this chapter but can be found in the literature (see Ashwal et al., 2006b, 2010; Munson, Schroth, & Ernst, 2006). Newer MRI technologies that show increased sensitivity to the structural effects of pediatric TBI include susceptibility-weighted MR imaging (Ashwal et al., 2006a) and diffusion tensor imaging (Yuan et al., 2007). Imaging techniques such as functional MRI (Kramer et al., 2008), proton magnetic resonance spectroscopy (Ashwal et al., 2006a; Babikian et al., 2006), positron emission tomography, and single-photon emission CT are able to assess brain function directly (Munson et al., 2006).

Neuroimaging studies in children with TBI generally indicate that the greater the structural or functional abnormalities, the greater the morbidity (Brenner et al., 2003).

Moreover, studies have also shown predictable brain–behavior relationships in children with TBI. For instance, frontal lesions have been associated with poorer social outcomes (Levin et al., 2004), and brain activation on working memory tasks is altered in frontal regions following TBI (Newsome et al., 2008). However, brain–behavior relationships based on adult models are not necessarily applicable after childhood TBI. For instance, frontal lesion volume does not consistently predict attention or executive function (Power et al., 2007; Slomine et al., 2002), and fronto-temporal lesions do not predict memory performance better than lesions outside those regions (Salorio et al., 2005).

Non-Injury-Related Influences

Most previous studies of the prediction of outcomes following childhood TBI have emphasized injury-related variables, even though injury severity fails to account for most of the variance in postinjury outcomes. More recently, research has begun to focus on non-injury-related influences. For instance, children's premorbid functioning may be an important determinant of the outcomes of childhood TBI. Yeates and colleagues showed that premorbid attention problems increased the risk of an increase in postinjury attention problems among children with moderate to severe TBI (Yeates et al., 2005). These findings are consistent with theories of cognitive and brain reserve capacity, which suggest that children's vulnerability to neurological insults varies as a function of their preinjury cognitive abilities and brain integrity (Dennis et al., 2007).

Environmental influences are another source of non-injury-related variance in outcomes following TBI. General measures of socioeconomic status and family demographics are consistent predictors of outcomes, as are more specific measures of family status and the social environment. However, research shows that the family environment actually moderates the impact of TBI, by buffering or exacerbating its direct, neurologically based consequences (Taylor et al., 2002; Yeates et al., 1997b, 2004, 2010). Thus, the effects of severe TBI relative to orthopedic injuries are more pronounced for children from dysfunctional families than for children from more functional families. Interestingly, the relative importance of injury severity and family environment varies across outcome domains, with injury severity playing a larger role for cognitive outcomes and the family environment assuming more importance for behavioral and functional outcomes.

The treatment and intervention that children receive is another potentially critical environmental influence on recovery from TBI. Unfortunately, research on treatment and intervention effectiveness is very sparse. Guidelines for acute medical management of childhood TBI are not based on rigorous evaluation through randomized controlled trials, and we do not know whether acute medical care affects long-term outcomes (Adelson, 2010; Adelson et al., 2003; McLean et al., 1995). Comprehensive reviews of inpatient and outpatient rehabilitation also highlight the relative paucity of empirical evidence (Anderson & Catroppa, 2006; Ylvisaker et al., 2005a). Even less is known regarding the effectiveness of educational interventions for children with TBI (Ylvisaker et al., 2001). Research regarding treatment for the psychosocial and cognitive sequelae of pediatric TBI is also relatively limited (Donders, 2007), although some empirical support exists for certain treatments of behavioral and social problems (Warschausky et al., 1999; Ylvisaker et al., 2005b, 2007). Cognitive remediation programs have been developed for pediatric TBI, but few have been the focus of empirical validation (Butler, 2007; Catroppa & Anderson, 2006; Laatsch et al., 2007; Van't Hooft, 2010).

ISSUES IN FORENSIC NEUROPSYCHOLOGICAL ASSESSMENT OF TRAUMATIC BRAIN INJURY

The forensic neuropsychological evaluation of children with moderate to severe TBI raises a number of issues that are unique to the forensic context (Donders, 2005). Some of the issues also arise in the forensic neuropsychological evaluation of adults with TBI (Bigler & Brooks, 2009; Ruff, 2009) or are characteristic of forensic neuropsychological evaluations of children in general (Dennis, 1989; Wills & Sweet, 2006). Many of the pertinent issues are reviewed in the other chapters in this volume. The following is therefore not intended to be a comprehensive review of forensic neuropsychological evaluation in general, but instead to highlight certain key issues that have often arisen in the author's experience of doing forensic evaluations of children with TBI.

Assessing Premorbid Status

The estimation of premorbid neuropsychological functioning is often of major importance in forensic evaluations of pediatric TBI (Donders, 2005; Wills & Sweet, 2006). Neuropsychologists attempt to estimate premorbid functioning to gauge the magnitude of postinjury neuropsychological impairment and to make predictions about children's long-term prognosis. This process is especially problematic in children as compared to adults, because children have less relevant history on which to base estimates of premorbid functioning.

One means of estimating premorbid functioning is to collect pertinent information retrospectively. For instance, school records frequently contain the results of group achievement testing and other indicators of cognitive ability (Baade & Schoenberg, 2004; Wright, Strand, & Wonders, 2005). Similarly, parent and teacher ratings of premorbid school performance also might yield valid estimates. However, school records do not always contain relevant information, and the quality of the information varies from school to school. Moreover, complete school records may not always be available, particularly for children who have attended multiple schools. Ratings from previous teachers also may be difficult to obtain after a TBI, particularly if an extended period of time has elapsed since the injury. Thus, parent ratings are often the only retrospective source of information that can be elicited routinely. Yet parent ratings of premorbid functioning are clearly vulnerable to a variety of biases, particularly when obtained long after an injury has occurred (Angold et al., 1996).

Rather than relying on retrospective data, neuropsychologists may be able to use current information to estimate premorbid neuropsychological functioning. Two methods have received empirical attention. The first involves the use of sociodemographic variables such as parental or sibling educational attainment, family income, and ethnic status, which are known to be correlated with children's IQ. The other method involves tests of skills such as vocabulary and word reading that are known to be related to IQ and that are thought to be relatively stable despite acute brain injury. Some research has combined the two approaches, using sociodemographic variables and concurrent measures of skills such as word recognition in multiple regression analyses to predict premorbid functioning; both types of variables can make independent contributions to the prediction of IQ and neuropsychological functioning (Schoenberg et al., 2007, 2008; Yeates & Taylor, 1997a). Unfortunately, these methods generally are not very precise, and they may not yield estimates that are sufficiently accurate for individual clinical cases.

For children injured during infancy and early childhood, who have no premorbid school history and for whom concurrent measures are likely to be affected by severe TBI, the only approach that may be available for estimating premorbid functioning (or what a child's level of functioning would have been absent the injury) is to rely on sociodemographic variables, and such methods are not terribly accurate. However, neuropsychologists may be able to rely in part on the fact that children are most likely to function in the "average" range, which can be defined as the interquartile range of standard scores from 90 to 110 (i.e., 25th to 75th percentile). Thus, the best estimate of premorbid functioning for any child, absent evidence to the contrary, is that it would be average. For children injured during infancy and early childhood, therefore, a reasonable starting assumption is that a child would have functioned at an average level, although the neuropsychologist should look carefully for demographic factors (e.g., unusually low or high socioeconomic status; familial mental retardation) that would increase the likelihood that a child's functioning would have fallen outside that range.

Test Selection

The selection of neuropsychological tests for a forensic evaluation is a multifaceted process that depends on numerous considerations (Wills & Sweet, 2006). In the context of evaluations of children with moderate to severe TBI, one important factor in the selection of tests is to evaluate functions that are known to be particularly vulnerable to TBI (Donders, 2005). Thus, tests of processing speed, attention, memory, and executive functions should always be included. At the same time, the inclusion of tests that are likely to be less vulnerable to TBI is also important, because it can help determine the extent and specificity of impairment. Tests of basic language abilities and previously acquired academic skills (e.g., word recognition) are germane in this context. Although deficits can occur on such measures following moderate to severe TBI, they would generally not be expected to exceed those found on measures of processing speed, attention, memory, and executive functions.

Motivation and Effort

Traditionally, neuropsychologists have evaluated children's motivation and effort to perform subjectively, based on their impressions of the child's engagement in testing. However, such impressions are known to be potentially inaccurate, because children are capable of deception, and poor test effort is not uncommon (Faust, Hart, & Guilmette, 1988; Lu & Boone, 2002). Thus, the use of formal tests of effort or motivation has recently been explored in children (see Chapter 7). Studies have examined the validity of measures such as the Word Memory Test (Courtney, Dinkins, Allen, & Kuroski, 2003), Medical Symptom Validity Test (Green, 2004), Computerized Assessment of Response Bias (Courtney et al., 2003), and Test of Memory Malingering (Donders, 2005b).

Effort testing probably should be a routine part of forensic neuropsychological evaluations in cases of childhood TBI, at least for children who are old enough to complete such testing validly. Of course, poor performance on effort tests does not necessarily imply a child is malingering, and poor performance on any one test is insufficient to determine biased responding (Slick, Sherman, & Iverson, 1999). Failed performance on an effort test does, however, raise questions about the validity of other test results and warrants further investigation (see Chapters 6 and 7).

Alternative Explanations

One of the more challenging aspects of forensic neuropsychological evaluation is attempting to determine whether a specific injury accounts for any deficits that are detected. In forensic cases, if a child with a TBI shows neuropsychological deficits, the plaintiffs will argue that the impairment was caused or worsened by the injury, whereas the defendants will want to suggest that the child's problems existed prior to the injury or can be accounted for by other factors. It is incumbent on the neuropsychologist to consider other risk factors that may provide alternative explanations for a child's deficits before concluding that the TBI plays a causal role. The need to consider alternative explanations highlights the importance of collecting a detailed history that includes information about the child's family, birth, developmental, school, psychosocial, and medical background (Yeates & Taylor, 2001).

The existence of other risk factors does not necessarily preclude a causal contribution of a TBI to neuropsychological deficits or poor functional outcomes. For instance, although children's premorbid functioning helps accounts for postinjury performance deficits, in some cases poor premorbid functioning may actually increase the likelihood of postinjury problems (Fay et al., 2010; Yeates et al., 2005). Similarly, deficits in children's adaptive and behavioral functioning are more likely following TBI when children come from a disadvantaged family environment (Taylor et al., 1999, 2002; Yeates et al., 1997, 2004, 2010). Thus, some risk factors can actually exacerbate the effects of TBI, and the neuropsychologist must attempt to decide whether the presence of such risk factors accounts for all of a child's deficits, contributes to them but does not fully explain them, or in fact exacerbates the effects of the TBI. Such decisions require a thorough evaluation, combined with an awareness of the existing research literature (Wills & Sweet, 2006).

Tests Versus Behaviors

Neuropsychological tests have clearly demonstrated validity in assessing central nervous system dysfunction in childhood, as well as in predicting functional outcomes (Taylor & Schatschneider, 1992). That is, neuropsychological tests have both neurological and ecological validity. Nevertheless, concerns can still be raised about the ability of neuropsychological tests to document certain types of brain injury, particularly damage to the frontal lobes, as well as their capacity to predict the full range of functional outcomes (Farmer & Eakman, 1995; Silver, 2000). Psychometric instruments may not detect the declines in executive functions or in emotional and behavioral regulation that often follow from TBI and that have substantial implications for everyday functioning.

Psychometric testing also cannot be used to assess some of the most important outcomes following TBI, including social competence, behavioral adjustment, and adaptive functioning. The latter outcomes are generally assessed via direct observation, as well as by administering rating scales and interviews. Notably, many commonly used rating scales, such as the Child Behavior Checklist (Achenbach, 1991), were not developed for use with children with TBI and may prove misleading or insensitive when used in that population (Drotar, Stein, & Perrin, 1995). The use of rating scales that are more specifically targeted to children with TBI may be more informative (Yeates et al., 2001). Regardless, neuropsychologists should not draw conclusions about the effects of TBI based solely on test performance, but instead within a broader context that reflects a careful review of a child's history as well as direct and indirect behavioral observations (Yeates & Taylor, 2001).

Predicting Long-Term Outcomes

In forensic cases, neuropsychologists are often asked to offer opinions about whether neuropsychological deficits are permanent and to what extent TBI and its associated deficits predict long-term outcomes such as employability, educational and vocational attainment, and functional independence. Longitudinal studies of children with TBI suggest that their neuropsychological and functional outcomes are relatively stable after the first few years post injury, with many but not all children demonstrating persistent deficits (Fay et al., 2009). Moreover, as noted earlier, the small but growing literature on long-term adult outcomes suggests that moderate to severe TBI puts children at risk of poor adult outcomes in a variety of domains (Anderson et al., 2009, 2010; Asikainen et al., 1996; Cattelani et al., 1998; Jonsson et al., 2004; Klonoff et al., 1995; Koskiniemi et al., 1995; Nybo et al., 2004).

Of course, neuropsychologists should acknowledge that not all children with moderate to severe TBI will demonstrate persistent neuropsychological deficits or poor adult outcomes. Moreover, they also should acknowledge that the ability to predict eventual outcomes is likely to be a function of both a child's age at the time of testing and the amount of time that has passed since the injury. Evaluations of children at younger ages provide less foundation for predicting outcomes, both because neuropsychological functioning is less stable in younger children and because the eventual outcomes will occur further in the future. Similarly, evaluations soon after an injury may document acute deficits, but they may not be as predictive of eventual outcomes as later assessments, which can more accurately reflect the extent of a child's recovery. Both of these considerations argue for conducting forensic neuropsychological evaluations several years post injury, especially when injuries involve young children.

Groups Versus Individuals

As noted already, competent forensic evaluation of children with TBI depends in part on an awareness of the relevant research literature. However, neuropsychologists must be cognizant that most of the research on childhood TBI is based on comparisons of group means using a variable-centered approach, and the results of such comparisons may or may not generalize to individual children. Children with moderate to severe TBI display substantial variation in outcomes that reflect the interplay of injury characteristics, non-injury-related influences, and developmental factors. Research using person-centered approaches reveals significant variability in the recovery trajectories that characterize individual children with moderate to severe TBI (Fay et al., 2009). Thus, neuropsychologists who conduct forensic evaluations of children with TBI should be careful not to overgeneralize the results of group studies to individual cases and should acknowledge that the extension of findings from such studies to individual cases is necessarily probabilistic.

CONCLUSIONS

Childhood TBI is a common cause of acquired disabilities, and hence it is a frequent source of personal injury litigation. Neuropsychologists can play a critical role in the evaluation of children with TBI in the forensic context, both to establish the extent of residual brain impairment and to make predictions about long-term functional outcomes. The forensic neuropsychological evaluation of moderate to severe TBI is a complex process, however, that involves multiple issues that are specific to the forensic context. Hence, neuropsychologists engaged in the forensic evaluation of children with TBI are ethically obligated to be informed not only about the scientific literature but also about specific issues arising in forensic evaluations and their attendant implications for clinical practice (Wills & Sweet, 2006).

REFERENCES

Adelson, P. D. (2010). Clinical trials for pediatric TBI. In V. A. Anderson & K. O. Yeates (Eds.). *Pediatric traumatic brain injury: New frontiers in clinical and translational research* (pp. 54–67). New York: Cambridge University Press.

Adelson, P. D., Bratton, S. L., Carney, N. A., Chesnut, R. M., du Coudray, H. E., Goldstein, B., . . . Wright, D. W. (2003). Guidelines for the acute medical management of severe traumatic brain injury in infants, children, and adolescents. Chapter 1: Introduction. *Pediatric Critical Care Medicine, 4*(Suppl 3), S2–S4.

Anderson, V., Brown, S., & Newitt, H. (2010). What contributes to quality of life in adult survivors of childhood traumatic brain injury? *Journal of Neurotrauma, 27*, 863–870.

Anderson, V., Brown, S., Newitt, H., & Hoile, H. (2009). Educational, vocational, psychosocial, and quality-of-life outcomes for adult survivors of childhood traumatic brain injury. *Journal of Head Trauma Rehabilitation, 24*, 303–312.

Anderson, V., & Catroppa, C. (2005). Recovery of executive skills following paediatric traumatic brain injury (TBI): A 2 year follow-up. *Brain Injury, 19*, 459–470.

Anderson, V., & Catroppa, C. (2006). Advances in postacute rehabilitation after childhood acquired brain injury: A focus on cognitive, behavioral, and social domains. *American Journal of Physical Medicine and Rehabilitation, 85*, 767–778.

Anderson, V. A., Catroppa, C., Morse, S., Haritou, F., & Rosenfeld, J. (2005a). Functional plasticity or vulnerability after early brain injury? *Pediatrics, 116*, 1374–1382.

Anderson, V., Catroppa, C., Morse, S., Haritou, F., & Rosenfeld, J. (2005b). Identifying factors contributing to child and family outcome at 30 months following traumatic brain injury in children. *Journal of Neurology, Neurosurgery and Psychiatry, 76*, 401–408.

Anderson, V. A., Morse, S., Catroppa, C., Haritou, F., & Rosenfeld, J. (2004). Thirty month outcome from early childhood head injury: A prospective analysis of neurobehavioural recovery. *Brain, 127*, 2608–2620.

Angold, A., Erkanli, A., Costello, E. J., & Rutter, M. (1996). Precision, reliability and accuracy in the dating of symptom onsets in child and adolescent psychopathology. *Journal of Child Psychology and Psychiatry, 37*, 657–64.

Asikainen, I., Kaste, M., & Sarna, S. (1996). Patients with traumatic brain injury referred to a rehabilitation and re-employment program: Social and professional outcomes for 508 Finnish patients 5 or more years after injury. *Brain Injury, 10*, 883–99.

Ashwal, S., Babikian, T., Gardner-Nichols, J., Freier. M. C., Tong, K. A., & Holshouser, B. A. (2006a). Susceptibility-weighted imaging and proton magnetic resonance spectroscopy in assessment of outcome after pediatric traumatic brain injury. *Archives of Physical Medicine and Rehabilitation, 87*, 50–58.

Ashwal, S., Holshouser, B. A., & Tong, K. A. (2006b). Use of advanced neuroimaging techniques in the evaluation of pediatric traumatic brain injury. *Developmental Neuroscience, 28*, 309–26.

Ashwal, S., Tong, K. A., Obenaus, A., & Holshouser, B. A. (2010). Advanced neuroimaging techniques in children with traumatic brain injury. In V. A. Anderson & K. O. Yeates (Eds.), *Pediatric traumatic brain injury: New frontiers in clinical and translational research* (pp. 68–93). New York: Cambridge University Press.

Asikainen, I., Kaste, M., & Sarna, S. (1996). Patients with traumatic brain injury referred to a rehabilitation and re-employment program: Social and professional outcomes for 508 Finnish patients 5 or more years after injury. *Brain Injury, 10*, 883–899.

Baade, L. E., & Schoenberg, M. R. (2004). A proposed method to estimate premorbid intelligence utilizing group achievement measures from school records. *Archives of Clinical Neuropsychology, 19*, 227–244.

Babikian, T., & Asarnow, R. (2009). Neurocognitive outcomes and recovery after pediatric TBI: Meta-analytic review of the literature. *Neuropsychology, 23*, 283–296.

Babikian, T., Freier, M. C., Ashwal, S., Riggs, M. L., Burley, T., & Holshouser, B. A. (2006). MR spectroscopy: Predicting long-term neuropsychological outcome following pediatric TBI. *Journal of Magnetic Resonance Imaging, 24*, 801–811.

Baron, I. S. (2008). Maturation into impairment: The merit of delayed settlement in pediatric forensic neuropsychology cases. In R. L. Heilbronner (Ed.), *Neuropsychology in the courtroom: Expert analysis of reports and testimony* (pp. 66–78). New York: Guilford Press.

Bawden, H. N., Knights, R. M., & Winogron, H. W. (1985). Speeded performance following head injury in children. *Journal of Clinical Neuropsychology, 7*, 39–54.

Bigler, E. D. (2003). Neurobiology and neuropathology underlie the neuropsychological deficits associated with traumatic brain injury. *Archives of Clinical Neuropsychology, 18*, 595–621.

Bigler, E. D. (2007). Anterior and middle cranial fossa in traumatic brain injury: Relevant neuroanatomy and neuropathology in the study of neuropsychological outcome. *Neuropsychology, 21,* 515–531.

Bigler, E. D., & Brooks, M. (2009). Traumatic brain injury and forensic neuropsychology. *Journal of Head Trauma Rehabilitation, 24,* 76–87.

Bloom, D.R., Levin, H.S., Ewing-Cobbs, L., Saunders, A. E., Song, J., Fletcher, J. M., & Kowatch, R. A. (2001). Lifetime and novel psychiatric disorders after pediatric traumatic brain injury. *Journal of the American Academy of Child and Adolescent Psychiatry, 40,* 572–579.

Bohnert, A. M., Parker, J. G., & Warschausky, S. A. (1997). Friendship and social adjustment of children following a traumatic brain injury: An exploratory investigation. *Developmental Neuropsychology, 13,* 477–486.

Brenner, T., Freier, M. C., Holshouser, B. A., Burley, T., & Ashwal, S. (2003). Predicting neuropsychologic outcome after traumatic brain injury in children. *Pediatric Neurology, 28,* 104–114.

Bruce, D. A. (1995). Pathophysiological responses of the child's brain. In S. H. Broman & M. E. Michel (Eds.), *Traumatic head injury in children* (pp. 40–51). New York: Oxford University Press.

Butler, R. W. (2007). Cognitive rehabilitation. In S. J. Hunter & J. Donders (Eds.), *Pediatric neuropsychological intervention* (pp. 444–464). New York, Cambridge University Press.

Cattelani, R., Lombardi, F., Brianti, R., & Mazzucchi, A. (1998). Traumatic brain injury in childhood: Intellectual, behavioural and social outcome into adulthood. *Brain Injury, 12,* 283–296.

Catroppa, C., & Anderson, V. (2002). Recovery in memory function in the first year following TBI in children. *Brain Injury, 16,* 369–384.

Catroppa, C., & Anderson, V. (2004). Recovery and predictors of language skills two years following pediatric traumatic brain injury. *Brain and Language, 88,* 68–78.

Catroppa, C., & Anderson, V. (2005). A prospective study of the recovery of attention from acute to 2 years post pediatric traumatic brain injury. *Journal of the International Neuropsychological Society, 11,* 84–98.

Catroppa, C., & Anderson, V. (2006). Planning, problem-solving, and organizational abilities in children following traumatic brain injury: Intervention techniques. *Pediatric Rehabilitation, 9,* 89–97.

Catroppa, C., & Anderson, V. (2007). Recovery in memory function, and its relationship to academic success, at 24 months following pediatric TBI. *Child Neuropsychology, 13,* 240–261.

Catroppa, C., Anderson, V. A., Morse, S. A., Haritou, F., & Rosenfeld, J. V. (2007). Children's attentional skills 5 years post-TBI. *Journal of Pediatric Psychology, 32,* 354–369.

Catroppa, C., Anderson, V. A., Morse, S. A., Haritou, F., & Rosenfeld, J. V. (2008). Outcome and predictors of functional recovery 5 years following pediatric traumatic brain injury. *Journal of Pediatric Psychology, 33,* 707–718.

Cattelani, R., Lombardi, F., Brianti, R., & Mazzucchi, A. (1998). Traumatic brain injury in childhood: Intellectual, behavioural and social outcome into adulthood. *Brain Injury, 12,* 283–296.

Chadwick, O., Rutter, M., Brown, G., Shaffer, D., & Traub, M. (1981). A prospective study of children with head injuries: II. Cognitive sequelae. *Psychological Medicine, 11,* 49–61.

Chapman, S. B., Sparks, G., Levin, H. S., Dennis, M., Roncadin, C., Zhang, L., & Song, J. (2004). Discourse macrolevel processing after severe pediatric traumatic brain injury. *Developmental Neuropsychology, 25,* 37–60.

Courtney, J. C., Dinkins, J. P., Allen, L. M., III, & Kuroski, K. (2003). Age related effects in children taking the Computerized Assessment of Response Bias and Word Memory Test. *Child Neuropsychology, 9,* 109–116.

Dennis, M. (1989). Assessing the neuropsychological abilities of children and adolescents for personal injury litigation. *The Clinical Neuropsychologist, 3,* 203–229.

Dennis, M., & Barnes, M. A. (1990). Knowing the meaning, getting the point, bridging the gap, and carrying the message: Aspects of discourse following closed head injury in childhood and adolescence. *Brain and Language, 39,* 428–446.

Dennis, M., Barnes, M. A., Wilkinson, M., & Humphreys, R. P. (1998). How children with head injury represent real and deceptive emotion in short narratives. *Brain and Language, 61,* 450–483.

Dennis, M., Guger, S., Roncadin, C., Barnes, M., & Schachar, R. (2001a). Attentional-inhibitory control and social-behavioral regulation after childhood closed head injury: Do biological, developmental, and recovery variables predict outcome? *Journal of the International Neuropsychological Society, 7,* 683–692.

Dennis, M., Purvis, K., Barnes, M. A., Wilkinson, M., & Winner, E. (2001b). Understanding of literal truth, ironic criticism, and deceptive praise following childhood head injury. *Brain and Language, 78,* 1–16.

Dennis, M., Wilkinson, M., Koski, L., & Humphreys, R. P. (1995). Attention deficits in the long term after childhood head injury. In S. H. Broman & M. E. Michel (Eds.), *Traumatic head injury in children* (pp. 165–187). New York: Oxford University Press.

Dennis, M., Yeates, K. O., Taylor, H. G., & Fletcher, J. M. (2007). Brain reserve capacity, cognitive reserve capacity, and age-based functional plasticity after congenital and acquired brain injury in children. In Y. Stern (Ed.), *Cognitive reserve* (pp. 53–83). New York: Taylor & Francis.

Donders, J. (2005a). Forensic aspects of pediatric traumatic brain injury. In G. J. Larrabee (Ed.), *Forensic neuropsychology: A scientific approach* (pp. 182–208). New York: Oxford University Press.

Donders, J. (2005b). Performance on the Test of Memory Malingering in a mixed pediatric sample. *Child Neuropsychology, 11,* 221–227.

Donders, J. (2007). Traumatic brain injury. In S. J. Hunter & J. Donders (Eds.), *Pediatric neuropsychological intervention* (pp. 91–111). New York: Cambridge University Press.

Drotar, D., Stein, R. E. K., & Perrin, E. C. (1995). Methodological issues in using the Child Behavior Checklist and its related instruments in clinical child psychology research. *Journal of Clinical Child Psychology, 24,* 184–192.

Ewing-Cobbs, L., & Barnes, M. (2002). Linguistic outcomes following traumatic brain injury in children. *Seminars in Pediatric Neurology, 9,* 209–217.

Ewing-Cobbs, L., Barnes, M., Fletcher, J. M., Levin, H. S., Swank, P. R., & Song, J. (2004a). Modeling of longitudinal academic achievement scores after pediatric traumatic brain injury. *Developmental Neuropsychology, 25,* 107–133.

Ewing-Cobbs, L., Fletcher, J. M., Levin, H. S., Hastings, P. Z., & Francis, D. J. (1996). Assessment of injury severity following closed head injury in children: Methodological issues. *Journal of the International Neuropsychological Society, 2,* 39.

Ewing-Cobbs, L., Fletcher, J. M., Levin, H. S., Iovino, I., & Miner, M. E. (1998a). Academic achievement and academic placement following traumatic brain injury in children and adolescents: A two-year longitudinal study. *Journal of Clinical and Experimental Neuropsychology, 20,* 769–81.

Ewing-Cobbs, L., Levin, H. S., Fletcher, J. M., Miner, M. E., & Eisenberg, H. M. (1990). The Children's Orientation and Amnesia Test: Relationship to severity of acute head injury and to recovery of memory. *Neurosurgery, 27,* 683–691.

Ewing-Cobbs, L., Prasad, M., Fletcher, J. M., Levin, H. S., Miner, M. E., & Eisenberg, H. M. (1998b). Attention after pediatric traumatic brain injury: A multidimensional assessment. *Child Neuropsychology, 4,* 35–48.

Ewing-Cobbs, L., Prasad, M. R., Kramer, L., Cox, C. S., Jr., Baumgartner, J., Fletcher, S., ... Swank, P. (2006). Late intellectual and academic outcomes following traumatic brain injury sustained during early childhood. *Journal of Neurosurgery, 105,* 2887–2896.

Ewing-Cobbs, L., Prasad, M. R., Landry, S. H., Kramer, L., & DeLeon, R. (2004b). Executive functions following traumatic brain injury in young children: A preliminary analysis. *Developmental Neuropsychology, 26,* 487–512.

Farkas, O., & Povlishock, J. T. (2007). Cellular and subcellular change evoked by diffuse traumatic brain injury: A complex web of change extending far beyond focal damage. *Progress in Brain Research, 161,* 43–59.

Farmer, J. E., & Eakman, A. M. (1995). The relationship between neuropsychological functioning and instrumental activities of daily living following acquired brain injury. *Applied Neuropsychology, 2,* 107–115.

Faust, D., Hart, K., & Guilmette, T. J. (1988). Pediatric malingering: The capacity of children to fake believable deficits on neuropsychological testing. *Journal of Consulting and Clinical Psychology, 56,* 578–582.

Fay, T. B., Yeates, K. O., Taylor, H. G., Bangert, B., Dietrich, A., Nuss, K. E., ... Wright, M. (2010). Cognitive reserve as a moderator of postconcussive symptoms in children with complicated and uncomplicated mild traumatic brain injury. *Journal of the International Neuropsychological Society, 16,* 94–105.

Fay, T. B., Yeates, K. O., Wade, S. L., Drotar, D., Stancin, T., & Taylor, H. G. (2009). Predicting longitudinal patterns of functional deficits in children with traumatic brain injury. *Neuropsychology, 23,* 271–282.

Fletcher, J. M., Ewing-Cobbs, L., Miner, M. E., Levin, H. S., & Eisenberg, H. M. (1990). Behavioral changes after closed head injury in children. *Journal of Consulting and Clinical Psychology, 58,* 93–98.

Ganesalingam, K., Sanson, A., Anderson, V., & Yeates, K. O. (2007). Self-regulation as a mediator of the effects of childhood traumatic brain injury on social and behavioral functioning. *Journal of the International Neuropsychological Society, 13,* 298–311.

Gerring, J. P., Slomine, B., Vasa, R. A., Grados, M., Chen, A., Rising, W., ... Ernst, M. (2002). Clinical predictors of posttraumatic stress disorder after closed head injury in children. *Journal of the American Academy of Child and Adolescent Psychiatry, 41,* 157–165.

Ghosh, A., Wilde, E. A., Hunter, J. V., Bigler, E. D., Chu, Z., Li, X., Vasquez, A. C., ... Levin, H. S. (2009). The relation between Glasgow Coma Scale score and later cerebral atrophy in pediatric traumatic brain injury. *Brain Injury, 23,* 228–233.

Giza, C. C., Mink, R. B., & Madikians, A. (2007). Pediatric traumatic brain injury: Not just little adults. *Current Opinions in Critical Care, 13,* 143–152.

Giza, C. C., & Prins, M. L. (2006). Is being plastic fantastic? Mechanisms of altered plasticity after developmental traumatic brain injury. *Developmental Neuroscience, 28,* 364–379.

Grados, M. A., Vasa, R. A., Riddle, M. A., Slomine, B. S., Salorio, C., Christensen, J., & Gerring, J. P. (2008). New onset obsessive-compulsive symptoms in children and adolescents with severe traumatic brain injury. *Depression and Anxiety, 25,* 398–407.

Green, P. (2004). *Manual for the Medical Symptom Validity Test*. Edmonton, AB: Green's Publishing.

Hanten, G., Wilde, E. A., Menefee, D. S., Li, X., Lane, S., Vasquez, C., ... Levin, H. S. (2008). Correlates of social problem solving during the first year after traumatic brain injury in children. *Neuropsychology, 22*, 357–370.

Janusz, J. A., Kirkwood, M. W., Yeates, K. O. & Taylor, H. G. (2002). Social problem-solving skills in children with traumatic brain injury: Long-term outcomes and prediction of social competence. *Child Neuropsychology, 8*, 179–194.

Jonsson, C. A., Horneman, G., & Emanuelson, I. (2004). Neuropsychological progress during 14 years after severe traumatic brain injury in childhood and adolescence. *Brain Injury, 18*, 921–934.

Keenan, H. T., & Bratton, S. L. (2006). Epidemiology and outcomes of pediatric traumatic brain injury. *Developmental Neuroscience, 28*, 256–263.

Kinsella, G., Prior, M., Sawyer, M., Ong, B., Murtagh, D., Eisenmajer, R., Bryan, D., Anderson, V., & Klug, G. (1997). Predictors and indicators of academic outcome in children 2 years following traumatic brain injury. *Journal of the International Neuropsychological Society, 3*, 608–616.

Klonoff, H., Clark, C., & Klonoff, P. S. (1995). Outcomes of head injuries from childhood to adulthood: A twenty-three year follow-up study. In S. H. Broman & M. E. Michel (Eds.), *Traumatic head injury in children* (pp. 219–234). New York: Oxford University Press.

Kochanek, P. M. (2006). Pediatric traumatic brain injury: Quo vadis? *Developmental Neuroscience, 28*, 244–255.

Koskiniemi, M., Kyykka, T., Nybo, T., & Jarho, L. (1995). Long-term outcome after severe brain injury in preschoolers is worse than expected. *Archives of Pediatric Adolescent Medicine, 149*, 249–254.

Kramer, M. E., Chiu, C. Y. P., Walz, N. C., Holland, S. K., Yuan, W., Karunanayaka, P., & Wade, S. L. (2008). Long-term neural processing of attention following early childhood traumatic brain injury: FMRI and neurobehavioral outcomes. *Journal of the International Neuropsychological Society, 14*, 424–435.

Kraus, J. F. (1995). Epidemiological features of brain injury in children: Occurrence, children at risk, causes and manner of injury, severity, and outcomes. In S. H. Broman & M. E. Michel (Eds.), *Traumatic head injury in children* (pp. 22–39). New York: Oxford University Press.

Kuhtz-Buschbeck, J. P., Hoppe, B., Golge, M., Dreesmann, M., Damm-Stunitz, U., & Ritz, A. (2003). Sensorimotor recovery in children after traumatic brain injury: Analyses of gait, gross motor, and fine motor skills. *Developmental Medicine and Child Neurology, 12*, 821–828.

Laatsch, L., Harrington, D., Hotz, G, Marcantuono, J., Mozzoni, M. P., Walsh, V., & Hersey, K. P. (2007). An evidence-based review of cognitive and behavioral rehabilitation treatment studies in children with acquired brain injury. *Journal of Head Trauma Rehabilitation, 22*, 248–256.

Langlois, J. A., Kegler, S. R., Butler, J. A., Gotsch, K. E., Johnson, R. L., Reichard, A. A., ... Thurman, D. J. (2003). Traumatic brain injury-related hospital discharges: Results from a 14-state surveillance system, 1997. *MMWR Surveillance Summaries, 52*, 1–18.

Langlois, J. A., Rutland-Brown, W., & Thomas, K. E. (2005). The incidence of traumatic brain injury among children in the United States: Differences by race. *Journal of Head Trauma Rehabilitation, 20*, 229–238.

Langlois, J. A., Rutland-Brown, W., & Thomas, K. E. (2006). *Traumatic brain injury in the United States: Emergency department visits, hospitalizations, and deaths.* Atlanta, GA: Centers for Disease Control and Prevention, National Center for Injury Prevention and Control.

Lehnung, M., Leplow, B., Herzog, A., Benz, B., Ritz, A., Stolze, H., . . . Ferstl, R. (2001). Children's spatial behavior is differentially affected after traumatic brain injury. *Child Neuropsychology, 7,* 59–71.

Levi, R. B., Drotar, D., Yeates, K. O., & Taylor, H. G. (1999). Posttraumatic stress symptoms in children following orthopedic or traumatic brain injury. *Journal of Clinical Child Psychology, 28,* 232–243.

Levin, H. S., & Eisenberg, H. M. (1979). Neuropsychological impairment after closed head injury in children and adolescents. *Journal of Pediatric Psychology, 4,* 389–402.

Levin, H. S., Fletcher, J. M., Kufera, J. A., Howard, H., Lilly, M. A., Mendelsohn, D., . . . Eisenberg, H. M. (1996). Dimensions of cognition measured by the Tower of London and other cognitive tasks in head-injured children and adolescents. *Developmental Neuropsychology, 12,* 17–34.

Levin, H. S., & Hanten, G. (2005). Executive functions after traumatic brain injury in children. *Pediatric Neurology, 33,* 79–93.

Levin, H., Hanten, G., Max, J, Li, X., Swank, P., Ewing-Cobbs, L., . . . Schachar, R. (2007). Symptoms of attention-deficit/hyperactivity disorder following traumatic brain injury in children. *Journal of Developmental and Behavioral Pediatrics, 28,* 108–118.

Levin, H. S., Madison, C. F., Bailey, C. B., Meyers, C. A., Eisenberg, H. M., & Guinto, F. C. (1983). Mutism after closed head injury. *Archives of Neurology, 40,* 601–606.

Levin, H. S., Mendelsohn, D., Lilly, M. A., Fletcher, J. M., Culhane, K. A., Chapman, S. B., . . . Eisenberg, H. M. (1994). Tower of London performance in relation to magnetic resonance imaging following closed head injury in children. *Neuropsychology, 8,* 171–179.

Levin, H. S., Song, J., Scheibel, R. S., Fletcher, J. M., Harward, H., Lilly, M., & Goldstein, F. (1997). Concept formation and problem solving following closed head injury in children. *Journal of the International Neuropsychological Society, 3,* 598–607.

Levin, H. S., Zhang, L., Dennis, M., Ewing-Cobbs, L., Schachar, R., Max, J., . . . Hunter, J. V. (2004). Psychosocial outcome of TBI in children with unilateral frontal lesions. *Journal of the International Neuropsychological Society, 10,* 305–316.

Light, R., Asarnow, R., Satz, P., Zaucha, K., McCleary, C., & Lewis, R. (1998). Mild TBI in children and adolescents: Behavior problems and academic outcomes. *Journal of Consulting and Clinical Psychology, 1998,* 1023–1029.

Lu, P. H., & Boone, K. B. (2002). Suspect cognitive symptoms in a 9-year-old child: Malingering by proxy? *Clinical Neuropsychologist, 16,* 90–96.

Luis, C. A., & Mittenberg, W. (2002). Mood and anxiety disorders following pediatric traumatic brain injury: A prospective study. *Journal of Clinical and Experimental Neuropsychology, 24,* 270–279.

Mangeot, S., Armstrong, K., Colvin, A. N., Yeates, K. O., & Taylor, H. G. (2002). Long-term executive function deficits in children with traumatic brain injuries: Assessment using the Behavior Rating Inventory of Executive Function (BRIEF). *Child Neuropsychology, 8,* 271–284.

Margulies, S., & Coats, B. (2010). Biomechanics of pediatric TBI. In V. A. Anderson & K. O. Yeates (Eds.), *Pediatric traumatic brain injury: New frontiers in clinical and translational research* (pp. 7–17). New York: Cambridge University Press.

Max, J. E., Castillo, C. S., Bokura, H., Robin, D. A., Lindgren, S. D., Smith, W. L., . . .
Mattheis, P. J. (1998a). Oppositional defiant disorder symptomatology after traumatic
brain injury: A prospective study. *Journal of Nervous and Mental Disease, 186,* 325–332.

Max, J. E., Koele, S. L., Castillo, C. C., Lindgren, S. D., Arndt, S., Bokura, H., . . . Sato, Y.
(2000). Personality change disorder in children and adolescents following traumatic
brain injury. *Journal of the International Neuropsychological Society, 6,* 279–289.

Max, J. E., Koele, S. L., Lindgren, S. D., Robin, D. A., Smith, W. L., Jr., Sato, Y., & Arndt, S.
(1998b). Adaptive functioning following traumatic brain injury and orthopedic injury:
A controlled study. *Archives of Physical Medicine and Rehabilitation, 79,* 893–899.

Max, J. E., Levin, H. S., Landis, J., Schachar, R., Saunders, A., Ewing-Cobbs, L., Chapman, S.,
& Dennis, M. (2005a). Predictors of personality change due to traumatic brain injury
in children and adolescents in the first six months after injury. *Journal of the American
Academy of Child and Adolescent Psychiatry, 44,* 434–442.

Max, J. E., Robin, D. A., Lindgren, S. D., Smith, W. L., Sato, Y., Mattheis, P. J., . . . Castillo, C. S.
(1997). TBI in children and adolescents: Psychiatric disorders at two years. *Journal of
the American Academy of Child and Adolescent Psychiatry, 36,* 1278–1285.

Max, J. E., Schachar, R. J., Levin, H. S., Ewing-Cobbs, L., Chapman, S. B., Dennis, M., . . .
Landis, J. (2005b). Predictors of secondary attention-deficit/hyperactivity disorder
in children and adolescents 6 to 24 months after traumatic brain injury. *Journal of the
American Academy of Child and Adolescent Psychiatry, 44,* 1041–1049.

McCarthy, M. L., MacKenzie, E. J., Durbin, D. R, Aitken, M. E., Jaffe, K. M., Paidas, C. N., . . .
Children's Health After Trauma Study Group. (2006). Health-related quality of life
during the first year after traumatic brain injury. *Archives of Pediatric and Adolescent
Medicine, 160,* 252–260.

McCauley, S. R., & Levin, H. S. (2004). Prospective memory in pediatric traumatic brain
injury: A preliminary study. *Developmental Neuropsychology, 25,* 5–20.

McDonald, C. M., Jaffe, K. M., Fay, G. C., Polissar N. L., Martin, K. M., Liao, S., & Rivara, J. B.
(1994). Comparison of indices of TBI severity as predictors of neurobehavioral outcomes in children. *Archives of Physical Medicine and Rehabilitation, 75,* 328–337.

McLean, D. E., Kaitz, E. S., Kennan, C. J., Dabney, K., Cawley, M. F., & Alexander, M. A.
(1995). Medical and surgical complications of pediatric brain injury. *Journal of Head
Trauma Rehabilitation, 10,* 1–12.

Merkley, T. L., Bigler, E. D., Wilde, E. A., McCauley, S. R., Hunter, J. V., & Levin, H. S.
(2008). Diffuse changes in cortical thickness in pediatric moderate-to-severe traumatic
brain injury. *Journal of Neurotrauma, 25,* 1343–1345.

Miller, L. M., & Donders, J. (2003). Prediction of educational outcome after pediatric
traumatic brain injury. *Rehabilitation Psychology, 48,* 237–241.

Munson, S., Schroth, E., & Ernst, M. (2006). The role of functional neuroimaging in pediatric brain injury. *Pediatrics, 117,* 1372–1381.

Nadebaum, C., Anderson, V., & Catroppa, C. (2007). Executive function outcomes following traumatic brain injury in young children: A five year follow-up. *Developmental
Neuropsychology, 32,* 703–728.

Newsome, M. R., Steinberg, J. L., Scheibel, R. S., Troyanskaya, M., Chu, Z., Hanten, G., . . .
Levin, H. S. (2008). Effects of traumatic brain injury on working memory-related brain
activation in adolescents. *Neuropsychology, 22,* 419–425.

Novack, T. A., Dillon, M. C., & Jackson, W. T. (1996). Neurochemical mechanisms in brain
injury and treatment: A review. *Journal of Clinical and Experimental Neuropsychology,
18,* 685–706.

Nybo, T., Sainio, M., & Muller, K. (2004). Stability of vocational outcome in adulthood after moderate to severe preschool brain injury. *Journal of the International Neuropsychological Society, 10*, 719–723.

Parslow, R. C., Morris, K. P., Tasker, R. C., Forsyth, R. J., & Hawley, C. A. (2005). Epidemiology of traumatic brain injury in children receiving intensive care in the UK. *Archives of Disease in Childhood, 90*, 1182–1187.

Poussaint, T. Y. & Moeller, M. D. (2002). Imaging of pediatric head trauma. *Neuroimaging Clinics of North America, 12*, 271–294.

Povlishock, J. T., & Katz, D. I. (2005). Update of neuropathology and neurological recovery after traumatic brain injury. *Journal of Head Trauma Rehabilitation, 20*, 76–94.

Power, T., Catroppa, C., Coleman, L., Ditchfield, M., & Anderson, V. (2007). Do lesion site and severity predict deficits in attentional control after preschool traumatic brain injury (TBI)? *Brain Injury, 21*, 279–292.

Roman, M. J., Delis, D. C., Willerman, L., Magulac, M., Demadura, T. L., de la Peña, J. L., . . . Kracun, M. (1998). Impact of pediatric TBI on components of verbal memory. *Journal of Clinical and Experimental Neuropsychology, 20*, 245–258.

Ruff, R. (2009). Best practice guidelines for forensic neuropsychological evaluations of patients with traumatic brain injury. *Journal of Head Trauma Rehabilitation, 24*, 131–140.

Saatman, K. E., Duhaime, A-C., Bullock, R., Mass, A. I. R., Valadka, A., Manley, G. T., & Workshop Scientific Team, Advisory Panel Members. (2008). Classification of traumatic brain injury for targeted therapies. *Journal of Neurotrauma, 25*, 719–738.

Salorio, C. F., Slomine, B. S., Grados M, A., Vasa, R. A., Christensen, J. R., & Gerring, J. P. (2005). Neuroanatomic correlates of CVLT-C performance following pediatric traumatic brain injury. *Journal of the International Neuropsychological Society, 11*, 686–696.

Schneier, A. J., Shields, B. J., Hostetler, S. G., Xiang, H., & Smith, G. A. (2006). Incidence of pediatric traumatic brain injury and associated hospital resource utilization in the United States. *Pediatrics, 118*, 483–492.

Schoenberg, M. R., Lange, R. T., Brickell, T. A., & Saklofske, D. H. (2007). Estimating premorbid general cognitive functioning for children and adolescents using the American Wechsler Intelligence Scale for Children-Fourth Edition: Demographic and current performance approaches. *Journal of Child Neurology, 22*, 379–388.

Schoenberg, M. R., Lange, R. T., Saklofske, D. H., Suarez, M., & Brickell, T. A. (2008). Validation of the Child Premorbid Intelligence Estimate method to predict premorbid Wechsler Intelligence Scale for Children-Fourth Edition Full Scale IQ among children with brain injury. *Psychological Assessment, 20*, 377–384.

Schwartz, L., Taylor, H. G., Drotar, D., Yeates, K. O., Wade, S. L. & Stancin, T. (2003). Long-term behavior problems following pediatric traumatic brain injury: Prevalence, predictors, and correlates. *Journal of Pediatric Psychology, 28*, 251–263.

Sesma, H. W., Slomine, B. S., Ding, R., & McCarthy, M. L. (2008). Executive functioning in the first year after pediatric traumatic brain injury. *Pediatrics, 121*, e1686–e1695.

Sigmund, G. A., Tong, K. A., Nickerson, J. P., Wall, C. J., Oyoyo, U., & Ashwal, S. (2007). Multimodality comparison of neuroimaging in pediatric traumatic brain injury. *Pediatric Neurology, 36*, 217–226.

Silver, C. H. (2000). Ecological validity of neuropsychological assessment in childhood traumatic brain injury. *Journal of Head Trauma Rehabilitation, 15*, 973–988.

Slick, D. J., Sherman, E. M., & Iverson, G. L. (1999). Diagnostic criteria for malingered neurocognitive dysfunction: Proposed standards for clinical practice and research. *Clinical Neuropsychologist, 13*, 545–561.

Slomine, B. S., Gerring, J. P., Grados, M. A., Vasa, R., Brady, K. D., Christensen, J. R., & Denckla, M. B. (2002). Performance on measures of executive function following pediatric traumatic brain injury. *Brain Injury, 16*, 759–772.

Stancin, T., Drotar, D., Taylor, H. G., Yeates, K. O., Wade, S. L., & Minich, N. M. (2002). Health-related quality of life of children and adolescents after traumatic brain injury. *Pediatrics,109*(2),e34.Availableat:http://pediatrics.aappublications.org/cgi/content/full/109/2/e34.

Statler, K. D. (2006). Pediatric posttraumatic seizures: Epidemiology, putative mechanisms of epileptogenesis and promising investigational progress. *Developmental Neuroscience, 28*, 354–363.

Taylor, H. G. (2010). Neurobehavioral outcomes of pediatric traumatic brain injury. In V. A. Anderson & K. O. Yeates (Eds.), *Pediatric traumatic brain injury: New frontiers in clinical and translational research*. New York: Cambridge University Press.

Taylor, H. G., & Alden, J. (1997). Age-related differences in outcome following childhood brain injury: An introduction and overview. *Journal of the International Neuropsychological Society, 3*, 555–567.

Taylor, H. G., & Schatschneider, C. (1992). Child neuropsychological assessment: A test of basic assumptions. The *Clinical Neuropsychologist, 6*, 259–275.

Taylor, H. G., Yeates, K. O., Wade, S. L., Drotar, D., Klein, S. K., & Stancin, T. (1999). Influences on first-year recovery from traumatic brain injury in children. *Neuropsychology, 13*, 76–89.

Taylor, H. G., Yeates, K. O., Wade, S. L., Drotar, D., Stancin, T., & Minich, N. (2002). A prospective study of long- and short-term outcomes after traumatic brain injury in children: Behavior and achievement. *Neuropsychology, 16*, 15–27.

Taylor, H. G., Yeates, K. O., Wade, S. L., Drotar, D., Stancin, T., & Montpetite, M. (2003). Long-term educational interventions after traumatic brain injury in children. *Rehabilitation Psychology, 48*, 227–236.

Teasdale, G., & Jennett, B. (1974). Assessment of coma and impaired consciousness: A practical scale. *Lancet, 2*, 81–84.

Thompson, N. M., Francis, D. J., Stuebing, K. K., Fletcher, J. M., Ewing-Cobbs, L., Miner, M. E., ... Eisenberg, H. (1994). Motor, visual-spatial, and somatosensory skills after TBI in children and adolescents: A study of change. *Neuropsychology, 8*, 333–342.

Van't Hooft, I. (2010). Neuropsychological rehabilitation in children with traumatic brain injuries. In V. A. Anderson & K. O. Yeates (Eds). *Pediatric traumatic brain injury: New frontiers in clinical and translational research* (pp. 169–178). New York: Cambridge University Press.

Vasa, R. A., Gerring, J. P., Grados, M., Slomine, B., Christensen, J. R., Rising, W., ... Riddle, M. A. (2002). Anxiety after severe pediatric closed head injury. *Journal of the American Academy of Child and Adolescent Psychiatry, 41*, 148–156.

Ward, H., Shum, D., Dick, B., McKinlay, L., & Baker-Tweney, S. (2004). Interview study of the effects of paediatric traumatic brain injury on memory. *Brain Injury, 18*, 471–495.

Ward, H., Shum, D., McKinlay, L., Baker, S., & Wallace, G. (2007). Prospective memory and pediatric traumatic brain injury: Effects of cognitive demand. *Child Neuropsychology, 13*, 219–239.

Ward, H., Shum, D., Wallace, G., & Boon, J. (2002). Pediatric traumatic brain injury and procedural memory. *Journal of Clinical and Experimental Neuropsychology, 24*, 458–470.

Warschausky, S., Kewman, D., & Kay, J. (1999). Empirically supported psychological and behavioral therapies in pediatric rehabilitation of TBI. *Journal of Head Trauma Rehabilitation, 14,* 373–383.

Wilde, E. A., Hunter, J. V., Newsome, M. R., Scheibel, R. S., Bigler, E. D., Johnson, J. L., ... Levin, H. S. (2005). Frontal and temporal morphometric findings on MRI in children after moderate to severe traumatic brain injury. *Journal of Neurotrauma, 22,* 333–344.

Wills, K. E., & Sweet, J. J. (2006). Neuropsychological considerations in forensic child assessment. In S. N. Sparta & G. P. Koocher (Eds.), *Forensic mental health assessment of children and adolescents* (pp. 260–284). New York: Oxford University Press.

Wright, I., Strand, S., & Wonders, S. (2005). Estimation of premorbid general cognitive abilities in children. *Educational and Child Psychology, 22,* 100–107.

Yeates, K. O. (2010). Traumatic brain injury. In K. O. Yeates, M. D. Ris, & H. G. Taylor (Eds)., *Pediatric neuropsychology: Research, theory, and practice* (pp. 92–116). New York: Guilford.

Yeates, K. O., Armstrong, K., Janusz, J., Taylor, H. G., Wade, S., Stancin, T., & Drotar, D. (2005). Long-term attention problems in children with traumatic brain injury. *Journal of the American Academy of Child and Adolescent Psychiatry, 44,* 574–584.

Yeates, K. O., Bigler, E. D., Dennis, M., Gerhardt, C. A., Rubin, K. H., Stancin, T., ... & Vannatta, K. (2007). Social outcomes in childhood brain disorder: A heuristic integration of social neuroscience and developmental psychology. *Psychological Bulletin, 133,* 535–556.

Yeates, K. O., Blumenstein, E., Patterson, C. M., & Delis, D. C. (1995). Verbal learning and memory following pediatric TBI. *Journal of the International Neuropsychological Society, 1,* 78–87.

Yeates, K. O., & Enrile, B. G. (2005). Implicit and explicit memory in children with congenital and acquired brain disorder. *Neuropsychology, 19,* 618–628.

Yeates, K. O., Patterson, C. M., Waber, D. P., & Bernstein, J. H. (2003). Constructional and figural memory skills following pediatric closed-head injury: Evaluation using the ROCF. In J. A. Knight & E. Kaplan (Eds.), *The handbook of Rey-Osterrieth Complex Figure usage: Clinical and research applications* (pp. 83–93). Odessa, FL: Psychological Assessment Resources.

Yeates, K. O., Swift, E., Taylor, H. G., Wade, S. L., Drotar, D., Stancin, T., & Minich, N. (2004). Short- and long-term social outcomes following pediatric traumatic brain injury. *Journal of the International Neuropsychological Society, 10,* 412–426.

Yeates, K. O., & Taylor, H. G. (2006). Behavior problems in school and their educational correlates among children with traumatic brain injury. *Exceptionality, 14,* 141–154.

Yeates, K. O., & Taylor, H. G. (1997a). Predicting premorbid neuropsychological functioning following pediatric traumatic brain injury. *Journal of Clinical and Experimental Neuropsychology, 19,* 825–837.

Yeates, K. O., & Taylor, H. G. (2001). Neuropsychological assessment of children. In J. J. W. Andrews, D. H. Saklofske, & H. L. Janzen (Eds.), *Handbook of psychoeducational assessment: Ability, achievement, and behavior in children* (pp. 415–450). New York: Academic Press.

Yeates, K. O., Taylor, H. G., Barry, C. T., Drotar, D., Wade, S. L., & Stancin, T. (2001). Neurobehavioral symptoms in childhood closed-head injuries: Changes in prevalence and correlates during the first year post-injury. *Journal of Pediatric Psychology, 26,* 79–91.

Yeates, K. O., Taylor, H. G., Drotar, D., Wade, S., Klein, S., & Stancin, T. (1997b). Premorbid family environment as a predictor of neurobehavioral outcomes following pediatric TBI. *Journal of the International Neuropsychological Society, 3,* 617–630.

Yeates, K. O., Taylor, H. G., Wade, S. L., Drotar, D., Stancin, T., & Minich, N. (2002). A prospective study of short- and long-term neuropsychological outcomes after traumatic brain injury in children. *Neuropsychology, 16,* 514–523.

Yeates, K. O., Taylor, H. G., Walz, N. C., Stancin, T., & Wade, S. L. (2010). The family environment as a moderator of psychosocial outcomes following traumatic brain injury in young children. *Neuropsychology, 24,* 345–356.

Ylvisaker, M., Adelson, D., Braga, L. W., Burnett, S. M., Glang, A., Feeney, T., ... Todis, B. (2005a). Rehabilitation and ongoing support after pediatric TBI: Twenty years of progress. *Journal of Head Trauma Rehabilitation, 20,* 90–104.

Ylvisaker, M., Todis, B., Glang, A., Urbanczyk, B., Franklin, C., DePompei, R., ... Tyler, J. S. (2001). Educating students with TBI: Themes and recommendations. *Journal of Head Trauma Rehabilitation, 16,* 76–93.

Ylvisaker, M., Turkstra, L. S., & Coelho, C. (2005b). Behavioral and social interventions for individuals with traumatic brain injury: A summary of the research with clinical implications. *Seminars in Speech and Language, 26,* 256–267.

Ylvisaker, M., Turkstra, L., Coehlo, C., Yorkston, K., Kennedy, M., Sohlberg, M. M., & Avery, J. (2007). Behavioural interventions for children and adults with behaviour disorders after TBI: A systematic review of the evidence. *Brain Injury, 21,* 769–805.

Yuan, W., Holland, S. K., Schmithorst, V. J., Walz, N. C., Cecil, K. M., Jones, B. V., ... Wade, S. L. (2007). Diffusion tensor MR imaging reveals persistent white matter alteration after traumatic brain injury experienced during early childhood. *American Journal of Neuroradiology, 28,* 1919–1925.

Chapter 12

Preinjury and Secondary Attention-Deficit/ Hyperactivity Disorder in Pediatric Traumatic Brain Injury Forensic Cases

JEFFREY E. MAX
RUSSELL J. SCHACHAR
TISHA J. ORNSTEIN

INTRODUCTION

Pediatric traumatic brain injury (TBI) is a major public health problem with an annual incidence of 400/100,000, and it is the foremost cause of disability and death in children in the United States (Langlois, Rutland-Brown, & Thomas, 2005). The distribution of brain injury by severity ranges between 80% and 90% for mild, 7% and 8% for moderate, and 5% and 8% for severe brain injury (Kraus, 1995). Psychiatric and neuropsychological complications are rated as more impairing and burdensome than physical disabilities (Di Scala, Osberg, Gans, Chin, & Grant, 1991). The civil justice system is the usual arena in which lawsuits related to pursuit of damages occur. To our knowledge, there is only one empiric research study of pediatric TBI in the civil justice system (Max, Bowers, Baldus, & Gaylor, 1998b). In the study, pediatric TBI ($n = 43$) and burn ($n = 51$) plaintiffs were ascertained through a survey of the U.S. civil justice system. The study involved a review of judicial opinions and verdict reporters in cases that resulted in an award of compensatory damages in all states from 1978 to 1988. The authors found that psychiatric disorders, almost exclusively internalizing disorders (e.g., anxiety), were present in approximately 25% of subjects in each group. Psychiatric symptoms were not related to the award amount. Significantly greater awards in the TBI group were accounted for by greater disability measures. Physical disability and total disability (including physical and quality of life limitations) were significantly and independently correlated with the award. Distribution of disorders was atypical compared with the authors' experience in pediatric TBI litigation and more important, compared with studies of consecutively hospitalized children, in that externalizing disorders (e.g., attention-deficit/hyperactivity disorder) were not commonly reported for either class of injuries (Max et al., 1998b).

In contrast to the dearth of pediatric TBI studies in the civil justice system, there is an expanding pediatric TBI knowledge base on psychiatric disorders and on neuropsychological problems in clinical populations. The reader is referred to recent comprehensive literature reviews of these areas (Max, 2011, 2010). In this chapter, we focus on attention-deficit/hyperactivity disorder (ADHD), which is one of the most important psychiatric disorders present in children who have a TBI. Our objective is to provide the reader with a working understanding of the following subject areas: (1) behavioral and neuropsychological features of developmental or preinjury ADHD; (2) behavioral and neuropsychological features of secondary ADHD or postinjury onset of ADHD; (3) complexity of individual plaintiffs with ADHD; (4) critical aspects of the conduct of the forensic case by both plaintiff's and defendant's psychiatric and neuropsychologist experts; and (5) pathway for lawyers to interact most expeditiously with their psychiatrist or neuropsychologist experts. We have chosen the vehicle of three case presentations in the course of the chapter to complement the research review of ADHD and to provide the reader with a more vivid picture of ADHD in the context of litigation after pediatric TBI. Identifying details and clinical details have been modified to preserve anonymity. Only the expert's formulation and conclusions regarding the case are presented. The cases therefore intentionally contain an admixture of history and interpretation.

BEHAVIORAL AND NEUROPSYCHOLOGICAL FEATURES OF DEVELOPMENTAL OR PREINJURY ADHD

Case 1: Luke: Preinjury ADHD (Composed by Plaintiff's Expert)

Luke is a 15-year-old male who suffered a severe TBI from a fall about 10 months before the forensic examination. The lowest postresuscitation Glasgow Coma Scale (GCS) score was 7. Computed tomography (CT) scan after the injury showed multiple small petechial hemorrhages particularly in the left parietal cortex and the largest hemorrhage was in the left thalamus and measured 10 mm in diameter. He presents with multiple behavioral problems, including conduct disorder; separation anxiety disorder in partial remission; attention-deficit/hyperactivity disorder, not otherwise specified; marijuana dependence; and maladaptive excessive use of alcohol. He has an earlier history of panic attacks associated with the separation anxiety disorder, a past history of major depressive disorder, a past history of enuresis, obsessive-compulsive traits, and a history of subthreshold vocal tics.

Luke's problems began around first grade with separation anxiety disorder leading to school absences. Absences were tolerated by his mother who had her own problems with anxiety and a history of substance abuse. Luke's father was unable to change this dynamic. School performance was complicated by co-occurring ADHD. Luke's functioning deteriorated over time due to these problems as well as multiple moves. Oppositional behavior and physically aggressive behavior leading to frank conduct disorder made his placement in regular school impossible and group home placement necessary. The relatively unsupervised environment in which he was raised, combined with a family history of substance abuse, has led to significant marijuana dependence and maladaptive use of alcohol. Periods of active juvenile justice and educational intervention have thus far not changed his behavior.

Luke's severe TBI has caused worsened attention and an inability to complete school work and process information as rapidly as before his injury. This is consistent with severe TBI and specifically with damage to the thalamus that was documented on CT scan. He appears to have had a significant problem with apathy after the TBI, which has resolved despite heavy use of marijuana, a substance known to induce lethargy when used regularly. His school academic program has minimal demands. All of these factors compounded by his truancy are leading him to fall further behind academically. He suffers from headaches and hearing deficits as a result of the TBI. Worsening of expressive language problems and balance problems are also reported to have resulted from the TBI. The problems are consistent with the documented transient hemiparesis at the time of injury and language problems noted during rehabilitation.

Luke's major problem is his delinquent behavior and conduct disorder. This problem, together with his other preinjury psychiatric disorders (ADHD; separation anxiety disorder, marijuana abuse, maladaptive alcohol use), is less likely to improve or resolve over the course of time due to his having suffered a severe TBI. This occurs because of a decrease in reserve brain function as a result of diffuse widespread brain damage.

Luke's function could improve from its current status with the enforcement of a strict consistent probation plan, well-supervised and individually tailored remedial education program, elimination of unsupervised time, elimination of truancy, specific treatment of substance abuse, and supervision of his taking psychotropic medication.

Review of Preinjury Attention-Deficit/Hyperactivity Disorder

Preinjury attention-deficit/hyperactivity disorder (PADHD) is a common psychiatric disorder in children with a prevalence of 3% to 5% (American Psychiatric Association, 2000). The disorder has a strong genetic component with an estimated 76% hereditability (Goodman & Stevenson, 1989). The diagnosis of ADHD is made clinically when the child manifests a constellation of inattentive symptoms and/or hyperactive/impulsive symptoms that cause impairment in the child's day-to-day life at home, at school, and in the community (American Psychiatric Association, 2000).

Current theories of PADHD focus on deficits in cognitive control that mediate attention and executive functions (EFs). Developmental cognitive theorists view EFs as (1) maintenance of a problem-solving set for future goals (Pennington, 1996); (2) organization of behavior over time (Denckla & Rudel, 1974); (3) orderly approaches to problems (Borkowski, 1996); (4) skillful use of strategies (Graham, 1996); (5) flexible and effective verbal self-regulation (Hayes, 1996); and (6) responses or actions that function to alter the probability of a subsequent response of the child (i.e., responsiveness to feedback) (Barkley, 1996); and they postulate that EFs depend on the maturation and integrity of the prefrontal region (Eslinger, 1996). Working memory and inhibition are fundamental, interactive processes involved in more complex skills such as problem solving, inferencing, planning, reading and aural comprehension, arithmetic, and self-regulation (Geary, 1993; Gernsbacher & Faust, 1991; Perfetti, 1985). Another type of executive function includes metacognitive skills (Hanten et al., 2004), which are integrative abilities enabling children to assess their knowledge, monitor their cognitive activities, and deploy strategies (Hanten et al., 2004; Leonesio & Nelson, 1990).

Children with PADHD show various EF deficits (Barkley, 1997a). Barkley (1997b) has proposed that the central cognitive deficit in childhood ADHD is behavioral disinhibition. Numerous studies have confirmed that poor inhibitory control is the cardinal deficit of childhood ADHD and is best characterized by an inability to inhibit unwanted responses (Schachar, Tannock, Marriott, & Logan, 1995), is affected in siblings of ADHD probands (Schachar et al., 2005), and serves as a marker for a particularly heritable subgroup of ADHD (Crosbie & Schachar, 2001). Moreover, the ADHD literature supports the conclusion that motor inhibition reflects a possible cognitive endophenotype in ADHD (Castellanos & Tannock, 2002).

In general, the current theory of ADHD is that multiple, interacting genetic and environmental influences add incrementally to the risk for ADHD. When the combined effects of these risk factors reach some threshold, the disorder is evident, causes impairment, and is diagnosed. There is clear evidence of the action of genetic risks in ADHD. Family studies show that ADHD runs in families. Studies of twins capitalize on the fact that identical (monozygotic; MZ) and fraternal (dizygotic; DZ) twins share 100% or 50% of their genes, respectively. If environmental influences are shared, twins are more similar and if they are not shared they tend to be less similar. Twin studies, in which similarity of MZ and DZ twins is compared for a trait like ADHD, show that the majority of ADHD variation is explained by unique genetic risks and nonshared environmental risks. Nonshared environmental risks are factors such as fetal exposure to drugs, alcohol, stress, or toxins.

Based on the robust response of ADHD patients to stimulant medication and the known effect of these drugs on neurotransmission, we have been looking for abnormalities in ADHD in the genes involved in neurotransmission. Several genes have been found to be associated with ADHD. However, to date, these risks account for very little of ADHD (Kuntsi, McLoughlin, & Asherson, 2006). Genome-wide scans have found several areas of the genome that might harbor ADHD risks, but none have been significant genome-wide. Genes do not code for complex traits such as the ones evident in Luke. Rather, they code for proteins that, during development, form the biological basis of brain function. There is considerable evidence for differences in brain structure in individuals with ADHD. Several of these differences lie in regions of the brain that are known to be themselves highly heritable. The action of the genes involved in ADHD could play themselves out in impaired abilities to think, problem solve, and in other functions broadly known as executive functions.

Measures of heritability of ADHD or any other trait could be inflated by gene–environment correlation (i.e., the tendency for people at genetic risk to have some attendant environmental risk). The following is an example. ADHD increases the risk for alcoholism and substance abuse disorder. A young woman affected with ADHD could develop a substance abuse disorder and expose her unborn child both to the genetic risks for ADHD and to the effects of fetal alcohol. Twin studies cannot easily separate these effects, although there are efforts underway to do just that.

Case 2: Elizabeth: Previously Unrecognized Preinjury ADHD (Composed by Defendant's Expert)

Elizabeth is a 16-year-old female who had a moderate TBI 30 months before the forensic evaluation. The lowest GCS score was 13. Elizabeth had a brief loss of consciousness and probable immediate seizure at the scene of the accident. CT scans after the accident showed bilateral temporal lobe and left frontal contusions, which cleared over time, and ultimately revealed, on magnetic resonance imaging (MRI), small contour abnormalities of the lateral aspect of the temporal lobes bilaterally suggestive of a small amount of encephalomalacia.

Elizabeth had a preinjury anxiety disorder, which required individual therapy. The therapist indicated that she had a lifelong tendency toward anxiety problems which preceded the stressors that precipitated the therapy at the time. Elizabeth appears to have had social anxiety, at least since age 9. The social anxiety has continued to the present, but it has been quite manageable. Elizabeth continues to have generalized anxiety symptomatology such as being self-conscious about her body, having muscle tension, restlessness, insomnia, preoccupation with her past actions and past behaviors, as well as clenching her teeth and jaw. The documentation reviewed also shows preinjury complaints of headache twice a week and frequent chest pain. Even by Elizabeth's report, these anxiety-related symptoms predated her injury and have continued to the present. Elizabeth is currently under stress because of the awareness that her lawsuit is coming closer to mediation or trial.

Within months after her injury, clinically significant obsessive-compulsive disorder became evident. Obsessive-compulsive disorder is infrequent following TBI, although obsessive-compulsive symptoms may not be uncommon (Grados et al., 2008). The obsessive-compulsive symptoms have markedly improved, probably related to the progression of time since the injury and in the absence of cognitive-behavioral therapy (CBT). However, her residual symptoms may improve further with CBT. This pattern of recovery has been described in the pediatric TBI literature. Elizabeth was predisposed to developing obsessive-compulsive disorder because of her personal history of anxiety disorder, including social anxiety and generalized anxiety symptomatology, before the injury. In addition, it appears that she has a family history of obsessive-compulsive disorder in a first-degree relative.

Elizabeth developed markedly inappropriate and disinhibited social behaviors such as making inappropriate remarks to strangers. She demonstrates a significant improvement in this problem and actively attempts to inhibit herself. Elizabeth has been able to keep her long-term friendships, attesting to her ability in the social realm. She would therefore not qualify for a diagnosis of disinhibited subtype of personality change due to TBI. Elizabeth also developed mood instability, which manifested itself mostly in angry outbursts within the context of her family. Although there were isolated incidents outside her family, the brunt of her anger was directed toward her siblings. This was not associated with any dangerous violent act. This symptomatology has also markedly improved, most probably related to the progression of time since the injury. This problem would be consistent with a diagnosis of personality change due to TBI, labile subtype, and it is in a residual phase at this point (i.e., not clinically significant although not completely resolved). It is significant to note that her individualized education plan recorded that her behavior does not interfere with her learning.

Elizabeth has attention-deficit/hyperactivity disorder, inattentive type. This is the one disorder, which has only recently been recognized in her. It has caused her significant impairment in her schoolwork. Treatment has only recently begun with atomoxetine. She has not had a trial of potentially the most helpful medications for this syndrome, that is, stimulant medication. There are multiple studies attesting to the effectiveness of stimulant medication for non-injury-related ADHD, and a few studies suggesting that ADHD related to TBI is responsive to stimulant medication. Review of school reports from kindergarten through eighth grade revealed overwhelming evidence of untreated ADHD present before the injury. Her report cards over the years were replete with repetitive comments, such as problems with homework completion, talking at inappropriate times, not respecting teacher or peers, trouble waiting her turn, calling out in class inappropriately, talkative, trouble listening, deficits in focus and organization, trouble following directions, trouble staying on task, making careless errors, rushing over work, and needing to slow down. It is striking to see the absence of her preinjury school reports quoted by her current and previous treatment providers. Without this preinjury academic documentation, one would easily reach the erroneous conclusion that her ADHD developed after the injury.

Elizabeth has used marijuana inappropriately. The use of marijuana at least three times per week up until recently probably affected her ability to concentrate and progress in her school work, at least to some degree. Quitting marijuana and getting treated for ADHD will probably result in significant improvements in ADHD symptomatology.

Elizabeth had symptoms of posttraumatic stress, which lasted several months after the injury and which have essentially resolved. She has minor avoidance of the intersection where she had the accident, but she has progressively pushed herself to the point that she has successfully crossed that road. Elizabeth's occasional self-injurious behavior, including cutting herself and bruising herself, is consistent with personality disorder traits. These traits are not associated with TBI and reflect developmental problems.

Research shows that a consistent predictor of postinjury psychiatric disorders after pediatric TBI is preinjury family dysfunction. Research also shows that postinjury behavioral disturbance is exacerbated by postinjury family problems. The record shows numerous examples of family difficulties over the years both preinjury and postinjury. Family therapy addressing both preinjury and postinjury family dysfunction would probably maximize Elizabeth's functioning.

It is doubtful that Elizabeth has a seizure disorder. Seizure disorders are rare after TBI, especially when the injury is not a penetrating injury. Even after severe traumatic brain injuries, the rate of seizures is no more than 10%. Since she has not had a seizure in the years since her injury, late-onset seizures are extremely unlikely.

Elizabeth's prognosis, given the aforementioned history of a moderate TBI, notable improvements in her obsessive-compulsive disorder, mood lability, and posttraumatic stress disorder symptomatology, cessation of marijuana use, her self-motivation to achieve goals, the impending final phase of her litigation, and anticipated treatment of preinjury ADHD, will allow her to function in society. I expect that she will gain employment at a level commensurate with her intellectual capacity, which is unchanged as a result of her TBI. She will require ongoing monitoring of residual obsessive-compulsive disorder should this not resolve completely, and she will require continued treatment of her preinjury ADHD.

POSTINJURY PROBLEMS INCLUDING BEHAVIORAL AND NEUROPSYCHOLOGICAL FEATURES OF POSTINJURY ADHD OR SECONDARY ADHD

Several studies have reported on the relationship between preinjury ADHD and the subsequent occurrence of a TBI in childhood (Gerring et al., 1998; Max et al., 1997b). Moreover, research studies have demonstrated that children develop ADHD post injury (secondary ADHD) (Gerring et al., 1998; Max et al., 1998a; Max et al., 2005b). Additionally, numerous psychiatric disorders have been reported to occur post injury. Several studies have documented the emergence of personality change due to TBI (PC) (Max et al., 2000; Max et al., 2005a), depression (Kirkwood et al., 2000; Max et al., 1998e), anxiety disorders (Vasa et al., 2002), including PTSD (Herskovits, Gerring, Davatzikos, & Bryan, 2002; Max et al., 1998d) and less commonly OCD (Grados et al., 2008). There is also indication of a relationship between severity of injury, PC, and adaptive and intellectual functioning decrements (Max et al., 2000). Furthermore, novel psychiatric disorders in children post TBI are significantly correlated with family psychiatric history and measures of family function (Max et al., 1997a).

Case 3: Isaac: Secondary ADHD (Composed by Plaintiff's Expert)

Isaac presents as an 8-year-old male with untreated ADHD with significant inattentive and hyperactive/impulsive symptoms. This is the direct result of his severe TBI from a motor vehicle accident at age 7, 16 months prior to the forensic evaluation. Isaac suffered a compound comminuted depressed fracture of left frontal bone and facial fractures. Head CT scan showed underlying hemorrhages in both frontal lobes. There was initially ventricular compression of the frontal horn, which resulted in some atrophy. In addition, a right frontal subdural hemorrhage, as well as a subarachnoid hemorrhage, and a right epidural hemorrhage were documented. The lowest postresuscitation GCS was 8. Estimated duration of impaired consciousness (injury until time of consistent following of simple commands) was about 43 hours. Follow-up scanning indicated bilateral frontal encephalomalacia.

His preinjury function was such that he performed well in a second grade gifted program but now his ADHD and associated cognitive and memory problems from his TBI have caused him to struggle academically. He has become aware of his difficulties at school and has begun to react by attempting to avoid school to reduce the perceived pressure. There is no family history of ADHD.

He had a higher than normal level of separation anxiety traits that has worsened to a mild form of separation anxiety disorder. This is related to his perceived vulnerability as a result of the life-threatening injury. Related to this are subthreshold anxious symptoms when riding in a car. The disorder has been perpetuated by his mother's wish to indulge him as a way to make up for his having suffered so much. The involvement of mother's new boyfriend seems to be a healthy influence and is already limiting the extent of this problem.

Isaac has other subthreshold symptoms consistent with the direct effect of brain injury. This includes emotional lability, disinhibition, perseveration, and immaturity.

Family dysfunction has possibly played a role in Isaac's relative lack of friends outside school and the unsatisfactory status of his friendships in school. Domestic arguments and the relative lack of a strong male role model have affected him subtly in the form of his becoming a "mama's boy" and have limited his confidence in socialization with peers. This could change over a period of months with his new family constellation.

Review of Secondary Attention-Deficit/Hyperactivity Disorder

ADHD is a common consequence of TBI in children and has recently come to be referred to as secondary ADHD. Secondary ADHD (SADHD) occurs in 15%–23% in studies of hospitalized children with TBI (Gerring et al., 1998; Max et al., 2005b, 2005c). SADHD is more likely to develop with more severe injuries and is also more likely when the child experiences intellectual and adaptive function deficits and comes from a home characterized by family dysfunction before the injury. A prospective study of attention-deficit hyperactivity (ADH) symptoms found a similar relationship with severity and that overall ADH symptoms were associated with lower preinjury family functioning (Max et al., 1998a). Another prospective study examining change in the number of ADHD symptoms found that inattentive symptoms were more prevalent and stable in children with preinjury ADHD than those with no preinjury ADHD (Levin et al., 2007). Change in hyperactive symptoms reflected greater and more frequent fluctuations in the children with no preinjury ADHD. Furthermore, in children with no preinjury ADHD, socioeconomic status predicted the onset of SADHD. Overall, inattentive and hyperactivity symptom counts were related to greater severity of injury in the children with no preinjury ADHD but not in the children with preinjury ADHD (Levin et al., 2007). A referred sample consisting of mostly severe TBI children had similar findings and the children with SADHD had greater "premorbid" psychosocial adversity (Gerring et al., 1998).

SADHD can follow severe TBI (Brown, Chadwick, Shaffer, Rutter, & Traub, 1981; Gerring et al., 1998; Max et al., 2004). After moderate TBI, SADHD has thus far been convincingly demonstrated only in the presence of preinjury ADHD traits

(Max et al., 2004). SADHD has also followed mild TBI and orthopedic injury (in the absence of brain injury) at similar rates (Max et al., 2004). Therefore attribution of brain injury as the primary etiological factor for SADHD after mild TBI remains uncertain pending larger controlled studies of mild TBI.

SADHD has been associated with thalamic or right putamen lesions (Gerring et al., 2000; Herskovits et al., 1999) and orbital frontal gyrus lesions (Max et al., 2005b). Therefore, lesions in varied locations along specific cortico-striatal-pallidal-thalamic spirals may generate a clinical syndrome of SADHD (Cummings, 1993).

One sees many executive function deficits following TBI. These deficits are likely to play a role in the development of the psychopathology (including SADHD), learning problems, and deficits in adaptive function seen after injury (Konrad, Gauggel, Manz, & Scholl, 2000; Schachar, Levin, Max, Purvis, & Chen, 2004; Slomine et al., 2005; Taylor et al., 1999; Wassenberg, Max, Lindgren, & Schatz, 2004; Yeates et al., 2005). Defining a neuropsychological profile of SADHD may provide important clues about neurobiological mechanisms involved in the expression of the syndrome. However, neurocognitive phenomenology associated with SADHD remains to be elucidated fully.

CONDUCT OF THE CASE: PSYCHIATRIC AND NEUROPSYCHOLOGICAL ASPECTS

Role of the Child and Adolescent Psychiatrist

Nurcombe has succinctly outlined how principles and practice of a child psychiatric forensic evaluation are quite distinct from those of a clinical evaluation (Nurcombe, 1993a). This author has also crisply described a recommended approach to expert witness testimony in court (Nurcombe, 1993b). A clear understanding by the expert witness of his or her role is essential. The following maxims have been provided to guide the evaluation (Nurcombe, 1993a): Be an informant, not an advocate; Evaluate, don't treat; Thoroughness and clarity supersede vigor of advocacy; Don't doctor the information, that is, oversimplify, delete facts or inferences that mitigate the force of their opinions, or claim greater certainty for their opinions than is justified; Don't claim more certainty than the data allow; Don't testify to the ultimate issue, rather gather information relevant to the ultimate issue for the court to decide.

An important task of the expert witness is to establish credibility. Except in the clearest of cases, "all or nothing" attributions of causation of psychiatric problems should be avoided. The case examples provided demonstrate typical complexity of TBI cases in the civil litigation arena. Regardless of whether the expert witness is retained by the plaintiff or defendant, a realistic and balanced formulation that addresses both sides of the argument will allow the principal thrust of the expert's opinion to come across as reasonable and valid. The better quality legal counsels favor working with an expert witness with these principles because it is preferable to hear the weakness of the case first from one's own expert and develop a legal strategy than to be surprised by opposing counsel later. An essential element for the expert witness to demonstrate is a deep and broad appreciation of the relevant scientific literature. Such expertise leads to the expression of the strongest possible multidimensional opinion by detailing the strengths of the case and identifying weaknesses in the expected opposing arguments. It is difficult for opposing counsel to disqualify the opinion of a well-read and well-practiced expert.

In addition to the previously noted general principles, there are several domains of specific relevance for the forensic expert in a pediatric TBI case. Comprehensive psychiatric and standardized neuropsychological assessments are essential for a full understanding of the case. Use of structured or semi-structured psychiatric interviews such as the Schedule for Affective Disorders and Schizophrenia for School-Age Children, Present and Lifetime Version (K-SADS-PL) (Kaufman et al., 1997) and Neuropsychiatric Rating Schedule (NPRS) (Max, Castillo, Lindgren, & Arndt, 1998c) indicate diligence and thoroughness on behalf of the expert witness but are not essential. Elicitation of a history of new postinjury symptoms is the cornerstone of every case. In particular, the development of personality change due to TBI provides the strongest evidence of TBI directly causing behavioral disturbance. The clinical presentation of this disorder involves new onset of clinically significant affective lability, rage, disinhibition, apathy, or paranoia. This disorder is a significant co-occurring syndrome of SADHD (Max et al., 2005c).

Additional common postinjury behavioral symptoms or syndromes include attention problems, SADHD, anxiety disorders, and depressive disorders. As noted previously, careful probing and documentation of evidence supporting the preinjury onset as well as the postinjury onset of specific symptomatology is crucial to each case. For example, documentation of preinjury ADHD even if it had not formally been diagnosed previously can alter the formulation of a case. Similarly, referencing records including school records that are incompatible with preinjury ADHD could be important in bolstering the justification that the inattentive and hyperactive/impulsive injured child in fact has SADHD. Surveillance video can be helpful to the expert at times. For example, in situations where posttraumatic stress symptoms of fear of roads or traffic are alleged, repeated surveillance video of an adolescent nonchalantly crossing a road can raise doubts. However, surveillance video of reckless or apparently impulsive crossing of a road may be consistent with the presence of preinjury ADHD or SADHD.

An often overlooked point in pediatric TBI cases directly linking behavioral change and injury is the improvement in or apparent resolution of preinjury disorders. For example, some children with preinjury ADHD, combined type, may no longer appear hyperactive or impulsive after a severe TBI. The reason for this is unclear but may be related to apathy, depression, or even motor problems. These children typically have worse attentional problems compared to their preinjury attentional abilities. Another example is the elimination of conduct disorder behaviors in some adolescents after severe TBI. The change seems to be related to apathy and/or executive function problems such that even simple planning of antisocial acts may be beyond the brain-injured individual. An ironic twist occurs at times after TBI such that some children and adolescents experience improvement in certain limited domains of functioning, find relief of symptoms of specific preinjury disorders, or even show improvement in overall functioning. This relatively favorable result may be found in situations of dire psychosocial adversity where there have been years of constraints preventing appropriate treatment of severe preinjury psychiatric disorders. The traumatic event sometimes is the unfortunate key to services that were previously beyond reach. Nevertheless, especially in the case of severe TBI, an extremely important point to make relates to the concept of reduction of cognitive or behavioral reserve in each individual. This implies that TBI has resulted in complications at several levels, for example, preinjury ADHD may now be less effectively treatable and the decline of cognitive reserves may result in lower long-term educational and employment achievement, or under stress, the child may prematurely reach his or her limits in using cognitive problem-solving strategies and decompensate behaviorally.

The expert will always note the presence or absence and role of adverse family and other psychosocial circumstances. The psychosocial milieu is particularly important for children who are dependent on adults for support and nurturance. While ironic twists of improved domains of functioning may occur in children from disadvantaged families, these children may be more affected by the same severity of TBI than a child from a more privileged social economic status. This has been termed the "double hazard" effect (Taylor et al., 1999). Family psychiatric history data are important in the development of an argument regarding the attribution of psychiatric disorders in the injured child. The absence of a family history of ADHD raises the possibility that the injured child presenting with ADHD actually has SADHD (Max et al., 2004). However, the presence of a family history of ADHD does not automatically imply that the injured child's ADHD is of preinjury onset. Consideration of the full clinical presentation, for example, timing of onset or worsening of symptoms, school records, and medical records, are necessary to determine whether the child has preinjury ADHD or SADHD. The expert witness is limited in his or her ability to document family psychiatric history unless a direct clinical evaluation of family members is allowed and/or access is provided to the psychiatric and school records of parents or siblings.

The quality of the child's social life can be informative. Documentation on changes in the quality and quantity of friendships can shed light on the effect of the TBI. In circumstances where seemingly exaggerated claims of disability are made, surveillance video of adolescents socializing in public can be enlightening.

Role of the Pediatric Neuropsychologist

The neuropsychological evaluation is an essential parallel and complementary assessment to the psychiatric evaluation. The major goals of the neuropsychological evaluation within a legal context are to identify whether and to what extent the TBI has produced (a) a pattern of cerebral pathology, (b) to determine whether a relationship exists between cerebral damage (if any) and measured cognitive ability, and (c) whether neuropsychological impairment translates into cognitive disability (the degree to which disordered functions impact an individual's daily functioning). A TBI can result in brain damage that affects a range of cognitive, behavioral, and personality characteristics. A neuropsychological assessment needs to reflect this diversity, keeping in mind, however, that the court is primarily interested in the consequences of the brain injury as reflected in the nature and degree of instrumental activities of daily living limitations.

The neuropsychological evaluation provides information relevant to psycho-social outcome; however, without information regarding what is known about the injury, the person sustaining the injury, and a host of preexisting emotional and environmental factors, the neuropsychological interpretation remains incomplete. This means that besides the information acquired from neurocognitive tests and psychological measures, in addition to embracing neuroimaging technology (i.e., a review of the medical records to help explain neuropsychological abnormalities), clinicians weigh information through direct observations or from caregiver interviews where changes have been identified in cognitive, emotional, and behavior spheres of functioning. The premorbid history is a highly relevant component of the neuropsychological process and important in the context of litigation. Such an evaluation provides a baseline against which to determine whether postinjury changes in functioning are the direct result of the impact per se. As such, an examination of the premorbid history can determine whether comorbid factors have contributed to performance or influenced preexistent difficulties. The diagnostic accuracy of a case is affected by whether premorbid factors have been taken into consideration.

The neuropsychologist is also interested in the changes observed post injury. Essentially, the neuropsychologist's task is to isolate factors associated with the TBI, to integrate this information to formulate probable causes, and to help guide formulation of treatment plans. The determination of postinjury changes in a child's functioning and how problems manifest at home and in school requires knowledge of normal development, the nature of the TBI, the cognitive deficiency characteristic of the nature and extent of the brain insult, a detailed account of the presenting problem, and measurement of behavioral, cognitive, and academic functioning.

RELATIONSHIP BETWEEN THE EXPERT WITNESS AND LEGAL COUNSEL

The relationship between the expert witness and legal counsel is important for the seamless progression of the case. Legal counsel should become conversant with review papers or chapters focused on psychiatric and neuropsychological aspects of pediatric TBI. He or she should retain a knowledgeable expert who is familiar with the scientific literature on pediatric TBI and the role of the expert witness. The expert should be able to educate legal counsel about the questions to ask to make his or her case as clearly and conclusively as possible. The expert should discuss with legal counsel the strengths and weaknesses of the case in order that the latter can make a more informed decision regarding litigation or settlement strategies. The legal counsel should inform the expert witness about the style of opposing counsel in depositions and in court if the case has not yet been settled. The expert witness should also be taught basics of expectations, dynamics, and limitations of typical juries in the service of providing the greatest fidelity in testimony and achieving a lasting impression upon the jury. Most commonly this will involve tailoring the style of testimony and the density of the content, as well as elimination of professional jargon.

CONCLUSION

ADHD is a common psychiatric disorder in childhood. Childhood psychiatric disorders, including preinjury ADHD, constitute a risk factor for a child having a TBI. Psychiatric disorders often arise as complications after pediatric TBI. There is no one psychiatric disorder that is an invariable result of brain injury. The presence of personality change due to TBI directly implicates the brain injury in the causation of the behavioral disturbance. SADHD is a significant co-occurring disorder with personality change due to TBI. Differentiation of PADHD and SADHD is important in civil litigation cases. The disorders can be differentiated by clinical features obtained through careful interviews of parents and child, review of school records, and review of medical records. Neurocognitive tests do not specifically identify individuals with PADHD or SADHD. Rather, such test results in a research setting may differentiate groups of children with PADHD versus normal controls or groups of children with SADHD versus normal controls. Additional neurocognitive research may provide clues to the differing pathophysiological mechanisms of PADHD and SADHD. The conduct of the forensic evaluation and expert testimony may be best achieved with informed and practiced expert witnesses and legal counsels.

REFERENCES

American Psychiatric Association. (2000). *Diagnostic and statistical manual of mental disorders* (4th ed., text rev.). Washington, DC: American Psychiatric Press.

Barkley, R. A. (1996). Critical issues in research on attention. In G. R. Lyon, & N. A. Krasnegor (Eds.), *Attention, memory, and executive function* (pp. 45–56). Baltimore, MD: Paul H. Brookes Publishing Co.

Barkley, R. A. (1997a). *ADHD and the nature of self-control.* New York: The Guilford Press.

Barkley, R. A. (1997b). Behavioral inhibition, sustained attention, and executive functions: constructing a unifying theory of ADHD. *Psychological Bulletin, 121*(1), 65–94.

Borkowski, J. G., & Burke, J.E, (1996). Theories, models, and measurements of executive functioning: An information processing perspective. In G. R. Lyon, & N. A. Krasnegor (Eds.), *Attention, memory, and executive function* (pp. 235–262). Baltimore, MD: Paul H. Brookes Publishing Co.

Brown, G., Chadwick, O., Shaffer, D., Rutter, M., & Traub, M. (1981). A prospective study of children with head injuries: III. Psychiatric sequelae. *Psychological Medicine, 11*(1), 63–78.

Castellanos, F. X., & Tannock, R. (2002). Neuroscience of attention-deficit/hyperactivity disorder: the search for endophenotypes. *Nature Reviews Neuroscience, 3*(8), 617–628.

Crosbie, J., & Schachar, R. (2001). Deficient inhibition as a marker for familial ADHD. *American Journal of Psychiatry, 158*(11), 1884–1890.

Cummings, J. L. (1993). Frontal-subcortical circuits and human behavior. *Archives of Neurology, 50*(8), 873–880.

Denckla, M. B., & Rudel, R. (1974). Rapid "automatized" naming of pictured objects, colors, letters and numbers by normal children. *Cortex, 10*(2), 186–202.

Di Scala, C., Osberg, J. S., Gans, B. M., Chin, L. J., & Grant, C. C. (1991). Children with traumatic head injury: Morbidity and postacute treatment. *Archives of Physical Medicine and Rehabilitation, 72*(9), 662–66.

Eslinger, P. J. (1996). Conceptualizing, describing, and measuring components of executive function: A summary. In G. R. Lyon & N. A. Krasnegor (Eds.), *Attention, memory, and executive function* (pp. 367–396). Baltimore, MD: Paul H. Brookes Publishing Co.

Geary, D. C. (1993). Mathematical disabilities: cognitive, neuropsychological, and genetic components. *Psychological Bulletin, 114*(2), 345–362.

Gernsbacher, M. A., & Faust, M. E. (1991). The mechanism of suppression: A component of general comprehension skill. *Journal of Experimental Psychology, Learning, Memory and Cognition, 17*(2), 245–262.

Gerring, J., Brady, K., Chen, A., Quinn, C., Herskovits, E., Bandeen-Roche, K., . . . Bryan, N. (2000). Neuroimaging variables related to development of secondary attention deficit hyperactivity disorder after closed head injury in children and adolescents. *Brain Injury, 14*(3), 205–218.

Gerring, J. P., Brady, K. D., Chen, A., Vasa, R., Grados, M., Bandeen-Roche, K. J., . . . Denckla, M. B. (1998). Premorbid prevalence of ADHD and development of secondary ADHD after closed head injury. *Journal of the American Academy of Child and Adolescent Psychiatry, 37*(6), 647–654.

Goodman, R., & Stevenson, J. (1989). A twin study of hyperactivity—II. The aetiological role of genes, family relationships and perinatal adversity. *Journal of Child Psychology and Psychiatry, 30*(5), 691–709.

Grados, M. A., Vasa, R. A., Riddle, M. A., Slomine, B. S., Salorio, C., Christensen, J., . . . Gerring, J. (2008). New onset obsessive-compulsive symptoms in children and adolescents with severe traumatic brain injury. *Depression and Anxiety, 25*(5), 398–407.

Graham, S., & Harris, K. R. (1996). Addressing problems in attention, memory, and executive functioning: An example from self-regulated strategy development. In G. R. Lyon & N. A. Krasnegor (Eds.), *Attention, memory, and executive function* (pp. 349–66). Baltimore, MD: Paul H. Brookes.

Hanten, G., Dennis, M., Zhang, L., Barnes, M., Roberson, G., Archibald, J., . . . Levin, H. S. (2004). Childhood head injury and metacognitive processes in language and memory. *Developmental Neuropsychology, 25*(1–2), 85–106.

Hayes, S. C., Gifford, E. V., & Ruckstuhl, L. E., Jr. (1996). Relational frame theory and executive function: A behavioral approach. In G. R. Lyon & N. A. Krasnegor (Eds.), *Attention, memory, and executive function* (pp. 279–305). Baltimore, MD: Paul H. Brookes.

Herskovits, E. H., Gerring, J. P., Davatzikos, C., & Bryan, R. N. (2002). Is the spatial distribution of brain lesions associated with closed- head injury in children predictive of subsequent development of posttraumatic stress disorder? *Radiology, 224*(2), 345–351.

Herskovits, E. H., Megalooikonomou, V., Davatzikos, C., Chen, A., Bryan, R. N., & Gerring, J. P. (1999). Is the spatial distribution of brain lesions associated with closed-head injury predictive of subsequent development of attention-deficit/hyperactivity disorder? Analysis with brain-image database. *Radiology, 213*(2), 389–394.

Kaufman, J., Birmaher, B., Brent, D., Rao, U., Flynn, C., Moreci, P., . . .Ryan, N. (1997). Schedule for Affective Disorders and Schizophrenia for School-Age Children-Present and Lifetime Version (K-SADS-PL): Initial reliability and validity data. *Journal of the American Academy of Child and Adolescent Psychiatry, 36*(7), 980–988.

Kirkwood, M., Janusz, J., Yeates, K. O., Taylor, H. G., Wade, S. L., Stancin, T., & Drotar, D. (2000). Prevalence and correlates of depressive symptoms following traumatic brain injuries in children. *Child Neuropsychology, 6*(3), 195–208.

Konrad, K., Gauggel, S., Manz, A., & Scholl, M. (2000). Inhibitory control in children with traumatic brain injury (TBI) and children with attention deficit/hyperactivity disorder (ADHD). *Brain Injury, 14*(10), 859–875.

Kraus, J. F. (1995). Epidemiological features of brain injury in children: Occurrence, children at risk, causes and manner of injury, severity, and outcomes. In S. H. Broman and M. E. Michel (Eds.), *Traumatic head injury in children* (pp. 22–39). New York: Oxford University Press.

Kuntsi, J., McLoughlin, G., & Asherson, P. (2006). Attention deficit hyperactivity disorder. *Neuromolecular Medicine, 8*(4), 461–484.

Langlois, J. A., Rutland-Brown, W., & Thomas, K. E. (2005). The incidence of traumatic brain injury among children in the United States: differences by race. *Journal of Head Trauma and Rehabilitation, 20*(3), 229–238.

Leonesio, R. J., & Nelson, T. O. (1990). Do different metamemory judgments tap the same underlying aspects of memory? *Journal of Experimental Psychology, Learning, Memory and Cognition, 16*(3), 464–467.

Levin, H., Hanten, G., Max, J., Li, X., Swank, P., Ewing-Cobbs, L., et al. (2007). Symptoms of attention-deficit/hyperactivity disorder following traumatic brain injury in children. *Journal of Developmental and Behavioral Pediatrics, 28*(2), 108–118.

Max, J. E. (2011). Children and adolescents: Traumatic brain injury. In J. M. Silver, T. W. McAllister, & S. C. Yudofsky (Eds.), *Textbook of traumatic brain injury-second edition* (pp. 438–450). Washington, D.C.: American Psychiatric Publishing, Inc.

Max, J. E., Arndt, S., Castillo, C. S., Bokura, H., Robin, D. A., Lindgren, S. A.,... Mattheis, P. J. (1998a). Attention-deficit hyperactivity symptomatology after traumatic brain injury: A prospective study. *Journal of the American Academy of Child and Adolescent Psychiatry, 37*(8), 841–847.

Max, J. E., Bowers, W. A., Baldus, D., & Gaylor, E. E. (1998b). Pediatric traumatic brain injury and burn patients in the civil justice system: The prevalence and impact of psychiatric symptomatology. *Journal of the American Academy of Psychiatry and the Law, 26*(2), 247–258.

Max, J. E., Castillo, C. S., Lindgren, S. D., & Arndt, S. (1998c). The Neuropsychiatric Rating Schedule: Reliability and validity. *Journal of the American Academy of Child and Adolescent Psychiatry, 37*(3), 297–304.

Max, J. E., Castillo, C. S., Robin, D. A., Lindgren, S. D., Smith, W. L., Sato, Y., & Arndt, S. (1998d). Posttraumatic stress symptomology after childhood traumatic brain injury. *Journal of Nervous Mental Disorders, 186,* 589–596.

Max, J. E., Ibrahim, F., & Levin, H. (2010). Neuropsychological outcomes of TBI in children. In R. D. Nass & Y. Frank (Ed.), *Cognitive and behavioral manifestations of pediatric diseases* (pp. 647–659). New York: Oxford University Press.

Max, J. E., Koele, S. L., Castillo, C. C., Lindgren, S. D., Arndt, S., Bokura, H.,... Sato, Y. (2000). Personality change disorder in children and adolescents following traumatic brain injury. *Journal of the International Neuropsychological Society, 6*(3), 279–289.

Max, J. E., Koele, S. L., Smith, W. L., Jr., Sato, Y., Lindgren, S. D., Robin, D. A.,... Arndt, S. (1998e). Psychiatric disorders in children and adolescents after severe traumatic brain injury: A controlled study. *Journal of the American Academy of Child and Adolescent Psychiatry, 37*(8), 832–840.

Max, J. E., Lansing, A. E., Koele, S. L., Castillo, C. C., Bokura, H., Schachar, R.,... Williams, K. E. (2004). Attention deficit hyperactivity disorder in children and adolescents following traumatic brain injury. *Developmental Neuropsychology, 25*(1–2), 159–177.

Max, J. E., Levin, H. S., Landis, J., Schachar, R., Saunders, A., Ewing-Cobbs, L.,... Dennis, M. (2005a). Predictors of personality change due to traumatic brain injury in children and adolescents in the first six months after injury. *Journal of the American Academy of Child and Adolescent Psychiatry, 44*(5), 434–442.

Max, J. E., Lindgren, S. D., Robin, D. A., Smith, W. L., Sato, Y., Mattheis, P. J., . . . Stierwalt, J. A. (1997a). Traumatic brain injury in children and adolescents: Psychiatric disorders in the second three months. *Journal of Nervous and Mental Disease, 185*(6), 394–401.

Max, J. E., Schachar, R. J., Levin, H. S., Ewing-Cobbs, L., Chapman, S. B., Dennis, M., . . . Landis, J. (2005b). Predictors of attention-deficit/hyperactivity disorder within 6 months after pediatric traumatic brain injury. *Journal of the American Academy of Child and Adolescent Psychiatry, 44*(10), 1032–1040.

Max, J. E., Schachar, R. J., Levin, H. S., Ewing-Cobbs, L., Chapman, S. B., Dennis, M., . . . Landis, J. (2005c). Predictors of secondary attention-deficit/hyperactivity disorder in children and adolescents 6 to 24 months after traumatic brain injury. *Journal of the American Academy of Child and Adolescent Psychiatry, 44*(10), 1041–1049.

Max, J. E., Smith, W. L., Jr., Sato, Y., Mattheis, P. J., Castillo, C. S., Lindgren, S. D., . . . Stierwalt, J. A. (1997b). Traumatic brain injury in children and adolescents: Psychiatric disorders in the first three months. *Journal of the American Academy of Child & Adolescent Psychiatry, 36*(1), 94–102.

Nurcombe, B. (1993a). The forensic evaluation. In G. Fritz, R. E. Mattison, B. Nurcombe, & A. Spirito (Eds.), *Child and adolescent mental health consultation in hospitals, schools, and courts* (pp. 257–274). Washington, DC: American Psychiatric Press.

Nurcombe, B. (1993b). Giving testimony as an expert witness. In G. Fritz, R. E. Mattison, B. Nurcombe, & A. Spirito (Eds.), *Child and adolescent mental health consultation in hospitals, schools, and courts* (pp. 275–290). Washington, DC: American Psychiatric Press.

Pennington, B. F., Bennetto, L., McAleer, O., & Roberts, R.J., Jr. (1996). Executive functions and working memory: Theoretical and measurement issues. In G. R. Lyon & N. A. Krasnegor (Eds.), *Attention, memory, and executive function* (pp. 327–348). Baltimore, MD: Paul H. Brookes.

Perfetti, C. A. (1985). *Reading ability.* New York: Oxford University Press.

Schachar, R., Levin, H. S., Max, J. E., Purvis, K., & Chen, S. (2004). Attention deficit hyperactivity disorder symptoms and response inhibition after closed head injury in children: Do preinjury behavior and injury severity predict outcome? *Developmental Neuropsychology, 25*(1–2), 179–198.

Schachar, R., Tannock, R., Marriott, M., & Logan, G. (1995). Deficient inhibitory control in attention deficit hyperactivity disorder. *Journal of Abnormal Child Psychology, 23*(4), 411–437.

Schachar, R. J., Crosbie, J., Barr, C. L., Ornstein, T. J., Kennedy, J., Malone, M., . . . Pathare, T. (2005). Inhibition of motor responses in siblings concordant and discordant for attention deficit hyperactivity disorder. *American Journal of Psychiatry, 162*(6), 1076–1082.

Slomine, B. S., Salorio, C. F., Grados, M. A., Vasa, R. A., Christensen, J. R., & Gerring, J. P. (2005). Differences in attention, executive functioning, and memory in children with and without ADHD after severe traumatic brain injury. *Journal of the International Neuropsychology Society, 11*(5), 645–653.

Taylor, H. G., Yeates, K. O., Wade, S. L., Drotar, D., Klein, S. K., & Stancin, T. (1999). Influences on first-year recovery from traumatic brain injury in children. *Neuropsychology, 13*(1), 76–89.

Vasa, R. A., Gerring, J. P., Grados, M., Slomine, B., Christensen, J. R., Rising, W., . . . Riddle, M. A. (2002). Anxiety after severe pediatric closed head injury. *Journal of the American Academy of Child and Adolescent Psychiatry, 41*(2), 148–156.

Wassenberg, R., Max, J. E., Lindgren, S. D., & Schatz, A. (2004). Sustained attention in children and adolescents after traumtaic brain injury: relation to severity of injury, adaptive functioning, ADHD and social background. *Brain Injury, 18*(8), 751–764.

Yeates, K. O., Armstrong, K., Janusz, J., Taylor, H. G., Wade, S., Stancin, T., & Drotar, D. (2005). Long-term attention problems in children with traumatic brain injury. *Journal of the American Academy of Child and Adolescent Psychiatry, 44*(6), 574–584.

Chapter 13

Independent Neuropsychological Evaluation of Children in Medical Malpractice Cases

IDA SUE BARON
JOEL E. MORGAN

INTRODUCTION

Negligent. Willful. Wanton. Reckless. Malicious. Such highly charged, negative, emotionally laden words as these are common accusations about the actions of medical practitioners in civil suits that seek to redress claims of wrongful acts that have allegedly damaged a patient. Physicians, like other health care workers, are liable for their professional activities. A patient who believes he or she was injured by the negligent or wrongful acts of a physician may file a civil suit in order to obtain financial or other restitution for the alleged wrongful practice act. This type of litigation is commonly referred to as medical malpractice.

In this chapter we will discuss fundamental aspects of neuropsychological consultation and expert professional services in forensic cases of alleged medical malpractice in pediatric populations. By virtue of their training in brain–behavior relationships, and knowledge of the range of effects on the developing organism consequent to central nervous system disruption, pediatric neuropsychologists are particularly well suited to offer opinions about the neurobehavioral status of children allegedly wrongfully injured due to a physician's malpractice. Either plaintiff or defense routinely retains neuropsychologists. The decision to accept or reject involvement in a case is a decision to be made after an initial discussion with the referral source, and it is an independent judgment as to whether one's training and experience are consonant with the attorney's request and the nature of the case.

This chapter will begin with a broad introduction, providing general information regarding neuropsychological consultation in a forensic context. We will discuss neuropsychological evaluation in medical malpractice cases, claims arising in infancy and childhood, and consider process and procedures related to the consultation examination, report, and testimony. We intend to provide a general guideline for the pediatric forensic neuropsychologist entering this arena for the first time and to serve as a reference for more experienced professionals. The reader may note that we have strong opinions regarding how the science of our discipline should be integrated into the work product in medical malpractice cases, with choices made in light of ethical standards and the importance of maintaining professional integrity and upholding the standards of our profession. It matters little to us whether we are retained by the plaintiff or defense. Applying our science with competence and diligence is our paramount concern and obligation. We understand that the results of our endeavors may ultimately matter little with regard to the outcome of any one case, and we recognize that we should have no invested interest in the final determination reached. Rather, we see it as our responsibility to find the (neuropsychological) truth and to tell that truth. The final judgment of the suit is the decision of the judge or jury, that is, the triers of law and fact.

In a medical malpractice suit, a claim is made that a breach of a standard of care (professional duty) by the defendant (health care provider) caused injury to the plaintiff (patient) and that this negligence resulted in damages. Thus, these cases take aim at core professional responsibilities and obligations of a practitioner and/or an institution. Should the plaintiff's case be successfully adjudicated, the medical malpractice suit may be interpreted by some as a censure of the defendant's competency, a breach of ethical responsibilities, and, if against a physician, a violation of this professional's sworn Hippocratic oath to keep [the sick] from harm and injustice. Moreover, there is a threat to the viability of continued professional practice and/or sustainability of medical practice by the physician, medical group, or hospital against whom the suit is filed. Yet, irrespective of which side succeeds, both the defendant(s) and plaintiff(s) typically experience a heavy emotional consequence. Thus, medical malpractice suits are among the most contentious and emotionally laden in forensic practice.

Arguably, in some instances medical malpractice cases may appear to be determined more by the experience of the attorney than the merits of the case. Not uncommonly, legitimate claims of liability (something untoward actually happened) are accompanied by assertions of damages in the form of cognitive and/or psychological sequelae that may, or may not, correctly characterize the plaintiff's condition. "Liability" in this context refers to the fact that a medical provider is obligated to compensate a patient-claimant for injuries. "Damages" refers to the substance and extent of said injuries (Danzon, 1985), to be redressed by some monetary award. In some malpractice contexts and/or jurisdictions, claims of emotional and psychological distress (pain and suffering allegedly associated with the medical malpractice claim) may be part of the civil complaint and the charges against the accused (doctor/hospital/other practitioners), that is, the defendant(s).

A malpractice suit may originate for a wide variety of reasons, such as plaintiff anger over loss, desire for retribution, perception of medical incompetence, desire to assign accountability for an unfortunate outcome, ignorance of the legal process and its potential negative impact on personal financial resources or its intrusiveness into ordinary life patterns over an extended period of time, or genuine instances of medical malpractice that result in serious damages. Examples of the latter from our own forensic experiences include an obstetrician's misdiagnosis of a pregnant woman that resulted in a mesentery artery hemorrhage with consequent severe interruption of blood flow to her fetus; the child survived but with extreme physical and cognitive impairment (see Appendix at the end of this chapter). Another case was of a lawsuit filed against a pediatric practice whose practitioners failed to attend to notification from a medical laboratory that a serious but treatable medical condition had been detected in an infant. Only when the child failed to make appropriate developmental progress was this error found, but by then it was too late to effectively treat the condition and permanent mental and physical impairments resulted.

While such instances of clear or acknowledged malpractice may be of greatest interest to a neuropsychologist who is willing to be an expert witness, clarity can be elusive. It should be highlighted that the expert neuropsychologist should not exceed the boundaries of competence and offer opinion about the medical care that was provided or decide, judge, or assess blame—that is the role of the court. Instances that are unclear are frequently encountered in this setting. Moreover, a medical malpractice suit may be initiated through court filing even when the claimed causal relationship cannot be documented in a thorough review of the scientific literature and with attention to the findings of evidence-based medical reports.

The neuropsychologist as forensic expert underscores a fundamental conflict between the practice of the law and the practice of neuropsychology. Attorneys advocate strongly for their clients, and winning the case has a higher priority than acknowledging truth (Greiffenstein & Cohen, 2005). The neuropsychologist is but one of a number of experts who will provide an objective opinion to the court—the trier of fact (the jury) and the trier of law (the judge). As for any of these experts, the neuropsychologist also fulfills a critical role in forensic proceedings since "[Neuropsychologist's] opinions can influence legal decisions and . . . public policy" (Greiffenstein, 2008, p. 933). Legal decisions change people's lives—often in dramatic ways for participants on each side.

With continued growth of the profession, the specific skill competencies of clinical neuropsychology specialists have been increasingly recognized by members of the legal profession. Neuropsychological testimony is increasingly relied upon when there is a need to provide expert opinion on the mental status of a claimant, and when allegations of cognitive/emotional damages have been articulated. Such expertise in evaluating cognitive functioning and emotional adjustment has led both plaintiff and defense attorneys to retain neuropsychologists (Sweet, Ecklund-Johnson, & Malina, 2008). Malpractice litigation typically begins with engagement of plaintiff experts, and it is followed by engagement of defense experts who then have an opportunity to also examine the plaintiff and provide a second opinion.

Discovery, one of a number of pretrial motions, is designed to "discover the other side's case" (Melton, Petrila, Poythress, & Slobogin, 1997). Within the context of civil litigation, discovery consists of numerous records, including the civil complaint; depositions (testimony of a witness) of plaintiffs, persons of interest, experts, and other potential witnesses; interrogatories (responses to written questions); and tangible evidence such as mental and physical examination reports and treatment/hospital records (Melton et al., 1997). The discovery period is when these documents and any other evidence relevant to the case are produced and exchanged between counsel, a crucial step. In some instances, the discovery process aborts the need to proceed to trial as mediation may occur, a settlement may be reached between the parties, or the defense moves for summary judgment, which, if granted, obviates the need for trial. Summary judgment refers to defense's assertion that the plaintiff has raised no genuine issues to be tried and asks the judge to rule in favor of the defense (Walston-Dunham, 2006).

NEUROPSYCHOLOGICAL EVALUATION IN MEDICAL MALPRACTICE LITIGATION

Acceptance of a medical malpractice case for which a neuropsychological evaluation is requested initiates an interesting dynamic in which the neuropsychologist, also a health care provider, acquires evidence that will ultimately influence judgment by others, that is, the trier of fact and the trier of law, about the professional practice of another health care provider. Each expert has a distinctive role related to discovery in forensic proceedings. Yet, as noted earlier, the neuropsychologist should not offer a judgmental opinion or diverge from the factual data to support the side that retained and pays the invoice. Rather, the neuropsychologist contributes to the discovery process in several pertinent ways. Neuropsychological methods allow for objective data collection and evidence-based conclusions that contribute to an expectedly contentious process that seeks to establish proximate cause and effect. An emphasis on evidence-based formulations, derived from well-established scientific principles, exemplifies essential professional ethics in forensic neuropsychological practice. Yet neuropsychologists involved in forensic matters know that despite presenting data that lead to scientifically sound conclusions, their conclusions may not always be effectively communicated under cross-examination by the opposing side; it is the role of an attorney in cross-examination to discredit the testimony of the other side's expert.

Irrespective of the rationale for a lawsuit, or the intellectual attacks that may be encountered, it is incumbent on the neuropsychologist to maintain professionalism, uphold ethical practice, and remain objective. More difficult is the need to refrain from reaching the types of conclusions that might be reached in a clinical context. Even though the neuropsychologist possesses extensive knowledge about the medical implications of neuropsychological data, boundaries of competence are firm within the forensic setting, and statements should not be offered that are the prerogative of the physician. To do so jeopardizes one's ability to serve in the agreed-upon expert role and potentially could undermine the case for the hiring attorney. The effectiveness of the neuropsychologist's work product is a function of clarity of methods, well-formulated conclusions reached through systematic consideration of the options, and procedures that allow for replicability to offset contention by the neuropsychologist expert on the opposing side, an almost inevitable occurrence in these cases. While the neuropsychologist should refrain from elaboration beyond what the data allow, it should be possible to generate conclusions based on appropriate test administration procedures and establishment of rapport with the plaintiff, acquired scientific knowledge through education and experience, selection of appropriate standardized test instruments that best enable assessment of brain–behavior functioning related to the condition of interest, use of appropriate normative data, and age-appropriate expectations for the child's behavior given chronological and mental ages. Understanding the diverse influences of a brain insult on developmental course, and potential deviations from the typical trajectory of neuropsychological maturation, is a specific and desirable skill the pediatric neuropsychologist brings to this venue.

At times an attorney may consult a neuropsychologist but may propose that duties be restricted to review of the pertinent records. In these instances, the neuropsychologist may be asked to provide analysis, commentary, and/or opinion about a case based only on a review of provided medical records, that is, without patient contact or examination. In accord with the American Psychological Association Ethical Principles and Code of Conduct (American Psychological Association, 2002), in such circumstances it is always necessary for the neuropsychologist to specifically articulate the restricted nature of the opinions rendered. At other times a retaining attorney may ask the neuropsychologist to restrict the professional role to that of an advisor. In this role, the neuropsychologist is retained to recommend types of questions counsel should consider asking when deposing opposing experts. Providing a primer of basic neuropsychological principles relevant to the case at hand is a common part of such consultation with attorneys, as is detection of exaggerated claims and inaccurate case formulation in the reports or deposition statements offered by the psychological expert on the opposing side. Irrespective of the specific role accepted by a neuropsychologist, adherence to ethical and scientific standards of the profession is expected.

MEDICAL MALPRACTICE CLAIMS ARISING IN INFANCY AND CHILDHOOD

Among the enormous range of reasons why a medical malpractice suit may be filed are those related to medical care in infancy or childhood. Malpractice claims related to care provided by specialists in obstetrics and neonatology have become a major threat to the health service delivery system (d'Aloja, Muller, Paribello, Demontis, & Faa, 2009). These physicians are at especially elevated risk for a lawsuit as a consequence of the high percentages of stillborn birth, maternal obstetric complications, fetal distress, neonatal encephalopathy, suspected or documented birth injury, and premature birth. For example, scientific uncertainty about when an hypoxic insult occurs, for example, during pregnancy, during labor, or after birth, has led to a higher percentage of civil lawsuit decisions likely to recognize a guilty medical behavior (d'Aloja et al., 2009). Such complications as breech birth, infection, trauma, or central nervous system malformation are among those conditions whose effects may not become fully apparent until the neonatal or perinatal period, or later. Such conditions, and others, may be attributed by the aggrieved plaintiff to medical error or incompetence. In childhood, cerebral palsy, traumatic brain injury, or any number of disorders not apparent or diagnosed earlier may be the basis for a lawsuit. Physicians treating pediatric patients may find themselves named in lawsuits related to their medication prescriptive authority, purported or real instances of misdiagnosis or missed diagnosis, or when diagnosis is delayed due to an initially innocuous or equivocal medical test result that is later interpreted as evidence of an incipient abnormality. This is an especially prevalent occurrence in the practice of radiologists. Psychiatrists who work in the public sector are also at greater risk for grievances and lawsuits than those in private practice (Miller, 1992). Surgeons' risk is related to both immediate and late effects of their procedures; although correction of a medical problem may result, there may be failure to achieve completely normal function over time.

Although a case may enter the judicial system related to early (obstetric or neo-natal) care, it is also likely that a neuropsychologist will be engaged as an expert for an older child or adolescent. Neuropsychologists need to be alert to the possibility that impairment may not yet be evident or completely understood in a young, actively maturing child. An accurate estimate of the full extent of such impairment may require greater elapsed time to best understand how the child will mature into his or her deficit(s) (Baron, 2008). In such cases, and when retained by the plaintiff, it is reasonable to offer a recommendation for delay of settlement that likely will be advantageous for the plaintiff whose range of impairment may be best appreci-ated at an older age. However, the legal process and insurance company financial limits may make such delay impractical. Moreover, there also needs to be thorough consideration of any intervening but unrelated occurrences in that interval of time up to when the lawsuit is brought that might better explain findings, including sociodemographic considerations, other illnesses or injury, and the wide range of potential contributory medical or psychological events.

It is also noted that lawsuits may be filed that have only vague circumstances documented, with ambiguous, unapparent, or nonexistent damages listed in an attempt to reap award even though the facts neither warrant the allegations nor the claim. These may be supported by attorneys who work on a commission basis and whose time is reimbursed as a percentage of a won judgment. In such circum-stance, the family may pursue a case without immediate financial burden but with opportunity to profit from a favorable judgment, or settlement, with no acknowl-edgment of guilt. Such common occurrences in malpractice litigation have long fueled the political fires of those calling for tort reform in the American judicial system. Yet it is worth noting that malpractice suits are an area of concern interna-tionally. For example, 167 cases among 960 malpractice claims filed in Turkey between 1996 and 2000 involved children under age 18; most were males (64.1%) and aged 6–12. More than half of the malpractices occurred in state hospitals (63.5%) related to nonsurgical interventions (58.7%); 63.5% were associated with crime, 59.3% with disease, and 31.7% with accidents. One-third of the children had infections, and 57.5% involved a death. Health staff was found at fault in nearly half (46.1%) of the claims, and cause of death reported before and after autopsies was conflicting in 13 of 19 children (68%) (Ozdemir, Ergonen, & Can, 2009).

PROCESS AND PROCEDURE

There are several specific issues to consider when a decision is made to conduct a forensic evaluation. The ability to apply one's scientific knowledge directly in a forensic matter may be rewarding for those who are comfortable answering direct questions about the nature and extent of disability or dysfunction consequent to the actions of a defendant. However, others avoid the real and imagined burdens imposed by the legal process, and a setting in which confrontation about one's scientific knowledge is routine.

In accepting a case of medical malpractice, the neuropsychologist allows for criticisms and direct attacks by an opposing attorney, and indirectly by that attorney's expert witnesses and consultants. Thus, a request for involvement in a medical malpractice case should initiate a number of careful considerations. It is sensible to accept only those cases for which one's training and experience have prepared one to understand the effects of the condition or disorder central to the case, and to contend with cross-examination that is intended to undermine one's credibility as an expert witness. For example, acceptance of a case that involves understanding the course and treatment of premature birth and outcome is unwise if one is unfamiliar with the extended range of preterm medical risk factors and the range of possible neurocognitive effects that have been reported after early birth, if one has not had sufficient clinical experience to use instruments appropriate for testing young children, or if one does not understand the range of options available that enhance the child's performance in a testing environment (Baron, 2004). Similarly, an understanding of peri- or postnatal traumatic brain injuries and their potential impact on the developing repertoire of cognitive, emotional, and behavioral functions is crucial in order to address these issues as they may arise in forensic context (Donders, 2008).

The "business" aspects of professional forensic consultation should be articulated and clarified early. It is necessary to establish conditions for one's involvement in the forensic process with the retaining attorney, including details regarding remuneration, and to document these in writing. With the child's family, it is important to obtain signed verification that the parents understand that a client relationship has been established with the attorney as the client, and that the usual clinical responsibilities associated when the patient and family are the clients is not applicable (see Chapters 1 and 2 for a more detailed discussion of these issues).

A thorough record review establishes the crucial chronological sequence of events leading up to the time of evaluation. One might also have been provided incomplete data, and any gaps in the timeline require follow-up with the hiring attorney, who serves as the conduit to the opposing attorney. It is not uncommon that as one reviews the records one will find conflicting data, for example, in reference to birth weight, length of time needed for resuscitation, or contradictory diagnoses. Just the suggestion of a specific diagnosis as a rule-out by one provider may later be presumed to be a formal diagnosis by another provider as the clinical course evolves and as multiple providers are consulted who have not thoroughly reviewed prior records, or who did not have access to such records. The neuropsychologist as record reviewer must pay careful attention to the sometimes obscure or unclear aspects found in the medical record. Thoroughness is important, as failure to be precise about conclusions reached in a review of records may prove problematic later, for example, during a deposition or at trial. The opposing attorney may ask what records were reviewed, whether every page of what was provided was read, and what information was requested but not provided. The question may be phrased to encourage the expert to admit reaching conclusions prior to actual patient contact.

Q: *With respect to the medical records you reviewed prior to your evaluation, did you reach any opinions as a neuropsychologist at that time?*

A: *I waited until I evaluated the plaintiff and had all the records and data that I needed to reach a conclusion.*

Reinterpretation of one's own data by the opposing side, along with submission of contradictory reports by opposing experts, can be expected. The neuropsychologist needs to be cautious and alert to attempts to deflect the import of conclusions that do not support the position taken by the opposing side. It is the objective of each side to diminish the impact of the expert on the other side concerning documentation of deficit or delay. It is not, for example, that the defense attorney does not recognize what plaintiff expert has done, but more that these data are crucial components of the case against their client and need to be deflected. It is the objective of the plaintiff attorney that the neuropsychological data be interpreted as unequivocal support for the allegations of damages secondary to malpractice and for remuneration for the liability and damages being sought.

Q: *(defense attorney to plaintiff expert) Doctor, you have opined that cognitive dysfunction is present and likely emanates from injuries allegedly attributable to my client's actions. Are you opining as to the cause of these so-called abnormalities; you are not a physician are you?*

A: *No, I am not a physician. Nevertheless, the cognitive dysfunction well documented in my thorough clinical examination is clearly associated with the cerebral damage noted on structural neuroimaging.*

It is not the neuropsychologist's place to opine regarding the domains of other medical experts, even if the neuropsychologist, for example, can read neuroimaging scans, interpret an electroencephalographic recording, or rely on years of experience to expound on the influence of neurological factors as they pertain to the plaintiff's particular condition. However, it is acceptable to rely on this experience to reaffirm the accuracy of one's own data and conclusions, while not making the misstep of venturing into the domain of another professional. This has the added benefit of helping defend against possible attempts by opposing counsel to have all of one's testimony excluded; some legal maneuvers may be more common in one jurisdiction than another.

Vocabulary is important. Attorneys may, for example, have a different understanding when neuropsychologists use a term common within professional discourse, for example, "behavior." Words that have clear definition for all concerned should be carefully chosen to communicate findings. This is especially true in depositions, when words are broadly interpreted and therefore subject to multiple interpretations. In these instances, clarification needs to be requested and definition provided.

Q: *Doctor what is meant by the descriptive term "low average"?*

A: *It is generally considered to be a standard score falling between the range of 80 and 89, or between the 9th and 24th percentiles.*

Q: *But "low average" is still average and therefore normal, is that not correct?*

A: *Not exactly. The lower the score, the less "normal" it is. For instance, most school districts use the 10th percentile as the cutoff for eligibility for special services, even though the 10th percentile is technically in the Low Average range. "Low average" is simply a descriptive term and doesn't imply what is "normal." One would have to consider the standard score/percentile.*

In reviewing records, consultant neuropsychologists should pay close attention to the medical record, the nature of the injury, the timing of the injury with respect to the presentation of symptoms, and supporting documentation of injury (e.g., imaging, laboratory results). Careful scrutiny is necessary to detect possibly relevant details as, for example, in the case of a child allegedly prescribed the wrong medication who then has seizures and goes into a coma, or when the medical record contains contradictory documentation of gestational age or birth weight. Records, including progress notes, may be informative with regard to mental status and neurological findings, for example, when a child emerged from a coma, about how effective antiepileptic medications were in relieving or controlling seizures, and whether any breakthrough seizures occurred. These bits of information may directly relate to how the child is currently functioning in the academic and home settings. A thorough inventory of what data were available and reviewed should be maintained.

Review of psychological or neuropsychological reports submitted by others is both crucial and often fascinating. Among the questions that arise in these reviews are whether the scores are accurately calculated and assigned, whether the summations about the data make sense given the data acquired, whether conclusions are appropriate in relation to the child's overall profile of functioning, and whether a sufficient range of tests was administered to support the stated conclusion. For example, executive dysfunction might be concluded without any evidence obtained through administration of specific tests of executive functioning or parental report on structured behavioral questionnaires. Similarly, sensory and motor tests allow for specific supportive conclusions about hemispheric integrity but may not have been administered even when presumptions that those regions are impaired are made. Or the descriptive ranges noted in a report may be inconsistent with standard practice, or they may be changed to provide a more pessimistic picture to the layperson. For example, low average performance may be alternatively labeled borderline or mildly retarded. In one case, the allegation that a middle-school-age child had suffered anoxia secondary to incorrect medication dosage was supported by a plaintiff neuropsychologist who routinely interpreted low average range scores as "impaired" (Greiffenstein, 2009); settlement was reached after this error and others in the plaintiff expert's report were pointed out.

Although more commonly addressed in adult neuropsychological practice, symptom validity measures may be administered to children and embedded features considered. Their administration may allow for greater assurance that the evaluation was indeed reliable and valid with respect to the child's cooperation and effort, an especially important assurance in the forensic context. Symptom validity testing in children is not yet routinely endorsed, but it is worthwhile and recommended in both child and adult forensic cases (Donders, 2005; Heilbronner, Sweet, Morgan, Larrabee, & Millis, 2009). Unfortunately, children may be easily influenced by parental coaching or suggestion, and they have been known to malinger (Flaro & Boone, 2009; McCaffrey & Lynch, 2009). (See Chapters 6 and 7 for a more detailed discussion of pediatric malingering and of symptom validity tests in children.)

It is appropriate to discuss the opposing expert's examination data, conclusions, and opinions, as well as point out errors of conceptualization, scoring, and interpretation along with reasons for differing opinions. In all forensic evaluations it is good practice to articulate that you have considered alternative explanations, diagnoses, and opinions, and to indicate why those you criticize are inaccurate and inappropriate from a data-driven, scientific perspective. Finding examples of neuropsychological conclusions that are unwarranted given the actual data is not a unique occurrence in forensic practice. Experts of either side may misstate the implications of their data, draw inappropriate or unwarranted inferences from data, ignore or minimize the importance of some data, not report data that did not support the desired position, or "bend" the findings to be in alignment with the referral source/retaining side. For example, in one of our cases, the examiner aged the child upward by several months since the child's chronological age was interpreted to be close enough to the older age normative data set to justify this unstandardized action. Doing this enabled the older age data set to be used to obtain lower scores, which had the effect of substantially lowering the child's overall performance; neither the plaintiff nor defense attorney had recognized this subtle attempt to support the plaintiff and the bias of the plaintiff expert. In another case, the psychologist noted the tests administered at the beginning of the evaluation report but only provided results for those specific scores that were judged to be indicative of poor performance, omitting report of all occurrences of intact functioning, and of tests that had been administered but were performed well. Such practices are unethical and unprofessional, but they do occur and need to be uncovered and reported when found. Professionalism, objectivity, courtesy, and respect for one's methods and the science of practice should not be compromised when the neuropsychologist assumes the role of expert witness or forensic consultant. Interpretation of facts as truly as possible, and without exaggeration or creation of forced suppositions, is the ideal.

The examination of the plaintiff and preparation of the report (if one is requested by counsel) should adhere to best professional practices. It is common practice in forensic contexts to discuss with the retaining attorney the results of record reviews prior to proceeding to an examination of the plaintiff. When the consultant neuropsychologist determines that the preponderance of the data will likely not support the referral source's position, whether plaintiff or defense, it is common practice to discuss one's opinion with the retaining attorney. At such time the decision is usually made as to whether a report should be prepared. If requested, the forensic report should be clear and consonant with the highest standards of our profession (American Academy of Clinical Neuropsychology, 2007). It is common for some beginning forensic practitioners to feel a "pull" toward assuming the role of advocate, looking for a way to support retaining counsel's case. Related to this is the lure of the financial ramifications, that is, the desire and expectation to be referred simi-lar cases if the attorney is satisfied. Succumbing to these considerations is always a mistake, and it is an important phenomenon in forensic neuropsychological practice that needs to be recognized. Best practice is simply to inform the attorneys that the review/exam will likely not be helpful to their case. Competent and ethical attorneys appreciate hearing an honest and truthful report, which helps them decide whether and how they should proceed.

It is the nature of forensic neuropsychological consultation that both begin-ners and experienced practitioners will experience some degree of performance anxiety at the prospect of appearing at a deposition or trial. Not surprisingly, experi-ence and solid preparation will alleviate much anxiety. Anticipating questions from opposing counsel, review of the depositions of others, and mock sessions with one's retaining attorney are often useful. Knowing the case well, in all its aspects, is critical preparation.

CONCLUSION

In conclusion, medical malpractice consultation for the pediatric neuropsycholo-gist is an interesting, challenging, and rewarding endeavor. The aim of this chapter was to aid those who wish to engage effectively in such professional activities. Toward that end we have summarized some of what we have learned in our own role as a neuropsychology expert in medical malpractice cases. Neuropsychologists have an important role to play in forensic matters, and our education and training have made us particularly suitable to carry out this responsibility with deserved pro-fessionalism and respect for all parties concerned.

APPENDIX: CASE PRESENTATION—PEDIATRIC MEDICAL MALPRACTICE

One of the authors (J. M.) was contacted by an attorney at a law firm that special-izes in the defense of physicians and other professionals against malpractice claims. The referral question was rather simple: "Doctor, plaintiffs [the child and parents] are claiming that this child will never function normally. They are asking for an exorbitant sum of money. Please examine the child and see if you concur with plaintiff experts."

The case was originally filed shortly after the child's birth as a civil action. The original filing concerned the alleged malpractice of the obstetrician who cared for D. B.'s mother, whose purported misdiagnosis resulted in life-altering harm to her fetus. During the sixth month of pregnancy, D. B.'s mother experienced sudden, acute, intense abdominal pain. The obstetrician allegedly did not correctly diagnose her spontaneous hemorrhage of the mesenteric artery. Consequently, the hemor-rhage severely reduced the supply of oxygenated blood that was required by the fetus, and D. B. was delivered by Cesarean section at 32 weeks of gestation. He sub-sequently was hospitalized for 4 months in a Neonatal Intensive Care Unit (NICU). After discharge from the NICU, he remained hospitalized for an additional 3 months. He required continuous in-home nursing care for the first 5 years of his life.

At the time of the defense neuropsychological evaluation, D. B. was a 9-year-old male with severe cognitive and physical disabilities. D. B.'s serious deficiencies extended to numerous areas of functioning. He had severe cerebral palsy (CP) and spastic quadriplegia. D. B. was wheel chair bound, controlling the wheel chair with movements of his head. Although his vision and audition were intact, he did not speak but communicated through a computer-assisted adaptive device that he controlled with left upper extremity movements. D. B. had a permanent tracheostomy and was fed through a gastrostomy tube. He attended the local elementary school, where he was a special education student.

The defense neuropsychology expert was provided with substantial records to review. Among these was a plaintiff neuropsychology expert's report noting that D. B. was essentially untestable because of his severe disabilities. The diagnoses were severe mental retardation, encephalopathy, and cerebral palsy. Other medical diagnoses included an inadequate gag and swallowing reflex, which resulted in feeding through a nasogastric tube.

The essence of the lawsuit concerned the fact that D. B. would need lifelong care, 24/7. The sums requested were into the seven figures. The plaintiff's neuropsychology expert opined that the boy would never develop normal cognitive or motor skills and would require lifelong care.

When evaluated by the defense's neuropsychology expert it was clear that the records reviewed and the plaintiff's neuropsychology expert's report were fundamentally correct—the child was untestable, had IQ values that were clearly in the retarded range, and, most unfortunately, would require lifelong care. In essence, the defense's expert agreed with the plaintiff's expert.

When the retaining defense attorney was informed of the findings, he was not surprised, expressed appreciation for the work, requested a report, and indicated that he hoped to settle the case, avoiding a trial.

In summary, when competent and ethical neuropsychologists accept a forensic case, they inform the retaining attorney that their examination results will be objective and therefore may not support their client's position. When examination results do not support the retaining attorney's case, some attorneys may ask the neuropsychologist to not write a report. "Thank you, doctor. Please don't write a report and send me your bill." Others, such as the defense attorney in this case, request a report, even though it provides no "help" for their client. It is relevant to consider how common it is in forensic neuropsychological practice for the neuropsychologist to feel advocacy pull, the implicit or explicit sense that he or she is expected to opine with the retaining side. Being mindful of these dynamics should be helpful in allowing the neuropsychologist to maintain professional independence and integrity.

REFERENCES

American Academy of Clinical Neuropsychology. (2007). American Academy of Clinical Neuropsychology (AACN) practice guidelines for neuropsychological assessment and consultation. *The Clinical Neuropsychologist, 21,* 209–231.

American Psychological Association (2002). Ethical principles of psychologists and code of conduct. *American Psychologist, 57,* 1060–1073.

Baron, I. S. (2004). *Neuropsychological evaluation of the child*. New York: Oxford University Press.

Baron, I. S. (2008). Maturation into impairment: The merit of delayed settlement in pediatric forensic neuropsychology cases. In R. L. Heilbronner (Ed.), *Neuropsychology in the courtroom: Expert analysis of reports and testimony* (pp. 67–78). New York: Guilford Press.

d'Aloja, E., Muller, M., Paribello, F., Demontis, R., & Faa, A. (2009). Neonatal asphyxia and forensic medicine. *Journal of Maternal-Fetal, and Neonatal Medicine, 22*(Suppl 3), 54–56.

Danzon, P. M. (1985). *Medical malpractice: Theory, evidence and public policy*. Cambridge, MA: Harvard University Press.

Donders, J. (2005). Performance on the Test of Memory Malingering in a mixed pediatric sample. *Child Neuropsychology, 11,* 221–227.

Donders, J. (2008). Traumatic brain injury of childhood. In J. E. Morgan & J. H. Ricker (Eds.), *Textbook of clinical neuropsychology* (pp. 158–170). New York: Psychology Press.

Flaro, L. & Boone, K. B. (2009). Using objective measures to detect noncredible cognitive test performance in children and adolescents. In J. E. Morgan & J. J. Sweet, (Eds.), *Neuropsychology of malingering casebook* (pp. 369–376). New York: Psychology Press/ American Academy of Clinical Neuropsychology.

Grieffenstein, M. F. (2008). Basics of forensic neuropsychology. In J. E. Morgan & J. H. Ricker, (Eds.), *Textbook of clinical neuropsychology* (pp. 905–941). New York: Psychology Press.

Greiffenstein, M. F. (2009). Clinical myths of forensic neuropsychology. *The Clinical Neuropsychologist, 23,* 286–296.

Greiffenstein, M. F., & Cohen, L. (2005). Neuropsychology and the law: Principles of productive attorney-neuropsychologist relations. In G. J. Larrabee (Ed.), *Forensic neuropsychology: A scientific approach*. New York: Oxford University Press.

Heilbronner, R. L., Sweet, J. J., Morgan, J. E., Larrabee, G. J. & Millis, S. R. (2009). American academy of clinical neuropsychology consensus conference statement on the neuropsychological assessment of effort, response bias and malingering. *The Clinical Neuropsychologist, 23,* 1093–1129.

McCaffrey, R. J., & Lynch, J. K. (2009). Malingering following documented brain injury: Neuropsychological evaluation of children in a forensic setting. In J. E. Morgan & J. J. Sweet, (Eds.), *Neuropsychology of malingering casebook* (pp. 377–385). New York: Psychology Press/ American Academy of Clinical Neuropsychology.

Melton, G. B., Petrila, J., Poythress, N. G., & Slobogin, C. (1997). *Psychological evaluation for the courts: A handbook for mental health professionals and lawyers* (2nd ed.). New York: Guilford.

Miller, R. D. (1992). Grievances and law suits against public mental health professionals: Cost of doing business? *Bulletin of the American Academy of Psychiatry and the Law, 20*(4), 395–408.

Ozdemir, M. H., Ergonen, T. A., & Can, I. O. (2009). Medical malpractice claims involving children. *Forensic Science International, 191*(1–3), 80–85.

Sweet, J. J., Ecklund-Johnson, E., & Malina, A. (2008). Forensic neuropsychology: An overview of issues and directions. In J. E. Morgan & J. H. Ricker (Eds.), *Textbook of clinical neuropsychology* (pp. 870–890). New York: Psychology Press.

Walston-Dunham, B. (2006). *Medical malpractice law and litigation*. Clifton Park, NY: Thompson.

Chapter 14

Neuropsychological Contributions to Independent Education Evaluations: Forensic Perspectives

LISA G. HAHN
JOEL E. MORGAN

INTRODUCTION

School-age children are the mainstay of pediatric neuropsychological practice and are typically referred for poor school performance, among other reasons. Not uncommonly, these children have been receiving special educational services and a private neuropsychological exam is requested in order to update the child's progress, or lack thereof, and provide recommendations for educational programming. Certainly, many children referred for private exams have not been receiving special educational services and the neuropsychological exam has been requested in order to determine their needs and eligibility for special education.

When the referral question concerns disputes regarding the provision of special educational services (e.g., "My attorney suggested I call" or "District would like to retain you"), the examination context may be said to be "forensic" in nature—that is, providing neuropsychological consultative services in legal matters—to attorneys, the courts, or the trier of facts (Greiffenstein, 2008). From a forensic perspective, neuropsychologists may be referred children by parents—displeased with the services provided to their child by the school, or by the district, as part of legal due process. Due process refers to a set of specific procedures for resolving disagreements with any of a school's processes or decisions regarding a student's identification, evaluation, educational placement or provision of a free, appropriate, public education (FAPE). It is increasingly common that children are referred for evaluation to neuropsychologists in such disputes—both by parents as well as school districts.

When conducting an evaluation in forensic neuropsychological contexts, an understanding of the law is necessary in order to provide a thorough evaluation that meets the criteria set forth by statute, in this case by federal and state special education departments. The Individuals with Disabilities Education Act (IDEIA/IDEA) of 2004, as established by Congress in Public Law 108–446, set the precedent for special education and provides explicit detail of definitions of key concepts such as "disability" as it pertains to educational services (IDEA, 2004). In this chapter, we will review the relevant laws and provide examples of the role a neuropsychologist may play within the field of legal-education law. In so doing, we hope to inform both beginning and seasoned neuropsychologists with some of the many things we have learned in doing a large number of these consultations over the years. Experience is a good teacher.

OVERVIEW OF INDIVIDUALS WITH DISABILITIES EDUCATION ACT

Prior to the elementary and secondary act of 1965, states were not required to ensure that children with disabilities received an education appropriate to their needs. Unfortunately some children with disabilities didn't even attend school because educational providers and programs were not made available to them. Since then many revisions have taken place and in 2004 the current version of the IDEA was implemented. In 2006, the final regulations for the amended IDEA were presented. The six basic principles of IDEA are as follows: FAPE, appropriate evaluation, individualized education program, least restrictive placement, parent/student participation in the decision-making process, and procedural due process.

The first principle—FAPE—is the basic premise of IDEA. IDEA was put in place to ensure that all children with disabilities have available to them a FAPE with special education and related services. The services are created to meet the students' unique needs and prepare them for future education and independent living. A FAPE means that all children with disabilities receive an individualized education program (IEP), that is, a program that is developed to meet the child's unique learning needs, is provided at public expense, and meets the standards of the state educational agency and IDEA. A FAPE begins with preschool and ends with secondary school education (age 21). A child with a disability may be diagnosed with a specific learning disability (SLD), mental retardation, autism, other medical/health disorder, neurological impairment, multiple disabilities, and so on. Each state has the right to set its own definition of a disability as well as create additional criteria as long as it is in accordance with IDEA's definition.

In addition, IDEA's definition of "special education" is considered to be an individualized education program developed to meet the unique needs of the child with a disability. This program is to be provided within the school the child would attend if a disability was not identified or within the least restrictive environment (LRE), either within the district or outside the district. Regardless of location, that is, within or outside the district, the district is required to provide funding for the special education program. However, if the district can provide a FAPE within one of their school settings, then an out-of-district placement (OOD) would not be required, regardless of how appropriate the parents may feel the OOD school is for their child's needs. In such cases where the district has an appropriate school/ program already in place, sending the student there, rather than to the OOD school, meets IDEA's requirement for "least restrictive" environment. Related services are also to be provided that may include speech and language therapy, physical therapy, occupational therapy, and counseling/psychological services, among others.

IDEA also was developed to ensure that the rights of children with disabilities and their parents were protected and to help states and federal agencies to provide appropriate education for children with disabilities. This act also lays out the necessity of assessing the effectiveness of the educational program for children with disabilities.

WHAT IS A "DISABILITY?"

The IDEA defines 13 categories of disability that are eligible for special education services. These include autism; deaf-blindness; deafness; emotional disturbance; hearing impairment; mental retardation; multiple disabilities; orthopedic impairment; other health impairment; SLD; speech or language impairment; traumatic brain injury; or visual impairment (including blindness). For most readers of this volume, the categories of mental retardation, autism, other health impaired (which includes attention-deficit/hyperactivity disorder [ADHD]), emotional disturbance, and especially SLD are most germane.

A SLD is defined by the IDEA as a disorder in one or more of the basic processes involved in understanding or in using language, spoken or written, that may manifest itself in difficulty listening, thinking, speaking, reading, writing, spelling, or doing mathematical calculations. Perceptual disabilities, brain injury, minimal brain dysfunction (an older term), dyslexia, and developmental aphasia are included. The term does not include learning problems associated with visual, hearing, or motor disabilities, mental retardation, emotional disturbance, or environmental, cultural, or economic disadvantage.

THE PROCESS OF DIAGNOSING A SPECIFIC LEARNING DISABILITY

The identification of a child with disabilities requires what is called "Child Find," a component of the IDEA. This occurs when a child is identified through a system that the state or school district has in place or by teachers or parents who request an evaluation. If the school requests an evaluation, then the parents must provide consent before testing can be initiated. Once consent is given, the school typically has 60 days to complete the evaluation. This time frame, however, may differ from state to state because each state has the right to set its own time frame. Indeed, there is great variability in the way states, and school districts within states, interpret the IDEA. Such latitude in interpretation is a result of the relatively vague language of these laws throughout states. The school's evaluation is conducted at no cost to the parents. A team of educational professionals, the Child Study Team (CST), will meet to discuss the child and his or her difficulties. The CST consists of a school psychologist, learning consultant, social worker, speech and language professional, and others. The evaluation typically consists of psychological, educational, and social work assessments. When appropriate, an occupational therapy or speech and language evaluation is also conducted and sometimes external consultants are sought, such as a child and adolescent psychiatrist or clinical neuropsychologist. The psychological evaluation must include a measure of intellectual ability (aptitude), often one of the Wechsler scales (Wechsler Intelligence Scale for Children–IV or Wechsler Adult Intelligence Scale–IV). Sometimes the psychological evaluation also includes a measure of emotional adjustment (projectives) and visual-motor skills (Bender Gestalt), and it must also include a classroom observation. Additional tests of other cognitive domains are typically not administered unless a neuropsychological evaluation is completed. The educational evaluation generally consists of an academic achievement test such as the Woodcock Johnson–III Tests of Academic Achievement or the Wechsler Individual Achievement Test-III. Achievement tests such as the Wide Range Achievement Test are deemed inappropriate for the purpose because of their lack of depth.

After the IQ and academic achievement testing is completed, the CST examines the results and, based on specific criteria, determines whether the child is eligible for an IEP due to a disability. The most common model utilized by schools to diagnose LD is the discrepancy model. This model uses a formula developed by the state to determine whether the child has a learning disability. This is based on the difference between the child's aptitude (i.e., intellectual functioning or IQ) and academic achievement, which is not due to lack of adequate instruction or exposure. The most common discrepancy model uses a difference of 1 ½ standard deviations to diagnose an LD. For example, a child with a Standard Score of 100 in verbal comprehension on the WISC-IV whose reading comprehension is a Standard Score of 78 meets this criterion and would be diagnosed with a reading disorder.

There are significant drawbacks to this approach and recently the discrepancy model has come under fire (Fletcher, Denton, & Francis, 2005). This is because quite often a child is not identified until she has begun to fall significantly behind her peers or has failed. Thus, this model is frequently titled the "wait to fail" approach because by the time the child is identified he has not acquired grade-level knowledge. Furthermore, in order to meet the criteria set forth with this model, the child's tested achievement needs to fall significantly below his IQ. Again, this typically leads to the wait to fail approach. Quite often this is what prompts parents to seek out an IEE. As parents observe their child struggling, they may request an evaluation from the district; however, the district does not have to provide this evaluation until the child is performing poorly (which is defined by the district as failing—but quite often for parents a drop in grades even from an A to a C usually leads to alarm). Rather than wait for their child to continue to fall further behind or risk failure, parents may opt to complete a private evaluation and then petition the district to develop or modify an IEP and provide appropriate services. To reduce the likelihood of the child failing before an evaluation is provided or services are placed, another model called response to intervention (RTI) (Fletcher & Vaughn, 2009) has been proposed that may alleviate the necessity of the student experiencing failure.

The RTI model focuses on early screening and effective instruction. This allows for interventions to be placed before the child has failed and also reduces the amount of time spent waiting for the evaluation and report from the involved professionals. That is, if a child is struggling, additional instruction may be provided first and his or her progress is monitored before a formal evaluation to assess the child for the IQ-achievement discrepancy is requested. RTI has been developed to address the issue set forth by IDEA that a LD is not diagnosed due to lack of exposure to appropriate instruction (Fletcher & Vaughn, 2009). Many professionals are proponents of this newer model for the aforementioned reasons. However, it is not instituted as frequently as the IQ-achievement discrepancy approach and thus we will focus on the use of the latter approach in the clinical cases described later in this chapter.

But no chapter in a book about neuropsychology would be complete without at least some discussion of the inadequacy of these models and the limited assessment methodology used. Let us assume that a child has either a significant IQ-achievement discrepancy or unexpectedly low achievement—thus qualifying him or her for special services under the IDEA. This model and methodology fail to answer the question as to why the child has such a discrepancy, that is, what cognitive processes are contributing to his or her failure to learn normally? Neuropsychological assessment, with its fundamental thoroughness, can answer such a question and potentially provide greater specifics for remediation/intervention (see footnote under "Vignettes" section).

THE INDIVIDUALIZED EDUCATION PROGRAM

If the child is found to be eligible, then the CST must develop an IEP within 30 days of completion of testing. The school must contact the parents and schedule a mutually convenient time for the meeting. The IDEA sets forth specific domains that must be covered in the IEP in order to ensure the child with disabilities receives appropriate services. The IEP is reviewed annually and testing is completed triennially. The IEP domains are as follows:

1. *Current educational performance:* This usually is based on classroom tests and assignments, individual tests that were administered to decide eligibility for services (e.g., Woodcock - Johnson), and observations by the parents, teachers, other school staff and professionals.

2. *Annual goals:* They are goals that a child can reasonably accomplish within a year and should be broken down into short-term objectives. This may include academic, social/behavioral, physical, or other needs. The objectives must be defined in measurable terms so that it is possible to determine whether the child has improved or not.

3. *Special education and related services:* The special education and related services deemed necessary are laid out in this section. This includes supplementary aids (i.e., laptop, etc.) and services that the child needs. Training or professional development for the educational providers is also included in this section.

4. *Participation with nondisabled children:* This section notes if the child will not participate in mainstreamed classes or school activities with nondisabled children.

5. *Participation in state and district-wide tests:* Because state and district achievement tests are routinely administered, the IEP must state any test administration modifications. If the test is not appropriate for the child, the IEP must state why and how the child will be tested instead.

6. *Dates and places:* The date of implementation for services, frequency of services, location, and length of time they will be offered is also included in the IEP.

7. *Transition service needs:* When the child reaches age 14, the IEP includes courses needed to reach the postschool goals. A statement of transition services is placed in the IEP when the child reaches age 16.

8. *Age of majority:* One year prior to the child reaching the age of majority, the IEP must include a statement that the student has been informed of his or her rights and when they will transfer to him or her.

9. *Measuring progress:* The IEP must state how the child's progress will be measured and how parents will be informed of that progress.

DUE PROCESS

As noted earlier, due process occurs when the parents (called the petitioners) and the district disagree with each other. An impartial hearing is scheduled to allow for resolution. A mediator may also be present to assist with finding a mutual agreement between the parents and the district. An impartial due process meeting also involves the parents and the district. But at this hearing a hearing officer is present to listen to each side's argument and then decide based on the law the most appropriate educational program for the child. The law is written in broad terms to protect the state and district such that the onus lies on the petitioner. It is very difficult to prove the district is not providing a FAPE because of how broadly the laws are written. Even though the parents may feel their child is not performing up to his or her potential, they may not have a strong case against the district. In our practice we have met with parents who feel their child is capable of earning A's in all courses. While the parents' expectations may in fact be consistent with their child's tested abilities, the responsibility does not lie with the district. The district is not responsible for the child who is not motivated and chooses not to complete his or her assignments or decides not to study. As long as the district is providing a FAPE and following IDEA, then the law remains on the side of the district. Nor does the law require that a student's performance be "optimal," or that his or her "strengths" be addressed. These may be desirable on the part of parents, but simply stated, the law does not work that way.

BEYOND LEARNING DISABILITY: OTHER
DIAGNOSTIC CONSIDERATIONS

Quite often teachers or parents may express concern about a child's acquisition of grade-level skills, but a LD may not be found or behavioral or health problems may be a concern. In this case there are several other possibilities that may be identified as the reason for the child's struggles. The child may suffer from ADHD or major depressive disorder, for example. Beyond psychiatric disorders, medical conditions may also be present (i.e., diabetes, Turner syndrome, etc.). In such cases, Section 504 comes into play as part of the Rehabilitation Act of 1973. This act states that a child cannot be discriminated against due to a disability. The term "disability" is defined as having a mental or physical impairment that substantially limits at least one major life activity and the child's ability to receive an appropriate education. If a child is diagnosed with a disability that is not a LD, then a Section 504 may be formulated and implemented. But the disability must significantly limit the child's ability with regard to academics; if not, then a Section 504 is not appropriate.

THE INDIVIDUALS WITH DISABILITIES EDUCATION ACT AND PRIVATE SCHOOLS

As the reader is already aware, IDEA provides a free and appropriate *public* school education, but what if a child is enrolled in a private school? Does IDEA still apply? Parents have the right to enroll their child in any school of their choice. This can be the public school or a private school, including a religious based school. Parents can also decide to home school their child. However, the IDEA changes when the child is not a participant in the public school system. If the parent chooses to enroll the child in a private school, then the school is not required to follow the laws of IDEA. Thus, the services the child receives, if any, may be different than those provided in the public school. Of course, if the public school system was unable to provide a FAPE for a child with disabilities, then the school district may enroll the child in the private school. In that scenario, IDEA does apply. The reason there is a difference is that private schools do not receive the same amount of government funding for educational programs as the public school system. This means that IDEA is not under the same requirements for children in private schools. In fact, under IDEA the private school setting is not required to provide the child with disabilities with the same services or any services at all.

What remains the same is the identification process. The "child find" system still applies and in order for a child to be eligible to receive services the same process must be followed regardless of enrollment in a private school. The CST will include representatives from the public school district in which the private school is located, and the child's parents and educational providers from the private school the child is enrolled in or will attend. Similar to the public school process, the CST will develop the child's program. The private school teachers and educational providers, however, do not have to meet the same expectations and qualifications as the special education teachers in the public school. Nor does the school have to provide the same services the public school would offer if the child is eligible under IDEA.

At times, a child may be enrolled in a private school with gifted students; however, the child's intellectual abilities and academic achievement may be average or low average. We see this in our practice. This is an unfortunate scenario because as previously stated the private school does not have to provide the same services as the public school would for the child. In this case, a private school may decide to make the appropriate services available for the child or the school may not.

Either way, the parent does not have a strong case against the school and in fact the parent cannot invoke due process because that right is forfeited once the child is enrolled in a private school by the parent. It is not uncommon that the child may be achieving at grade level but the private school population is achieving above grade level (this is also not uncommon in suburban school districts where the "average" student's abilities are actually above average). Thus, the expectations and work load are significantly beyond the child's abilities. Basically the child's abilities and the school's demands are mismatched. The parent then must decide to either have the child continue attending the private school or transfer the child to the public school system where IDEA applies. Once in the public school setting, however, the child may not be eligible for services if his or her academic achievement is at grade level. In the end, the decision remains with the parent as to what is right for his or her child.

WHY IS AN INDEPENDENT EDUCATION EVALUATION NECESSARY?

There are several ways in which a neuropsychologist may become involved in an IEE. First, as previously alluded to, a parent may choose to seek an evaluation from a professional outside of the district. Parents may feel this is necessary if their child is not doing well in school but has not yet met the school's criteria for testing. Another reason may be the school has completed its evaluation and did not find the child eligible for an IEP or Section 504 and the parents feel their child should qualify or needs services despite the school's testing results. This can happen because the district's evaluation often only includes an IQ test and measure of achievement, which obviously fails to take into account other cognitive domains. While scores from IQ and achievement measures are all that are needed to diagnose an LD, there certainly are other cognitive abilities that may interfere with a child's ability to learn or acquire knowledge. In this respect neuropsychology plays a key role. Our training allows us to answer the question that parents often pose: "Is there something else going on with my child? I understand he doesn't have a learning disability but why is he struggling so much in school?" A memory disorder may be present or visual-spatial/perceptual abnormality. The comprehensive neuropsychological evaluation can provide an in-depth answer to the parents' question. In this case, if the school has already completed its evaluation and determined the child is not eligible and then the parent requests an IEE, the district must pay for the IEE or show that its evaluation was appropriate at an impartial due process hearing. Another possible scenario may occur when the school has indeed provided an IEP but the parents feel the services are not adequate. In all of these instances a parent may opt to schedule an evaluation with a neuropsychologist in the community. However, sometimes a district may be struggling with how to provide the appropriate services to a child. Perhaps the child has exhausted the available interventions and is still not making gains. Then the district may opt to hire an independent evaluator who can assess for additional diagnoses outside of those provided by the psychological and educational evaluation. In this instance the district is responsible for paying the neuropsychologist's fee. Regardless of payment, the professional is sought to provide an independent opinion that is unbiased for either party and rests on the available scientific data. This is extremely important in all situations but of particular necessity if the parents are involved in mediation or due process with the district.

An IEE should include separate clinical interviews with the parent(s) and student, a comprehensive neuropsychological battery, and if possible a school observation. Time restrictions or other factors may interfere with completion of a school observation, but it is strongly suggested that one is completed in order to provide additional data about the student's current placement and performance. This also allows for more specific recommendations for the student.

In our practice a comprehensive neuropsychological battery typically includes tests of IQ, academic achievement, language, memory, fine motor, visual-spatial and executive function as well as behavioral questionnaires obtained from the parent(s) and child, and assessment of emotional adjustment. The battery approach is flexible with a core set of tests. We always cover all of the cognitive domains, but the actual measures may differ based on age, level of impairment, and strengths and weaknesses overall, as well as test results on the day of testing that may necessitate further testing in specific areas of cognition. See Table 14.1 for the recommended list of measures.

FORENSIC CAVEATS

As is true of all legal consultations for neuropsychologists, it does not matter which side retains you—whether parents or the district—you still do exactly the same job. Independent neuropsychological exams in this context strive for the truth, that is, the data. Whether one's assessment results are helpful to the referral source is incidental to the process. Beginning neuropsychologists working in forensic contexts are cautioned about "advocacy pull"—the implicit pull by retaining attorneys, parents, or districts to be a member of a team. This phenomenon is common in all forensic neuropsychological contexts. Remember: You are independent (Morgan, 2008).

The salience of symptom validity assessment issues in the neuropsychological literature over the past decade has predominantly concerned forensic assessment with adults. Recommendations by leading experts suggest the need for symptom validity assessment not only in all forensic contexts also but in clinical examinations (Heilbronner, Sweet, Morgan, Larrabee, & Millis, 2009). But adults are not alone in demonstrating poor effort on neuropsychological testing. Practicing pediatric neuropsychologists have known for some time that school-age children may not always put forth their best efforts in testing. This of course can occur for a variety of reasons, not the least of which may be malingering (Flaro & Boone, 2009; McCaffrey & Lynch, 2009). Thus, pediatric forensic neuropsychologists need to be aware of this issue and note that children as young as age 5 can perform normally on symptom validity tests (Donders, 2005). The reader will note that in the following case vignettes symptom validity tests were not administered, as these referrals occurred prior to recent prominence of these issues and recommendations.

VIGNETTES

To provide a better idea of how the laws apply to an IEE, we present several cases.

TABLE 14.1. Comprehensive Neuropsychological Battery

Domains and Tests

Intellectual Functioning
Wechsler Intelligence Scale for Children–Fourth Edition (WISC-IV)

Academic Achievement
Wechsler Individual Achievement Test–Third Edition (WIAT-III)
Or
Woodcock-Johnson Tests of Achievement–Third Edition (WJ-III)

Memory
California Verbal Learning Test–Children's Version (CVLT-C)/Second Edition (CVLT-II)
Rey-Osterrieth Complex Figure Test (ROCFT)
Wechsler Memory Scale (WMS)–Revised/Third Edition/Abbreviated
Wide Range Assessment of Memory and Learning–Second Edition (WRAML2)

Executive Function
D-KEFS Tower, D-KEFS Proverbs Test
Trail Making Test, Part A and B
Stroop
Conners' Continuous Performance Test
Auditory Consonant Trigrams Test
Wisconsin Card Sorting Test (WCST)
NEPSY-II
Delis-Kaplan Executive Function System (D-KEFS)
Letter Fluency
Category Fluency

Language
Boston Naming Test

Visual-Spatial
Judgment of Line Orientation (JLO)
Facial Recognition Test
Hooper Visual Organization Test (VOT)
The Beery-Buktenica Developmental Test of Visual-Motor Integration (VMI)

Fine-Motor
Grooved Pegboard Test
Finger Tapping

Behavioral/Personality
Minnesota Multiphasic Personality Inventory–Adolescent (MMPI-A)
Personality Inventory for Youth (PIY)
Personality Inventory for Children (PIC)
Behavior Assessment System for Children, Second Edition (BASC-2)

Case 1: A Learning Disability Complicated by Attention-Deficit/Hyperactivity Disorder

REFERRAL QUESTION

At the time of the evaluation, J.T. was a 13-year, 6-month-old female with a history of difficulty acquiring grade-level reading skills. She was enrolled in the seventh grade and was classified as communication impaired. J.T. had long-standing academic problems. According to her mother and teacher report, she struggled to keep up with the pace of the classroom. She was not a fluent reader and also had difficulty with math. Her reading resource room class for language arts and mathematics originally had five students, but during seventh grade the size was increased to reportedly more than 20 students. She received in-class support for science and social studies, as well as speech and language therapy twice a week. She also participated in an extended school year program of Wilson reading instruction 3 days per week for 1 hour for 6 weeks. Her parents had retained an attorney specializing in legal-education law because they believed their daughter required more intensive reading assistance than what the district was providing. An IEE was requested to provide updated testing results and recommendations.

BRIEF BACKGROUND HISTORY

J.T. was the younger of two children. Her parents both obtained higher educational degrees. There were no reported social problems with initiating or maintaining friendships, although the mother reported difficulties keeping up with peers during conversation. Her medical history was notable for a febrile seizure at age 5. Her early speech was described as unclear and gross motor skills reportedly were delayed. Family medical history was notable for cancer, hypertension, diabetes, heart disease, stroke, ADHD, and depression.

With regard to emotional and behavioral history, her mother noted J.T. easily and frequently became frustrated and angry because she had trouble keeping up with the pace of conversations. But she recovered quickly and preferred not to talk about it.

BEHAVIORAL OBSERVATIONS

J.T. easily separated from her mother and transitioned to the examining room. She was a timid and shy young lady; however, she readily answered the examiner's questions. She was very pleasant and cooperative throughout the evaluation, even when certain tasks were quite difficult for her. She appeared embarrassed if she did not know the answer to a question but usually with encouragement she would attempt to answer. She was very responsive to praise.

NEUROPSYCHOLOGICAL TEST RESULTS
For test results, see Table 14.2.

SUMMARY AND RECOMMENDATIONS
The comprehensive neuropsychological testing revealed weaknesses in numerous cognitive areas, including executive function (sustained attention, inhibition, selective inhibition, auditory attention, letter fluency, fine-motor dexterity, working memory, and retrieval of visual stimuli). Furthermore, significant language and reading impairment were noted. The profile was consistent with areas of severe weakness in the dominant (left) hemisphere, given the poor reading and fine motor skills, and bilateral frontal region given the executive dysfunction. In addition, weakness of the fronto-tempo-parietal system was also present given poor visual-spatial and visual learning skills. She also struggled to complete reading and writing

TABLE 14.2. J. T. Summary Sheet: Tests and Performance

Intellectual Functioning			Academic Functioning		
	SS	Percentile		Percentile	Grade Level
WISC-IV, FSIQ	84	14	WJ-III		
WISC-IV, VCI	94	34	Letter-Word	6	3.4
Similarities	9	37	Passage	<1	2.0
Vocabulary	8	25	Comprehension		
Comprehension	10	50	Word Attack	11	2.4
WISC-IV, PRI	82	12	Spelling	10	3.8
Block Design	5	5	Calculation	59	8.8
Picture Concepts	7	16	Applied Problems	31	6.0
Matrix Reasoning	9	37	Reading Fluency	18	5.0
WISC-IV, WMI	68	2	Math Fluency	46	7.8
Digit Span	4	2.3	Writing Fluency	9	4.6
Letter-Number	5	5	Broad Reading	5	3.4
Sequencing			Broad Math	41	7.3
WISC-IV, PSI	103	58	Broad Written	11	4.4
Coding	9	37	Basic Reading	7	3.0
Cancellation	12	75	Math Calculation	55	8.4
			Written Expression	14	4.9
Speech and Language			Academic Skills	12	4.5
Letter Fluency	1	<1	Academic Fluency	15	5.3
Category Fluency	9	37	Academic	15	3.9
Boston Naming Test	3	1	Application		

Visual-Perceptual		
Judgment of Line		
Orientation		6

2008 Performance	SS

Executive Function	
Continuous	
Performance Test	Inattentive, 4 out of 8 indicators
Auditory Consonants Trigram	4
Stroop	4
Trail Making Test A	44
Trail Making Test B	23

	SS
WISC-IV FSIQ	87
WISC-IV VCI	99
WISC-IV PRI	88
WISC-IV WMI	68
WISC-IV PSI	100
WIAT-II	
Word Reading	6
Reading Comprehension	<1
Pseudoword Decoding	2

Motor	
Grooved Pegboard	
Dominant Hand	6
Nondominant Hand	<1

(*Continued*)

TABLE 14.2. (Continued)

Intellectual Functioning			Academic Functioning		
	SS	Percentile		Percentile	Grade Level
Memory			Spelling	14	
CVLT-C Total	10	50	Written Expression	2	
Trials 1–5			Broad Reading	1	
CVLT-C Long Delay	7	16	Broad Math	27	
Free Recall			Written Language	5	
ROCFT Copy	3	1			
ROCFT Delay	2	<1			
WMS-R Logical	4	2			
Memory I					
WMS-R Logical	4	2			
Memory II					
WMS-R Visual	9	37			
Reproduction I					
WMS-R Visual	2	<1			
Reproduction II					
Emotional/Behavioral					
BASC-Parent	All domains WNL				
BASC-Child	All domains WNL				

NOTES: BASC, Behavior Assessment System for Children; CVLT-C, California Verbal Learning Test, Children's Version; FSIQ, Full Scale IQ; PRI, Perceptual Reasoning Index; PSI, Processing Speed Index; ROCFT, Rey-Osterrieth Complex Figure Test; SS, standard score; VCI, Verbal Comprehension Index; WIAT-II, Wechsler Individual Achievement Test; WISC-IV, Wechsler Intelligence Scale for Children, Fourth Edition; WJ-III, Woodcock-Johnson, Third Edition; WMI, Working Memory Index; WMS-R, Wechsler Memory Scale, Revised Edition; WNL, within normal limits.

tasks quickly and accurately. In sum, the following diagnoses were made: Reading Disorder, ADHD–Inattentive type, and Cognitive Disorder, NOS.

Given the array of learning disabilities and cognitive difficulties present, J.T. was at risk for developing an emotional disorder such as depression or anxiety. Clinical observations during the evaluation revealed a timid and soft-spoken young lady with low self-esteem. She was unsure of herself and hesitant to guess if she did not know an answer. She was responsive to positive reinforcement but seemed embarrassed of her cognitive difficulties. Her affect was flat. Her mother reported J.T. was aware of her struggles and the differences between herself and her peers. She, however, preferred not to speak of these differences. Her mother also reported her daughter encountered difficulty adapting to changing situations and recovering from difficult situations. She reported her daughter struggled to effectively communicate. Although J.T. denied any emotional problems on the BASC, her mood appeared to be mildly depressed. This was not of a clinical nature to meet criteria for a depressive disorder at this time. However, her parents and educational providers were strongly encouraged to keep an eye on her for possible emotional changes.

The aforementioned results clearly indicate that J.T. continues to qualify for special services with the presence of learning disability and cognitive impairment.[1] It was recommended that such services be incorporated immediately, including the summer months, into her learning environment to improve her academic success and ensure that she did not fall further behind her peers. The following recommendations were provided to assist with helping to increase her academic development:

1. J.T. should be placed in an academic environment that is small, structured, and provides multisensory instruction. Given her array of learning disabilities, specifically the severity of the reading disorder along with the presence of ADHD, she required slow-paced but intense academic instruction. To meet her emotional needs, she required a supportive and nurturing environment. It was imperative that J.T. be placed in an environment with other children with learning challenges such as hers in order to foster a feeling of acceptance and belonging rather than isolation or even being ostracized due to her different learning needs.

2. J.T.'s reading skills were severely behind her peers. She needed small group instruction (no more than four students; preferably one-to-one) on a daily basis for at least an hour to assist with reading and writing. Instruction should begin immediately following the end of the school year through an extended school year program that is provided for the entire summer on a daily basis. Working with a professional trained in a multisensory method such as the Wilson or Orton Gillingham methods was strongly suggested. It was imperative that this type of training continue in order to provide J.T. with the intense therapy she needed as well as consistency in teaching/learning style. Clearly, J.T. had failed to make adequate gains in her current program and was almost 6 years behind her peers in reading comprehension. The small group instruction in her current academic setting, which originally consisted of five students, had reportedly grown to 20 students. Even a group of five students was too large for J.T. given her severe reading disorder. J.T. was entering the eighth grade, yet she was reading at the 3.9 grade level. We recommended that if J.T.'s current academic placement could not provide the necessary intensive reading training program, then an out-of-district placement needed to be considered.

1. It should be noted that a "learning disability" to a neuropsychologist always suggests the presence of cognitive impairment of one or more areas of cognition. While in legal terms an IQ-achievement discrepancy may suffice to define a "learning disability," knowledge of what is causing unexpectedly low achievement usually cannot be discerned on the basis of an IQ test and an achievement test alone, without thorough cognitive assessment. Similarly, the school system's reliance on IQ to assess cognition is inadequate for comprehensive neuropsychological assessment (Baron, 2003). It may answer the "what" question, but not the "why."

3. She should receive handouts, outlines, and notes, minimizing the need for her to write in class. The handouts or worksheets should not incorporate significant amounts of visual material. Simple handouts were best, given that she was easily overwhelmed with visual stimuli.

4. Given the presence of ADHD, several accommodations should be provided to reduce J.T.'s distractibility.

   a. Preferential seating should be provided.
   b. Directions/instructions should be repeated and provided in written format.
   c. Her teachers should review her homework assignments with her prior to her leaving the classroom.

5. To adequately meet J.T.'s unique learning needs, she required training in metacognitive strategies. This training should be implemented in each subject so that she learns different ways to approach the different activities that require organization and to integrate self-monitoring techniques to improve attention. Assisting her with creating a plan or breaking down projects into small steps was optimal. In addition, working with J.T. on study skills to help improve her visual and verbal learning/memory was suggested. For example, teaching J.T. how to create note cards and rehearse will assist her with memorization of rote material.

6. J.T.'s parents should consult with their physician about the possibility of pharmacological treatment for ADHD.

7. It was strongly suggested that J.T. undergo a repeat neuropsychological evaluation in approximately 1 year. This would be helpful to reassess her cognitive abilities after the aforementioned recommendations have been implemented and provide an informed assessment of potential progress or continued areas of weakness, particularly in the reading domain.

8. If J.T.'s mood and behavior appear to change, a consultation with a pediatric psychologist should be scheduled to assess for depression or another emotional disorder.

Follow-Up

Following the completion of the aforementioned evaluation, the child's parents and attorney entered due process with the district. After reviewing the neuropsychological results, the district agreed to place J.T. in a private school for children with learning disabilities. The last update we received from the parents indicated that J.T. was making progress with her reading acquisition skills.

Case 2: Only Mild Cognitive Difficulties—What to Do?

Referral Question

C.W. was a 7-year, 7-month-old male enrolled in second grade at the time of the evaluation. He was referred by his parents due to difficulty acquiring grade-level reading skills. His parents reported their son's reading was slow and labored. They first noticed in kindergarten that C.W. was having trouble with reading. Then in first grade he worked with a reading specialist but at the end of first grade his grade equivalent was reported to be 1.5 and services were discontinued because he failed to meet the 1.5 standard deviation discrepancy requirement. However, his phoneme awareness reportedly continued to be poor, and he skipped or substituted sounds and words when reading.

BRIEF BACKGROUND HISTORY

C.W. was a twin born at 38 weeks gestational age. His mother's pregnancy was complicated by gestational diabetes. He weighed 5 pounds, 11 ounces at birth and his Apgar scores were reported to be 9. He was placed in an incubator for 1 day and phototherapy was used to treat jaundice. Developmental milestones were generally accomplished within normal time frames. He suffered from enuresis and colic. He had speech articulation and stuttering difficulties. He also had difficulty learning to ride a bike because he was afraid of falling or crashing. Family medical history was notable for cancer, heart disease, and hypertension.

With regard to emotional and behavioral history, C.W. was described as very sweet and full of a lot of energy by his parents. He was able to relate well to others. His parents noted he was aware of his reading difficulties, and they were concerned about his self-esteem.

BEHAVIORAL OBSERVATIONS

C.W. appeared slightly anxious to separate from his parents and enter the examiner's office. Once seated, however, he readily answered the examiner's questions and appeared comfortable. He smiled easily and was very pleasant. He appeared to enjoy the challenges of testing and worked very hard on every task. He desired to please and exhibited a perfectionistic style. When offered a break or snack, he preferred to continue working. When he was unsure of an answer, he often whispered to himself or lowered his voice. Aside from these observations, his spontaneous speech was fluent, grammatical, and free of paraphasic errors. We observed mild articulation problems. There was no evidence for clinically significant aphasia or an underlying thought disorder during testing. Furthermore, there was no evidence of frank neurobehavioral anomalies such as dysphasia, dystaxia, or gait or balance disturbance.

NEUROPSYCHOLOGICAL TEST RESULTS

For test results, see Table 14.3.

SUMMARY AND RECOMMENDATIONS

C.W. completed comprehensive neuropsychological testing that revealed overall average cognitive abilities. His intellectual functioning was in the average range and academic achievement was average and did not suggest the presence of a learning disorder. Furthermore, his language and visual-perceptual skills were intact. His performance did, however, suggest several areas of weakness, namely in the area of executive functioning (e.g., attention, nondominant hand fine motor dexterity,

TABLE 14.3. C.W. Summary Sheet: Tests and Performance

Intellectual Functioning			Academic Functioning		
	SS	Percentile		Percentile	Grade Level
WISC-IV, FSIQ	111	77	WJ-III		
WISC-IV, VCI	108	70	Letter-Word	57	2.5
Similarities	11	63	Passage	30	1.8
Vocabulary	10	50	Comprehension		
Comprehension	14	91	Word Attack	42	1.9
WISC-IV, PRI	112	79	Spelling	47	2.0
Block Design	13	84	Numerical	43	2.1
Picture Concepts	13	84	Operations		
Matrix Reasoning	10	50	Broad Reading	48	2.3
WISC-IV, WMI	99	47	Basic Reading	50	2.3
Digit Span	10	50	Math	50	2.3
Letter-Number	10	50	Calculation		
Sequencing			Skills		
WISC-IV, PSI	112	79	Academic	50	2.3
Coding	11	63	Skills		
Symbol Search	13	84	Academic	67	2.9
			Fluency		
Speech and			**Memory**	SS	
Language			WRAML2	10	50
Letter Fluency		91	Verbal Learning		
Category		31	WRAML2	7	16
Fluency			Verbal Learning		
Boston Naming		64	Recall		
Test			WRAML2	10	50
			Picture Memory		
Visual-Perceptual			WRAML2	12	75
Judgment of Line		27	Picture Memory		
Orientation			Recall		
Executive Function			WRAML2	14	91
Continuous		Inattentive,	Story Memory.		
Performance Test		6 out of 8	WRAML2	14	91
		indicators	Story Memory		
Stroop		38	Recall		
Trail Making		71	ROCFT Copy		79
Test, Version A			ROCFT		23
			Delay		
			Emotional/Behavioral		
			BASC-II	All domains WNL	

TABLE 14.3. (Continued)

Trail Making Test, Version B	10
Motor	
Grooved Pegboard	**Percentile**
Dominant Hand	44
Nondominant Hand	18

NOTES: BASC-II, Behavior Assessment System for Children, Second Edition; FSIQ, Full Scale IQ; PRI, Perceptual Reasoning Index; PSI, Processing Speed Index; ROCFT, Rey-Osterrieth Complex Figure Test; SS, standard score; VCI, Verbal Comprehension Index; WISC-IV, Wechsler Intelligence Scale for Children, Fourth Edition; WJ-III, Woodcock-Johnson, Third Edition; WMI, Working Memory Index; WNL, within normal limits; WRAML2, Wide Range Assessment of Memory and Learning, Second Edition.

and retrieval of visual and verbal [lists] information). This indicated bilateral weakness of the frontal regions. Behavioral observations indicated that although C.W.'s reading ability tested average, he struggled to read unfamiliar words. This was consistent with mild weakness in the dominant (left) hemisphere language region. In sum, mild reading and phoneme problems as well mild attention/multi-tasking difficulties were present. These areas of weakness were mild and did not warrant a diagnosis at the time of the evaluation.

This is a common scenario that we see in our practice. The child's areas of weakness are mild and therefore the district is not required by law to provide special services, especially if eligibility is based upon the discrepancy model. We generally recommend a 504 plan or informal accommodations but educate the parents that the district very clearly does not have to do so. Rather, the child's parents were encouraged to begin private tutoring for their son. Additional recommendations included

1. Although C.W's word-reading and passage comprehension were average, qualitatively his reading was somewhat dysfluent and slow, and he struggled to comprehend information. Working with a reading tutor to improve his reading abilities and comprehension was strongly suggested. Training in metacognitive strategies was also recommended to assist with multitasking and attention. In addition, sessions should integrate training to improve his list learning and complex visual information memory.

2. The parents and examiners noted C.W.'s strong desire to do well on academic tasks and a perfectionistic tendency that may indicate mild anxiety. His parents also reported he was aware of his academic weaknesses, and he often compared himself to his twin brother. Since it is not uncommon for children with such difficulties to also develop emotional disorders such as depression and anxiety, his parents were encouraged to keep an eye on his mood and if they noticed a change in his behavior a consultation with a pediatric psychologist would be helpful.

Case 3: A Teen Diagnosed With Posttraumatic Stress Disorder

REFERRAL QUESTION

D.F. was a 15-year, 10-month-old male adolescent who was referred for a neuropsychological evaluation by his parents at the suggestion of their son's psychologist to further evaluate his emotional functioning in light of a diagnosis of major depression. He was in the 10th grade and recently was transferred to a therapeutic day school; however, he had refused to attend the new school and had missed a total of 31 days of school that year. He was failing most subjects and reported "school was a waste of time." He had a long history of poor academic achievement beginning during his middle school years; he was previously an excellent student achieving honor roll from fourth grade through seventh grade. A 504 plan was implemented during ninth grade following a diagnosis of ADHD. His parents were also interested in understanding his cognitive abilities and academic skills in order to determine his strengths and weaknesses given that he had never completed a neurocognitive evaluation.

BRIEF BACKGROUND HISTORY

D.F. was the middle of three children and resided with his parents and siblings. His relationship with his siblings was described as "cordial." D.F. was described as a very social child before entering middle school. He enjoyed spending time with peers. However, during his middle school years he began to withdraw from social interactions with both peers and family members. Since then he had isolated himself and chose to spend time alone or with his family. When he was spending time with his family (i.e., going out to dinner, etc.), he typically read a book. He reported he spent time playing on the computer and "interacted" with peers using instant messaging. During the past year, he began to participate in rock climbing. D.F. previously enjoyed golf and competed at the state level. He was described as having been extremely motivated, enthusiastic, and competitive about golf and usually spent about 20 hours a week practicing.

D.F.'s early history was unremarkable. He was carried full term and reportedly achieved all of his developmental milestones within appropriate time frames. He was toilet trained during the day at 3 years of age but required a synthetic hormone to assist with bladder control at night. Medical history was noncontributory. Historically, D.F. suffered from a great deal of somatic complaints yet frequent medical workups had been negative. He often complained of headaches, frequent diarrhea, and stomach pain. He also reportedly would sleep for days at a time and then would remain awake for close to an entire day. This occurred in cycles, and when he remained in bed he had been observed to neglect his personal hygiene. D.F. reported he preferred to be awake at night and sleep during the day. Although a general history of difficulty sleeping was noted by his parents, reportedly his sleep habits worsened since middle school. He also would bite his nails and used pliers, scissors, and push pins on his nails. He picked at bug bites until they bled, prolonging the healing process. He was noted to be a picky eater but seemed to prefer carbohydrates. At times he would eat very large quantities of food and other times hardly eat at all.

Family medical history was notable for stroke, hypertension, substance abuse, and possible undiagnosed bipolar disorder (maternal grandmother). There was a family history of suicide (paternal grandmother). D.F.'s cousin was diagnosed with pervasive developmental disorder and additional comorbid diagnoses and had been hospitalized psychiatrically several times for aggressive and suicidal behavior.

D.F. was diagnosed with major depression in eighth grade and was prescribed a selective serotonin reuptake inhibitor (SSRI). As previously mentioned, his father described his son as an easy-going, social, and very responsible child. Prior to eighth grade, D.F. reportedly loved spending time with his family and friends. He readily responded to positive praise and always aimed to please his parents and other adults in his life. He was a highly motivated student, earned good grades, and was a rising star academically. He enjoyed golf and was quite an accomplished athlete, including winning several state championship awards and winning second place in the state overall. However, during his middle school years there was a drastic change in D.F.'s behavior and personality. He slowly withdrew from friends, then his grades began to drop, he started to isolate himself from his family, and finally he began to refuse to attend school. According to his father, D.F.'s whole outlook on life changed for the worse, and he began to complain of many physical complaints and somatic problems, which were not diagnosable after medical workups. He also had missed 31 days of school during the 10th grade. He was failing most courses. He stated he preferred to be alone in his room. He reported the only activity he enjoyed was rock climbing. In the past, D.F. was prescribed sleep aids. Of note, during the clinical interview D.F. denied feeling depressed or anxious. He stated he was never depressed.

Mr. F. reported a few months prior to this drastic change he and his wife found out that their son was reportedly being verbally and physically abused by his golf coach. When this came to their attention through an outside source, D.F. was removed from the team. It was around this time that D.F.'s personality and behavior changed. The F's believe something even more significant may have happened, but they have been unable to get their son to confide in them. Since then, on numerous occasions they noted that their son's behavior regressed and he seemed to be urinating in his bedroom. They replaced the bedroom carpet due to the strong urine smell and sometimes found plastic bottles full of urine in his room. D.F. was enrolled in psychotherapy with several therapists, and all reported there was something related to his time playing golf that seemed to have been very traumatic; however, he would not reveal what exactly happened. His most recent psychologist reported to the parents he felt D.F. was starting to feel comfortable about sharing what happened, but then he abruptly refused to return to treatment. He has not been in psychotherapy since then.

D.F.'s parents reported they attempted to implement numerous behavior modification programs to increase school attendance, to no avail. At the time of the evaluation, the parents were fearful their son would deteriorate even further unless an appropriate program was put in place. They were concerned that if they didn't immediately provide intensive treatment for their son that he would never successfully overcome what happened to him. Furthermore, because he had missed 31 days of school he was in danger of retention.

D.F. was diagnosed with ADHD in 2007. He was prescribed Concerta during the ninth grade but was not taking any medication for ADHD at the time of the evaluation.

BEHAVIORAL OBSERVATIONS

D.F. was compliant and readily answered the examiner's questions during the interview until the examiner inquired about psychotherapy. He noted he "may" have seen a therapist in the past but was unwilling to disclose the reason. It was difficult to establish rapport with him after this. During the testing, he did not like to guess when he didn't know the answer to a question, even with encouragement. At times he appeared resistant to cooperating with the testing directions and demands. He perseverated on different topics—often repeatedly asking why a certain task was important given his current situation. His demeanor did appear to change for the better after the lunch break in that he was more cooperative and attempted to initiate conversations with the examiner. However, when a different examiner entered the room he engaged in the resistant behavior again. Mental status examination revealed a generally constricted affect. He appeared guarded, defensive most times, particularly when questioned about psychological treatment, school, and related issues. Though he denied experiencing depression during the examination day and for that matter at any time in the past, he did appear to be clearly dysphoric to the examiners. When specifically queried about staying in bed all day with the covers over his head, he admitted that this was true but he continued to deny that this was a result of depression, sad feelings, low mood, and the like. At times it was noted that D.F.'s effort was reduced, specifically during verbal tasks. He was generally unresponsive to encouragement or reminders of the importance of trying his best on all tasks. Overall, his results were considered to reflect reliable and valid indices of his current level of neuropsychological and psychological functioning but may be slightly low estimates of his optimum abilities.

NEUROPSYCHOLOGICAL TEST RESULTS

For test results, see Table 14.4.

SUMMARY AND RECOMMENDATIONS

D.F. completed comprehensive neuropsychological testing that revealed mostly intact neurocognitive functioning with very mild relative weaknesses. His intellectual functioning was in the superior range and academic achievement was generally above average except for a few areas. His verbal learning and memory and motor skills were intact as were his visual-spatial abilities. There were a few areas of mild weakness that were notable. Although his word reading and phoneme awareness were in the average range, when compared to his superior range reading comprehension these were areas of relative weakness. His average verbal comprehension on the WISC-IV was also a relative weakness in light of his high average to superior abilities in other domains. D.F. had some difficulty with complex visual stimuli. Given the appearance of reduced effort selectively on the exam, these areas of "relative weakness" may be underestimates of his abilities. In sum, D.F.'s academic achievement and intellectual functioning were at least average if not superior,

TABLE 14.4. D.F. Summary Sheet: Tests and Performance

Intellectual Functioning	SS	Percentile
WISC-IV, FSIQ	120	91
WISC-IV, VCI	102	55
Similarities	10	50
Vocabulary	12	75
Comprehension	10	50
WISC-IV, PRI	117	87
Block Design	8	25
Picture Concepts	13	84
Matrix Reasoning	17	99
WISC-IV, WMI	123	94
Digit Span	14	91
Letter-Number Sequencing	15	95
WISC-IV, PSI	123	94
Coding	13	84
Symbol Search	14	91
Speech and Language	**SS**	**Percentile**
Letter Fluency		79
Category Fluency		77
Boston Naming Test		69
Visual-Perceptual		**Percentile**
Judgment of Line Orientation		56
Executive Function		**Percentile**
Continuous Performance Test		WNL
Auditory Consonants Trigram		42

Academic Functioning		
WJ-III	**Percentile**	**Grade Level**
Letter-Word	49	
Passage Comprehension	97	
Word Attack	31	
Spelling	91	
Numerical Operations	78	
Applied Problems	79	
Reading Fluency	99	
Math Fluency	94	
Writing Fluency	92	
Broad Reading	98	>18.0
Broad Math	88	>18.0
Broad Written Lang.	97	>18.0
Basic Reading	47	8.9
Math Calc. Skills	91	>18.0
Written Expression	98	>18.0
Memory	**SS**	**Percentile**
WMS-R Logical Memory I		35
WMS-R Logical Memory II		31
WMS-R Visual Reproduction I		27
WMS-R Visual Reproduction II		66
CVLT-C Trial 1		16
CVLT-C Trial 2		84
CVLT-C Trial 1–5 Total		50

(*Continued*)

TABLE 14.4. (Continued)

Intellectual Functioning	SS	Percentile	Academic Functioning	
Trail Making Test, Version A		76	CVLT-C Long Delay	69
Trail Making Test, Version B		84	ROCFT Copy	69
Motor			ROCFT Delay	21
Grooved Pegboard		**Percentile**	**Emotional/ Behavioral**	
Dominant Hand		58	MMPI-A	All domains WNL
Nondominant Hand		31		

NOTES: CVLT-C, California Verbal Learning Test, Children's Version; FSIQ, Full Scale IQ; LM, Logical Memory; MMPI-A, Minnesota Multiphasic Personality Inventory, Adolescent Version; PRI, Perceptual Reasoning Index; PSI, Processing Speed Index; ROCFT, Rey-Osterrieth Complex Figure Test; SS, standard score; WISC-IV, Wechsler Intelligence Scale for Children, Fourth Edition; VCI, Verbal Comprehension Index; VR, Visual Reproduction; WJ-III, Woodcock-Johnson, Third Edition; WMI, Working Memory Index; WMS-R, Wechsler Memory Scale, Revised Edition; WNL, within normal limits.

suggesting he was very capable of earning at least average grades. His poor academic performance was likely related to other factors. He did not evidence cognitive impairment of any kind; ADHD was not supported diagnostically by the results of this examination.

As previously mentioned, D.F.'s intellectual functioning and academic achievement were average to superior. His overall neurocognitive profile indicated intact cognitive functioning. Yet D.F. was failing in school and refused to attend school. His behavior appeared to be linked to unknown incidents that occurred with his golf coach several years ago. Prior to these incidents he was described as outgoing, very responsive to adult guidance, and desiring to please others. But during sixth grade D.F.'s parents learned their son's golf coach was verbally and physically abusing their son. He slowly withdrew from his friends, isolated himself from his family, regressed behaviorally, and refused to attend school. He spent days at a time in bed disregarding his personal hygiene and then would spend days awake. Although he had participated in therapy with several different therapists, when one began to get close to understanding what happened he evidenced resistance, became fearful, and discontinued treatment. He refused to disclose the details of the incident to his parents, siblings, or any other adults or friends. This behavior is not uncommon in children who are victims of abuse because they typically feel that the adults and friends in their life have let them down because no one could protect them from the traumatic abuse. As is so common in such cases, D.F. was unable to trust anyone for fear something might happen again or he would be let down like he was in the past. These dynamics were mostly outside of his awareness, far too painful to think about. He was so fearful of letting someone in that he pushed everyone away. Most likely, he feared that if someone knew what he went through, that person would reject him and he could not handle that. To cope with the pain and fear, he built a wall around himself to protect him from reexperiencing the deep traumatic pain that occurred years ago. Some may interpret his behavior as oppositional or defiant, but this appeared purely defensive, his only way of protecting himself. He did not possess any other coping skills to deal with his pain. He was in desperate need of intense therapy to work with and heal his pain. This was a young boy who was suffering from posttraumatic stress disorder (PTSD). Despite his denial, the results of the examination were consistent with the presence of severe depression. The family history of suicide in a relative underscored the seriousness of the findings and the need for substantive, immediate, and intensive professional psychotherapeutic intervention.

The presence of PTSD qualified D.F. for special educational services, under the category of Emotional Disturbed. In our clinical opinion, D.F. required a therapeutic residential facility; however, the district by law did not have to provide this type of setting. Instead the district only needed to begin to provide psychological assistance in the least restrictive environment and if implementation of such services was ineffective, then the district would need to consider placement in a therapeutic residential facility. Thus, the initial recommendation was to place D.F. in a therapeutic day program. While the district and parents were working to locate an appropriate placement, home instruction was recommended to begin immediately due to the significant number of school days D.F. had already missed. We also recommended that D.F. be included in the search for the new school, rather than having the decision foisted upon him. Individual psychotherapy was clearly needed and recommended to help him to accept school attendance as a normal, necessary, and appropriate alternative to his current situation of withdrawal, refusal, depression, and denial. We believed all of these educational components were necessary in order to make D.F. available for learning.

The therapeutic day school should provide a challenging academic curriculum commensurate with D.F.'s high-level cognitive abilities; a supportive and integrated therapeutic intervention program provides throughout the day; trained and experienced mental health and academic professionals; and individual and group therapy to help identify and resolve emotional issues, learn appropriative and adaptive coping skills, and develop insight. Implementation of a behavioral plan that was consistent both in his academic setting and home environment was necessary. D.F. required a structured environment with clear rules and consequences for his school refusal behaviors. Consultation with a behavioral consultant to assist in developing a plan for both school and home was strongly recommended. In addition, therapy should focus on the creation of a strong therapeutic rapport with D.F. that provides a safe environment for him. We noted that it could take a considerable period of time for D.F. to feel comfortable with a therapist and develop a strong therapeutic rapport. He would likely be resistant to opening up to a therapist initially, but this would improve with the right "mix" of D.F. and the therapist. This was noted to be the key to helping D.F. adjust to and develop appropriate coping skills to handle the traumatic event. Enrollment in group therapy for teens suffering from PTSD was also strongly encouraged. We stated that without therapy D.F. may not overcome the trauma and was at great risk of continuing down the path of isolation, withdrawal, and failure that began several years ago.

In addition, the academic environment needed to provide multisensory instruction with positive reinforcement. D.F. had experienced a significant degree of academic failure and thus had lost interest in and motivation to apply himself to his school work. He required a positive and nurturing environment where he could experience success. His teachers needed to be aware of his emotional struggles in that he was suffering from PTSD and his behaviors were not of a defiant nature but rather due to his limited coping skills. With this, the academic atmosphere needed to be at a level commensurate with his high-level abilities, offering interesting and challenging opportunities for academic development.

D.F.'s teachers were encouraged to provide simple handouts to assist him with his difficulty in breaking down complex visual stimuli.

D.F. enjoyed rock climbing, and that appeared to be his only social interaction. He stated he was comfortable with the members of his rock climbing team. We strongly encouraged D.F. to continue this activity as it was a very positive sign that he had sought out an activity that also required socialization with others. Rock climbing appeared to be his only outlet at the time of the evaluation, and it likely carried great therapeutic value for him.

We also noted that parenting a teenager can be trying under typical circumstances, but handling the emotions related to the knowledge that one's child has experienced a traumatic event was extremely difficult. D.F.'s parents were encouraged to participate in therapy together so that they could develop new ways to work with their son and create a therapeutic environment for him in their home.

We stressed to the district that it was going to take an integrated, coordinated effort of a team of mental health and educational professionals to assist D.F. in accepting a return to school given his emotionally fragile state, despite his seeming appearance. He was clearly vulnerable for further decompensation, deeper depression, complete withdrawal, and possibly worse. We noted that he should not return to the public school system, a place where he no doubt endured serious emotional and/or physical trauma and humiliation. He required an educational environment that was supportive and emotionally therapeutic. Without appropriate placement and intervention his condition will surely worsen.

FOLLOW-UP

D.F.'s parents and legal-education attorney met with the district and an agreement was reached to enroll D.F. in a therapeutic day school with his input. A program was chosen by D.F. and his parents with the district's approval. D.F. attended 2 days of school, a Thursday and Friday, and then refused to return after the weekend. We were contacted by D.F.'s parents to provide further guidance on how to handle the situation. At that time, we stated it was necessary to enroll D.F. in a therapeutic residential program. The attorney worked with the district to obtain an agreement for the new plan. This was reached within a day and D.F. was enrolled in a local residential program. The parents contacted us a few weeks after he began the program to report that he was adjusting well, although he continued to be resistant to therapy.

In this case, the district was extremely cooperative and worked quickly with the parents and attorney to find the appropriate placement for D.F. This is not always the case. The district did not need to fund an out-of-district placement so quickly because the law clearly states their in-district plan must first be implemented and if that fails then another plan may be put in place. However, it appeared that the district understood the severity of D.F.'s psychological status and the dire seriousness of his current state. Rather than implementing different plans based on the law, the district was willing to initially try a therapeutic day program but responded to the urgent nature of the situation when that setting failed. Given the potential for greater decompensation or even suicidal ideation, it behooved the district to work quickly to find the appropriate placement for their student.

Case 4: A Medical Disorder

Referral Question
A.B. was referred for the evaluation at the suggestion of his therapist due to academic difficulties, specifically trouble with reading comprehension. His parents indicated that some prior testing scores were low and that he needed improvement in several academic areas. In addition, he appeared to be taking more time in school to do various tasks than his peers. He was diagnosed with type 1 diabetes at the age of 2 ½.

Brief Background History
A.B. was an 8-year, 9-month-old male and was enrolled in the third grade at the time of the evaluation. He resided in an intact family and both parents earned higher education degrees.

Developmental and medical history revealed that A.B. was carried full term and weighed 6 pounds, 9 ounces at birth; his condition was described as very good. He reportedly reached his developmental milestones within normal limits. Medical history was notable for a diagnosis of type 1 insulin dependent diabetes at the age of 2 ½. A.B. reported that when he experienced low blood sugar he felt fatigued. Family medical history was remarkable for cancer, heart disease, diabetes, and depression.

Socially and emotionally, A.B. was reported to be doing fairly well though he is described by his parents as a somewhat emotional child. They had observed occasional nervous twitches or ticking. He seemed enthusiastic about most everything and loved sports and other activities. His parents reported that he required considerable parental time and energy as a result of his medical issue.

Educational history noted he was not receiving special educational services at the time of the evaluation. A.B. noted he did not like reading and particularly found reading comprehension to be somewhat hard.

Behavioral Observations
A.B. was generally cooperative and easily engaged in conversation with the examiner. At times some nervous ticking/twitching was observed. His mood was generally neutral, and his affect appeared to be appropriate and within a full range of emotions. As noted, a few times during the testing he became more overtly nervous, but this did not appear to affect his overall performance.

Neuropsychological Test Results
For test results, see Table 14.5.

TABLE 14.5. A.B. Summary Sheet: Tests and Performance

Intellectual Functioning	SS	Percentile	Academic Functioning		
WISC-IV, FSIQ	97	42	**WIAT-II**	**SS**	**Percentile**
WISC-IV, VCI	96	39	Word Reading	109	73
Similarities	9	37	Reading Comprehension	102	55
Vocabulary	10	50	Decoding	112	79
Comprehension	9	37	Spelling	106	66
Information	12	75	Numerical Operations	107	686
WISC-IV, PRI	98	45	Basic Reading	106	66
Block Design	7	16	**WJ-III**		
Picture Concepts	10	50	Reading Fluency	105	63
Matrix Reasoning	12	75	Math Fluency	111	77
Picture Completion	5	5	Writing Fluency	116	86
WISC-IV, WMI	99	47	Academic Fluency	110	74
Digit Span	9	37	**Memory**	**SS**	**Percentile**
Letter-Number Sequencing	11	63	WRAML2 Verbal Learning		31
WISC-IV, PSI	97	42	WRAML2 Verbal Learning Recall		84
Coding	10	50	WRAML2 Picture Memory		5
Symbol Search	9	37	WRAML2 Picture Memory Recall		25
Speech and Language	**SS**	**Percentile**	ROCFT Copy		4
Letter Fluency		20	ROCFT Delay		3
Category Fluency		31	**Emotional/ Behavioral**		
Boston Naming Test		26	BASC-II	All domains WNL	
Visual-Perceptual		**Percentile**			
Visual-Motor Integration		37			
Executive Function		**Percentile**			
Continuous Performance Test		WNL			
Stroop		3			
Auditory Consonants Trigram		16			
Trail Making Test, Version A		83			
Trail Making Test, Version B		88			
Motor					
Grooved Pegboard		**Percentile**			

TABLE 14.5. (Continued)

Intellectual Functioning	SS	Percentile	Academic Functioning
Dominant Hand		44	
Nondominant Hand		42	

NOTES: BASC-II, Behavior Assessment System for Children, Second Edition; FSIQ, Full Scale IQ; PRI, Perceptual Reasoning Index; PSI, Processing Speed Index; ROCFT, Rey-Osterreith Complex Figure Test; SS, standard score; VCI, Verbal Comprehension Index; WIAT-II, Wechsler Individual Achievement Test; WISC-IV, Wechsler Intelligence Scale for Children, Fourth Edition; WJ-III, Woodcock-Johnson, Third Edition; WMI, Working Memory Index; WNL, within normal limits; WRAML2, Wide Range Assessment of Memory and Learning, Second Edition.

SUMMARY

The results of the evaluation found generally average IQ scores with selected areas of weakness noted in terms of some aspects of visuospatial processing and visual attention and reasoning. Verbal skills, working memory, and processing speed on the WISC-IV were all average or better. Similarly, A.B. was found to be making appropriate and acceptable progress of academic achievement across all areas of reading, math, spelling, and academic fluency/speed of academic operations. Overall, these scores did not corroborate reports of difficulties that A.B. was having in school as he was a bright youngster who was making appropriately expected academic progress.

However, in this case, A.B.'s difficulties in school were explained by other findings in the evaluation. Issues concerning language processing, visuospatial and perceptual processing, and learning and memory were noted that, taken together, were likely to be causing the difficulties with efficiency and academic performance that A.B. was experiencing. In the area of language functioning, A.B. was found to have slight difficulty on the Letter Fluency exam reflective of weak word retrieval skills, and in terms of rapid automatic naming, reflecting that he labored with visual-verbal associations. The findings were consistent with slow word retrieval skills and reduced efficiency in visual-verbal processing and suggested mild dysfunction of the dominant hemisphere. The findings explained his reading issues.

In addition, A.B. had difficulty with selected areas of executive functioning. Although visual attention was found to be quite good, auditory attention was much more variable and he had difficulty with inhibitory controls required in gating out or blocking interfering stimuli. Mild visual perceptual impairment was also noted with extremely weak visuomotor integration, poor visuomotor planning, poor organization, and difficulty with placement and planning on the page.

Although verbal learning and memory was found to be intact, more variability was found with visual learning and memory where scores fell as low as the 5th percentile.

Taken together there appeared to be weakness of selected cortical systems in the dominant hemisphere subserving language skills, in the frontal region responsible for aspects of attention and executive skills, and in the nondominant (right) hemisphere subserving visuospatial, perceptual, and visuomotor integration skills.

The weaknesses noted were likely to be consistent with what is often seen among children with type 1 diabetes, which does seem to affect cognitive functioning. In that vein, it should be noted from a more positive perspective that the finding that A.B. demonstrated with selective weakness in these cognitive areas was relatively mild compared to many other children with diabetes.

Overall, the results were best characterized in terms of a nonspecific cognitive disorder or a learning disability, not otherwise specified.

In this case, A.B. was not eligible for school-based services because of his adequate and average academic achievement test scores; therefore, the best approach to deal with A.B.'s difficulties was in the private domain. A.B.'s parents were encouraged to continue private tutoring.

Emotionally and behaviorally A.B. was found to be a pleasant, sweet, cooperative, and unassuming child. His parents completed the BASC-II Parent Rating Scale and there were no elevations on any of the behavioral or emotional scales that would suggest the presence of any type of emotional or behavioral concern. However, A.B. was noted to be somewhat anxious in testing, and his twitching or ticking appeared to be associated with those anxious times. Nevertheless, A.B.'s level of anxiety did not reach a threshold that would be consistent with the presence of a disorder. His parents of course were advised to keep an eye on this and to take note of any increase in his anxious tendencies, particularly around school work and having subjective difficulties.

In this particular case, the parents decided against taking this up with the district given that their son was not in fact eligible for services. To the best of our knowledge, A.B. continued with private tutoring and did well academically.

DISCUSSION

As can be seen, the law is clearly written in favor of the state and district. Despite this, there are times where an IEE is valuable and relevant. The role of the IEE is to provide a thorough understanding of a child's neurocognitive and psychological strengths and weaknesses in relation to his academic functioning. At all times, the evaluator must remain unbiased and present their opinion based solely on the available data. There are times where it is obvious that a child would benefit from special services yet based on the law the district is not required to provide any additional assistance.

Experience is a great teacher. Experienced pediatric neuropsychologists working in the education-law domain will note that some parents are unaware of the laws that govern eligibility and provision of services. Similarly, some parents are convinced of greater impairment or psychopathology in their child than there actually is, while others tend to under "diagnose" their children. This may be particularly true of fathers relative to mothers, at least in our experience. Some parents are convinced their child is "gifted" and particularly "special." When assessment results fail to confirm these notions, neuropsychologists may struggle to convince well-meaning, but seriously misinformed parents. Some parents present themselves as knowing more than the neuropsychologist—the "expert" they retained! Then, some parents present a plethora of issues in their child, where testing indicates normal functioning and interactions with the parents suggest significant psychopathology in the parent. Truly, these issues seen in pediatric neuropsychology practice are not unique to the legal-education arena, but the "forensic" context heightens one's awareness of these issues. In all cases, the neuropsychologist must use great clinical skills in dealing with the children, parents, and districts—as well as attorneys—in resolving these clinical issues. One final word of advice, not unique to the topic of this chapter, but of singular importance: Always do your best work; always have the best interests of children in mind.

REFERENCES

Baron, I. S. (2003). *Neuropsychological evaluation of the child*. New York: Oxford University Press.

Donders, J. (2005). Performance on the Test of Memory Malingering in a mixed pediatric sample. *Child Neuropsychology, 11*, 221–227.

Flaro, L., & Boone, K. (2009). Using objective effort measures to detect noncredible cognitive test performance in children and adolescents. In J. E. Morgan & J. J. Sweet (Eds.), *Neuropsychology of malingering casebook*. New York: Psychology Press.

Fletcher, J. M., Denton, C., & Francis, D. J. (2005). Validity of alternative approaches for the identification of LD: Operationalizing unexpected underachievement. *Journal of Learning Disabilities, 38*, 545–552.

Fletcher, J. M., & Vaughn, S. (2009). Response to intervention: Preventing and remediating academic difficulties. *Child Development Perspectives, 3*(1), 30–37.

Grieffenstein, M. F. (2008). Basics of forensic neuropsychology. In J. E. Morgan & J. H. Ricker (Eds.), *Textbook of clinical neuropsychology* (pp. 905–941). New York: Psychology Press.

Heilbronner, R. L., Sweet, J. J., Morgan, J. E., Larrabee, G. J., & Millis, S. R. (2009). American academy of clinical neuropsychology consensus conference statement on the neuropsychological assessment of effort, response bias and malingering. *The Clinical Neuropsychologist, 23*, 1093–1129.

Individuals with Disabilities Education Improvement Act of 2004 (IDEIA). P.L. 108–446 (2004).

McCaffrey R. J., & Lynch, J. K. (2009). Malingering following documented brain injury: Neuropsychological evaluation of children in a forensic setting. In J. E. Morgan & J. J. Sweet (Eds.), *Neuropsychology of malingering casebook*. New York: Psychology Press.

Morgan, J. E. (2008). Non-credible competence: How to handle "newbies," "wannabies," and forensic "experts" who know better or should know better. In R. L. Heilbronner (Ed.), *Neuropsychology in the courtroom*. New York: Guilford.

SELECTED WEB SITES

http://www.nichcy.org/Pages/Home.aspx
http://www.nichcy.org/reauth/IDEA2004regulations.pdf
http://idea.ed.gov
http://www.reading.org.

PART THREE

The Pediatric Forensic Toolbox

Note: These templates in Exhibits A–I represent a sample of the forms that may be useful in conducting pediatric forensic evaluations. However, these forms and the information within each form may not apply to all practice circumstances or jurisdictions, and therefore should be modified as needed for clinical use.

EXHIBIT A. SAMPLE CONSULTANT–ATTORNEY AGREEMENT

{Insert Letterhead}

CONSULTANT–ATTORNEY AGREEMENT

This agreement is entered into between Dr. Smith, the consultant, and {insert name of attorney and law firm}, the client-attorney.

The purpose of this agreement is to procure the services of the consultant in relation to the case of {insert name of child or file} (Client File #).

Dr. Smith will provide services to the client-attorney as an independent professional. Payment to Dr. Smith is not dependent upon the findings that Dr. Smith renders, or on the outcome of any legal action, mediation, arbitration, or the amount or terms of any settlement of the underlying legal cause, nor on any contractual arrangement between the client-attorney and any other person or party.

The client-attorney has had the opportunity to investigate and verify Dr. Smith's credentials, and agrees that Dr. Smith is qualified to perform the services in this contract.

Retainer

At the time of the execution of this agreement, the client-attorney shall tender to Dr. Smith a non-refundable retainer in the amount of $_____ ($___/hour x ___ hours). This fee will cover initial case review and consultation, to be paid in advance. The retainer is required prior to any work being initiated. The client-attorney shall not identify Dr. Smith as either a testifying or non-testifying expert until such time as the retainer has been paid.

Billings for services performed or expenses incurred shall be charged against the retainer until it is depleted. Should initial case review require additional time beyond ____ hours, each additional hour beyond the initial ___ hours will be billed at the rate of $____ per hour, and is due immediately.

Fees

Services after the initial case review and consultation will consist of, but may not be limited to, client and collateral interview, examination, record review, telephone calls, letters, reports, travel time, testimony preparation, and testimony. Time is prorated to the next highest quarter hour.

After payment of the retainer, further work will require another advance of $_____ due immediately. Each time the advance is depleted, a subsequent advance of $_____ is due immediately, against which each additional hour will be billed. Unlike the initial retainer, the unused portion of any of these subsequent advances will be returned should Dr. Smith's services no longer be needed. Estimates of time anticipated to be spent on a case will be gladly provided on request.

The fees for services provided by Dr. Smith and staff are as follows:

Consultant Fees. Except as outlined herein, the client-attorney shall compensate Dr. Smith at the rate of $____ per hour for all tasks performed under this agreement. Courtroom testimony time, travel time and courtroom waiting time will be charged as a full day at $\_\_\_\_ x 8 hours ($____), or half-day at $\_\_\_\_ x 4 hours ($____).

Psychometrist Fees. Psychometrist fees are $____ per hour.

Cancelled and Missed Appointments

Appointment times are reserved in advance, and 48 hours notice is required for cancellations and rescheduling. Appointments missed or cancelled without 48 hour notice will be billed for a 4-hour flat fee for consultant time ($____). To cancel appointments within business hours, call 555–555-5555. To cancel appointments outside of business hours, call 555–555-5556.

Cancellation of courtroom testimony at less than 48 hours notice will result in a minimum billing of 2 hours. Cancellation of courtroom testimony with less than 24 hours notice will result in a minimum billing of 4 hours. Same-day cancellation will result in full-day fee.

Terms of Engagement

The client-attorney is responsible for payments to Dr. Smith as outlined in this contract, regardless of any arrangement the client-attorney has with any party or parties he or she represents. Dr. Smith will issue bills on a monthly basis, or whatever other interval is deemed appropriate. Bills are due on receipt, and shall be considered delinquent if unpaid more than 30 days after their date of issuance. Interest shall accrue to any delinquent balance at the maximum rate permitted by law, not to exceed 1.5 percent per month. In the event that a bill remains unpaid for 60 or more days after the date of issuance, Dr. Smith shall have the unrestricted right to resign from performing additional services for the client-attorney on any and all cases that Dr. Smith is working on for the client-attorney's firm.

Signatures

Signature below indicates agreement to the terms outlined above.

The client-attorney should sign both copies of this document and return one copy to Dr. Smith.

Client-Attorney Name (please print):	Consultant: Dr. Smith
Client-Attorney Signature:	Consultant Signature:
Date:	Date:

EXHIBIT B. SAMPLE PEDIATRIC FORENSIC INFORMED CONSENT FORM (SHORT VERSION)

{Insert Letterhead}

INFORMED CONSENT FOR NEUROPSYCHOLOGICAL ASSESSMENT

Referral Source

This Forensic Neuropsychological Evaluation is being conducted at the request of {insert name of attorney, court, insurance company, etc.}.

Nature and Purpose

In most cases, this evaluation is intended for use in some type of a legal proceeding. The goal of neuropsychological evaluations is to clarify the nature and extent of problems/changes with thinking skills such as attention, memory, language, problem solving, as well as emotional state and behavior. It is common when someone is injured in an accident or is going through an administrative process (e.g., seeking disability benefits or testing accommodations) for the insurance carrier, attorney, trier of fact, administrative body, or other third party to request an examination by an expert neuropsychologist of their choosing.

The neuropsychological examination includes an interview, where questions are asked about background, current medical symptoms, and other relevant matters. Additionally, standardized tests and other techniques are commonly used to determine general knowledge, academic abilities, drawing or design construction skills, ability to learn word lists or stories, problem-solving skills, and/or other mental abilities. In addition, questions about mood, interests, and other aspects of emotional state, personality, and behavior are typically asked. It is very important that questions are answered as accurately as possible. Problems should not be minimized or exaggerated. It is also essential that one's best effort is given during the testing. Part of the examination will assess honesty and effort.

Participation in this evaluation is voluntary and will not be performed without relevant signatures on this document. You also have the right to stop the evaluation at any time; however, there may be legal consequences if you stop the evaluation. Therefore, it would be in your best interest to consult with an attorney before doing so.

If, at any time, you have a question about any aspect of the evaluation or these procedures, please feel free to ask me. In addition, if at any time a break is needed, please let me know and we will stop.

Foreseeable Risks and Benefits

For some people, neuropsychological examinations can cause fatigue, frustration, and anxiousness. An attempt will be made to help minimize these factors. The results of this examination may either support or not support your legal claim.

Limits of Confidentiality

The confidentiality of the evaluation and the results is determined by the rules of the legal/administrative system. If your attorney has requested this evaluation, he/she will receive a copy of my report and will control how it is to be used and who has access to it. If an attorney other than your attorney has requested the evaluation, all involved attorneys and their staffs, a minimum, will have access to the results. Should the case proceed to trial, those involved in the trial will be exposed to the results of the examination, and the court record will be available for anyone to review. If the purpose of the evaluation is to address a different, administrative matter, those persons involved in the administrative process will have access to the evaluation results. Beyond the above, confidential information obtained during the examination can ordinarily be released only with written permission. The results of this examination will be forwarded to {insert name of attorney, court, insurance company, etc.}.

There are some special circumstances that can limit confidentiality, including, but not limited to, (a) a statement of intent to harm yourself or others, (b) statements indicating harm, abuse, or neglect of children or vulnerable adults, (c) any statement concerning participation in terrorist activities, and (d) a subpoena from a court of law.

Observation and Recording

Parents are typically invited to participate in clinical interviews. Additional third parties, such as attorneys, may be allowed to be present during clinical interviews, and such interviews may be recorded, with the permission of the neuropsychologist. In contrast, the professional performing the neuropsychological testing and the person undergoing the testing are the only ones permitted in the room during the testing. Recording of neuropsychological testing is not permitted.

Feedback

You will not receive the results or a copy of the report directly from this office. However, it may be possible for you to receive a copy of the results from the referral source.

I have read and agree with the nature and purpose of this examination and to each of the points listed above. I have had an opportunity to clarify any questions and discuss any points of concern before signing.

_____   _____
Examinee Signature   Date

_____   _____
Parent/Guardian or Authorized Surrogate   Date

NOTE: Form provided by Bush, MacAllister, and Goldberg (authors of Chapter 2, this volume).

EXHIBIT C. SAMPLE PEDIATRIC FORENSIC INFORMED CONSENT FORM (LONGER VERSION)

{Insert Letterhead}

INFORMED CONSENT FOR NEUROPSYCHOLOGICAL ASSESSMENT

{insert attorney or other retaining party}, has referred your child, {insert child's name}, for an *independent neuropsychological assessment* by Dr. Smith, a psychologist registered in the State/Province of {insert name of State or Province} (Reg.# _____). Apart from providing independent assessments, Dr. Smith is not in any way associated with this law firm.

What is a Neuropsychological Assessment?

Neuropsychological assessment is a process for evaluating cognitive functions, such as intelligence, problem solving, language, attention, learning and memory. Emotional adjustment and life stress are also evaluated. No invasive procedures are involved and the examination will not be physically painful.

The products of the assessment include Dr. Smith's professional opinions about:

+ The nature, extent, causes, and outcome of any brain injury or brain dysfunction that your child may have
+ The nature, extent, causes, and impact of any emotional/adjustment problems that your child may have
+ The nature and extent of any factors that may impact on the validity of the assessment, such as poor effort.

Why has a Neuropsychological Assessment been requested?

This assessment is meant to inform parties involved in an existing or potential civil legal proceeding, and is not being carried out for any other purpose. Consequently, Dr. Smith will not provide your child with any psychological treatment or care and will not discuss any aspect of diagnosis or treatment with your family. Dr. Smith will not discuss any aspect of any legal proceeding with your family except as necessary for conducting this assessment. Normally, Dr. Smith will not be in direct contact with your family after s/he has completed the assessment. Please refer any questions or comments that your family may have after the assessment to your lawyer.

What will happen during the assessment?

Dr. Smith's assessments typically take two days. The assessments normally include:

+ Interviews with you and possibly other people who know your child (e.g., teacher)

- Questionnaires completed by you and possibly other people who know your child (e.g., teacher)
- Observations of your child's behavior during the assessment
- Tests of cognitive functions such as intelligence, problem solving ability, language, attention, learning and memory
- Measures of your child's emotional state and level of psychological adjustment

Dr. Smith will also review all available records (e.g., medical, legal, educational).

What is my role and my child's role in the evaluation?

You and your child must answer truthfully and completely to any questions asked by Dr. Smith. You must respond honestly to all questionnaires. Dr. Smith will report any significant differences between what you or your child reported and what others say or have said or written about your child.

What happens after the assessment is completed?

Dr. Smith will usually write a report that includes:

- A description of any particular cognitive or emotional problems that your child may have
- Dr. Smith's opinion about what may have caused any cognitive or emotional problems that your child may have

The report may include other types of opinions or recommendations if these are requested by the referring party.

Who will receive copies of Dr. Smith's report?

The report will be sent to {insert attorney or other retaining party}. The report may also be shared with other parties involved in your child's court case such as the opposing lawyers and their assistants, officers of the court, judges, or juries. The results of the assessment may also become part of the public legal record. *Dr. Smith will not convey the results of his or her assessment directly to your family*. Please consult with your lawyer if you want to know the results of this assessment. If one of your child's health care providers requires a copy of Dr. Smith's report, you should arrange to have a copy sent by your lawyer.

In what other ways will information on my child be shared?

Dr. Smith may discuss his or her findings or any other information obtained during the assessment with {insert attorney or other retaining party}. Dr. Smith may also be required to give a deposition or testify in court regarding this assessment.

In accordance with legal and ethical standards of psychological practice, Dr. Smith may share his or her report or other information obtained during this assessment with persons who are <u>not</u> parties to your child's court case (e.g., police) if:

- Your child's statements or behavior or your statements or behavior suggest that a he/she or another child may be abused, neglected, or otherwise harmed
- Your child's statements or behavior suggest that your child is likely to harm him/herself or someone else
- A judge hearing a different court case orders Dr. Smith to turn over records or orders and have him/her testify about your child

In these cases, information about your child that is relevant to the specific concern will be shared with authorities and others as required by law or as necessary to protect those who may need it.

What are the possible consequences of my child's participation in this assessment?

Your child's participation in the assessment may lead to significant consequences. <u>The results of this assessment may not support your child's litigation</u>. The results of this assessment may become publicly available if it is presented in court.

Is my child's participation in this assessment voluntary?

You and your child have the right to refuse to participate in this assessment. Your child may also stop participating in the assessment at any time.

Do not sign below if you do not understand any part of this document or do not agree to any part of this document.

I, _____, by signing below, give my full and informed consent to have my child participate in a neuropsychological assessment conducted by Dr. Smith as described above. My initials above indicate that I have read and understand the meaning of each corresponding section, and that any questions I had about this assessment have been explained to my satisfaction. By signing below, I authorize Dr. Smith to send a report of this assessment to the law corporation {insert attorney or other retaining party} and to discuss the assessment with them as needed. I understand that I am entitled to have a copy of this consent form.

_____   _____
Signed   Date

_____   _____
Witness   Date

This assessment took place at the offices of: _____

_____

_____

_____

_____

_____

_____

_____

_____ I have received a copy of this consent form

EXHIBIT D. SAMPLE LETTER TO PARENTS ABOUT
NEUROPSYCHOLOGICAL ASSESSMENT

{Insert Letterhead}

Dear {insert parent or guardian name},

Following our recent telephone conversation, this is to confirm {insert child's name}'s neuropsychological assessment on {insert date and time}, at the request of {insert attorney or other retaining party}. Please plan to be at our office for approximately 7 hours on your appointment day. As we discussed, we may need to see {insert child's name} for an additional session if further testing is required.

Please let your child know that this is not a typical doctor's visit (e.g., there are no needles or medical examinations). Your child will be asked to participate in activities that help us understand more about thinking, learning, and remembering abilities. Your child may be asked to assemble puzzles, draw pictures, solve problems, and similar activiies.

We are located at {insert address}. Parking is located at {insert parking details}. See attached map for office location.

On the day of your appointment, please bring copies of the following that we may keep:

1. Your child's most recent school report card and year-end report cards for previous years.
2. Your child's Individualized Education Plan (IEP) or other relevant school documents, if your child has these.
3. Glasses or hearing aids if your child needs them.
4. A lunch and/or snack for yourself and your child.

Enclosed are questionnaires to be completed by {insert child's name}'s classroom teacher. Please sign and complete the enclosed *Consent Form for Release of School Information* (see Exhibit F, this volume) and give it and the questionnaires to the teacher along with the self-addressed stamped envelope.

We look forward to meeting with you and {insert child's name}. Please contact us or your attorney should you have any further questions regarding this assessment.

Sincerely,

EXHIBIT E. SAMPLE LETTER TO TEACHER ABOUT NEUROPSYCHOLOGICAL ASSESSMENT

{Insert Letterhead}

Re: {insert child's name}

Dear Teacher,

We have scheduled a neuropsychological assessment with your student {insert child's name}, as part of a neuropsychological evaluation for legal purposes requested by {insert attorney or retaining party}, and with the consent of your student's parents or guardian. To help us with our assessment, could you kindly complete the enclosed forms and return them to us as soon as possible. Your observations of {insert child's name} will form an important part of this assessment and we appreciate the time and effort you spend on completing these questionnaires. Please find enclosed a *Consent for Release of Information* which has been signed by the parent or guardian, and which is intended for your school's records. The following items are enclosed:

- *Consent Form for Release of School Information* (see Exhibit F, this volume), signed by the parent or guardian and to be retained by the school for your records
- {insert list of questionnaires enclosed}

Thank you for your assistance in our assessment. Please do not hesitate to contact us at {insert contact information} should you have any questions.

Sincerely,

EXHIBIT F. SAMPLE CONSENT FORM FOR RELEASE OF INFORMATION FROM SCHOOL

{Insert Letterhead}

CONSENT FORM FOR RELEASE OF SCHOOL INFORMATION

I hereby authorize {insert name of school and school board}
to release any or all educational data, including information labelled "confidential"
(e.g., achievement test results, psychoeducational assessments, speech and
language reports, *including raw test data*) to Dr. Smith regarding:

_____

Name of Child/Adolescent

_____

Date

_____

Signature of Parent/Guardian

_____

Signature of Child (when appropriate)

_____

Signature of Witness

NOTE: This form is to be signed by the parent and retained by the school

EXHIBIT G. CHECKLIST FOR A PEDIATRIC INDEPENDENT NEUROPSYCHOLOGICAL EVALUATION INTERVIEW

General

- Purpose and overview of evaluation
- Consent procedures.

Preinjury

- Birth and early development
- School achievement and school placements prior to injury (grade by grade)
- General medical health, physical functioning, childhood illnesses
- Other head injuries or accidents
- Specific queries re: definite or suspected history or signs of ADHD, behavior problems or learning difficulties

Injury Details

- Details of injury (including loss of consciousness, post-traumatic amnesia, length of retrograde amnesia, postinjury medical complications, pain, medications, hospitalizations)
- Chronology of postinjury symptoms (onset, course, resolution)

Postinjury Course

- Course of recovery (improvement, plateauing, worsening)
- Cognitive functioning
- Physical functioning
- School functioning
- Emotional and behavioral functioning (with specific queries re: post-traumatic stress disorder, anxiety, depression, friendships/social interactions; in older adolescents, sexual activity and substance use)
- Results of prior evaluations
- Results of prior interventions
- Extracurricular activities and career goals
- Expectations for outcome

Family History

- Parental occupation, education, family background
- Family medical history—query ADHD, learning disorders, psychiatric (bipolar, depression), chronic pain; problems with the law; substance abuse
- Family coping and family conflict

Child Interview

- Understanding of the evaluation
- Understanding of the accident
- Course of recovery (improvement, plateauing, worsening)
- Physical functioning
- Cognitive functioning
- School functioning
- Emotional and behavioral functioning
- Query post-traumatic stress disorder, anxiety, depression (in older adolescents, sexual activity and substance use)
- Social functioning
- Home situation, relationship with parents, teachers
- Extracurricular activities
- Career goals
- Expectations for outcome

EXHIBIT H. SAMPLE TRAUMATIC BRAIN INJURY INTERVIEW FORM

TRAUMATIC BRAIN INJURY INTERVIEW: EXAMINEE AND/OR COLLATERAL INFORMANT'S DESCRIPTION OF ACCIDENT/INJURY

Name: _____ Date: _____
Interviewer: _____
Date of Accident: _____ Time of Accident: _____
Place of Accident: _____

Overview Of The Accident/Injury

Last memory prior to accident
Memory of accident itself
Loss of consciousness (onset, length, resolution)
First memories after accident
Posttraumatic amnesia (onset, length, resolution)

Symptoms And Course Over Time

Dizziness
Vertigo
Diplopia
Headache
Nausea
Tinnitus
Other

Posttraumatic Stress Symptoms

Flashbacks
Nightmares
Fear/anxiety/avoidance

Functional Impact of Accident/Injury

Perceived impact on school functioning
Perceived impact on emotional and behavioral functioning
Perceived impact on activities of daily living and functional independence
Perceived impact on social and recreational activities
Perceived impact on activities of daily living

EXHIBIT I. SAMPLE BACKGROUND AND HISTORY QUESTIONNAIRE

Dear Parents/Guardian: The following is a detailed questionnaire on your child's development, medical history, and current functioning at home and at school. This information will be integrated with the testing results in order to provide a better picture of your child's abilities as well as any problem areas. Please fill out this questionnaire as completely as you can.

CHILD'S FAMILY

Child's Name: _____ Today's Date: _____

Birthdate: _____ Age: _____ Grade: _____ Name of School: _____

Birth Country: _____ Age on arrival in
Canada if born elsewhere: _____

Person filing out this form: ☐ Mother ☐ Father ☐ Stepmother ☐ Stepfather ☐
Other: _____

City of residence: _____ Home phone #: _____
Work phone #: _____

Biological Mother's Name: _____ Age: _____
Highest Grade Completed: _____

Number of Years of Education: _____
Degree/Diploma (if applicable): _____

Occupation: _____

Biological Father's Name: _____ Age: _____ Highest
Grade Completed: _____

Number of Years of Education: _____
Degree/Diploma (if applicable): _____

Occupation: _____

Marital status of biological parents: ☐ Married ☐ Separated ☐ Divorced ☐ Widowed
☐ Other: _____

If biological parents are separated or divorced:

How old was this child when the separation occurred? _____

Who has legal custody of the child? (Check one) ☐ Mother ☐ Father ☐ Joint/Both
☐ Other: _____

Stepparent's Name: _____ Age: _____
Occupation: _____

If this child is not living with __either__ biological parent:

Reason: _____

☐ Adoptive parents ☐ Foster parents ☐ Other family members ☐ Group home
☐ Other: _____
Name(s) of legal guardian(s): _____

List all people currently living in your child's household:

Name   Relationship to Child   Age

_____

_____

_____

_____

_____

_____

If any brothers or sisters are living outside the home, list their names and ages:

_____

_____

Primary language spoken in the home: _____

Other languages spoken in the home: _____

If your child's first language is not English, please complete the following:

Child's first language: _____ Age at
which your child learned English: _____

Behavior Checklist (Current)

Place a check mark (✓) next to behaviors that you believe your child <u>currently</u> exhibits to an excessive or exaggerated degree when compared to other children his or her age.

Sleeping and Eating

- ❑ Nightmares
- ❑ Sleepwalking
- ❑ Trouble sleeping (describe):
- ❑ _____
       _____

  Eats poorly
- ❑ Picky eater
- ❑ Eats excessively

Social Development

- ❑ Prefers to be alone
- ❑ Shy or timid
- ❑ More interested in objects than in people

- ❑ Difficulty making friends
- ❑ Plays or socializes with younger children
- ❑ Teased by other children
- ❑ Bullies other children
- ❑ Does not seek friendships with peers
- ❑ Not sought our for friendship by peers
- ❑ Does not play or socialize with other children outside of school
- ❑ Difficulty seeing another person's point of view
- ❑ Doesn't empathize with others
- ❑ Overly trusting of others
- ❑ Easily taken advantage of

- ❑ Overly familiar with people
- ❑ Doesn't appreciate humour
- ❑ Overly attached to certain people

Behavior

- ❑ Stubborn
- ❑ Irritable
- ❑ Frequent tantrums
- ❑ Strikes out at others
- ❑ Throws things at others
- ❑ Destroys things
- ❑ Angry or resentful
- ❑ Oppositional
- ❑ Negativistic
- ❑ Lying
- ❑ Argues with adults
- ❑ Low frustration threshold
- ❑ Blames others for own mistakes
- ❑ Daredevil behavior
- ❑ Runs away
- ❑ Needs a lot of supervision
- ❑ Impulsive (does things without thinking)
- ❑ Talks excessively
- ❑ Skips school
- ❑ Interrupts frequently
- ❑ Purposely harms or injures self
- ❑ Dangerous to self or others (e.g., running into street) describe:

  _____
  _____

- ❑ Talks about killing self (describe):

  _____
  _____

- ❑ Unusual fears, habits or mannerisms (describe):

  _____
  _____
  _____

- ❑ Steals

- ❑ Depressed
- ❑ Cries frequently
- ❑ Excessively worried and anxious
- ❑ Overly preoccupied with details
- ❑ Overly attached to certain objects
- ❑ Not affected by praise
- ❑ Not affected by negative consequences
- ❑ Drug abuse
- ❑ Alcohol abuse
- ❑ Sexually active

Other Problems

- ❑ Wets bed
- ❑ Wets self during the day
- ❑ Poor bowel control (soils self)
- ❑ Motor/Vocal tics
- ❑ Overreacts to noises
- ❑ Overreacts to touch
- ❑ Fails to react to loud noise
- ❑ Poor sense of danger
- ❑ Has blank spells
- ❑ Sloppy table manners
- ❑ Bangs head
- ❑ Bites nails
- ❑ Picks nose
- ❑ Sucks thumb
- ❑ Masturbation in public places
- ❑ Excessive daydreaming and fantasy life

Motor Skills

- ❑ Poor fine motor coordination
- ❑ Poor gross motor coordination
- ❑ Clumsy
- ❑ Cannot tie shoes
- ❑ Cannot dress self
- ❑ Difficulty walking
- ❑ Difficulty running
- ❑ Cannot throw or catch

BEHAVIOR CHECKLIST (IF YOUR CHILD IS BEING ASSESSED DUE TO AN INJURY OR ACCIDENT, PLEASE COMPLETE WITH REGARD TO PREINJURY FUNCTIONING)

Place a check mark (✓) next to behaviors that you believe your child exhibited to an excessive or exaggerated degree, <u>prior to his or her injury</u>, when compared to other children his or her age.

Sleeping and Eating

- ❑ Nightmares
- ❑ Sleepwalking
- ❑ Trouble sleeping (describe):
  _____
  _____
- ❑ _____
  _____
  _____
- ❑ Eats poorly
- ❑ Picky eater
- ❑ Eats excessively

Social Development

- ❑ Prefers to be alone
- ❑ Shy or timid
- ❑ More interested in objects than in people
- ❑ Difficulty making friends
- ❑ Plays or socializes with younger children
- ❑ Teased by other children
- ❑ Bullies other children
- ❑ Does not seek friendships with peers
- ❑ Not sought our for friendship by peers
- ❑ Does not play or socialize with other children outside of school
- ❑ Difficulty seeing another person's point of view
- ❑ Doesn't empathize with others
- ❑ Overly trusting of others
- ❑ Easily taken advantage of
- ❑ Overly familiar with people
- ❑ Doesn't appreciate humour
- ❑ Overly attached to certain people

Behavior

- ❑ Stubborn
- ❑ Irritable
- ❑ Frequent tantrums
- ❑ Strikes out at others
- ❑ Throws things at others
- ❑ Destroys things
- ❑ Angry or resentful
- ❑ Oppositional
- ❑ Negativistic
- ❑ Lying
- ❑ Argues with adults
- ❑ Low frustration threshold
- ❑ Blames others for own mistakes
- ❑ Daredevil behavior
- ❑ Runs away
- ❑ Needs a lot of supervision
- ❑ Impulsive (does things without thinking)
- ❑ Talks excessively
- ❑ Skips school
- ❑ Interrupts frequently
- ❑ Purposely harms or injures self
- ❑ Dangerous to self or others (e.g., running into street) describe:
  _____
  _____
- ❑ Talks about killing self (describe):
  _____
  _____
- ❑ Unusual fears, habits or mannerisms (describe):
  _____
  _____
- ❑ Steals
- ❑ Depressed

- ❑ Cries frequently
- ❑ Excessively worried and anxious
- ❑ Overly preoccupied with details
- ❑ Overly attached to certain objects
- ❑ Not affected by praise
- ❑ Not affected by negative consequences
- ❑ Drug abuse
- ❑ Alcohol abuse
- ❑ Sexually active

- ❑ Poor sense of danger
- ❑ Has blank spells
- ❑ Sloppy table manners
- ❑ Bangs head
- ❑ Bites nails
- ❑ Picks nose
- ❑ Sucks thumb
- ❑ Masturbation in public places
- ❑ Excessive daydreaming and fantasy life

Motor Skills

Other Problems

- ❑ Wets bed
- ❑ Wets self during the day
- ❑ Poor bowel control (soils self)
- ❑ Motor/Vocal tics
- ❑ Overreacts to noises
- ❑ Overreacts to touch
- ❑ Fails to react to loud noise

- ❑ Poor fine motor coordination
- ❑ Poor gross motor coordination
- ❑ Clumsy
- ❑ Cannot tie shoes
- ❑ Cannot dress self
- ❑ Difficulty walking
- ❑ Difficulty running
- ❑ Cannot throw or catch

EDUCATION PROGRAM

Does your child have an individual education plan (IEP) or modified learning program? ❑ Yes ❑ No

If yes, when was the IEP created? _____

If yes, are you satisfied with the IEP? ❑ Yes ❑ No

If not satisfied, please explain: _____

Has your child been held back a grade? ❑ Yes ❑ No

If yes, what grade(s) and why? _____

Is your child's curriculum modified? ❑ Yes ❑ No

If yes, please describe: _____

Is your child in any special education classes? ❑ Yes ❑ No

If yes, please describe: _____

Is your child receiving assistance at school? ❑ Yes ❑ No

If yes, please describe: _____

Has your child been suspended or expelled from school? ❑ Yes ❑ No

If yes, please describe: _____

Has your child ever received tutoring? ❑ Yes ❑ No

If yes, please describe: _____

Rate your child's academic performance relative to other children <u>of the same age</u>. Please estimate the grade level your child is functioning at in the given area if he or she is above or below average.

	Above Average	Average	Below Average	Impaired	Grade Level
Handwriting	☐	☐	☐	☐	_____
Spelling	☐	☐	☐	☐	_____
Punctuation	☐	☐	☐	☐	_____
Vocabulary	☐	☐	☐	☐	_____
Grammar	☐	☐	☐	☐	_____
Reading speed	☐	☐	☐	☐	_____
Reading comprehension	☐	☐	☐	☐	_____
Math skills	☐	☐	☐	☐	_____

Check any problems **reported from school**:

- ☐ Difficulty sustaining attention
- ☐ Easily distracted
- ☐ Daydreaming
- ☐ Fidgeting/restless
- ☐ Frequently gets out of seat
- ☐ Difficulty working quietly
- ☐ Difficulty working independently
- ☐ Doesn't want to be called on
- ☐ Blurts out answers
- ☐ Difficulty following instructions
- ☐ Doesn't cooperate well in group activities
- ☐ Doesn't respect the rights of others
- ☐ Shifts from one activity to another
- ☐ Does better in a one-to-one relationship
- ☐ Won't wait his/her turn
- ☐ Teased by other children
- ☐ Talking back
- ☐ Refusing to do work
- ☐ Bullies other children
- ☐ Fighting
- ☐ Messy/disorganized
- ☐ Does not like school
- ☐ Truant
- ☐ Excessively tired or sleepy

Describe briefly other classroom or school problems if applicable: _____

_____

_____

COGNITIVE SKILLS

Rate your child's cognitive skills relative to other children of the <u>same age</u>.

	Above Average	Average	Below Average	Impaired
Speech	☐	☐	☐	☐
Comprehension of speech	☐	☐	☐	☐
Problem solving	☐	☐	☐	☐
Attention span	☐	☐	☐	☐
Memory for events	☐	☐	☐	☐
Organisational skills	☐	☐	☐	☐
Memory for facts	☐	☐	☐	☐
Learning from experience	☐	☐	☐	☐
Conceptual thinking	☐	☐	☐	☐
Overall Intelligence	☐	☐	☐	☐

Check any specific problems:

- ☐ Poor articulation
- ☐ Difficulty finding words to express self
- ☐ Disorganized speech
- ☐ Ungrammatical speech
- ☐ Talks like a younger child
- ☐ Slow learner
- ☐ Forgets to do things
- ☐ Easily distracted
- ☐ Frequently forgets instructions
- ☐ Frequently loses belongings
- ☐ Difficulty planning tasks
- ☐ Doesn't foresee consequences of actions
- ☐ Slow thinking

Describe briefly any other cognitive problems that your child may have: _____

_____

_____

Describe any special skills or abilities that your child may have: _____

_____

_____

DEVELOPMENTAL HISTORY

If your child is adopted, please fill in as much of the following information as you are aware of.

During pregnancy, did the mother of this child:

Take any medication? ☐ Yes ☐ No

If yes, what kind? _____

Smoke? ☐ Yes ☐ No

If yes, how many cigarettes each day? _____

Drink alcoholic beverages? ☐ Yes ☐ No

If yes, what kind? _____

Approximately how much alcohol was consumed each day? _____

Use drugs? ☐ Yes ☐ No

If yes, what kind? _____

How often were drugs used?

List any complications during pregnancy (excessive vomiting, excessive staining/ blood loss, threatened miscarriage, infections, toxemia, fainting, dizziness, etc.):

Duration of pregnancy (weeks): _____ Duration of labor (hours): _____ Apgars: _____/_____

Were there any indications of fetal distress: ☐ Yes ☐ No

If yes on any of other above, for what reason? _____

Check any that apply to the birth: ☐ Labor induced ☐ Forceps ☐ Breech ☐ Caesarean

If yes on any of other above, for what reason? _____

What was your child's birth weight? _____

Check any that apply following birth: ☐ Jaundice ☐ Breathing problems ☐ Incubator ☐ Birth defect

If yes, please describe:_____

Were there any other complications? ☐ Yes ☐ No

If yes, please describe: _____

Was there any maternal depression during the immediate postnatal period?

If yes, please describe: _____

Were there any feeding problems? ☐ Yes ☐ No

If yes, please describe: _____

Were there any sleeping problems? ☐ Yes ☐ No

If yes, please describe: _____

Were there any growth or development problems during the first few years of life? ☐ Yes ☐ No

If yes, please describe: _____

Were any of the following present (to a significant degree) during infancy or the first few years of life?

☐ Unusually quiet or inactive

☐ Did not like to be held or cuddled

☐ Not alert

☐ Difficult to soothe

☐ Colic

☐ Excessive restlessness

☐ Excessive sleep

☐ Diminished sleep

☐ Headbanging

☐ Constantly into everything

☐ Excessive number of accidents compared to other children

Please indicate the approximate age in months or years at which your child showed the following behaviors. If you feel that you child was early or late in showing a listed behavior, please indicate by checking the appropriate box. Check never if your child has never shown the listed behavior.

	Age	Early	Late	Never		Age	Early	Late	Never
Smiled	____	☐	☐	☐	Tied shoelaces	____	☐	☐	☐
Rolled over	____	☐	☐	☐	Dressed self	____	☐	☐	☐
Sat alone	____	☐	☐	☐	Fed self	____	☐	☐	☐
Crawled	____	☐	☐	☐	Bladder trained, day	____	☐	☐	☐
Walked	____	☐	☐	☐	Bladder trained, night	____	☐	☐	☐
Ran	____	☐	☐	☐	Bowel trained	____	☐	☐	☐
Babbled	____	☐	☐	☐	Rode tricycle	____	☐	☐	☐
First word	____	☐	☐	☐	Rode bicycle	____	☐	☐	☐
Sentences	____	☐	☐	☐					

CURRENT MEDICATIONS

Medication	Reason Taken	Dosage (If known)	Start Date

List **all** medications that your child is currently taking:

Medical History

Date of last physical examination: _____

Date of last vision examination: _____

Date of last hearing examination: _____

Place a check next to any illness or condition that your child has had. When you check an item, also note the approximate date of the illness (if you prefer, you can simply indicate the child's age at illness).

Illness or condition	Date(s)/age(s)	Illness or condition	Date(s)/age(s)
☐ Measles	_____	☐ Ear infection	_____
☐ German measles	_____	☐ Dizziness	_____
☐ Mumps	_____	☐ Severe headaches	_____
☐ Chicken pox	_____	☐ Rheumatic fever	_____
☐ Whooping cough	_____	☐ Tuberculosis	_____
☐ Diphtheria	_____	☐ Bone or joint disease	_____
☐ Scarlet fever	_____	☐ Sexually transmitted disease	_____
☐ Meningitis	_____	☐ Anaemia	_____
☐ Pneumonia	_____	☐ Jaundice/hepatitis	_____
☐ Encephalitis	_____	☐ Diabetes	_____
☐ High fever	_____	☐ Cancer	_____
☐ Seizures	_____	☐ High blood pressure	_____
☐ Allergy	_____	☐ Heart disease	_____
☐ Hay fever	_____	☐ Asthma	_____
☐ Injuries to head	_____	☐ Bleeding problems	_____
☐ Broken bones	_____	☐ Eczema or hives	_____
☐ Hospitalizations	_____	☐ Suicide attempt	_____
☐ Operations	_____	☐ Alcohol abuse	_____
☐ Otitis media	_____	☐ Drug abuse	_____
☐ Visual problems	_____	☐ Physical abuse	_____
☐ Fainting spells	_____	☐ Sexual abuse	_____
☐ Loss of consciousness	_____	☐ Paralysis	_____
☐ Poisoning	_____	☐ Stomach pumped	_____

Family Medical History

Place a check next to any illness or condition that any member of the immediate family (i.e., brothers, sisters, aunts, uncles, cousins, grandparents) has had. Please note the family member's relationship to the child.

Condition	Relationship to child	Condition	Relationship to child
☐ Seizures or Epilepsy	_____	☐ Neurological illness	_____
☐ Attention deficit	_____	☐ Mental illness	_____
☐ Hyperactivity	_____	☐ Depression or anxiety	_____
☐ Learning disabilities	_____	☐ Tics or Tourette's syndrome	_____
☐ Mental retardation	_____	☐ Alcohol or drug abuse	_____
☐ Childhood behavior problems	_____	☐ Suicide attempt	_____

Does your child wear glasses? ☐ Yes ☐ No

If yes, please list prescription or describe (e.g., nearsighted): _____

Does your child have a hearing problem? ☐ Yes ☐ No

If yes, please describe): _____

Does your child use a hearing aid? ☐ Yes ☐ No

List had any previous assessments that your child has had:

	Dates of Testing	Name of Examiner
Psychiatric	_____	_____
Psychological	_____	_____
Neuropsychological	_____	_____
Educational	_____	_____
Speech Pathology	_____	_____

Have there been any recent stressors that you think may be contributing to your child's difficulties (e.g., illness, deaths, operations, accidents, separations, divorce of parents, parent changed job, changed schools, family moved, family financial problems, remarriage, sexual trauma, other losses)?_____

List any form of psychological/psychiatric treatment that your child has had (e.g., psychotherapy, family therapy, inpatient or residential treatment):

Type of Treatment	Dates	Name of Therapist
_____	_____	_____
_____	_____	_____
_____	_____	_____

OTHER INFORMATION

What are your child's favourite activities: _____

_____

List any special interests that your child has: _____

_____

List any sports your child plays: _____

Has your child ever been in trouble with the law? ☐ Yes ☐ No

If yes, please describe briefly: _____

_____

_____

What disciplinary techniques do you usually use when your child behaves inappropriately? Place a check next to each technique that you usually use.

- ☐ Ignore problem behavior
- ☐ Scold child
- ☐ Take away some activity or food
- ☐ Threaten child
- ☐ Reason with child

- ☐ Redirect child's interest
- ☐ Don't use any technique
- ☐ Tell child to sit on chair
- ☐ Send child to his/her room
- ☐ Spank child

Which disciplinary techniques are usually effective, and with what types of problem(s)? _____

_____

Which disciplinary techniques are usually ineffective, and with what types of problems? _____

_____

On the average, what percentage of the time does your child comply with requests or commands? _____

_____

What have you found to be the most satisfactory ways of helping your child? _____

_____

What are your child's assets or strengths? _____

_____

Is there any other information that you think that may help me in assessing your
child? _____

_____

_____

_____

_____

_____

_____

_____

_____

_____

_____

_____

_____

_____

_____

_____

_____

_____

INDEX